BECOMING
CHINA'S
BITCH

BECOMING
CHINA'S
BITCH

———————— AND ————————

NINE MORE CATASTROPHES
WE MUST AVOID RIGHT NOW

A Manifesto for the Radical Center

PETER D. KIERNAN

TURNER

Turner Publishing Company

200 4th Avenue North • Suite 950
Nashville, Tennessee 37219

445 Park Avenue • 9th Floor
New York, NY 10022

www.turnerpublishing.com

BECOMING CHINA'S BITCH:
AND NINE MORE CATASTROPHES WE MUST AVOID RIGHT NOW

Cover design by Gina Binkley
Dust jacket design by Mike Penticost
Interior design by Kym Whitley
Cover image: "American Flag Firecrackers," courtesy of
Getty Images/Jan Cobb Photography Ltd.
Bill O'Reilly letter excerpt on page 14 used with permission by *The Circle*.

Library of Congress Cataloging-in-Publication Data

Kiernan, Peter D.
Becoming China's bitch : and nine more catastrophes we must avoid right now : a
manifesto for the radical center / Peter D. Kiernan.
p. cm.
ISBN 978-1-61858-005-4
1. United States--Economic conditions--2009. 2. United States--Social condi-
tions--21st century. 3. United States--Foreign economic relations--China. 4.
China--Foreign economic relations--United States. I. Title.
HC106.84.K56 2012
330.973--dc23
2011046504

Printed in the United States of America

12 13 14 15 16 17 18—0 9 8 7 6 5 4 3 2 1

To Eaddo and our young adults Eaddy, Mareill, Lacy, and Peter.

My Steel Magnolias

Contents

PART I: WHY ARE WE POLARIZED?
FIVE FACTORS THAT FREEZE US FROM DOING THE RIGHT THING

PART II: TEN CATASTROPHES WE MUST AVOID

Acknowledgments

To Eaddo, my wife for most of my life: Meeting you was like popping the cork of my first bottle of champagne. Spending life with you is like drinking it . . . You are not just my soul mate, you are my soul.

To my extraordinary young adults: Eaddy, Mareill, Lacy, and Peter. You are our reason for living. How lucky are parents when the apples from our tree fall up? I will try and live up to the example you set. I adore you all.

To my parents: you guide me every day and I am still your loving work in process. I miss you both so much.

To my six siblings: John, Casey, Greg, Mike, Stephen, and Amy, I love you and remind you that if you tell on me, turnabout is fair play. You are my first circle and I live for our reunions with your spouses, in-laws, outlaws, heirs, and assigns. To Jean, Boo, Lawson, Garrett, Ross, and CJ, the Southern charms of my inherited Hayes family. And to my dearly departed in-laws, Eaddy and Lawson, both your names and your traditions carry on.

What's more fun than being Uncle Pete twenty-one times over?

For Sheafe, who believed in me as a rough-cut Williams sophomore.

For so many others who believed along the way, you helped me in breathtaking ways. God bless you.

For those who did not believe, I am sorry to say you helped, too, in direct proportion to the degree of your disbelief. In my youth I might have told you to pound sand, but today I know our battles hardened me. Here's an ironic hint: you significantly increased my will to make it, contrary to your hopes. And that really makes me happy. So what the heck, go pound sand.

To Ian Jackman, whose wit and skilled editorial insights match an equally good humor and passion for this book. To Todd Bottorff, Diane

Gedymin, and Christina Huffines at Turner Publishing for believing in both the Bitch and the writer, and for bringing this moment to pass.

To John McConnell who manages with dexterity and fun, and Steve Ross of Abrams Artists Agency for taking a risk on me when the end was nowhere in sight. For Wil Surratt of CNN for seeing life in the blank screen. And to Patty Sardinas for keeping my life sane.

___ INTRODUCTION ___

A RECENT VERMONT TOWN HALL MEETING began with a simple premise: a microphone stand in the front of the room, a gathering of townspeople, and no agenda. One by one, folks approached the open mike. Each began in measured, halting tones. Time and time again, as they warmed to their subject, their voices rose, veins bulged, until person after person wound up bellowing their belligerent position on subjects ranging from the price of cigarillos to global warming. Venting and spewing, they continued until their energy was spent. Then they wordlessly returned to their seats.

THERE ARE NO FOREGONE CONCLUSIONS.

Except one: If you ignore problems with all your might, you cannot make them evaporate.

Instead problems blossom into full-blown crises. Perversely, we seem to crave them.

The lives of most Americans must be lacking the excitement of the early days—that frisson of fear when our neighborhood had a cholera outbreak or when we played the roulette game of childbirth. We could breathe black air and in our wood-framed, gaslit cities, fret over constant threat of fire.

We run the country as if we crave the calamity of yesteryear—constantly lurching to the brink. Sometimes we're able to pull back from the maw, other times we let problems play out to the level of full-blown catastrophe.

Like the burghers of that Vermont town, we'd much rather stand in a room and yell than constructively work toward solutions.

We enjoy scaring ourselves. Brinksmanship in the House is covered like tropical depressions on the Weather Channel. Are we caught in a Category Five hurricane? Or thrilling to a Six? Try watching CNBC's market storm trackers without holding your breath and grabbing your wallet. Or Fox News without running for the fallout shelter. We're addicted to every derivative of tsunami though most of us have never seen one. So we manufacture artificial amber alerts—stand-offs like "Debt Ceiling" fiascos that allow politicians to posture and sound concerned. All this scaremongering does is obscure genuine problems, which for many of us is actually kind of nice. It's how we prefer it.

We have become a frozen tableau of contrasts. We are rich, with poverty rates at all-time highs. Homeownership is higher here than anywhere in the world, and our homelessness keeps breaking records. Almost 40 percent of adults and 20 percent of kids are obese, and more Americans will go without food today than at any time since the framers.

We are frozen in other ways.

Some call our polarization and inability to unite against problems a crisis in governance. It's no crisis. It's a self-inflicted wound. The first part of this book delves into the real reasons we are glaciated like an almond in a piece of toffee. Things are different today. Our refrigeration is much more than a frosted duopoly. There is an infrastructure of divide which has been crafted over decades. And if you do not understand how it works, you can never thaw out.

We've also become so anodyne to the real problems that we either falsify new ones or worse, we treat them like dry cleaning and have them done for us.

So if you are here to be diverted from the real issues, once again, wrong place. There are plenty of books that can serve you non-problems, false crises, and a pabulum diet of *aren't-you-terrific*. Try one of them.

This isn't a book that will tell you that the left or the right has a monopoly on good ideas. Not a single poll was taken in writing it. It's not a book about

China exactly. It's about how America got diverted and lost momentum, and a dragon leapt into the breach. It's also about getting our mojo back.

I don't really care if you agree with me on everything. This isn't that kind of book.

What I do care about is your willingness to face ten catastrophes we've allowed to go too far. Together we could come up with ten more, but these are ten biggies we need to address, right now. Actually, yesterday.

As with any makeover, the first step is admitting we have a problem.

If you deny these ten are major problems, then I ask you to consider something potentially painful—that you, my friend, are part of the problem. We need to get past the stage of denial. We're here to get things done.

It is time for you to take a new approach to your country and develop solutions yourself. That's where we may differ. I say turn one way, you say another. We will and should debate the approach. But let's at least agree to cease focusing on non-issues—those pointless diversions that we and the government waste endless time debating—and save our energies for the true challenges.

Meanwhile, our leaders have lost the ability to ask us to do something really basic, really American.

They so rarely ask us to just pitch in and help.

And that is precisely what I'm asking you to do.

You don't need to be a senator to make change in this country—quite the opposite. What I love about the Tea Party movement is not its position on most issues, or even its grassroots beginnings. It's that many of the members have never been political or social activists before now, until they heard the bell go off.

This book is your opening gong.

You can do it too. I've chosen to be an agent of change. I'm a naturally impatient man and I like to get things done. I've deliberately stayed out of the political arena, in large part because I want results. I confess, I thought hard about a career in politics. But instead I'm running towards problems, not running for office. (That's a Chris Christie no.)

I've been able to make things happen in any number of areas that mean a lot to me: charter schools, hunger, homelessness, disability and paralysis, stem cells, health-care reform, and more, because I have framed the terms of my own debate. So can you.

For better or worse, I have shown up, staked my ground, pissed some people off, and gotten things done. Children got educated, the hungry fed, the sick cared for, the poor housed, and every once in a while, I got to experience the unremitting joy of watching a paralyzed kid get up from a wheelchair and walk. You can do that too.

I am also a card-carrying member of a discredited class, with a couple of dozen years plus on Wall Street. We made a hell of a mess, for sure. But we had plenty of collaborators, and I see the end of their fingers pointing at us. So be it. We owe the world—including some of the pointers—a collective apology. But we can only rehabilitate if we're allowed to use our talents for good. That's the best way we can say "I'm sorry."

Class-war slurs on Wall Streeters must feel pretty terrific. But the time has come to focus specifically on the few bad guys and let the rest of business get back to doing its job.

I must admit, business has a broken brand. Pretty shabby considering we are branding experts. One way we can get our groove back is by taking the right kind of businesslike approach to solving the nation's problems. I think doing that is the key to a business rebirth in America.

As a nation of activists and societal participants, we all need to redefine the traditional affiliation we have with our government. That metamorphosis starts with changing our relationship with our politicians, which has devolved to they act, we react. Or worse, they fail to act until it is almost or actually too late, then we suffer the consequences.

If you want to return America to its former greatness, essentially you have three choices—two political and one social—none of them easy. The two political choices are that you can work to reform and build a voice with your politicians and your party, or you can try to form an alternative party. It's the classic choice of the lady or the tiger. The third choice is to actually do something to help people in need beyond just writing a check.

The task facing anyone creating a new third party in U.S. politics is Sisyphean. You push your platform almost to the top of the hill only to have it tumble back on you. Most politicians who step completely outside the tent are decried as traitors and ruthlessly dealt with. One look at how popular Governor Charlie Crist fared as an Independent candidate for the U.S. Senate in Florida should give you a clue. He was gone in a flash.

Sure, there have been a few Independent governors and 20 Independent victories in Congress over the last half century. But Independents don't have real staying power because if the parties don't crush you, then they steal your ideas. When George Wallace brought some disaffected Democrats to his Independent bandwagon, Richard Nixon countered with his unctuous Southern Strategy to woo Mason-Dixon Democrats who had tired of LBJ's civil rights rhetoric. And when Ross Perot's charts and graphs started making too much sense to Independent voters in 1992, he found himself with 19 percent of the vote. The following election cycle, both parties stole from his playbook, and Perot sank in the early going.

It may take a billionaire like Michael Bloomberg to create an Independent party, but mere mortals created the Tea Party. The American people deserve better than a slip and slide from the duopoly parties—because two sizes don't fit all.

The political parties have been operating essentially the same way since the Lincoln presidency. We need office holders who are not solely dependent on the patronage or the ideology of the Republicans or Democrats. We need fresh thinkers.

And they are you.

Which leads to the most annoying question anyone can ask: "So what are you?"

"Hey, what is this guy, a libertarian, a socialist, a Republican, a moderate . . . a what?" I say, when it's smart to be conservative, I pick a conservative solution. And when the intelligent outcome requires a liberal interpretation, then that's what I am.

In short, I am a common-sense American. And if I have to be pinned down like a butterfly on wax then call me a Radical Centrist.

So what does *that* mean? It means that polarized purists who push the spectrum even farther out rarely have a solution that consistently works, even as they demand consistent orthodoxy from their followers. It means that living between the extremes is where most Americans reside. That's our home. It also means something pretty obvious:

Ideology is not always helpful in solving problems in the real world.

We're electing people who are so driven by ideology they sign mandates or pledges (like promising not to raise taxes) before they reach office and fatally compromise their ability to solve problems.

So resist anyone who says, "You're not Republican enough." And, "You're not with the party line." In fact, take them as compliments. The party line is never the solution because it's more about the party than the solution.

Today's politicians have become ingenious at long division. When you divide a two-year term into a twenty-year problem, the answer is . . . you are off the hook—so vexing quandaries go unresolved.

I say be radical in your interventions and thoughtful in parsing through problems. And the more emotional the subject, the more likely an ideologue has hijacked reason from the argument. That's where you need the courage of a radical. It used to be the extremes were hard to maintain. Today balance is the challenge. Being a uniter is the home of the brave.

Okay, so once you've managed to think like a Radical Centrist, what's next?

First and foremost, use your voting franchise to elect better candidates.

Let's face it. Most of the folks who represent you, particularly at state and local levels, are not people you would ever hire into your company. Nor would you delegate running your household to them. Can you imagine working for them? So why would you ever consider voting for them?

Second, stand by your candidates when they do something brave.

It stands to reason that not every issue will fall neatly along party lines. A congresswoman in Seattle may have different priorities from a congressman in Arkansas, whatever the party.

If they cross party lines it is certain the Speaker or the minority leader will rain down on the treasonous member. Will you protect them?

Third, don't vote like an invertebrate—have the backbone and fervor for change. Charter schools bubbled up from individuals and educators dissatisfied with what school boards were offering. After local groups showed that charter schools could work, then government created the construct.

Local power brought us community banks and credit unions. Local organizations are the main infrastructure in feeding the homeless. Nobody national tucks in their blanket.

Fourth, for God's sake, take some responsibility and push for regional authority. Some believe all politics is local. Well, schooling, hunger, homelessness, and quite a bit of health-care delivery are as local as a home team. So how does our irresponsibility manifest itself? We wait for the government, often the federal government, to act on everything and to cater to all our needs.

It's also time to insist your fellow Americans take more personal responsibility. I think we are far better at guarding our rights than at living up to responsibilities. As a nation we have become expert at delineating: "Here is how I just got screwed."

Here's a news flash—nobody really cares. They think they just got screwed too.

Instead of tabulating our tragedies , why don't we stop a few things?

Regulations never die—especially the really dumb ones. Get moving on them.

Stop feeding the media machine that has helped support the polarization we all find abhorrent. If "talking" heads are instead screaming, change the channel. Find some real reporting and real dialogue. Vote with your eyeballs.

Responsibility will eliminate some of the most corrosive entitlements. If you are indigent, we need to find a way to help you. But if you lived well but saved nothing for health care because it is a God-given right, you missed a generation. Perhaps once upon a time it was such a right. After World War II, there were forty workers for each retiree on Social Security. By 2030, each retiree will theoretically be supported by two workers. That's like every working family getting a new grandma.

The age wave is washing over us, and we don't have water wings.

Most of the rest of the world has figured out what is just dawning on us today. The government can't take care of everything unless tax rates are absurdly high and everyone is hard at work. This is the new reality. Get used to it.

Finally, get in global gear. China and India know a lot more about us than we know about them. And they like it that way. Do you have any idea where presidential or national candidates stand on the emerging economic powers? Let's be sure Obama is the last president elected where we have no idea where the candidate stands on China.

OUR NATION WAS ONCE FILLED with uniters. The key to forming a pluralist democracy was not intolerance or unremitting belligerence. As a nation, in the end we somehow found the humility to allow people of different faiths and backgrounds to be equal participants in finding a common solution, especially during partisan times. Looking back, don't you agree that on people matters sooner or later America always got it right? What's missing now?

As Ben Franklin purportedly said, "Compromisers don't make great heroes, but they do make great democracies."

Policy arguments have been hijacked by the outlying voices of the far right and liberal left. Ossification and inefficiency of decision making at all levels of government and society are the result. Real and positive change, often change that the majority of Americans want, is difficult at best, and impossible in any sensible time frame.

The debate freezes us like a specimen in the ice. Paralysis leads to bad law. And civil rights are trampled in the process.

In the first part of this book, we look at the forces that sustain and preserve paralysis; then we look at ten catastrophes we can avoid if we act soon enough. It's essential to understand that none of these bad outcomes is a fait accompli. Again, the only foregone conclusions are the ones we fail to address.

Nothing less than a revolution will lead this nation back to the center. Oldsmobile moderates will never break the logjam. Tip O'Neill once said, "Moderates, they are always around when you don't need them." We don't need them now. We need immoderates.

We need a Che, a Martin, a Reagan, a John, a Rush for the Center. Otherwise we will never get back there. But we need more than a voice or a solitary leader. We need a movement. And like any movement, it must be driven by the people.

To make this trip you will have to embrace that central independent streak that led your ancestors here. For we are all immigrants.

And we are about to take a trip.

It is an Odyssey of courage, a journey to the American soul.

Please come with me. Read this book and join the provocation.

I dare you.

BECOMING
CHINA'S
BITCH

PART I

WHY ARE WE POLARIZED?

FIVE FACTORS THAT FREEZE US FROM DOING THE RIGHT THING

FACTOR ONE
Genesis: The Shot Heard 'Round the Dial

IT WAS A STEAMY MAY DAY, *high noon at the cement ("see-ment")
plant on the outskirts of Fort Worth. Every noontime was the same. Radio
blaring, the crowd quiet, and The Voice giving homily. Everywhere there
were Camels, Luckies, Pall Malls, and big thermoses of instant, the caffeine-
nicotine-routine. Lunch was eaten, stories were suspended; it was hushed as a
chapel. Dust in the room, dust in the air, dust in the drive . . . dust.*

But that May day, the radio just went dead.

*A stunned silence filled the lunchroom. In the quiet was a pause so preg-
nant it had come full term. Paul Harvey was speaking. More precisely, he was
not speaking.*

"Mr. President, I love you . . . but you're wrong."

*It was 1970, and the object of his inflection was Richard Milhous Nixon.
The most trusted man in America had just told one of the least trusted that the
Vietnam War was doomed to fail and it was time to leave.*

*And then Mr. Harvey, possessor of the most golden voice on the airwaves,
did the most assertive thing a radio man could do, the thing that had nearly
gotten him fired time after fateful time, the thing which was the most powerful
and articulate statement he could make:*

He fell silent.

*In that dead air, at the cement plant in Fort Worth and at lunchrooms all
over our nation, Paul Harvey gave his 14 million listeners a gift few broadcasters would dare to give: A moment of silence to think it over.*

THE VOICE

1970. AMERICA'S TIMBERS WERE SHIVERING. Vietnam vexations; racial agonies; military-industrial complex paranoia and the Cold War created a culture in which discord fought tooth and nail with status quo.

Americans turned to voices in the darkness like Paul Harvey and Norman Rockwell. Music, art, books, poems, and dance rang with echoes of fifties Beat writers. Kerouac was on the road, Ferlinghetti explored the vast confusion, and Allen Ginsberg howled. The national search went beyond beatnik. City Lights books made way for Haight Ashbury. The Naked Lunch became the Summer of Love. The counterculture was captured on a popular button that said: "I am a human being, do not fold, spindle or mutilate."

But while revolution was in the air, the counterculture's luster was being extinguished by the shooting of Kent State students, Charles Manson's Helter Skelter, and the Aging of Aquarius. Pete Hamill wrote in the *Times* that the counterculture was "just another media fraud."

It wasn't a fraud—just an un-Civil War.

At the time, I presumed changes were permanent. How young must I have been to be so fooled?

People sought refuge, many in recreational narcotics. Others found another narcotic entirely; subtle but no less addictive: The exclusionary safe zone of cocooning with those who think just like you do.

That poisonous analgesic is the subject of this whole book.

You can't be a Radical Centrist without understanding what you are fighting. To fully grasp today's paralysis you must understand how centrifugal forces whirl us to extremes. It's not just a radio voice, or a cable channel, or a Tea Party.

Too many pundits pontificate today without context, and any damn idea sounds reasonable with no context. Polarization's now all over the TV, but radio has long been a bellower's pulpit, dating from Father Coughlin in the 1930s. But by 1971, something profound was happening.

For decades, Cronkite delivered the cold hard facts to the nation like he was transmitting from Mount Rushmore. But in the hinterlands, journalistic truth was changing. New broadcast talents were emerging, sharing their views, delivering their own versions of truth. Operating independently, without central tenets or rigid ideology, they were changing the medium. They fed a growing need to have our opinions represented and promoted by national media.

Trust in objectivity was replaced by safety in numbers.

In the late seventies, the remedy contained trace amounts of polarity. By the early eighties the storm gathered force, swirling us to extremes, building like a hurricane offshore. The nineties made it a Category Five. Landfall came with the Millennium.

Since 2000, the storm's whistle at the windows has grown to a roar. It's the growl of a mighty brute.

Polarization has captured us, and our national soul is what's for supper.

This book is the escape plan.

To make our break we must pay a price: We need to know how we got here and we need radical change. Fasten your seat belts.

Remember, the storm began as most do: just a puff of air, like the breeze of a broadcaster's voice. Back then in the Fort Worth lunchroom and all across our nation, murmurs carried on the wind, meek unnoticed whispers, mere suspicions of themselves.

They whispered change.

SAGES OF TV HISTORY CONTEND the second that the hammer hit on Vietnam was when CBS's Uncle Walter declared the war unwinnable. Cronkite had the bully pulpit of Tiffany Network news, the momentum of Murrow, and the power of Paley.

Cronkite was called the most trusted man in TV and he may well have been. He called the T.O.D. on JFK in Dallas in '63. But he was also one of the great momentum players of all time. With that huge NASA following telling us T-minus three-two-one and "That's the way it is." He was trusted like a remote high priest, a pontiff of the people-granting benediction.

Which is why you need to consider Paul Harvey, a voice and attitude forged in Tulsa and hammered out across our middle in towns like Salinas and Kalamazoo. He won his listeners one at a time in the perennially threatened world of radio.

He wasn't drive time, shock jock, or Jack Benny. He invented the 10 P.M. news slot. He spoke in bursts and pauses, always with the voice, the voice, the voice. Not from the rice paddies or the convention floor, not live via satellite, not from mission control, but direct from Chicago—in the nation's heart.

Harvey dressed up for the radio in his coat and tie and retreated to his windowless Wacker Drive basement studio. There, on an old Selectric, he rat-a-tat typed each phrase and from the bunker beamed his catchy lyricism, his patriotic stories, his "Good Day" Paul Harvey News and Comment. His writing was forged every dawn the way a baker makes fresh bread: homey, warm, respectful, loving.

And when he beamed out at noon through the ABC Radio Network to those thousands of affiliates in ragweed towns between the coasts, an odd thing happened.

America stopped and listened.

Like no other broadcaster before or since, Paul Harvey, and his wife and partner he called Angel, tapped directly into our soul. And at cement plants, mechanic shops, and luncheonettes all over our nation, the shushers among us did their shushing precisely at 11:59:59.

Paul Harvey was sharing:

"America's six percent of this planet's mothers cannot bear enough baby boys to police Asia, and our nation cannot bleed to death trying."

Listen to his coup-de-gras: "And quite frankly Mr. President, out here in the unterrified nine-tenths of this country that's still country, we don't think there is anything in Indochina worth that."

Harvey's closing sentence was the sentence of death for the domino theory.

Invading Cambodia was too much even for patriot Paul. In the May silence, Nixon lost the powerful middle. Headlights of the silent majority dimmed, the quiet of that broadcast was a silence heard round the world. It was deafening.

Harvey gave Americans the time to think followed by a heartwarming "Good Day." And it was over.

Peace accords and the retreat with honor were simply ambassadorial benedictions.

Paul Harvey had called it the Time-Of-Death for the Vietnam War. 12:15 P.M., May 1, 1970. And the war ended.

GENTLE GIANTS

IN EVERY WALK OF LIFE you find them, gentlemen giants. In baseball it was Hank Aaron or Cal Ripken Jr. In movies it was Jimmy Stewart or Tom Hanks. In comedy—Bill Cosby or Robin Williams. Okay, it was Bill Cosby. Okay, never mind comedy. Let's stick with Jimmy Stewart.

In radio it was Paul Harvey. Like legendary test pilot Chuck Yeager, Paul changed the face of things without realizing it. They both had "the right stuff."

Plain old radio has been impossible to kill. Wave after wave of technology has tried: TV, video, movies, cable, Internet, DTV, satellite radio, wireless, Palms, CrackBerries, iPods, iPads, iPhones, and every other "i" that Steve Jobs tried to dot. Radio soldiers on like kudzu on our consciousness.

Harvey had to endure labels, often directed at him from the twin coasts. He suffered, like Norman Rockwell, from the misapprehension that his work was the house wine of the Republican Party. The man himself was indifferent to labels, but in a pinch, would acknowledge Christian, patriot, or loyal American.

But categorizations are all too easy. Paul Harvey had got to the center of things.

According to the *New York Times,* by the Monday after his intervention, Harvey had received over 25,000 letters at his home in River Forest, Illinois—a two-day record that still stands in that community 40 years later. In fifteen minutes this right-wing voice, this flag-waving patriot, this God-fearing Republican had summoned his courage, loosed the bounds, and found the radical center.

Harvey and Rockwell's popularity led them there because that's where the people live. Each spoke to the heart of America. It was a mutual love affair.

Rockwell found his own centered perspective in the mid-sixties. And when the moment struck, he brought us home too. Derided as a propagandist for some homey ideal, Rockwell spent 50 years illustrating America on the cover of the *Saturday Evening Post*.

His "Four Freedoms" paintings ("Of Worship," "Of Speech," "From Want," and "From Fear") buttressed by an unending fund of boys gone fishin', girls acourtin', soldiers returnin', and Americans being Americ'n, all illustrated a love of a country and her people.

But in fresh pastures at *Look* magazine, Rockwell found a brave inner spark exhibited in unflinching paintings of race in our nation that were far from his Stockbridge-in-trade maple syrupy New England scenes.

"The Problem We All Live With" depicts little Ruby Bridges, being led to her classes by federal marshals in 1960 to integrate the New Orleans school system. An ethnic screed is scrawled across the wall, and juice from a just-tossed tomato runs like blood down the whitewash. As an older woman, Ruby told me that painting captured the moment like no photograph could have, because Rockwell painted it.

In works like this, "Southern Justice" and "Negro In the Suburbs," Rockwell's brush swept across the canvas and led us where we needed to go as a nation: The radical center. Rockwell gave us his Fifth Freedom: "From racial injustice."

These two men found their Centrist voice in complex times.

The Impressionists

THE RIGID ACADÉMIE FRANÇAISE LAID down very strict rules delineating the differences between professional and amateur paintings in the eighteenth century.

The Art Mandarins decreed that true artists must create a "licked surface," concealing any evidence of brushstrokes. Viewers could sink their attention fully into the image without being diverted by the artist's process. Artists should be invisible in their art.

Those were the rules.

The Impressionists gleefully rejected everything the Academy required. Color took primacy over line. Using globs of paint, sometimes applied with their own fingers, Impressionists sculpted a painterly, color-splashed surface that dared viewers to consider the artist an integral part of the process. And while the Louvre fumed, audiences thrilled at the riot of color and interpretation. Art would never be the same.

In the 1960s the Mandarins of News decreed their own licked surface and the dogma of editorial neutrality was no less strict. Apart from peeks behind the curtain, as when Cronkite removed his glasses and woefully announced the death of John F. Kennedy, the anchorman was considered a sacred vessel who sanctified each broadcast with total objectivity.

It was the news maker's creed.

Yet all across the nation, impressionists of a different sort were experimenting and inserting themselves into the process, their canvas the radio. Their beliefs varied, but they shared a passion for showing their colors and their brushstrokes more than their objectivity. Arrayed to the right and to the left, impressionists let loose the bounds of serving as writers, sportscasters, DJs, comedians even, to find their voices as political and social commentators—a new opinionator class. But as popular as they became, their slanted approach to the day's events meant traditional media simply couldn't accommodate their art. Pent up, their views became more strident, until some became more important than the news they covered.

A daring MO for talk radio and news was about to be born. Like every artistic revolution, news impressionists were cultivating their craft, breeding a new way of doing things, with little knowledge of one another or of how fate would one day cause them to collide.

Make no mistake though—a collision was coming.

IN A PLACID INDUSTRIAL TOWN, McKeesport, PA, a Top 40 station jock with the newly minted sobriquet of Jeff Christie was spinning the latest hits. He was all rock and chatter, but like the vinyl records he played, his life was spinning in place. He wanted more.

Christie found himself a minstrel for the next decade, wandering from station to station in the Midwest, spinning tunes with 'tude, until he settled in Kansas City, Missouri.

No matter how many times he moved, however, it was always the same old song, so Christie quit radio altogether, taking instead a promotion job with the Kansas City Royals . . . hardly the stuff of revolution.

But thunder often rolls before it claps.

A big break came when a Sacramento station was looking to fill the slot vacated by the notorious Morton Downey Jr. Christie had tired of baseball and jumped at the chance.

Downey had a real edge that could play both ways. Echoing his antics, the boys in programming escaped the sameness of the Top 40 playlist (and the payola) by creating a fresh niche for the newcomer: a news talk format on the AM dial.

The boys at the promo desk wanted him to be keeping it real, so when he relinquished his Top 40 style, away with it went the Jeff Christie handle too. He would go with his given name instead: Rush Hudson Limbaugh III.

Expectations were muted and early returns mixed. Would this new guy somehow catch on? They had no idea.

Across the country, with different styles, in different media, were more Impressionists. Most had never heard of one another. Some came before Rush, and a great many later.

There was no place for them on the major TV networks. Radio was their Off-Off-Off-Broadway. And though they were making their debuts, they were still just voices in the wilderness playing to sparse audiences, like a traveling revue in search of a director.

Imagine the playbill: an extraordinary cast of true characters. To know the story, you have to know them.

OUT ON LONG ISLAND, A Levittown boy was making his way in the world. All along the route he had a trademark attitude. He was big for his age, and tough. He was possessed, too, of a swagger and a surety and an Irish wit that sometimes called the good sisters of Saint Brigid to knock him down a peg. He was a fast thinker, a faster talker, a football punter, and a pitcher with some smoke. He was a bundle of energy and opinions, and shy about neither.

In Mineola is a private Catholic boys' school with a reputation for tough schooling and strong athletics. Their players were known for being well coached, well drilled, and especially well conditioned. They were also known for that Chaminade attitude, which meant two things: Chaminade boys won a lot of games, and they created a few controversies.

This young man thrived on both diets.

The turn toward the '70s was Vietnam trickle-down. College unrest prompted high school unrest and schools like Chaminade were not exempted. In fact, schools with an unyielding commitment to principles were suspected of deeper and darker motives. Icons made good targets in those days.

Everywhere there were questions, imputations, and doubts.

The Irish American boy was drawn to Marist College in Poughkeepsie after graduation. It was, like many colleges in the late '60s, experimenting. Coeducation had just commenced at the traditionally all-male enclave and the school's newspaper, *The Circle,* was devoting increasing ink to spiraling events surrounding Vietnam. Football triumphs and tragedies simply weren't enough to hold the attention of '60s youth.

At Marist our young man played football, studied in England his junior year, and displayed a marked tendency to challenge administrators, coaches, teachers, and fellow students. The story is told that when he originally applied to spend a semester abroad, the good Marist fathers encouraged a yearlong commitment instead. If this tale is true, it was probably the first time in history that the teachers requested a sabbatical for a student.

Myth or fact, let's note that that story is never told by the boy himself.

From London, in December 1969, the student challenged *The Circle* when it published an editorial supporting an immediate withdrawal from Vietnam. The letter's close is like looking into a crystal ball. Peer deeply inside the excerpt and picture the young man writing it.

December 4, 1969

Gentlemen:

I have just finished reading your editorial. . . . I am appalled at the inaccuracy of some of your statements. You stated: "The American people can not wait for the South to take over the war. . . . They want immediate withdrawal. . . ."

This statement is simply not true. According to a Time-Louis Harris poll, 36% of the American people advocate an immediate withdrawal. In my estimation, this figure pulls up considerably short of the American people in total.

". . . Let's face it, idealists; it would be to Nixon's personal benefit to pull out now. He would be hailed as a peace-maker. . . . But maybe Tricky-Dick is getting a kick-back from the napalm factory and wants to keep us there to amass a fortune for himself.

The Vietnam situation is terrible. But sometimes, terrible situations don't get less terrible if you run away from them. Sometimes they get more terrible. Maybe there is another way besides direct withdrawal. May be."

Alertly yours,

Bill O'Reilly
London, Eng.

This wasn't so much a letter as it was an echo, with reverberations down the decades since it was alertly penned.

Bill O'Reilly may be the smartest of the bunch. He has brought that unvarnished Chaminade attitude and brainpower to his work and he's maintained what many opinionators lose over time: the ability to surprise. Bill is a simmering presence on the tube. He sparkles when he is in a gentle mood. But it's perversely appealing to search the screen for O'Reilly's tells. Sometimes it is a curl of the lip, or a nervous tilt of the head; sometimes he angles his shoulders toward the viewer, or more arousing, towards an errant or imperfect guest. When the pointer finger goes up we are in the zone. Even when we disagree, we want him to vent, we need him to rant. Sometimes especially when we disagree with him.

O'Reilly is no "licked surface." He owns the screen.

His voice takes on a withering superiority like he's delivering gospel truth with an uppercut as a side order. It's hot off the presses, but it sure ain't news. It's actually a bit scary.

Delivering his talking points, his voice becomes ambrosial. It lulls you into a comfortable stupor. And even when you disagree, you are left with the clear impression he is fighting for your own good.

And for some viewers, he is willing to say out loud what they are thinking or fearing inside.

That makes O'Reilly a tonic if you are feeling a little disenfranchised, a little diminished, a little bullied by life. And these days there are plenty of us who just want to be told he is on our side.

O'Reilly delivers news theatrics with appalling effectiveness. When they are good, he has the capacity to elevate. But in a darker light, when his opinion draws us into the shadows, O'Reilly's shaping of the truth can alienate and terrify. And we must always be mindful of the difference.

AT 6:30 ONE TEHRAN MORNING in 1979, students cut the chains on the U.S. embassy gates and breezed past guards who wouldn't use deadly force against them. Within minutes, hundreds of supporters flooded the compound.

What began as a student-led sit-in meant to span hours became a 444-day occupation. Not a shot was fired, yet this incident reverberated like a magnitude ten earthquake.

The globe watched, transfixed, as President Carter chose not to deliver the expected presidential ultimatum. In measured tones, he requested release of the 53 hostages on humanitarian grounds. Ayatollah called the U.S. "The Great Satan," while Americans boiled with frustration.

A hundred humiliating days and a million miles away from the Iranian student protests, 8,500 people huddled in the cold to watch a hockey game. Resentment simmered beneath the ice, nevertheless.

The site that February evening was the Lake Placid Arena and these were the XIII Winter Olympic Games.

Less than six months before, an aloof and distant coach named Herb Brooks had stitched together a group of strangers from Minnesota to Boston and a dozen frozen places in between. He had subjected these young players to a conditioning regime the likes of which no U.S. Hockey Team had ever experienced. Three days before the opening ceremony the scrappy Americans lost 10–3 to a polished Soviet Union ice machine.

No one was surprised, least of all the Americans.

Many of the Soviets, four-time defending Gold Medal winners, had played together every day for a decade. Lake Placid gold was theirs to lose.

Late in the third period the Soviets unsurprisingly led three goals to two.

Suddenly, in 81 seconds, the axis of the game and the globe tilted. The Americans flick-flicked their way into the lead with back-to-back twine tickles by Mark Johnson and Captain Mike Eruzione.

There were ten minutes left to play.

Never before or after in sport have ten simple minutes crawled in such plodding tick-tick-tick agony. The key was to keep the Soviets off balance. Brooks sensed that the defending champions had no respect for the American team.

He used their thinly disguised disdain to his advantage.

One 21-year-old arriviste to sports broadcasting saw the imbroglio on ice as a powerful metaphor for our nation and the world. This was much more than a hockey game. He could feel it. And that is how he reported it.

Others got more air under their wings that night. Announcer Al Michaels led the triumphant chorus ("Do you believe in miracles?"). But the younger apprentice felt something stir as stars and bars waved and red-shirted Russians leaned on their sticks like they were shovels in the gulag. In that frozen joyous moment, he was a broadcaster with the larger view.

The young opinionator had his own cut at the ball.

There was superiority in the way he reported.

Whatever the game, he saw it better, played it better, won it better, and saw it in context better than you. He was the arbiter. He was the game. And victory and defeat wasn't theirs or ours.

It was his and he was giving it to you.

And here's the scary part. In a very real way, he was right about it all. (Just ask him.)

A sports nut since his teen years high on a hill in Hastings-on-Hudson, he cut his teeth as a play-by-play announcer for WHTR of Hackley School fame. Continuing at Cornell, he honed his craft as Sports Director on student-run radio and landed himself a job at UPI and RKO Radio.

He parlayed that experience into a 1980 Olympics gig, at that fateful game during that winter of our discontent. Years later, after successful stints at KTLA in Los Angeles, and three times winning the Best Sportscaster by the California AP, after co-hosting ESPN's *Sports Center,* and leading Fox Sports in a similar endeavor, he would list first among the top-five moments in a two-decade sports casting career the reaction of the crowd and of the nation to the "Miracle on Ice."

Keith Olbermann's nightly *Countdown* show (from 2003-11 on MSNBC, now on Current TV) is truly a contact sport. It comes at you fast, loaded with historical references, pop culture analogies, and the fire hose of his opinions, especially the gentle chiding called "The Worst Person in the World."

Keith's snarky asides are funny in the way a razor slice is funny. They cut but they don't maim. You have to appreciate the show biz, the leer, the smug histrionics, the shameless promotion of self and show. They are calculated to bind or cleave—nothing in between.

Ratings rose with rants and feuds with O'Reilly, Chris Matthews, and anybody in between. Does calling the vice president a "war criminal" generate heat? For years he was MSNBC's top-rated show. At least until the *Countdown* ran out.

Before long, bombast was back on Al Gore's lumbering Current TV (if you can find it), where he proved that gardening leave had not softened him. Describing Reagan during a "Worst Person in the World" segment in 2009, Olbermann intoned: "Reagan's dead. He was a lousy president."

———————

AT DARTMOUTH, THE WHITE MOUNTAINS snuggery for liberal arts, a cloistered poetess sharpened her pen. From the great North came an Indian war cry, an alternative, well-funded howl that crossed the quadrangles like a chilly breeze.

The Dartmouth Review seeks the hearts and minds of Hanover, the support of a cadre of loyal alums—many long, long gone from their days in the mountains—and unaffiliated readers throughout our nation.

In a 25th anniversary paean to the review, William F. Buckley lovingly wrote: "A vibrant joyful provocative challenge to the regnant but brittle liberalism for which American colleges are renowned."

In modest offices, a woman toiled. Recently of Glastonbury, the first woman to serve as editor-in-chief, monitored illicit recordings and made a discovery: homosexuals in their midst. Was outing these young gay students to their parents the "vibrant joyful provocative challenge" Buckley was seeking? For that is what she did. In her collegian quest to dequeer Dartmouth she wrote that gay activists were "cheerleaders for latent campus sodomites."

Beautiful, poised, fierce, unafraid, and thin; years later she would soften on gays when her brother decloseted—a nice bend toward the center.

Where does meanness take her? She has become the most listened-to woman in political talk radio. She has penned four number-one *New York Times* bestsellers, most recently *The Obama Diaries,* and she's heard on hundreds of radio stations, sometimes substituting for O'Reilly.

When she guests on *Imus,* it's like watching a flirtatious dance of the praying mantis, where the female devours her mate after he has impregnated her. Armed with a UVA law degree and biting intelligence, she drifts into more popular fare, circling ever closer to shock jock territory. But powerful native intelligence courses through her. Even when she sounds foolish, she is nobody's fool.

A sharp stiletto voice matches her slicing wit. Her Imus sessions are less a dialogue than a blues jam where one icy guitarist riffs until the other takes turn.

Something in her style of play tells you she will always have the last word.

"The *Review* made me who I am," Laura Ingraham was quoted in the *New York Sun* as saying. The *Review* has reportedly asked for a blood test.

CULTIVATING AN ATTITUDE WIRY AS the sagebrush of his desert youth, he was always on the move.

His tombstone might read "nee in Riverside, California," but this cowpoke was reared on the Willows, a dusty scrub of Prescott, Arizona cattle ranch. The boy changed schools often, because he needed to.

He joined the Marines as a bugler. His cowpoke heart inhabited a dusty never land between country and rock and roll where chords bend slow like a Texas ramble, and "sang" is said in the present tense.

Discharged at 19, he began a parade of jobs like an argument of insidious intent—window dresser, rockabilly musician, DJ, uranium and copper miner, brakeman for the mighty Southern Pacific Railroad.

He stuck with music and got himself on the radio. Disturbed by an awful DJ on air one morning, he sauntered into the station, unearthed the manager from the back room, and demanded a chance to prove he was better.

In 1968, the sleepy burg of Palmdale, California, had a brand-new talent armed with a chip on his shoulder. Somewhere along the way he got fired by saying "hell" on air in Stockton, California—as if anyone alive could tell the difference between the two places—but the can of worms was opened.

During a particularly memorable on-air bit when he ordered 1,200 hamburgers from a fast-food restaurant, with specific instructions on their preparation, the young DJ helped to precipitate a new FCC ruling requiring stations to ID themselves when phoning listeners.

I guess you might call him a public servant. The boys at the commission were on to him early. But they would never contain him. Ensconced in Cleveland, his acid tongue brought steady listeners.

In 1971, he moved to WNBC and became a huge hit while the King of All Media was still struggling with high school geometry. Plagued by the demon twins of success and addiction, the star got fired in 1977 and returned to Cleveland; then back to New York and his addictions. The circle was unbroken.

But his morning show thrived. When all-sports network FAN bought WNBC, the station experimented with something beyond just more sports dreck: a comedic, news-oriented talk morning show.

John Donald Imus Jr. blossomed once he dropped the music and let himself go. Perhaps the market was thirsting for social and political commentary, perhaps it was the biting repartee Imus carried in his holster, but he was rustling listeners like cattle while Opie and Anthony were still in diapers.

Imus's magic was more obvious than his cowboy hat, yet also subtler.

Don Imus was and is an extraordinary interviewer. He has the cranky ability to be endearing and to pull shockingly frank answers from even the most coiffed and guarded politicians. And he can suddenly turn scary. Nothing is predictable.

It's not that he is a relaxing guy. There is something trapped inside that wheezing, rattling body he is carting around. He's nice like Bette Davis used to be nice—amazed and interested until you trip some invisible trap. Then he leaps like you used a wire hanger. But when he is blessed by benevolent moods, brought on by a euphoric country rhapsody he might have just spun, or by a fawning comment from his devoted team, then he blossoms like a mimosa.

And just like the mimosa he can clam up at the first chill of the evening.

It's a combination of relaxation and fear. So an interview is like an audience with Caprice. Will the subject survive and be warmed, or be flayed like a desert varmint? And it's not just the subject who might explode, Imus lights his own fuse at the beginning of every interview.

That's why they watch. And it's why they visit too.

Is there something vaguely idiotic about presidential contenders referring to him as "I-man"?

For all the bluster, Imus is rarely stingy with his support, particularly if you come at him straight. Arrogance and self-importance are the twin kisses of death, and Imus has an obsessive's penchant for staying with the whipping for weeks and months after the affront occurred. Imus has paid his own price for being the embodiment of the First Amendment. Nobody likes truth well told.

And Imus ran off the rails, con gusto.

Should the Clintons have been shocked that Imus went for the bait when he spoke at the White House Correspondents dinner? When you run your car right up to the edge of the cliff, you can expect the front wheel to slip over the edge a few times.

For decades the I-man escaped disaster, even as he courted it. But his raw talent was bigger than the raw nerves he kept hitting. So, many people who spoke with him shared insights of great consequence. And people listened.

He had always been worth the risk.

But that calculus changed, and when the Rutgers women went to the hoop against Tennessee, Imus said the wrong thing, got hit with a charging penalty, and was benched.

He was finished at CBS.

But, he was hardly finished. Americans love a comeback, especially from a cantankerous pioneer and a noted philanthropist who spends his free hours helping kids with cancer.

Imus is different from the opinionators. He and Charlie Rose possess unique skills to draw the best out of their interviews. Like good lovers they take their time, they know when to pounce, when to cajole. Their opinions matter—you know where Imus stands, at least at that moment. But they have a way of letting their opinions simmer, like a land mine beneath the surface. Their opinions are potent, not menacing, ever-present without being domineering. So their interviews are more like dialogues than debates.

My hunch is that, come full circle, candidates at the next election will return to Imus's parlor, and all sides of the argument will simmer in his steely glare. Because he isn't right or left—he's a centrifugal force: sometimes whirling dervish, sometimes wheezing cowboy. But Imus is the best interviewer on air today.

I wouldn't bet against him.

Amazons of the Iliad mated with vanquished male foes and occasional neighbors keeping only the female children they bore. You can't say they didn't have a sense of humor, even if they did have a sense of Homer.

Talk television has its own Amazon, who thrives, by her own admission, on a diet of chardonnay and cigarettes. She has gotten pretty adept at dispatching men. She is a polemicist in the tradition of Greek warlike orators and of a great many modern-day assholes.

Only, this warrior princess is funny.

Besides, her friends say they really enjoy her, with the phrase: "She is nothing like you'd imagine her to be." Truth is that still leaves a lot of room. Wow, can she be annihilatory.

Which is part of her charm . . . ?

And which probably explains why she gets fired so often, and why they always seem to hire her back.

Frankly, she often becomes the issue, almost to the complete dilution of whatever subject she is covering. Like an armed Amazon, she overwhelms the material.

An incident when a group of Muslims were expelled from a U.S. Airways flight because other passengers expressed worries sparked a call for Muslims to boycott the airline. On her Web site in 2006, after six imams removed from a flight called for a boycott of the airline involved, our antidote to Michael Moore was compelled to write: "If only we could get Muslims to boycott all airlines we could dispense with airport security altogether."

Ms. Right confesses confusion about multicultural outreach "to people who want to murder us."

She earned herself the ultimate adversarial accolade Al Franken could muster. He called her "a lying liar" and a "telebimbo," the latter a tough call since Coulter earns almost nothing from TV appearances, her paychecks coming from writing and speeches.

I think she goes on TV because she is an enema for rage, and because she enjoys confusing people even when she is being crystal clear. Anyone who has witnessed her in action knows she is fearless and comfortable, fully unburdening herself of moral outrage.

But is it all an act?

She is the picture of glee when she gets to deliver one of her notorious Philippics: a fiery, damning speech. But her style raises the question: Is she a net positive or a net negative for the right wing she celebrates with her Swiftian satire?

Ann Coulter was raised in the wilds of New Canaan, Connecticut, by her union-busting lawyer father and her mom, a gracious lady of the Kentucky South. Dinner table discussion must have been of the kill-or-be-killed variety, especially with two domineering brothers.

At Cornell she developed twin reputations as the fastest mouth in the east and the most fun friend you could have. Later at Michigan Law School and during a multiyear stint as a corporate attorney she kept both crowns.

That is key to understanding Ann Coulter. She is fiery *and* fun.

In the pundit fraternity, one woman stands forth with a consuming self-confidence and a scorching tongue. But even at her most outré there is always a smirk.

So if she makes you rage, ask yourself the difficult question: Is the joke on you? If you take her too literally, have you missed the satire? Remember, she's trying to push your buttons and nobody does it better. And if she sets you off, nothing delights her more.

It is a matter of indifference whether she amuses or enrages you. At her best, she does both. In 2007, she told the *New York Observer*, "If we took away women's right to vote, we'd never have to worry about another Democrat President. It's kind of a pipe dream; it's a personal fantasy of mine."

Ann was on MSNBC their very first day. But she'd been busy way before that.

Working behind the scenes as legal advisor to Paula Jones when she proceeded to file suit against Bill Clinton for sexual harassment, Coulter wanted to forestall a settlement. Fact is Coulter wanted Clinton taken down. Settlement was gender treason.

It was Coulter who unmasked Clinton's "distinguishing characteristic"— a recognizably bent penis.

But her attempts to pin that tail on the president were scuttled by a settlement rumored to be seven figures. Coulter considered Jones' compromise an act of sedition. She and others had labored on the case pro bono and the settlement was pro boner as far as Ann was concerned.

Ann was also on the periphery of the Linda Tripp/Monica Lewinsky imbroglio, proving, if nothing else, that she has a strong stomach.

Let's face it, Ann finds trouble.

MSNBC fired her for describing Pamela Harriman, U.S. Ambassador to France, during her memorial service, as one of those women who "used men to work their way up."

Which means they fired her for telling the truth.

With Ann there simply is no middle ground.

"Even Islamic terrorists don't hate America like liberals do. They don't have the energy. If they had that much energy they'd have indoor plumbing by now" (from her bestseller *Slander*).

She's most comfortable casting the right as besieged patriots beset by liberal "weepers" bent on destroying the nation: "Guns are our friends because in a country without guns, I'm what's known as prey . . ."—and later,

"As the saying goes: God made man and woman. Colonel Colt made them equal." She is a talk-show Taser.

Disdainful about abortion clinic workers afraid for their safety, she wrote, "The casualty figures are seven murdered abortionists to 30 million murdered babies."

Which brings us to a bit of a sore subject.

The woman is occasionally unburdened by the facts. If you Google "Ann Coulter lies," you routinely turn up about three million entries. Okay, I get it. Throwing scorching thunderbolts does not mean providing point-by-point forensic rebuttal to your positions.

But is it too much to ask for a bit more obsession with the facts?

The right-wing power positions have long been held by the George Will's and the William Kristol's; and Rush is the undisputed heavyweight.

So where does our glamazon fit in? There is no easy answer because she is smart but not learned, profound but not citable, and assured but not convincing. She is also a complete wild card. If you had a TV show, would you have her as a guest, knowing she might harangue 9/11 widows?

But there is something incandescent about Ann Coulter. For every viewer who complains that she coarsens our culture, there are dozens who find her irresistible. For every one who finds her shrill, there are others who find that her truth resonates with theirs.

THE FIRST CHILL WINDS BLEW fast along the Housatonic River. It was September 11, 1974. High on Aspetuck Hill, Canterbury School dozed in dawn breezes. In a few hours the Catholic New England boarding school would buzz with the energy of returning boys on opening day. The air was clear and crisp.

That same morning, the air could not have been more different in Charleston, South Carolina, steamy with a tenacious ground fog. The house was bedlam. As the youngest of eleven in a close-knit Irish Catholic family, the ten-year-old boy could never have imagined how the day would unfold.

The father was taking the boy's two eldest brothers to Canterbury. All around Charlotte a dense ground fog blurred the lines of reality and the flight crew of their plane strained visually to find the Douglas Airport landing strip. The pilot pitched in just short of the runway in spite of the instruments' directions. The impact was so jarring that the aircraft lost control, smashed into pieces, and exploded into flames.

That September 11 morning, 71 souls perished including James, Peter, and Paul Colbert, leaving a widow and nine children, the youngest of whom, ten-year-old Stephen, would never be the same.

As a teen, the boy found solace in Tolkien, science fiction, and imagineering games like Dungeons and Dragons. His passions led him to Northwestern University School of Communication. Stephen imagined himself as a dramatic actor but ultimately took a job at the famed Second City selling souvenirs. When the touring company was looking for an understudy for rising star Steve Carell, they found an excitable and talented backup in Stephen Tyrone Colbert.

A comedy career was born. He didn't have to look very far for material and a lifelong mentor.

He met a stand-up comedian, occasional actor, and puppeteer for children in New York City. The comedian had appeared in a bevy of forgettable roles in even more forgettable movies. "I can be in 20 movies," said Jon Stewart, "but I will never be an actor."

One day the dominoes just fell on the *Late Late Show*—after producer David Letterman of World Wide Pants dropped Tom Snyder's drawers, Craig Kilborn was tapped to replace him, leaving a gaping hole in Comedy Central's less-than-signature daily newscast. Stewart moved up and took the reins himself. Immediately the show became more news oriented, topical, and biting.

More important, people started watching.

Stephen Colbert worked briefly at *Saturday Night Live* and later *Good Morning America,* where only one of his humorous segments ever made it on air. He went to Comedy Central on trial, then became a correspondent on *The Daily Show* with Jon Stewart.

Though they were kindred spirits, Colbert wanted his own show. In

2005 he left to create a parody of personality-driven political opinion shows, to the extent that they weren't already parodies of themselves.

Colbert and Stewart redefined political satire. Drawing on a long history of political cartoons, both comedians found the unfair ground from which to puncture pomposity. But increasingly their fake news desks kept intersecting with the real news. I am not a journalist, but I play one on TV.

Using caricature and current events, these comedians found a way to info-tain America's youth. They also found a way to poke holes in the polar punditry. In 2004 Stewart appeared on CNN's *Crossfire* and took hosts Paul Begala (lefty) and Tucker Carlson (bow tie = righty, obviously) by surprise. He asked point blank why they wasted half an hour a day yelling at each other.

"What you do is not honest. What you do is partisan hackery . . ."

"You're doing theater, when you should be doing debate . . ."

When CNN brass dumped Carlson a few weeks later, Stewart's pointed commentary was cited as part of the problem. Something funny had slipped into the water. Humorists were building credibility even as professional news opinionators were losing it.

Stewart and Colbert's 2010 "Rally to Restore Sanity and/or Fear in Washington, D.C." was a direct send up of Glenn Beck's "Restoring Honor Rally" and Al Sharpton's "Reclaim the Dream" rally. A comedian posing as a Conservative teamed with a comedian making fun of the whole process sounds like an implausible draw.

Over 200,000 people showed up.

Was it too much free time, or are Americans that hard up for entertainment? Humor with edge was gaining an edge. It was through-the-looking-glass news comedy. Right was becoming left, and left was getting left out. News was becoming a jumbled soup. And humor both defrosted and polarized the discussion, depending on the day.

Roll over, Cronkite—surveys show the overwhelming majority of men and women under 35 list *The Daily Show* as their primary source of TV news.

THE BLAKE SCHOOL PREPARES MINNEAPOLIS'S sons and daughters for the rigors of "out east."

From here issued a couple of young men, partners in comedy crime, each underneath a nimbus of late '60s hair. They were irreverent, had an edge, and possessed a prepster's propensity to tilt at authority. They moved to a Minneapolis dinner theater called Dudley Riggs's Brave New Workshop, the country's oldest satirical comedy theater, and after stints at Harvard, which led eventually to a graduation and starvation on the East coast, the two were finally discovered.

Their irreverence led them to the scrappy halls of a New York comedy producer's lair while splitting a miserly $350 per week in salary. They represented a totally fresh and often obnoxious way of looking at life. They were an instant hit.

It was a new dawn for political comedy. It was acidic; it was topical to the minute. It was live!

Their satire knew no boundaries other than some anemic censors. The twisted pair gained prominence, ushering in a period where '70s cynicism devoured '60s naiveté every Saturday night. One, named Tom Davis, spent more time behind the camera. The other was focused on many things, but chief among them, voting for me, Al Franken.

Presciently, that bit played to rave reviews on *SNL*. It led him to cross over at the century's turn to liberal commentary on *Air America*. His biting humor took new shape in a series of books with subtle subtext like *Rush Limbaugh Is a Big Fat Idiot*, *The Truth (with jokes)*, and the ever so oblique *Lies and the Lying Liars Who Tell Them: A Fair and Balanced Look at the Right*.

Franken has had five bestsellers. Clearly subtlety sells.

Unlike the other Impressionists, Franken always joked that he was planning to run . . . until it was no joke. Could this be Colbert, Maher, and Stewart on steroids? How effective could a career funny man be in the most exclusive club in the world?

Coming from the no-holds-barred world of *SNL*, where slicing wit and painful candor are coin of the realm, could a parody writer succeed in the all-too-serious world inside the Beltway where straight talk and openness are scarce commodities?

Franken spoke with clear understanding about these challenges during his campaign. He knew that celebrity is a magnet in our culture that can sometimes pull an odd candidate over the finish line. He was not afraid to apologize for his biting sarcasm, but he would not retreat from the keen insights that had brought him success as a comedian.

"Let me tell you what a satirist does. A satirist looks at a situation and sees the inconsistencies and the hypocrisies and absurdities, and cuts through the baloney and gets to the truth. And I think that's pretty good training for the U.S. Senate. Don't you?"

ALL ACROSS THE NATION MORE Impressionists painted at their easels.

Imagine an Irish Catholic kid from Philly so desperate to be in Washington he started out as a police officer assigned to the Capitol. Hired away from his security duties by Ralph Nader, the young man performed proctology exams on politicians' financial disclosures, as he said, to "break these little stories that ruined their lives for a month and *maybe* end up on the front page." He grew tired of the work and crossed over—he wrote speeches for Carter and labored for years as Speaker Tip O'Neill's right hand, or should I say left, against Reagan.

Unbridled passion for political commentary brought him to television until a forerunner channel of MSNBC gave Chris Matthews his first show, which by 1997 evolved into *Hardball.* Calling him shrill misses the point entirely. Matthews has an unvarnished love of the game. *Hardball* shows are like a gushing fan-zine. His distinction is that he is so obviously pro-politician. He spits out historical references like a trick-or-treater on a sugar high. He dresses left but will take a punch at a phony of any stripe like he was schooled at an Irish pub as much as at Holy Cross. He's too old a hand to be an out-and-out groupie, but soaring liberal rhetoric still gives him a thrill up his leg.

A LONG ISLANDER REARED IN a town framed by Garden City and Hempstead dropped out of NYU and Adelphi and he drifted west. Picking up work as a bartender and general contractor in Santa Barbara, he managed to get a volunteer radio show at the local university, though he wasn't a student. In a matter of months he was canceled because he told a lesbian caller, "I feel sorry for your child." Displaced, he responded by placing ads in radio publications calling himself "the most talked about college radio host in America."

He found radio work in Alabama and then shortly after spent four years at "The Talk of Atlanta"—WGST. Fox News impresario Roger Ailes hired the combative radio man to do a political dustup version of "Jane, you ignorant slut," blade point to blade counterpoint gabfest, with a file folder name of *Hannity and LTBD,* meaning, of course, Sean Hannity and a Liberal To Be Determined.

Colmes never stood a chance—by 2008 the cheese stood alone.

Carrying dual citizenship in the U.S. and Ireland, Sean Hannity may well be the most powerful voice and ringleader of right-leaning talk, armed with major TV, radio, and Internet presence. His enormous profile stems from an almost annoying consistency—does he really believe every bit of it? He also boasts an impatient likability. He explains things to you like your older brother would, which frames a universal familiarity—Sean Hannity dated your cousin, he played on your office softball team, you were altar boys together.

Sean can come over for a barbecue and not ruin the afternoon, even if you voted Democratic in every election since FDR.

Suddenly, there were dozens of these aces, liberals, and conservatives, with a few yucksters in between. They were gaining attention but were a long way from freezing us in our tracks.

Conservatives surged, taking the Top Five radio talk slots. A few years ago you never heard of 'em. Today the names roll off the tongue like a conservative Davis Cup Team: Rush Limbaugh, Sean Hannity, Glenn Beck, Mark Levin, Michael Savage.

Beck, like Rush, was a Top 40 DJ whose morning zoo antics regarding a radio rival's wife and her miscarriage almost lost him his own carriage.

Mark Levin, a Phi Beta Magna and JD from Temple, began contributing to Rush and Sean before carving his own scathing niche. Intriguingly, he is far more temperate in print. His books are thoroughly researched, not personality cult. He is piercingly smart, but when he rears on the radio, he can peel the bark off a birch, even a John Birch.

Savage was buddies with poets Allen Ginsberg and Lawrence Ferlinghetti. Stranger still, he was keeper of Timothy Leary's gatehouse in Millbrook, New York, before taking his own trip to the conservative right.

Some Impressionists achieved rock-star status and matching W-2's. Some became proper nouns, others became verbs—but they are all part of the nation's vocabulary.

But individual artists don't make movements. Government and big media delivered decisive blows.

The Fairness Doctrine was a 1949 FCC mandate that required all points of view be aired by licensees (as opposed to Equal Time, which was for politicians). The Doctrine had precisely the opposite effect its drafters intended. Structured to ensure wide-ranging perspectives, it turned broadcasters timid. Edgy perspectives never made it on air.

Was the Doctrine's 1987 repeal a catalyst? Without question. But regulations don't make movements either.

Patrons and salons make movements. Seismic shifts in technology make movements. Swerves in consumer sentiment make movements. Massive financial incentives support movements.

Forget your perfect storm. We were witnessing a polarizing Big Bang. The connection of detonator to battery was the simple confluence of need and want.

Impressionist proselytizing reached such a fever that people turned for news to satirists and stand-up comedians who might end up in the Senate.

It wasn't their humor so much as the fresh thinking. People tired of opinionators throwing the same ideological pitch over and over. Fake news desks were permissioned to go farther, just as Thomas Nast took political cartoons to high art.

Oscar Wilde said never confuse the public interest with what's interesting to the public. We wanted their outrageous opinions as much as they needed to share them. Ratings became heat-seeking missiles. And if missiles flew too close to the sun, opinionators repotted. In the genre of farce, banished news talkers became news. Their Napoleonic exiles, their trails of tears, and their resurrections were chronicled like modern Greek tragedies.

For the middle earth of old-school journalism, life became a ball of confusion.

It takes more than a gaggle of artists to create a movement this powerful.

It takes three things: want, need, and someone to light the fuse.

What creates the nation's thirst for such sharp opinion? It requires a marinated populace, grown timid and forlorn by attack and retreat politics. It takes a dark and unseen enemy plotting against us. It takes a nagging instinct that the nation is adrift. It takes the sense that our rights and privileges and what we are justly due are melting like an ice cap beneath a polar bear's feet.

It takes a vast collective insult.

Umbrage has replaced baseball as our national pastime. We have developed an emotional need to storm off *The View.*

We retreat to our corner and let Angelo Dundee towel us off. We gargle, we swish, we spit—then we pound our gloves together and wait for the opening bell.

If it takes a village to raise a child, what does it take to raise a ruckus?

A bunch of polar-opposite gabbers could not freeze us all on their own. Bounced from the Louvre, the Impressionists needed shelter from the storm. Talk mavens were no different. Without a platform they were clanging gongs and clashing cymbals incapable of freezing anything. Something profound was necessary to let their work flourish. ⸳

It took a grand enabler, a superb impresario, to give this factor life—one man above all, who institutionalized the Impressionists and gave them a platform while a small band of impresarios and daredevils drove the movement. First, he needed a historical moment, a coming together of technology and media, to flourish.

It all began in the narrow straits of the Dardanelles during a nasty bit of World War I business known forever by a single haunting name: Gallipoli.

AFTER GENESIS: THE PUPPET MASTERS

BRITAIN AND ITS ALLIES WERE *flagging in 1915 during World War I. A brash young Admiralty Lord, Winston Churchill, pressed to execute a plan to drive through Turkey to secure a sea route to mother Russia to subjugate the Huns from the East.*

It was a bold plan with a single basic flaw—it could not be accomplished.

The Admiralty's concept was to drive across the narrow straits of Darda-nelles to the high cliffs of Gallipoli, and overcome dispirited Turks by sending wave after wave of Anzacs (Australia and New Zealand Armies) headlong into Turkish fire. It was annihilation.

Anzac casualties exceeded 50 percent, yet General Ian Hamilton's posts from the front carried rosy projections of glorious victory and spoke little of the squalid conditions or the massacre of Anzac boys.

Deprivation in the camps was carried back home by rumor and innuendo. A wary Australian Prime Minister dispatched Keith Murdoch, the stuttering son of a Calvinist minister, to monitor undelivered mail in the region. Re-pulsed by what he saw, and frustrated by Hamilton's censorship of his press dispatches, Murdoch headed back via London with a letter from another jour-nalist describing the deplorable conditions of the doomed campaign. Alerted to the plan, Hamilton had Murdoch arrested on arrival and deprived of his report. Seething, Murdoch composed his own 8,000-word letter, imperfect in memory and accuracy but compensating in its passions.

Murdoch's letter was a thunderclap and was copied and retold across the British Empire. General Hamilton was relieved of his command and the doomed campaign was suspended.

The igniting letter brought Keith Murdoch notoriety and an offer to serve as editor of The Melbourne Herald. *With the Gallipoli Letter, a press dynasty was born.*

Murdoch's energetic son, Rupert, watched intently from the sidelines at Oxford, and then was schooled at the knee of Lord Beaverbrook, a tabloid magnate from the grand duchy of Fleet Street.

Young Murdoch joined the family news business in Australia and, like his father, veered his whole career between the respectability of the broadsheet and the call of the populist tabloid.

Rupert learned both worlds from his father and Lord Beaverbrook, and a more lasting lesson too. At sixty-five, his ailing father was pried from his perch as Chairman of the Herald Organization. For all his power, he wasn't the owner. Rupert never forgot the difference.

IN A LIFETIME OF BOLD moves, ownership was the mantra. Borrow heavily, consolidate expenses, defray the debt, and reload. It was a classic loan-to-own stratagem, and it was Murdoch's creed.

First in Britain was the *News of the World* and, in the late '60s, a daily, *The Sun,* gave Murdoch the highest circulation newspaper in England. He became the most feared and powerful newsman in the United Kingdom. The mighty would kowtow to him; prime ministers would fall under his powerful sway. Murdoch piled victory upon victory until the bottom fell out and Hackergate claimed the life of the *News of the World.* (*NOW* journalists hacked teenager Milly Dowler's voice mail after she was murdered walking home from school.)

Do you have any idea how hard it is to disgrace a British tabloid?

In 1973, the peripatetic Murdoch made his first forays into the U.S. market. He acquired the *San Antonio Express* and the *San Antonio Evening News,* which he immediately took down-market to challenge the local tabloid the SA *Light.* The next year he founded the *National Star,* a supermarket tabloid, and went up against the *National Enquirer.* In 1976 he acquired ailing tabloid the *New York Post,* from Dolly Schiff. He is rumored to have lost more money on that one holding than anyone has ever lost on a single publishing property—something like a million dollars a week. After 35 years that adds up.

In the United Kingdom, having bought the nation's papers of record, the *Times* and *Sunday Times,* Murdoch launched Sky TV as a satellite network. In February of 1989 he created Europe's first 24-hour news channel, Sky News. Building on the success of his four-channel launch, he merged Sky TV with major competitor BSkyB in 1990. His ultimate plan for gaining complete control over BSkyB was scuttled by the hacking scandal that took down *News of the World*.

Murdoch became a virtual magnate, having naturalized as a U.S. citizen in 1985. While it's difficult to find an area of the media he didn't revolutionize, U.S. network television is perhaps the most dramatic. Nothing could match the oligopoly of the Big Three before Murdoch. Despite declining audiences, the networks consistently increased up-front sales of TV time. Networks augmented their distribution and cash flow through owned and operated TV stations; and achieved national coverage of 100 percent by signing affiliates in markets major and small.

Murdoch's plan was executed with such certainty and relative swiftness we all marveled. I was involved in some of the transactions and witnessed others from the sidelines. Most stunning was the unmitigated gall of the plan.

Rupert bought 50 percent of Twentieth Century Fox, a TV and movie production studio. In 1985 Rupert Murdoch's family-controlled News Corporation acquired John Kluge's Metromedia TV stations for $1.55 billion. By October, Murdoch had the temerity to call his play, like Babe Ruth pointing to the center-field wall. He was starting a fourth network. His stations reached barely 22 percent of the U.S. He had no network programming: no shows, no news, and no sports. What affiliates could possibly be interested?

It was laughable.

Murdoch was obsessed with this old-fashioned Fleet Street brawl. It was a time of pirates and buccaneers. The whirling dervish of the capital markets was a key ingredient because the stakes were too big for anyone to afford on their own. Success at a minimum called for home currency billions, unending confidence, luck . . . and loads of debt.

Friends would become owners, competitors friends, and partners mortal enemies.

Regulators strained to keep pace with advances in technology and ingenuity. In the all-out war for control of the world's living room, no aspect of communication was left untouched, from our mail to our entertainment, our sports, and our news. That precious bit of household real estate occupied by the TV set were the cliffs along the Dardanelles.

Media entrepreneurs assaulted households through telephone and cable wires, and through radio, TV, and cellular spectrum. Messages blitzed us through every media orifice. Storage technologies created wave after wave of repurposed and new content.

The infrastructure wars of these media masters recast an entire industry. Without these great enablers, the Impressionists would have remained fringe players.

CABLE WARS WERE FOUGHT BY men like Bob Magness, cottonseed salesman and sometime rancher, who sold his stock, the kind that comes in head, not certificates, and started a cable system in Memphis, Texas. The town's chief attractions were that it was remote and devoid of any other attractions.

By day, Bob strung cable and at night on the dinner table his wife Betsy did the books. Before long they had persuaded 700 subscribers to join their system.

Nothing about their business felt like a huge idea. But Magness persevered, hiring a Yale math whiz with a PhD from Johns Hopkins named John Malone who had done stints at Bell Labs and McKinsey and ran Jerrold Electronics for General Instrument.

From their new home base in the burgeoning cable mecca in Denver, Magness as Chairman and Malone as CEO shared motel rooms as they traversed the country looking for financing to grow their business.

It was a pride-swallowing grind, and it made them tough.

And then something very special happened.

Cable evolved from providing TV to remote locations to something far more dynamic: a subscription-based pay-television service. Suddenly channels like HBO, Showtime, and Ted Turner's CNN gave television consumers choices. Basic and enhanced payment tiers were created. For the first time, TV came with a menu.

Viewer choice and narrowcasting became the new watchwords. And

. while advertising played a role in some services, it was that consumer impulse to subscribe that paid the freight.

It was Beaverbrook's circulation war games revisited. Content dictated the way viewers used their cable sets. It was like a giant news-barking bake-off, and the stakes were enormous. The rush was on to rewire the nation another time.

The third wire was upon us.

Generations earlier, electrical wires were strung across our nation from centers of power generation to every home. Then the second wire ran from major telephone switching systems to every house. Cable ushered in the information superhighway: voice, data, video. Satellite distribution played a major role in bringing content to cable. Advances in earth dish technology would provide satellite pathways to the living room.

John Malone guided the most amazing build-out in our nation's history. From the mid '70s to the mid '90s, TCI would start, acquire, or invest in over 650 companies. They would soon pass one in four U.S. households. But Malone was far from just a layer of pipe.

Through TCI and programming spin-off Liberty Media, Malone would direct or strongly influence dozens and dozens of cable channels around the world. He had command over content and the pipe that carried it, which made him a dangerously powerful man. He was everywhere, and was as nimble in the capital markets as he was in his cerebellum.

Time after time when the scrum cleared, Malone had the ball. There was almost no chess move anywhere in media without him. Knight to Malone 6. Checkmate.

Fellow cable mavens like Brian and Ralph Roberts of Comcast, Amos Hostetter of Continental Cablevision, and the Dolans of Cablevision had uncovered a marvelous business model: a utility with growth. Protected by the regional authority of near-monopoly in a community, cable giants used high-yield financing and bank debt to lever up their consistent cash flows. But unlike electrical and gas utilities, cable had a special gift: new services— which meant new revenues and higher margins.

The cable geniuses recognized that they were in the railway business.

Once the rails were laid down, profits came from running more and more items down the track.

Now there was a new target: fat subscribers who bought multiple tiers of content—and the better the content, the stickier the subscriber. That's where the Impressionists came in. Cable needed them to fatten up their subscribers.

In the center of the cable ring was the Operations PhD, Malone. Rarely brash, he was always considering, weighing, and balancing alternatives.

Think of 3D chess and you have a sense of Malone's intellect—clinical, unemotional, and extraordinarily comfortable with enormous complexity. Listening to Malone dissect a four-handed transaction with careful attention to tax treatment, cross-border issues, and different regulatory regimes was like hearing a virtuoso play an instrument. He could carry these interlocking concepts in his head the way you and I might carry a tune.

He had a gift.

There was one more thing. It was quiet, but unmistakable.

The man had one of the fiercest determinations to beat competitors that I have ever seen.

But for all of Malone's clinical calculations and Murdoch's drive to see around the corner, there was another player on the stage—so unpredictable, so outspoken, so brash, that his act seemed death-defying.

Which was just the way he liked it.

AT 24, AFTER HIS FATHER'S suicide, Ted Turner inherited a foundering billboard business. Bound by an airtight contract to sell the business, Turner stunned his would-be acquirer by offering to buy him out, despite the fact that he didn't have a dime. For the first time, but not the last, Ted saw no obvious way out of the company's mess so he plunged further in. He bought the business on a prayer.

But stabilizing billboard cash flows was an hors d'oeuvre. Hungrily Ted lurched toward TV, buying a money-losing and semi-redundant Atlanta

UHF TV station—improbably succeeding by running ancient movies and Hawks and Braves games.

With the advent of cable, Ted broke all the rules. He created a new hybrid, a Superstation—blanketing North America by satellite from 22,000 miles above. Atlanta uber alles.

To succeed, Ted needed just three things: He needed to get carriage on the right satellite so cable operators could carry his Superstation. Cable was starved for nationwide programming, even if it was the Atlanta Braves. Cable leaders were persuaded by Ted's "almost childlike logic." Malone described a first meeting with Ted crawling around on Malone's office floor imploring, "Whose feet do I gotta kiss to get picked up on your systems?"

Next he needed an uplink to reach that transponder—another million out of pocket.

And finally Ted needed a friend. His Superstation pissed off most of the free world. Mere mortals aren't smart enough to get in that much trouble.

Syndicators flipped. Going regional was one thing, but a national footprint broke all the barriers. Syndicators buy by the yard and sell by the inch. Turner buys an inch worth of fabric and covers the whole nation with it.

Major League Baseball was apoplectic, a contagion that soon spread to all the other sports leagues. Turner had turned order into bedlam.

Broadcast networks were livid, too, as were their affiliates, since a network station could be broadcasting a show at the same time Ted was, in every market in the country.

The man had to be stopped.

If you and I pissed off Hollywood, the FCC, the syndicators, virtually every sports league, the Big Three TV networks, all their owned and operated station managers, and every local affiliate across the USA, we might be a bit defensive.

Not Ted.

He played offense.

He threatened to buy each of the Big Three. When Nielsen wouldn't track his "Fourth Network," he sued them for restraint of trade. When regulators tried to pin him down, Ted always wriggled free.

And the more his swashbuckling annoyed people, the more he became a folk hero. Even when he badgered his way into every major cable system, the TV networks did nothing.

At the time, the Big Three were each spending $200 to $300 million just to air a 30-minute newscast at night and morning shows like *Today* and *Good Morning America.* They defined winning as beating the ratings of the other two networks.

Cable was barely an afterthought.

From the sidelines, the Big Three watched Discovery, USA, MTV, HBO, Nickelodeon, VH1, and The Weather Channel get launched. (ABC took a minority stake when Hearst and others launched ESPN, and later exercised their option for control.)

Meanwhile, Turner's TBS didn't even have a news department. Typically their "anchor" would read the news required by regulators at 3 A.M.

He gamely decided that he could launch a 24/7 news network for about one-tenth of what the Big Three were paying. His news channel planned a budget of $30 million a year.

There was just one problem. Ted didn't have $30 million to spend, even once, not to mention every year, but he plunged ahead anyway, to make a preemptive strike. A recently vacated Jewish Country Club became CNN's Atlanta headquarters.

Fore!

Ted reserved a transponder on RCA's Satcom III, the hot new launch bird of choice, and then turned his attention to the single thing that would define CNN: how to keep news flowing 24/7. To smash network news hegemony he sought news and editorial commentary across the political spectrum. It was a flier, but after a rocky start (including Satcom III being lost in space and ABC announcing, then folding a look-alike channel) it worked.

Cable's smaller audiences meant advertising revenue alone couldn't sustain the channel. CNN required subscription revenue to survive. Turner needed cable as much as cable needed him.

Over the next decade Turner, Malone, and Murdoch circled each other and intertwined with more arias than an Italian opera. Each would attempt to buy all three networks. And they loved to play in each other's backyards. Together, and apart, these men created the infrastructure that fed the news talk revolution.

In the world of talk, Murdoch wanted the point position. Others played for media power and net worth. Murdoch played for political might.

As a programmer, Murdoch had not wandered far from Lord Beaverbrook. Shows like *When Animals Attack!* drew derision from establishment players. Programming at a halting one-night-per-season pace, Murdoch steadily found affiliates among hundreds of independent TV stations across the country despite negligible ratings. His first shows like *The Late Show with Joan Rivers* were paltry. In mid '87 *Married with Children* gained prime-time traction in a low tabloid sort of way.

It took Homer Simpson to bring Murdoch a Top 30 show.

Undaunted, Murdoch kept buying capacity. He acquired Ron Perelman's New World Stations and others owned by Chris Craft Group. By 1993, all seven nights were programmed.

As the stakes were raised, Murdoch got bolder. Spending a billion to lure the NFL from CBS, Fox finally had the appearance of a true network. All it lacked was news. Local affiliates produced their own programming or did without.

Murdoch had been searching for someone to drive a stake into the heart of network news. Desert Storm proved that CNN had the "of the moment" market, as did every school shooting, tornado, and amber alert. But day in and day out nothing could touch the Big Three for gravitas.

Murdoch approached Malone suggesting they buy CNN together. After Time Warner won the prize asset, there was wailing and gnashing of teeth. Bill Gates, hardly the emotive type, described himself as "crushed" that he did not emerge victorious with CNN.

CNN was the fourth news outlet, and few people saw room for a fifth.

Murdoch was frustrated, too, but not stymied.

His greatest competitive strength at the time was the capacity of his competitors to underestimate him. And underestimate him they did.

Instinctively he knew he needed an inside partner to match his outsider's zeal and ambition. He found an unlikely cohort in a former executive producer of *The Mike Douglas Show,* Roger Ailes.

The two formed an extraordinary partnership—unusual because partnership is hardly in Murdoch's nature and Ailes pulls no punches.

When Richard Nixon derided television as a gimmick, Ailes, age 27, reportedly told him if he kept believing that, he would lose. Ailes told Nixon, "The camera doesn't like you." A few days later he was working for the campaign.

After Ronald Reagan's first disastrous debate with Walter Mondale, Mike Deaver brought in Ailes as coach, prompting Nancy to grouse, "Just what we need, another consultant."

Ailes' genius was finding the key issue and going directly to it. "The American people are simple, not simpletons. They are smart and want their concerns addressed." They wanted simple reassurance that Reagan hadn't passed his "sell by" date.

Quickly, Ailes got to the point: "Mr. President, what is your goal in the second debate?"

Every head in the room swiveled to Ailes and then back to the president. There was a pause. "Well. Mondale's saying some things that aren't true and I've got to correct the record."

Ailes locked in on the great leader.

"Mr. President, there are five strategies you can choose from. You can attack, counterattack, defend, sell, or ignore. You've picked defense, which is the weakest possible position. If you do that, you will lose again."

At that moment there were effectively just two people in the crowded room. Ailes told Reagan, "You didn't get elected on details, you got elected on themes. Every time a question is asked, relate it to one of your themes. You know enough facts and it's too late to learn new ones now. . . ."

The Gipper won the next skirmish and sailed into the presidency.

Years later, Ailes was widely credited with George H. W. Bush's come-from-behind victory over Michael Dukakis. While much is made of Willie Horton, it was Ailes' "Revolving Door" ad shot in a Utah prison showing a parade of prisoners returning from work release that shifted public perception of Dukakis.

Searching for the next mountain, Ailes went from the message to the medium.

He became President of fledgling cable network CNBC and by 1994 his new venture, *America's Talking,* transplanted Rush and other talk mavens from radio to the small screen—the body rejected them.

Frustrated over CNN, Bill Gates persuaded NBC to drop *America's Talking* and launch MSNBC (called MSLSD by Mark Levin) on their transponder.

America's Talking unplugged was Murdoch's opportunity.

Like Gates, Murdoch knew little about TV news, but he knew one thing: cable news was recutting the diamond right under the collective noses of the Big Three. Murdoch scoffed at Gates' partnership with NBC and decided to go it alone.

But he needed his own foil. Someone who knew TV, who had a keen sense of messaging—someone willing to take it farther than Murdoch was willing to go. Tabloid TV was calling.

Ailes was the perfect counterpoint. Fox News, founded in 1996, combined all of Murdoch's and Ailes's life lessons.

It was Lord Beaverbrook, assailing and counterprogramming—taking on the broadcast establishment.

Ailes's genius was to appeal to an unserved market, one that ABC, NBC, CBS, and CNN missed: the conservative view. The bumptious impresario tapped into a nationwide urge that had been all but ignored. No less an eminence than the late Peter Jennings conceded, "Perhaps we have missed the conservative view for too many years."

Casting Ailes as Lord Voldemort misses the essential point. Ailes loudly protested in 2010 on *This Week* on ABC, "I am not in politics, I am in ratings. We're winning." Back in '03, he told the *Daily News,* "We're not programming to conservatives. We're just not eliminating their point of view." His strategy to program journalism under the banner "fair and balanced" immediately put the rest of the gang off balance.

"We report, you decide" became the mantra, because Ailes believed the

Big Three talked down to the viewer. Fox News is delivered across the breakfast table like a televisual Fleet Street tabloid—complete with banner headlines and "Remember the *Maine*," homage to God and country.

CNN went to war immediately. Joining ranks with parent Time Warner, they blocked carriage of the pubescent news channel. Unlike broadcast networks, the first battle in cable news is not about programming, it's about living rooms. If you're distributed by the cable operator into the home, you have a shot. If you are not invited into the living room, you're in the dead room.

Murdoch was born to play underdog and he did so with relish. Fox News launched with 17 million subscribers, none in New York or Los Angeles, compared to CNBC's 22 and CNN's 70 plus million. They were every inch a dark horse.

Ailes led at night with opinion, featuring the *O'Reilly Report* (now *The Factor*) and the *Crier Report* featuring Catherine Crier, and a half-hearted attempt at balanced programming with *Hannity and Colmes.*

By 2002 Fox News surged past CNN in ratings, propelled by programming and the nationalism coursing through American veins in the aftermath of 9/11. Just as Desert Storm made CNN, Operation Iraqi Freedom marked Fox's moment. At the height of the Iraq conflict, Fox enjoyed as much as a 300 percent increase in viewership, averaging 3.3 million eyeballs a day.

Ponderous news organizations watched like world-weary members of the House of Lords as the outbreaks drew viewers to the House of Commons on cable. Animosities played out in plain sight. O'Reilly and Geraldo bellowed at each other, while over at MSNBC, liberals Chris Matthews and Olbermann walked on each other's lines.

Talk formats evolved from one-on-one debate, to panels, to *Hollywood Squares*–style hoot fests. Personal insults rather than dialogue became the norm.

CNBC went liberal after dark: Rachel Maddow joined Matthews and Olbermann. Fox News dismissed them as the chattering class elites.

Gravity sought the lowest common denominator.

Morning zoo disc spinner Glenn Beck found a reasonable following at

CNN. But calling Obama a traitor at Fox in 2008 elevated him to a media brand, stuffed to the plimsoll line with apocalypse and conspiracy. He regularly attracted two million viewers even as he alienated advertisers and News Corp brass.

Branding himself like Oprah, Beck's $9.95 *Insider Extreme* Web service earned more than double his Fox earnings, *Forbes* reports. GB-TV delivered via the Internet is on the horizon—the first Impressionist turned impresario. The King of All Media, Howard Stern, had plowed that field in a massive payday with aspiring Sirius satellite radio.

No wonder more people turned to humor journalists for their news.

Fox News surged. When Scott Brown won a special election in Massachusetts, over six million viewers tuned in—more eyeballs than CNN, MSNBC, and CNBC together. Ailes built a cash flow juggernaut, exceeding the income-generating capabilities of *all* other broadcast news programs combined.

With profits came dangerous precedents . . . and megatrends.

POLARIZING MEDIA MEGATRENDS

THE REVOLVING DOOR OF POLITICIANS to lobbying firms and Think Tanks found yet another egress: TV news.

Sarah Palin, Mike Huckabee, and Newt Gingrich became Fox News paid political analysts. All but Palin were one-time Republican presidential candidates (Newt's back). MSNBC's Harold Ford Jr. left the network to run, then quit, the U.S. Senate race in New York, only to return again like a TV MacArthur.

In *The Making of the President,* John F. Kennedy was viewed like a product manufactured by the media. Celebrity politicians as paid analysts mean two things: More politically charged news, and endless televised political branding—Energizer bunnies that never stop banging the drum.

Part-time pundits get visibility and dinero, and the viewers get an automatic affinity group.

Politicians have crossed this bridge and back before. Pat Buchanan notoriously co-hosted CNN's *Crossfire* in the '90s, even as he paused for a station break to run for president twice. And Ronald Reagan sandwiched radio and newspaper gigs between his California governorship and his 1980 run for the Oval Office.

A piercing example of the problem occurred when Fox's Chris Wallace promoted an "exclusive" interview with Sarah Palin, failing to mention in the promo that she was an employee of the network.

A second TV-polarizing megatrend comes courtesy of the Supreme Court: the *Citizens United v. Federal Election Commission* decision tears down a wall that has stood for a century between corporations and electoral politics. The ruling also liberates labor unions to spend freely on advertising. Their coffers pale in comparison to those of major corporations, but unions understand advocacy.

To be fair, major publicly held corporations like General Motors or General Electric are unlikely to lavish huge sums on campaign commercials for a particular candidate for fear of alienating any stakeholders. But it is likely that unions, trade associations, and myriad third-party groups and lobbying initiatives, like the U.S. Chamber of Commerce or the National Rifle Association, will see massive inflows.

A final megatrend, apart from the Internet tsunami, is that the end of network news as we know it may be at hand.

As 2010 opened, ABC News was faced with a most unusual challenge: survival. The necessary decision to furlough 25 percent of its workforce followed similar moves over the prior 20 months at CBS and NBC News.

Here are the facts: network news costs are completely out of line with declining viewership (21.6 million in 2010 versus 50 million-plus in 1980) and falling advertising revenues. Not surprisingly, all the networks have pursued a survival strategy that will not work.

Firing every third person and pining for a rebound is flawed—hope is a very bad strategy.

NBC is the only one of the Big Three with a cable news channel, MS-NBC, and a business/talk channel, CNBC, which ensure steady subscription revenues to support their costly network news operation.

Sadly, CBS and ABC have no such offsets to their sea of red ink. Are these bastions of serious news about to fall away to the benefit of the tabloid channels? Unlikely. But consolidation is as inevitable as the tides. Two likely brides are CNN and Bloomberg, both solidly profitable. When one goes, the other will follow expensively.

What exactly is their incentive to marry ABC News or CBS News? Neither network news business makes much money, neither is growing, even as they cost-cut their way to prosperity. Will the bigger marquee name or the bigger earner control the news?

I borrow Warren Buffett's golden rule: "He who has the gold makes the rules."

Network news is a falling knife. But no network CEO wants to shut out the lights on their news legacy. The days are numbered for network news divisions lacking cable or digital revenues. Old media companies pray surging digital fortunes will replace disappearing eyeballs and peeling profits. Record companies stacked 99-cent songs as fast as they fed into MP3s, but their business suffered for a simple reason: losses trumped the mountain of 99-cent gains.

Lest Cable get too cocky, the Internet tolls for thee.

Today, 75 percent of Americans hear breaking news via e-mail or social networking sites. Studies still show broadcast cable as the most sought-after news source, but they used to say the same about the Big Three.

The Internet has transformed news. Stroll through blogs, chat rooms, even bulletin boards—it's a coliseum of venting, plural voices, and digital lynchings.

Every netizen is a one-man CNN. And you are editor-in-chief. Do you seek shelter with people who see things exactly like you do? Or do you pull your own wagon?

Dozens of talk-show mavens skillfully promote their ideas. Some are pure geniuses, many are not.

They are players on a stage. It's show business, folks—a ratings game aimed at viewers, subscribers, and sometimes advertisers. Hundreds of advertisers have identified shows with which they refuse to associate. Talk mavens don't care. In the new model, advertiser boycott is no cause for alarm.

What is cause for alarm is that dialogue and discourse have disappeared even as decibels rise. Peer deep into the screen, beyond the wires, the spectrum, and the airwaves. Beasts lurk within—puppet masters who harness massive cash flows to bend the shape of the river.

Once we feared the military-industrial complex. Today's version is the media-talk complex, a multibillion-dollar cash machine designed to whirl us to extremes.

It is the ultimate one-sided transaction disguised as a two-way exchange; a freezing factor, a palliative elixir for a collective angst—endless talk and a bankruptcy of listening. Nothing ever gets resolved, just a repeated philosophical pitch thrown over and over like an eternal baseball game in Hell.

The problem is not that you are watching. It's that you are frozen to your couch. Nighttime talk is junk food for your cerebellum. It makes you an intellectual slob. If you only watch people who agree with you it's time for Tae Bo on your brain.

Declare intellectual Chapter 11 and seek protection from talk. Try a listening channel instead. All listening, all the time. Listen to someone whose opinions you loathe. Go to a Tea Party function. Occupy something other than your family room or your IP address. Engage with someone you completely disagree with.

That won't sell tabloids, but it will unite us.

But if you can only be happy watching people who think like you do—don't worry, you can always go back. The strings of the puppet masters are still attached to you.

Factor Two

Democracy Under the Influence (DUI): Lobbyists in the Kitchen

IT IS THE BEST OF TIMES; *and the worst of times. Washington has always been a city of two tales.*

One story starts far from the District's metes and bounds; the other, right there on K Street. Washington has forever been a town trussed up by its own struggles. But for all its duality, the troubles always begin far from the Beltway, then wend their way back.

Deep in the swampy back roads of bayou Louisiana sits a town that time might have forgotten named Elton. In the land of Huey Long, where every man's a king, Elton boasted its own principality.

The Coushata Indian Tribal Nation has a story we have heard before, but this time with a surprise ending. Siding with the British against an indifferent settler populace in our earliest days, the Creek Nation, including the Coushata, were remanded to Georgia where they eked out a farming existence until their land became prized. Treaties repudiated, the Creek were sent to Alabama where the tribe endured its own civil war.

Split again, the Coushata found succor on the shores of the Kinder River farther west, in Louisiana. They were still not quite home. Squatters began to homestead on these Indian territories, tightening on the Coushata like a noose.

Exasperated, the enterprising tribe decided to pool its resources and purchase a plot of land just north of a tiny backwater near Elton. What follows is a sad tale of land placed in trust by the federal government around the opening of the twentieth century.

In the 1930s the Bureau of Indian Affairs took responsibility for the health and education of the tribe. Then more pressing matters caused the federal agency to turn away. The trust dissolved, the land was gone, the tribe struggled and scraped by.

In a final attempt to reclaim its sovereignty the Coushata fought the federal government and were granted a miserly 140 acres. It was 1988 and after generations of grim tribulation, they were finally home.

In the 1990s the tribe applied to Louisiana authorities to establish a casino on their sovereign land. Disputes followed, naturally, but tax exemption was ultimately granted. After one last federal fracas over the land, the tribe prevailed and by 1995 the Grand Casino opened with great fanfare.

Steve Wynn has nothing to worry about.

The casino is modest by every measure save one: The pride of the tribal leaders. Louisiana, which is stringent about few things, is very restrictive of gambling within its boundaries. The small casino prospered.

After the long struggle things were good with the tribe. So good in fact that other tribes took notice. Using the same playbook, the Tigua carved out a piece of land inside the city limits of El Paso, Texas, where they created the Speaking Rock Casino.

Back in the bayou, the Coushata grew nervous.

It's hard to explain what happened next, and harder to fully comprehend. But the primal fear of the tribe seemed to magically attract people with malevolent intention from another tribe entirely. This one does its hunting and gathering along K Street in the nation's capital.

Washington baffles outsiders. It's a foreign and complex world where clues and signals, like wind talker code, guide the players from skirmish to skirmish.

That civic planners designated two non-contiguous meandering streets "K Street" gives a cartoonish peek into the confusing and backhanded battles that lobbyists wage in the foggy bottoms and riverbanks of Washington. Northern K Street is the real K Street, and in a city of unwritten secrets, you just have to know which one's which.

K Street is home to nearly 15,000 lobbyists who have grown their practice into a $3.5 billion-a-year business.

How it is that lobbyist Jack Abramoff found the Coushata is lost in lore.

But the dark and stocky operator coolly explained to the troubled tribal leadership that he could find ways to shut the Tigua Tribe's rival operation down. It was a matter of killing legislation, something his access enabled him to do. His starting retainer was $120,000 a month with additional fees and contributions to be determined. Abramoff assured the beleaguered tribe he could silence the Speaking Rock.

The campaign was entirely concealed.

How does such a clandestine action work?

Ralph Reed secretly accepted payments from Abramoff and associates so that he and his Christian Coalition and other organizations would conduct anti-gambling campaigns. The money flowed through nonprofits to disguise its sources because Reed never wanted a path leading from his name to Abramoff's.

The money was cleansed and bore no markings . . . or so Reed thought.

No matter how disguised the trail, Reed forgot one thing. Pissed-off Indians make excellent trackers.

But Ralph Reed was rarely lacking in confidence.

"I do guerrilla warfare." Reed once boasted to a reporter in describing how he works as a political operative. "I paint my face and travel at night. You don't know it's over until you are in a body bag."

The Tigua never saw the attack coming. Like a midnight raid, by the time the Texas tribe found out, the die was cast. Their casino was shuttered as promised.

In the real world that is where the story ends. The Coushata triumph and the Speaking Rock is silenced. But K Street is not the real world.

So the story is just starting to get interesting. Abramoff was connected. From his Pennsylvania Avenue restaurant Signatures, a green-and-gold awninged speakeasy boasting walls of rare documents including a signed replica of Gerald Ford's Nixon pardon, Abramoff hosted the city's elite. Most just went to be seen, yet in this salon were strung the simple connections that would create Abramoff's expansive web.

He possessed a simple but hard-won asset: access.

It wasn't long before the terrors of the Tigua drew Abramoff and his team to El Paso. Guilelessly, Abramoff explained his position.

Someone clearly had it in for the Tigua casino, he explained, failing to mention that someone was him. The armies of the night had gathered in secret and the Tigua Nation needed a true friend in the process. Abramoff assured them he was the only one they could trust.

Without his help, he cautioned, their casino would never reopen. A vehicle was necessary, Abramoff explained, in order to give voice to the Speaking Rock.

The strategy was exquisite in its dark effectiveness—secretly shut down their casino; then get retained by the same tribe to reopen it.

His initial retainer was supported by a payment of $5 million.

FORGET EVERYTHING PEOPLE HAVE TOLD you about lobbyists.

Their role has evolved over the decades as they've crawled from the primordial ooze to the office complex. Lobbyists are like the Blackwater mercenaries of legislative process and their role is almost universally misunderstood.

So your simple choice is to figure out how the game is played or remain blissfully ignorant.

Being a Radical Centrist means having the courage to probe.

For lobbyists it is the best of times. Business is booming. The magnitude of their influence will shock you. Their scale, scope, and growth are immense and mission critical. Lobbyists are an absolute governing necessity, particularly on the state level.

"We can't live with them, can't live without them."

We need lobbyists to make good law; we just need to manage them more effectively.

They are magnets for debate: we can't even agree on how they got their name. America lays claim to the moniker. Since that very first day when a man on a mission approached Ulysses S. Grant, who was enjoying brandy and a cigar in the lobby of the Willard Hotel, the term *lobbyist* was hatched to describe using chummy proximity to gain undue influence.

Never to be outdone, the British claim the term describes their heritage of hallway badinage in the Houses of Parliament between MPs, Peers, Lords, and Commoners.

Whatever the etymology, peddling influence has exploded into a multi-billion-dollar industry. Few people have a precise sense of how vast and integral lobbying has become to our state and federal government—to the extent that we cannot possibly manage without professional lobbyists. And by becoming indispensable, lobbyists gain extraordinary access.

THE BEST OF TIMES

SO WHAT IS THE OTHER story? If Abramoff is the worst of times, then what is the best of times in lobbying today? It is a new breed of player, many far from K Street confines, a new style of influencer, less colorful perhaps but in many ways more powerful.

And a lot less dark. You won't find them hiding in the long grass with the snakes. They are more apt to be working the canyons of Wall Street or peering for hours into a flat screen.

Preston Baldwin tossed his boyish mop of hair to one side and buttoned his suit. Standing about five-and-a-half feet tall, his outsized personality and charm nevertheless gave everyone the impression they were speaking to him eye to eye. As he watched the Capitol's morning bustle blossom in a riotous explosion of clicking heels and thumbed BlackBerries, Preston soothed himself. Today was a day for action and he was more than ready.

Schooled at the University of Virginia, Preston had honed his craft working for companies like UST, the smokeless tobacco crowd that brought you Skoal, Happy Days Mint, and the endless pinches between cheek and gum. He had developed a clinical remove, learned the ways of Washington, studying how the older lobbyists did their kabuki dance of twisting arms, slapping backs, and picking up the tab. It was an art, a craft requiring an apprentice's attention.

First he learned a lot about how they did what they did; then chose to do everything differently.

And he tried something even rarer; he read every word of every bill in which his clients were involved. He read liner notes and briefing memos. He asked around. He became the change.

When he met with legislators and their overworked staff he knew more than just the strengths and weaknesses of the bill. He had the legislative war game all mapped out. Blending the old and the new, Preston looked for strategic value add: structural shifts in important districts, predictive voting patterns, reaction models for various interest groups; where you could get hurt, where it didn't matter.

Most important for those seeking re-election, which was everyone, he could tell you whether you needed to vote or not.

Lobbying has become a professional sport.

But the bull's-eye is moving from K Street's center of the universe, much like Wall Street broadened across the land to Main Street. Professionals like Preston have moved their focus to places where they can have impact free of the beltway's intestinal blockage. Imagine advising a big-box retailer on a policy initiative in all 50 states. Such an undertaking cannot be reduced to twisting arms and zero-sum gains. No winner takes all.

The business of lobbying has become a classic advisory game—complex and consultative, it's centered around trying to assess the flow of things and put your client at the center of the solution. These major multistate programs are where the big changes in lobbying are headed. And execution requires critical mass—so lobbying is a growth industry.

For so many in the new breed, the District is a drained pipe—so balkanized that all their energy is sapped just trying to maintain status quo.

Ironically, the framers' intent for states' rights and the Tenth Amendment has come full circle, but not for the reason they envisioned. The cause is stalemate in Washington.

Today, Preston advises clients never to make a decision until they have to. The game is no longer about architecting victory for the benefit of a corporate client to the exclusion of all else.

Lobbying has evolved into a government-relations consulting practice for finding what can be done; it requires a broader lens, greater patience, and a willingness to coach legislators—not pick their pockets.

For the new breed of lobbyist like Preston, representing corporate clients involves carefully finding a solution that works for both sides. Doing so means working diligently to find a middle ground.

If you are a lawmaker and a bill is dying, yet you need to support it to gain favor with a constituency, Preston can coach you on the best way to cast your toothless vote and gain credit at home while the doomed measure sails over the falls. Or if a bill is certain to pass, and your home district hates the measure, he advises the most sophisticated way to vote nay or yea.

Preston has a way of knowing what makes you look and feel your best. He's the ultimate beauty regime. And, if you are an activist, trading your vote or a provision for support elsewhere (and by this definition, everyone in the game is an activist), he can probability weight the outcomes, evaluate scenario analyses of each trade, and show you the dispersion of returns on every branch of the decision tree. In the corridors of power he paints legislators their risk portrait, evaluates their potential losses and gains, and gauges the tolerance for the compromises that make government hum. Balancing corporate clients with legislative realities, he is like a hedge fund czar.

He is the change—a skillful marriage of the old and the new. Close, trusted, and shrewd, he blends the science of governing with research and persuasion. And despite the charm offensive, he is the ultimate political scientist. And he is everywhere.

SO JUST HOW BIG ARE we talking here?

Six billion dollars was spent on lobbying over the last two years, with nearly 15,000 lobbyists handling the U.S. Congress and the federal government alone. Yet these massive numbers still do not come close to conveying the influence lobbyists enjoy.

People tend to think of lobbyists as exclusively focused on representatives and senators; they couldn't be more wrong. Lobbyists amble through every trail and tributary of the federal government's agency structure.

Take, for example, the Industry Trade Advisory Committees, or ITACs, which propagate throughout the federal branch. These powerful commissions outlast elected officials and represent the apparatus of government. They have been a magnet for inquiry of late, but ITACs have longevity and survival instincts. These committees advise the federal government on a wide variety of policy areas. The president does not appoint their members but instead they are chosen by the federal agencies themselves.

Lobbyists call that a port of entry.

Agency regulation has as much to do with how the government operates and how companies and individuals are expected to behave as it does with any laws enacted by Congress. Yet, these commissions work completely under the radar screens of even the closest watchers of our government.

How many ITACs are there? While no one knows precisely where all of these panels and commissions are, estimates are that they number around 1,000 and include a membership of more than 60,000 people. A significant number of these members are registered lobbyists and a surprising number of lobbyists actually chair the commissions on which they serve.

Rightfully, the Obama administration is concerned about these highly influential panels and commissions carrying so many lobbyists among their members. What's more illuminating than obvious concern over spheres of influence is that on many commissions, lobbyists play a key role in generating many of the documents and policy pieces that are the work of the committee.

In lobbying there is a law of the jungle: Propinquity is the key to longevity.

We'll see how effective the administration is at governing the ITACs, but first they have to find them.

Counting up the number of companies pressuring the federal branch is another way to uncover lobbyist impact. Since the dizzying array of federal regulations critically affects profits, corporations are active lobbyers. The number peaked at over 2,000 companies under the Bush administration. And, proving that not all politics is local, nearly 700 companies from 79 other countries have lobbied the federal government in the last decade.

Powerful forces work throughout the District. They contribute to polarity and the death of common sense even as they grease the wheels of government. Worse, they prohibit any hope of nimble reaction. Like a philodendron, they are almost impossible to kill.

After the tragedy at Virginia Tech in 2007, in which a crazed gunman systematically murdered and wounded students, staff, and faculty at the university, why was there nary a whisper of debate in the *Congressional Record* about an assault weapons law ban?

Laws get made by influencers, and influencers have money to make things happen. We have moved from an electorate to a Selectorate. And we have created a system in which many legislators do not tackle problems that they do not have to solve. It has become too risky to do so.

No single thing about lobbyists should trouble you more than the notorious *revolving door*. The government, military, and corporate worlds have developed very porous membranes at their adjacencies.

Right after he left Congress, Wilbert "Billy" Tauzin II, a former Cajun representative, went from shepherding the Medical Prescription Drug Bill through Congress to joining the lobbying organization PhRMA, a trade group representing the pharmaceutical industry, as its new $2 million-a-year CEO. There was no necessity for a training program. He had the other side's playbook—he had written it.

Tauzin began political life as a conservative Democrat but later switched to the Republican Party because he felt conservative viewpoints were no longer welcome in the Democratic Party. Tauzin is not a man discomforted by changing sides. He has lots of company.

Why is the *revolving door* so powerful?

Former members of Congress retain access to the members-only dining facilities, gymnasiums, cloakrooms, and the chamber floors. They can boldly go where no others dare. More than access is the steady flow.

Of the 100 most recent members to leave Congress for private life, over 40 percent have become lobbyists. In a six-year period, more than 2,200 former federal employees, including 273 former White House staffers and nearly 250 former members of Congress, have registered as federal lobbyists. A reasonable question is, how much influence can these people have once they gain access?

Look at the federal and state legislation process. For years I have heard House members hold their lapels and reassuringly declare that they have introduced legislation. Typically the declaration is made as if it were written on a tablet.

Listeners have a tendency to react with respect and a bit of awe. But the facts may alter that reverential response.

According to *Roll Call*, the 110th Congress was the busiest since 1980, in terms of bills introduced—14,000. Hillary Clinton led the pack, introducing a piece of legislation nearly every day that Congress was in session during her period as New York senator. From that robust flood of introduction, 449, only about three percent, trickled into law and nearly a third of those were ceremonial, naming buildings for a dignitary or declarations of a name for a day. That compared with 121 such bills in the 109th Congress.

Ceremony is clearly on the rise. How reassuring for the republic.

Volume of bills passed is not indicative of workload, however, since Congress increasingly bundles measures into jumbo omnibus bills. One result of this trend toward packaged legislation is that unrelated programs and regulations are swooped up in a single act, and that's before earmarks worm their way in. Few people, if anyone, can be expected to have command of all the subject matter in an omnibus bill.

Lobbyists play a very important role in informing legislators of all of the aspects of a particular bill. They are uniquely positioned to do so. (Some of the verbiage is theirs.)

For the 535 members of Congress and their combined staff of 30,000 there simply isn't time to manage it all. Increasingly, matters are outsourced to lobbyists who are frequently supplying position papers and many are providing specific language for legislation.

The best lobbyists have elevated their game.

What most lay people regard as lobbying, actual communication and advocating with government officials, represents the smallest portion of a lobbyist's time. Most is spent researching and analyzing complex and constantly evolving proposals, attending endless regulatory and congressional hearings, building ventures and coalitions with like-minded groups, and something new and different: Game Theory.

Made popular in the movie *A Beautiful Mind,* Game Theory is a branch of applied mathematics and social science which attempts to capture behavior in strategic situations in which an individual's success in making choices is affected by the choices of others. John Nash, a Nobel Prize–winning economist, developed a theory of equilibrium, though it was hard to find in his own life. In equilibrium, each player begins with a strategy that they are unlikely to change. As moves are made, consequences both intended and otherwise occur.

In complex legislation, having a sense of the consequences and reactions of your game counterparts and the other stakeholders is crucial. Game theorists imagine simultaneous moves on the chessboard and how they affect lawmakers. This is a complex world with meaningful sway in the results. The very best lobbyists educate not just legislators, but everyone with a stake in the outcome.

This new breed of talent is a long way from the caricature of the gout-hobbled, steak and port, "winer and diner" of overfed lawmakers. Today's lobbyist is a highly sophisticated professional whose organizations earn billions in revenues with a direct involvement in governing the country.

Lobbyists aspire to be the Fourth Branch of the government, but they are closer to the back office.

Yet they escape real scrutiny. To put things in context, the amount spent each year on lobbying is routinely more than double what is given to federal candidates and committees in campaign contributions. Yet campaign finance reform gets all the attention.

On the state level, lobbyists arguably play an even larger role.

Consider the state legislator: fully six state legislative bodies meet biennially. That's right: every two years. Only six to eight meet in something that feels like a yearlong session, and most states meet for 60 to 90 days a year.

It's a part-time job, with a difference.

State governments routinely review 1,500 to 2,000 pieces of legislation resulting in between 100 and 500 bills in a compressed period. Even when divided by committees the workload sums to 50 bills per committee.

The difference is this part-time job has a full-time workload. That means that state representatives desperately need help. And they get it.

Only with the support of lobbyists can these part-time government leaders facilitate the passage of all these laws. Many will admit, as will members of the U.S. Congress, that they cannot possibly read all of the legislation before they pass it.

It gets worse.

Lobbyists are not only integral to passing laws; they also handle the purse strings. By chairing, controlling, and influencing what are known as PACs and 527s, they can influence both issues and election outcomes.

PACs, or Political Action Committees, raise and spend money to help elect and defeat candidates. The innovation of PACs was first used to help FDR win re-election essentially from the "voluntary" contributions of union members.

Leadership PACs are funds raised by politicians with the aim of funding other candidates' campaigns. Lobbyists have served as treasurers of over 800 PACs in the last decade and have spent over a half a billion dollars.

As for Leadership PACs, at least 79 members of Congress have appointed lobbyists to head their campaign committees or leadership PACs in the last decade.

Stop and think about the result: lobbyists are attempting to influence legislators even as they chair committees which give money to some of those very legislators' campaigns.

Thank goodness they can keep the Chinese wall in their head because the rest of us would have too much trouble keeping ourselves from being conflicted.

As for 527s, they are a different breed of influencing organization. These groups tend to be more issue-oriented than candidate-driven, though the Swift Boat Group pushed the envelope by going directly after John Kerry and ran into difficulty because of it.

What results from all of this influencing is a mixed bag. Clearly lobbyists have created the grease for the cogs of government. That combination of command of the subject matter, money, and access are integral to the process of governing.

But increasingly, at both the federal and congressional levels, lobbying firms and their lobbyist professionals are categorizable as Democratic or Republican, right or left. They are an outsourced battalion that can grease the works or polarize with equal skill.

Particularly with the advent of omnibus legislation, they are indispensable resources for understanding a bill and its implications. With competing stakeholders each engaging their political muscle, we fight to a standoff with greater frequency.

Remember, it is far easier to kill legislation than to make it.

That's why fewer than nine percent of the proposed bills never see daylight.

And lobbyists are skilled at telling legislators what the probabilities are of passage of controversial bills. They can tell who will be angered, who will forgive, and who will never forget.

For members holding elective office, those insights are a matter of political survival; and someone sharing that judgment is a friend indeed.

So the game has gotten more like chess and a lot less like a friendly checkers match. All this complexity cleaves the lobbyist to Congress.

The problem with lobbying today is not so much what is illegal but what is legal and sanctified. So much of what goes on in Washington lies in the loopholes. Money is flowing everywhere.

At least 30 American corporations spent more money on lobbying than they paid in federal income taxes between 2008 and 2010. Lobbyists have silent partners, nonprofits, and fuzzy connections.

It is the nexus of money and influence that is the age-old magnet for misjudgment. The system encourages corruption because it requires a certain pragmatism to get things accomplished.

The system also enables opposing players to maneuver to stalemate, because they each employ their own supporting cast of lobbyists.

The most important missing piece is that much of the work is clandestine.

The Worst of Times

BY THE TIME JACK ABRAMOFF was finished with the Coushata and Tigua, the two tribes had paid nearly $36 million to cancel each other out. Estimates of the total take for Abramoff's extensive Indian casino work were in the neighborhood of $82 million.

The final number is elusive because money was paid in fees and contributions to Abramoff-selected charities and nonprofits with strong Republican ties. The lobbyist advised tribes in Mississippi, Louisiana, and Michigan to hire an associate's company, Capital Campaign Strategies, LLC, for grassroots public relations work while hiding the fact that he would receive half of the profits. He also brokered lucrative jobs for congressional aides at powerful lobbying firms in exchange for legislative favors. As reported in the *Washington Post* in 2004, a review of Abramoff's charity Capital Athletic Foundation showed it took in millions for "needy and deserving" kids' sports programs over four years and spent less than one percent of its revenue on them.

Abramoff concocted an extraordinary three-ring circus of lobbying, political fundraising, and nonprofit work. When he was in the first two rings he was clearly a partisan, and in the third he would suddenly become nonpartisan.

It was an amazing parlor trick, and he moved from one sphere to the other with such dexterity, people never felt a border was crossed.

All this ring mastering brings us back to the vital currency of the story—access. And in the political world of strange bedfellows, Abramoff used his access to create a very strange pair indeed.

He had come to know Bob Ney, a Wonderbread Republican Congressman from Ohio, in the day-to-day business of building rapport with lawmakers. Golfing weekends in Scotland and entertaining Sundays at football super boxes brought Ney into Abramoff's parlor. He also hired Ney's Chief of Staff to join his firm. Ney and Abramoff developed a rapport.

It was soon time to repay the debt.

The Tigua sent their lieutenant governor, Carlos Hissa, to Washington to meet with Congressman Ney. That session would haunt Ney for the rest of his days.

He and Chief of Staff Neil Volz were hard at work on a bill that was an antidote to the Florida 2000 hanging chad fiasco. They were calling the bill the heartwarming "Help America Vote Act." It was an ideal cover for Abramoff's clients.

As co-sponsor Ney had a lot riding on the bill. But there was always room for a last-minute addendum; it was done all the time. Ney gave the tribal leader clear assurances that the deal was struck and the casino would soon reopen. "Just leave it to me."

How many bad decisions commence with that line?

How do these riders and earmarks work?

Earmarks were designated funding requests for specific projects, which were added to bills. What began as small addenda to a bill after debate by the legislature exploded into a gigantic source of non-reviewed funding. Earmarks became a currency of corruption, and you could run a small nation with the proceeds they generated.

In the 1950s when Eisenhower passed his first Highway Transportation Bill there were two specific projects earmarked for construction. In a 2006 transportation bill there were well over 6,000 earmarks added without debate or scrutiny summing to over $24 billion.

The good times couldn't last forever.

In 2011 House Republicans and the President issued a moratorium. Earmarks had reached half of one percent of all federal funding without real review. They weren't all fatty pork, but they brought home the bacon for lobbyists. For fees and a few hundred thousand or at worst a few million, massive projects could fall into the laps of interested parties . . . tantalizing returns on investment.

Lobbyists dashed to fill the breach. Within 90 days of earmarks getting a speeding ticket, the *Washington Post* reported the emergence of "phonemarking," where legislators called agencies with specific local funding requests.

Our trusted enablers were right in the thick of things, prompting the calls.

If it walks like an earmark . . .

Back when he was sitting across the table from an earnest Tigua Indian visitor, Bob Ney had every reason to believe what he was predicting would come to pass. In the fullness of time, the "Help America Vote Act" was signed by President Bush.

Soon after there was joy in El Paso and the Tigua Casino reopened.

In the real world the story might end happily there. But in the Abramoff world a stranger turn occurred. Abramoff prospered at the edges, finding folks on the periphery who needed:

ACCESS.

Clients had money and Abramoff made his fortune trading one for the other.

The winds of fate blew the lobbyist far out into the western Pacific, as far from Ney's Ohio as you could find on the globe.

The Northern Mariana Islands claim, among their many virtues, to be a U.S. territory. My father was stationed there on the island of Saipan during the Second World War.

Despite the helpful designation of American territory, there are certain U.S. laws which do not apply there. A small number of local mandarins like it that way.

In sections of the island sweatshops staffed with densely packed young ladies churn out garments with labels which justifiably read, "Made in the USA."

Local mandarins like the label too.

It was the best of both worlds. Emerging nation manufacturing economics married to the ability to say, "Crafted with Pride in the USA."

As business improved, conditions in the shops worsened. American authorities turned a deaf ear. After years of substandard circumstances and pay, workers summoned their courage and complained to U.S. officials. That's when Al Stayman, head of the State Department's Marianas Office, got involved. Stayman's intercession led to the drafting of a bill that had the simple goal of improving conditions and the compensation of workers in this American territory.

Anxiety spread like influenza among the sweatshop owners.

Once again, anxiety drew malevolence. Jack Abramoff had an uncanny ability to insert himself into troubled situations and solve them for hire.

Abramoff's chief contact on the Marianas matter was House majority whip Tom DeLay of Texas, and later of *Dancing with the Stars*.

DeLay and his family traveled all-expenses paid to the Marianas. I have watched videotape of Abramoff's enveloping hug of welcome at the airport. DeLay was whisked away to golf and beach excursions and as near as anyone can recall never saw the inside of a sweatshop.

But the results of his trip were long lasting. For the next ten years, the Marianas Worker Protection Bill (ultimately introduced as the Northern Marianas Human Dignity Act) never saw the inside of the House Chambers. DeLay proved the master of delay.

The Marianas vacation began a drip feed of benefits for DeLay from Abramoff—he played a major role in DeLay's well-financed and successful run for Whip. DeLay also enjoyed all-expenses-paid trips to Scotland for a week of golf at Saint Andrews, as well as trips to Russia and South Korea.

One trip on the Gulfstream to Scotland makes for most interesting reading. The itinerary called for teeing up at seven courses in five days. In between were sumptuous meals and grand old hotels. The costs for an adventure in the heather were determined by federal prosecutors to exceed $150,000 but for the Republican lawmakers the trip was free of charge. Abramoff paid for the freebie with someone else's money—the Capital Athletic Foundation, a charity he created to fund inner-city youth athletic programs. Most of the donations came from lobbying clients like six Indian tribes who had other connections to Abramoff.

Things between the master lobbyist and the Majority Whip had gotten very cozy indeed.

Distance is hard to maintain when you state, as DeLay did in 1997, "When one of my closest and dearest friends, Jack Abramoff, your most able representative in Washington, D.C., invited me to the islands I wanted to see firsthand the free-market success and progress and reform you have made."

All was well with the world. Casinos buzzed, sweatshops hummed, money changed hands, and all the while Abramoff raked in the fees.

Just who was Jack Abramoff?

A College Republican leader with Grover Norquist (who later got a majority of Republican legislators to sign his no tax increase pledge) and Ralph Reed, a young Abramoff espoused extreme free market dogma. He was a fragrant personality even then.

This sometime movie producer was a square-jawed, boxy weight-lifting champion at Beverly Hills High School. The young conservative spent time as President of Regency Entertainment Group but was drawn to the District and the lobbying world by catching the Gingrich wave of the mid-nineties.

Cutting his teeth at Preston, Gates—a well-regarded conservative law firm—it wasn't long before Abramoff's wanderlust took him elsewhere.

He landed at Greenberg Traurig, where he plied his trade as an independent operator; that is until the bottom fell out.

He was named to the 2001 Bush transition team as an advisor to the Department of Interior, which oversees Native American issues. Though in 2006, after Abramoff was convicted, at a press conference the President spoke reassuringly: "I, frankly, don't even remember having my picture taken with the guy. I don't know him."

Abramoff once produced political action thrillers like *Red Scorpion* with funding from South Africa's apartheid regime. The forgettable action figure movie features Dolph Lundgren as muscle-bound protagonist. When Lundgren is questioned on capture "Are you out of your mind?" he coolly responds, "No, just out of bullets."

It might serve as a fitting epitaph. The trouble began as trouble often does, innocently enough—a limited inquiry into Indian casinos.

The Justice Department found a secret weapon in Tom Rodgers, a Native American and former Democratic staffer working for the Saginaw Chippewa Tribe. Someone at the tribe had questioned Abramoff's billing practices and was shocked at the threats that resulted. Rodgers worked for years in obscurity plotting ways to bring the lobbyist to justice.

He had a target-rich environment.

Shortly after Abramoff had purchased a fleet of casino boats in Florida called SunCruz, the former owner was murdered gangland-style. It had been a very trying negotiation. To help expedite the sale, Abramoff prevailed upon Ney to criticize former SunCruz owner, Gus Boulis, in statements placed in the *Congressional Record.* Ney also lavished praise on the new owner when the sale went through.

If this all sounds like a bad movie, Hollywood agreed—Kevin Spacey starred in the satire, *Casino Jack.* Both Abramoff and the film were released about the same time. But in the city of two tales nothing ever strains credulity. Justice compiled its evidence with great care. The connective tissue led them everywhere.

The news hit like a bombshell and provided the best smorgasbord of editorial outrage since Woodstein took down Nixon.

The *Washington Post* won a Pulitzer for its coverage of what it termed "the biggest scandal in Congressional history."

Jack Abramoff pleaded guilty to three federal felony counts on conspiracy, mail fraud, and tax evasion. He was also found guilty of fraud in the SunCruz casino purchase; plus two more felony counts. He spent three-and-a-half years in prison, a sentence lightened by his cooperation and admission to bribing at least 20 members of Congress.

Several news stations ominously foretold, "A lot of members of Congress will be losing sleep tonight."

What's been the nuclear fallout?

Bob Ney pleaded guilty to corruption charges and spent 17 months of a 30-month sentence in federal penitentiary.

That's it.

No one else in Congress was tried or imprisoned. A few may have lost sleep but they are still at their posts. Admittedly Tom DeLay lost his Majority Leader position and ultimately turned to life as a celebutard. Justice declined after six years to prosecute him on Abramoff, but dirty laundry in campaign finance landed him a three-year stretch in 2011—another great dancer behind bars.

And Ralph Reed put his political career in his own style of body bag, as he lost an election for Georgia Lieutenant Governor in a landslide.

A great many Americans were tickled by the news.

For a few months after release to a halfway house in 2010, Abramoff briefly rehabilitated at a kosher pizzeria in a Maryland strip mall until the dough ran out. There is no awning outside.

He is most certainly out of bullets. Except that he claims to have bribed at least 20 members of the nation's legislature . . . which makes him a man to be feared.

We were all expecting fireworks. The Abramoff Scandal was the greatest disappointment since Geraldo opened Al Capone's tomb.

Taking down Ney meant the Abramoff matter ended not with a bang, but a wimp.

You call this a "Blockbuster Corruption Scandal"? What happened to the "long list"? Was it overblown?

I think the opposite may well be true. It is simply too hard to prove the negative, but there was influence peddled, and everyone knows it. You vote in favor of a special interest. Something nice comes your way. It happens every day.

And the mere fact that a charity of murky connection to that special interest is a contributor or hired a staff member is too tenuous to prove anything.

Abramoff represents one part of Washington's city with two tales. Was he a rotten apple or an indication of a spoiled bunch?

Both tales are true. And that is why the duality continues and why Americans mistrust the process.

So what do Americans surmise about the world of lobbying? Most Americans don't want a Congress member that is too "small c" catholic representing their interests. They just want their share.

They rightfully suspect that the vast majority of the men and women who conduct lobbying as it exists today are not Jack Abramoffs or anything close. But without supervision and regulation, it is easy to see how exclusive access can be thoroughly and blatantly abused.

Americans also recognize that there is an indefinite opportunity for corruption. Washington is like Long Island Sound. It lacks sufficient flow to cleanse itself of poisons and toxins. Lobbyists tend to linger longer than elected officials. And for errant legislators and executive branch members, there are many safe nooks and harbors where they can hide.

So what can a Radical Centrist do? We need a concerted policy initiative to reform the lobbying industry. These four ideas are a great place for government to commence healing itself:

- All ITACs should be centrally registered; we know almost nothing about them.
- Real-time daily notice of lobbying contacts would shed sunlight.
- All nonprofits involving funding via lobbyists should be identified.
- Legislative reform governing the use of nonprofits as advocacy funders is way past due. PACs funding political campaigns should not be chaired by lobbyists.

We have outsourced huge parts of the governing of our nation to lobbyists who simultaneously advocate for, fund, and write the laws. They are on all sides of the equation. Elected officials come and go, but the lobbying apparatus remains, sustaining the great divide and directing the legislative process.

And that Game Theory calculus simply does not add up.

FACTOR THREE

The Ultimate Backstage Pass: Thought-Provoking Think Tanks

V LADIMIR PUTIN WAS STRIPPED TO *the waist and flexing; his pale and hairless chest still bore some of the musculature that he had hammered to steel as a boy. He was running for President. His handlers wanted an action figure, not a polished politician. The role was hardly a stretch because, until the moment of that photograph, Putin had never spent a single second campaigning in his entire life.*

Or maybe he had never stopped.

In school, the young man refused to attend German classes because the Nazis had wounded his father and killed his grandfather and uncles. In a pragmatic shift, which would begin to mark his determined steady rise, as an adult, Putin relented and became fluent in the language and transferred to Germany as a KGB man at the time of the fall of the Berlin Wall.

It was Boris Yeltsin who asked the young operative to spend three years in Dresden earning his chops. He was watching.

In a gray hillside villa hovering over the Elbe, young Putin spent the waning eighties convincing people to spy on the West. He toiled for nearly two decades as a mid-level KGB agent but rose only to the rank of Lieutenant Colonel. His next posting was back at his hometown of St. Petersburg working for a former law school professor, Anatoly Sobchak, who became the first democratically elected mayor of St. Petersburg in 1991. It pleased Putin to be home despite the changes he encountered. As a boy, he had known the city as Leningrad. At the same time that Sobchak was elected, the city's name was changed back to its imperial title. Russia was evolving.

As an "in the background" aide to Sobchak, Putin was never much of a public figure. But his years of living on the seam of East/West confrontation during the dying days of the Cold War taught him many lessons about survival.

Sobchak was ill-prepared for leadership and chafed with the newly reconstituted legislature, the Duma, from his first days in office. His "grey cardinal," as Putin was labeled, was Sobchak's frequent dispatch for mending relations. Putin was an efficient and stealthy repairman—two attributes highly prized by the Russian hierarchy.

When Sobchak was unsurprisingly defeated in 1996, Putin moved to Moscow at the behest of an intrigued and watchful Boris Yeltsin. Once again he was assigned a mid-level job, but this time at the Kremlin.

In no time, for reasons obvious to a tiny few, Putin's fortunes began to change, and quickly.

In 1997, he became director of the Federal Security Service, the domestic successor to the KGB. He became deputy chief of Presidential staff, completed a Ph.D.-equivalent dissertation, and was named head of the Kremlin Security Council . . . all within ten months.

He was just getting warmed up. By August of 1998, barely two years after he had arrived in Moscow, Putin was Prime Minister. And on the last day of the twentieth century, just fourteen months later, he was acting President of Russia.

Putin had never made a single campaign stop. Even by modern Russian standards, his secretive and swift advancement was meteoric. Three months later, the "grey cardinal" won 53 percent of the vote in the presidential election. He was marketed as an action hero, their very own 007, and won the hearts and minds of his countrymen. Helped by rising worldwide gas prices and a booming economy, Putin went on to lead the nation for a second term.

Along the way he learned a thing or two about orchestration, so when he was foreclosed from running again by term-limit laws, he did what he had been taught.

He watched, identified his successor, and when the moment arose, he acted. At the moment of truth, Putin turned to his Chief of Staff, Dmitry Medvedev, a fixture from their St. Petersburg city government days together. Medvedev had served in numerous roles, including Chairman of the Board of Gazprom, the world's largest natural gas company. Putin had developed Medvedev with even more care than he had himself been nurtured by Yeltsin.

Medvedev handily won the election, and in a triumph of orchestration, the "subordinate" role of Prime Minister went smoothly and serenely to his mentor, Putin.

Medvedev's Gazprom training was important to Putin. He was always shrewd in his cultivation of the new tycoons and he kept them on a fairly tight leash. Recalcitrants found themselves imprisoned or otherwise diminished.

The timing was apt because of Russia's resurgence on the world economic stage which was boosted in large measure by its oil wealth, but for real optionality even more so by the nation's staggeringly abundant fields of proven, undeveloped reserves.

Much of Russia's supply of oil is buried deep in the ground many thousands of miles from refinery and transportation capacity. But any student of energy politics knows latency means power, particularly when oil carries triple-digit per barrel pricing on light sweet crude.

Though $140 oil was a blip on the chart, warning signs of "Christmases to come" were not lost on American leaders concerned about access to strategic oil reserves. Russia was no longer the aging Communist Superpower with a GDP that was an insignificant fraction of the world's output. It was now a card-carrying member of the BRICs (including Brazil, India, China, and South Africa) and a potential player in any axis of oil supremacy.

After the clownish and besotted array of leaders from Khrushchev to Brezhnev, the latter of whose length of term as General Secretary was only exceeded by Stalin himself, to Chernenko, who was so ill as a leader he barely survived it a year, Russia was back as a major global player.

American lawmakers took notice. It was important to know Russia, and equally important to know Medvedev.

Few in the highest echelons of the U.S. government had intersected with Putin, but almost no one knew his chosen successor. That was the lawmaker's dilemma.

As a mid-level legislator or Energy Department operative, there was little practical likelihood of an audience with the new Russian leader. Someone with convening power would be necessary to make this vital introduction.

Democracies work in funny ways. Russia, which never really had a democracy, elects men who don't campaign. The presidency has been passed on with a succession that the tsars might find familiar. In September 2011, Putin's surprise announcement: He was running again in 2012. Even Russians found his degree of orchestration overwhelming, and they took to the Moscow streets. It might portend a change, but remember that before celebrating a Russian Spring, Muscovites rarely experience Spring of any kind.

But for anyone here who would act superior, our democracy works in some funny ways too. And not always in ways that look very democratic. The keys here, just as in Moscow, London, Canberra, or Katmandu, are access to power, clear thinking, and orchestration from behind closed doors.

––––––––––––––––––

FIRST LESSON ON THINK TANKS: They aren't what you think.

When newly minted Russian President Dmitry Medvedev made a lightning trip to Washington for an economic summit in 2008, it was a Council on Foreign Relations session moderated by Madeline Albright that brought many Congress members together with the new President for the first time. The Council provided the access, the introductions, and the venue. The Council fielded the questions and managed the process. For both sides the meeting was a necessity.

Ten days earlier, just after Obama was elected, Medvedev spoke from Russia and warned the president-elect not to follow through on the Bush administration's plan to install a missile defense system in Europe. In a move right out of the Cold-War playbook, he said Russia would deploy its own short-range missiles near the Polish border if Obama did.

Medvedev sounded less bellicose when he spoke on U.S. soil—even if the U.S. and Russia couldn't find common ground on many issues, he said he thought they could work together to create a partnership in the future. What was notable was that Medvedev chose to make his first public appearance in the U.S. at a Think Tank—a recognizably formal and accredited setting but not a governmental one. Not officially anyway.

Think Tanks do a lot of thinking, sure, but they do much much more. They have convening power, extraordinary reach, and unprecedented access. In recent decades, these institutes have grown enormously in capacity and scope, including financially.

They are the fourth branch of government, nothing less. Sorry to disappoint the lobbyists who aspire to the crown.

Begun as universities without students 100 years ago, the first Think Tanks were often the brainchildren of wealthy benefactors. Their names are recognizable: The Carnegie Endowment for International Peace (1910), The Conference Board (1916), The Institute for Government Research (1916) (which merged in 1927 with the Robert Brookings Graduate School for Economics and Government and another institute to form Brookings), The Hoover Institution (1919), and The Council on Foreign Relations (1921).

As the decades have passed, each of these early Think Tanks has taken on a decidedly different focus and cast. And they have all grown in size, wealth, and influence. Today, Brookings has more than 200 resident and visiting scholars and over $200 million in endowment. The organization produces a new book every ten business days and frequently testifies before Congress, dispersing its long-range and intermediate thinking throughout the government.

The RAND Corporation (an acronym for Research And Development) began in 1945 with a grant for two engineers from Douglas Aircraft to study German V1 and V2 rockets for the Army Air Forces. Today, RAND continues to receive the bulk of its $100 million plus annual budget from the Army/Air Force/Secretary of Defense, but its work is no longer confined to national policy issues.

In 2007, Carnegie announced a reorganization designed to create the first truly global Think Tank, boasting offices in Moscow, Brussels, Beirut, and Beijing. Carnegie publishes, among other things, the influential bi-monthly *Foreign Policy* magazine, and its Conference on International

Proliferation is considered the preeminent global event on nuclear weapons and technology.

The Council on Foreign Relations publishes *Foreign Affairs* and counts among its members most of the Presidents and Secretaries of State of the last 75 years. These are not accidental tourists. Listen to their president Richard Haass speak on international security, Asian developments, or our policy in the Middle East and you recognize a man of prodigious ability backed by an armada of brilliant researchers and a marquis list of members.

Think Tanks are influential for a reason.

Not enough has been written about these highly persuasive and well-run organizations. They are an odd blend of being at once highly public and quoted, but at the same time opaque; sometimes front and center and other times stealth. But they cannot be ignored. They are skilled, packed with extraordinary talent (far more intellectually potent than any government organization), articulate, forceful, persuasive, and very well financed.

Think Tanks have evolved along with the increasing sophistication and complexity of our government. In order to maintain their tax-exempt status, there are strict rules against lobbying that Think Tanks must follow. But that leaves plenty of room for outsized clout. Adopting the mores of the university and to support their scholarly credentials, Think Tanks refer to those performing the research and writing their position papers as Fellows, Policy Analysts, and Distinguished Scholars.

Some Think Tanks function inside the government like the Congressional Research Service and the Congressional Budget Office. Some, like the RAND Corporation and the Urban Institute, rely heavily on government funding. But the more typical independent institutes can trace their roots to the early 1900s when Andrew Carnegie and Robert Brookings (a Saint Louis businessman) formed politically "neutral" research initiatives to explore the facts behind the issues and provide insight to policy makers. These original Think Tanks were staunchly independent and continue to thrive to this day.

Never confuse independence with objectivity.

Respective Think Tanks on the right and left have educated and trained thousands of Congressional staffers, government and agency operatives, and aspiring political candidates. They provide position papers, write and undertake research for speeches, and provide platform materials for political parties. While it appears that the right-leaning institutes have been more thoughtful and strategic in carving up the issues to be addressed, liberal work has gotten more vigorous in recent years.

Over time, Think Tanks have evolved to focus on the three biggies: research, marketing, and media. Some, like Brookings, have a natural focus on the medium- to longer term, whereas the Heritage Foundation has developed a skill at delivering what policy makers need to know now.

These organizations are the hidden persuaders. Largely unregulated, they are fortified by major endowments to fund their research. The next time you hear a freshman political aspirant display his breadth of knowledge by holding forth with great fervor on an esoteric element of foreign or domestic policy, you can rest assured the position was molded and shaped in large measure by the intellectual might of a major Think Tank.

The potent Heritage Foundation is a model of the modern Think Tank—rich, independent, and highly opinionated. It was created in 1973 when brewer Joseph Coors gave a seed grant of $250,000 to two former congressional aides with a commitment to begin to influence policy and roll back the liberal welfare state. Heritage saw the role of the Think Tank more broadly: Its aim was to change policy, not simply to comment on it.

The work of Heritage became two-fold: to influence the policy discussions throughout the government and to market its message to conservative voters. Close to 66 percent of its income is generated by over 250,000 conservative donors and foundations, the largest being a $20 million donation from billionaire Richard Mellon Scaife, currently Foundation vice-chairman.

With a staff of 130 and over two-dozen visiting and residential scholars, Heritage has become an extraordinary force for the conservative view. While some dispute the relative scholarly credentials of Heritage, its frequency of media citations and its ability to gain access to policy makers with timely information makes it an organization to watch carefully.

When Reagan was elected, Heritage produced a "Mandate for Leadership," calling for deregulation, spending hikes for defense, and cuts in social programs. The document became a blueprint for the Reagan administration.

During the Bush administration, The Heritage Foundation claimed to be involved in every piece of major legislation brought before Congress.

Heritage doesn't pretend to be anything other than it is. On a recent visit to its Web site, a banner advertising foundation memberships featured pictures of Rush Limbaugh and Sean Hannity. "Help Heritage Keep the Conservative Momentum Growing," ran the site headline.

The media landscape has been dominated for years by conservative and centrist Think Tanks like Heritage, but left-leaning organizations now boast two members of the top 10: The Center for American Progress (CAP) and The Economic Policy Institute. ("Progressive Ideas for a Strong, Just, and Free America," runs the banner on the CAP site. CAP also has an Artist-in-Residence, something Heritage lacks.)

Headed by John Podesta, former Clinton Chief of Staff, CAP has become the standard bearer for the liberal position on the Iraq and Afghanistan wars. The hit-driven nature and timeliness of research on Iraq explains a great deal of the surge by CAP in the last few years.

How can a Think Tank like the Heritage Foundation or CAP influence policy without lobbying?

Though the line can sometimes be fine, consider the often-debated topic of gun control: Lobbyists aggressively advocate to members of the government of the need for freedom with guns. Interest groups and lobbyists hold forth with great ability and fervor representing gun owners, manufacturers, and dealers. The NRA is one particularly vocal and effective such effort, though there are many others.

The Think Tank's number-one job is to educate policy makers while also molding public opinion through seminars, books, media citations, and appearances. The Think Tanks may do exhaustive work in support of the Second Amendment (the right to bear arms), they may inform on gun statistics and trends, they may inform of police presence and crime rates but they just cannot represent gun manufacturers and gun owners and speak on their behalf.

The Heritage Foundation, for example, publishes articles written by law professors from respected universities in defense of a broad interpretation of the Second Amendment on its Web site. It is scholarly material, sourced from an academic institution, and it is in support of a particular point of view. Many of the Heritage fellows also testify before congressional committees, and are identified as Heritage Foundation members as they do so.

In the marketplace of ideas, Think Tanks have become the brokers.

These institutions are constantly meeting, both formally and informally, with members of Congress and are always looking for ways to influence the policy debate. When Obama became President, the Carnegie Endowment developed so many studies that they created a special Web site entitled "Advice to the President," with reports on everything from the situation in Afghanistan to the details of economic policy.

To get a clearer glimpse of how Think Tanks work, think of policy as a cycle: Some Think Tanks do extraordinary amounts of research. Search the Heritage site for content and the research is divided by date, seven formats (blog posts to congressional testimonies), and no fewer than 28 publications: "America at Risk Memos," "White Papers," and "Obama Tax Hike Series" included. Others are far more effective at gaining access with pointed information at key points in the cycle. Each of these Think Tanks works to shape the political agenda, to contribute to policy formulation with analysis of impact, and now more than ever, to assist in the implementation.

Anyone dismissing these organizations as aggregated policy wonks has clearly missed the growing trend toward activism in the Think Tank world. They are the brains behind our government. What began as the incubator of ideas for policy has become a full-fledged support system for the governing of our nation and the determination of policy. An integral part of the role Think Tanks play is the hiring of former members of the administration and the supply of new talent for the new administrations.

For generations, Britain has maintained a government-in-waiting (a "Shadow Cabinet") ready for the time a political party falls out of power (they need to be on standby—under British rules, an election can be called at any time). With fixed political terms of office, the United States doesn't need such a formal construct, but the staffing of senior Fellows and Distinguished Scholars is close to a shadow government.

The Bush administration, for example, took Vice President Dick Cheney from the American Enterprise Institute and Condoleezza Rice from the Hoover Institution. It's another example of the revolving door that so frequently blurs the lines between government and the private sector.

Think Tanks today are not only focused inside the Beltway, but a major part of their work is in gaining media support and attention for their reports and research.

The 25 most quoted Think Tanks are cited almost 28,000 times a year in the news media. Yet this number understates their impact because the number of newspapers has been shrinking. Think Tanks claim hundreds of thousands of instances every year in which their research, though not cited, has directed the thinking of journalists and reporters. Be assured, their work is everywhere, even when they are not specifically cited.

By almost any measure, Brookings leads the league in media citations. And across the universe of Think Tanks the centrist view has become the largest proportion of citations at 47 percent, with conservative at 37 percent, and progressive at 16 percent.

But centrist is a vague construct in the Think Tank world. These are soft labels but there has been a clear rise in the centrists at the expense of the conservatives. It is important to remember that the work of Think Tanks is offered as research and their experts are rarely given an ideological label to help people put the research into context.

When was the last time you saw the phrase, "As conservative Think Tank the Heritage Foundation advocated . . ."? You won't. But whenever you see a Think Tank's citation, question it, or at least consider the source.

Even the description of their output as research is open to refutation.

Real research is systematic, blind and/or peer reviewed, and employs an easily replicable methodology. It's not unusual for research articles in the world of academics to be openly debated at convocations, conferences, and seminars. Not so the research of Think Tanks.

Today many Think Tanks repackage and repurpose existing research and market it to policy makers and newspaper reporters, and even get the material entered as testimony. The Heritage Foundation specializes in hand-delivered two-page briefing notes to Congressional and Executive leadership. Often, such well-timed materials create an ongoing advisory and dialogue. But, besides making lawmakers look smart, Think Tanks' true expertise is getting their ideas in the room when they aren't there.

Every decade has its Think Tank. The Brookings Institution so frustrated Richard Nixon that the President told his aides he had the urge to firebomb their Washington building. They didn't. The 1980s were a different sort of boom decade for the Heritage Foundation, and they continue to wield considerable influence today.

Long after Reagan left the stage, Ed Meese, Jack Kemp, and William Bennett carried the Conservative baton. After the Bush administration, the American Enterprise Institute brought Paul Wolfowitz and John Bolton to its Fellowship; so impactful has the Center for American Progress become that President Obama named its leader John Podesta to lead his transition team.

Do the right-wing Think Tanks work together? Some have called the conservative Think Tanks a "Mighty Wurlitzer," but they more closely resemble a network. Many of the same names lead the funding: Lynde and Harry Bradley Foundation, William E. Simon Foundation and the Olin Foundation, the Smith Richardson Foundation, and the Koch Foundation.

This network of Think Tanks and advocacy organizations number in the hundreds, and some care is taken to orchestrate areas of focus and study. The organ does seem to grind out a lot of synchronous sound.

While the Heritage Foundation makes a bold play for pushing the conservative agenda, another right-leaning organization, The American Enterprise Institute (AEI), makes a play for nonpartisanship while still pushing a similar conservative approach: limited government, deregulated enterprise, individual liberty and responsibility.

By a very significant margin, AEI is the most prolific supplier of signed op-ed pieces on the *Wall Street Journal*'s editorial page; more than one a week in recent years.

The *New York Times,* with a decidedly more liberal cant, chooses Brookings and the centrist New America Foundation, both sort of Center-left organizations. CAP has chosen to pursue its own sites or affiliates over op-ed pages to promulgate its findings.

Whatever line they push, Think Tanks have the ability to infiltrate, influence, and get in very deep. They use every marketing and promotion tool at their behest to promote their research. Op-ed pages, seminars, direct mail, blogs and Internet sites, round table discussions, retreats, training, book publishing, expert testimony, and magazine articles target the populace.

The rest of their energy is directed at the Selectorate—those federal and legislative leaders who have the ability to implement policy.

These are the politics of the elite, the Selectorate not the electorate. They have become a dark necessity for governing. Congressional and federal staffs are typically stretched too thin to take the time, presuming they had the financial and intellectual capacity, to generate the same work product.

Taken as a whole, Think Tanks play a vital role in the running of our government. They have the funding and the human capital and expertise to do exhaustive, applied research to support major initiatives. We just have to make sure we read the fine print on the packaging.

We need to remember that Think Tanks are not the same as the educational institutions they resemble in so many ways. If a university does research, it can be assumed it does so without bias, focusing only on the results of objective study. But most Think Tanks have a predisposition one way or another, to the right or the left. They are cited tens of thousands of times in the media with little, if any, acknowledgement that the work is determinedly partisan. That's not to say that they are cooking the books, but as we know, you can prove anything (immigration helps/hurts the economy; the climate is changing/not changing; Albert Pujols is as good as/not as good as Babe Ruth) with statistics.

Think Tanks are an ever-present, unelected part of the political system. Although not allowed to lobby in the strictest sense of the term, they provide ammunition that lobbyists can utilize in their ongoing assault of influence. As such, they're not so much problem-solving as policy-making, and that's not the same thing at all.

There is a thick frozen layer of permafrost between the citizenry and Washington. Think Tanks are like reinforcing Rebar in that frigid soil. They provide the ultimate backstage pass, available to such a scarce few they define the term *Selectorate*. Funded by benefactors with an urge to put their thoughts in the center ring, these are clubs which are expensive to join.

Bottom line: Anyone looking to find the center of things must be thoroughly versed in the world of Think Tanks. Because wherever there is a room with decision makers, Think Tanks have found a way in.

You haven't.

And in all likelihood, you won't.

FACTOR FOUR

Predator or Pray: Wayward Christian Soldiers

LATER IN HIS LIFE, BILL *Buckley repaired, as he did each year, to Switzerland for the writing "season." Author of more than fifty books, he was an odd man to carry the cross. But he was about to take it up . . . again.*

One of ten children, William F. Buckley Jr. was born in 1925 into a peripatetic and Arcadian existence to William Sr., a staunchly Irish lawyer and oil investor, and Aloise Josephine Antonia Steiner, a woman of inestimable affection from New Orleans. His mother was a daily communicant and though his father's faith was not extrovert, it was at least a matter of clan, if not conviction.

Young William was schooled in Paris, Britain, and at home in Sharon, Connecticut, in a house that boasted no fewer than five pianos. Whatever the faith of his parents, Buckley was naturally argumentative and seemed born to carry the cross.

Buckley was a prolific author and he was paid an advance in the eighties to pen a book entitled, Why I Am Still a Catholic. *When he sat down to write, one thing occurred to him immediately, and something else a good deal later.*

What smacked him first was the nagging sensation that there was one too many words in the title. The irritant of course was the word "still," implying that remaining Catholic is extraordinary. Buckley dispensed with the offending designation and wrote a chapter or two until he put down his pen and promptly returned the publisher's advance. Why?

A second "slower release" notion had occurred to him.

He confessed to two things: He admitted to having "inadequate resources" to write a book about his faith. It's an occupational hazard for anyone who has written about Catholicism because, like it says in the song "Embraceable You," how do you get your arms around it?

He also admitted to something worse: Feeling rotten about capitulating. But the guilt which beset him was not about disappointing his publisher or his erstwhile reader, but rather his Almighty Editor in Chief.

Bill Buckley baptized the religious conservative movement in 1951 with his first book, God and Man at Yale. *Not long after, the deity moved on from New Haven. God left too.*

Can you blame him? Not a decent bagel in the place.

What began as a treatise on the demise of religion in the liberal arts college was swept up by the blossoming Christian search engine and drawn to the bosom of the conservative movement. Buckley may have set the modern precedent for binding these two forces together. And what God has joined together . . .

Buckley found a detractor in no less than Henry Sloane Coffin, furniture heir and President of the Union Theological Seminary. A member of the Yale Board of Trustees, he dismissed Buckley and his book as Catholic misrepresentation of a traditionally Protestant institution. "He should have attended Fordham," Coffin sniffed.

Most college students aren't clever enough to get in that kind of trouble, but Buckley was a force, and his book was the opening salvo in a fresh new tango between conservatism and religion that drew each other into close embrace.

In 1955, Buckley and others created the National Review, *at a moment in our history when conservative intellectuals were considered a genetic impossibility. The* Review *continues today—a flourishing conservative magazine which Buckley edited in some fashion until he joined his maker in 2008.*

Undaunted by his earlier attempts, Buckley once more took up the cudgel and completed a faith-based initiative all his own with the work Nearer, My God *(1997), taking as its title a fragment of the wonderful hymn. He still had incomplete confidence in his ability to deliver satisfactory handiwork to the man upstairs.*

There is plenty of food for debate and discourse in Buckley's writings; he'd be disappointed otherwise. But there is a kernel of an idea, just a sentence fragment really, that seems to launch a thousand polarizing ships: "There is today another God," Buckley argued, "and it is multiculturalism." Time has proven the notion as much more than a kernel. It is a new reality.

Another passage captures passions that have an Inherit the Wind *feel: "We are not accidental biological accretions. We are creatures of a divine plan."*

And those two concepts have drawn God out of the heavens and into the political discourse in ways that split rather than unite. Buckley found himself binding together the great power of the Almighty with the Conservative movement. What he was asking was the profound question:

Is religion as adaptable as politics?

WHEN YOU INVOLVE THE CREATOR in any political debate you need to appreciate the grand sweep; he paints on a very big canvas. You've got to start with the big picture, and religious census is a great way to direct the discussion.

There are about two billion Christians on the planet, who make up just under a third of the global population, and over half of these consider themselves Catholic. The number of adherents in the nation of Islam is over one and a half billion—more than the number of Catholics and 70 percent as large as the Christians. Islam is a huge and powerful faith and is the world's fastest growing religion. Until 9/11, most Americans paid no heed to the Muslims of the world, but in the years that followed the tragedy, both Muslims and non-Muslims alike have shown that Islam's teachings are capable of being misused and misunderstood.

Hindus are next in demographic size, topping 900 million.

Judaism by contrast has about 14 million adherents. Clearly genocide in Germany and Russia were crushing to the propagation of that religion. One simply has to marvel at the extraordinary accomplishments and influence from this comparatively small group of believers. Striking, too, is the fact that the majority of the world's Jews live outside Eretz Israel. The largest community lives in the U.S., with 5.7 million. About five million Jews live in Israel.

The United States has a fascinating religious demographic apart from being home to the largest community of Jews. Nearly 80 percent of American adults consider themselves Christian. The number-one religious group in the United States is Catholic—about 67 million, and the number-two is lapsed Catholics. The next largest is the Southern Baptist Convention with 16 million members split over 42,000 churches.

Powerful trends are bringing historic fluidity to religion in America. We have created a unique theological ecosystem where religions compete, adapt, and, much like a cellular phone call pinging between transmitters, Americans drift seamlessly from one congregation to another.

According to the Pew Forum, 28 percent of American adults have left the faith in which they were raised in favor of another religion—or increasingly to no religion at all. If the definition allows shifts within Protestantism, then the number jumps to 44 percent.

To answer Buckley's profound question, religion in America has become a moveable feast. If religions prove inflexible, people change. As with any Exodus there are consequences for the wanderers.

Change was our founding principle and it has never been more pronounced than with today's young adults.

Adding to the churn are the powerful implications of a growing trend of interfaith marriages. Between one-third and one-half of American marriages in any given year are interfaith or involve a partner with no faith at all. The trend means young people particularly have gained comfort with religious pluralism.

But it also sets the tone for The Great Irony of American Religion:

As a nation we want those in government to have religious beliefs but with all this chopping and changing, most powerful religions are losing ground in America. The fastest growing group is the unaffiliated—the none-of-the-aboves are now topping 16 percent of adults. We want politicians of faith even as we shift and leave the faith ourselves.

Despite all of the pluralism there is ample evidence of increasing polarization. Churn means that we are searching for the like-minded—and we are forming potent clusters who share a common outlook on religious, social, and political matters. Some of these clusters feed on themselves, and delight in being divisive and dogmatic.

Fluidity and polarization make strange bedfellows. I know firsthand. I live in a divided household.

I was born an Irish Catholic and raised by devout parents. My wife is a Southern belle and lifelong Episcopalian.

Three decades of circling each other in wedded bliss have taught me that the only difference between the Church of Rome and the Church of England is that the former is infallible . . . and the latter is never wrong.

So much religious discussion swirls between those who claim some God-given link to infallibility and others who are never wrong. The Radical Centrist knows that God doesn't take sides even though the deity is routinely asked to do so (especially by athletes who point skyward after a score, as if God's running a believers-only fantasy team). Yet there are many who believe God isn't neutral.

We are surrounded by increasingly strident observation of the religious in secular governance. Lately the clarion call of Dominionism declares that Christians have a God given right to rule all earthly institutions, or at least those based in the USA.

Dominionism's domination is kind of like Islamism's right to rule the world, except with more bake sales.

The fierceness and the dividing language calls to mind the title of that most prized spiritual, "The Battle Hymn of the Republic." Fallible or not, it's hard in all the discourse not to see the battle lines being drawn.

Before we arch against the weaponizing of religion, there is a central question to consider: Is it possible to separate religion from politics? A stumper like that requires some careful analysis, something religious debate rarely encounters.

What Would Jefferson Do?

Let's start with a few facts.

Our Constitution is one of the oldest written constitutions on earth and the first in any country to be approved by its people in a representative vote.

Constitutional ratification was not a foregone conclusion—Rhode Island held the only referendum and the people of the Ocean State voted it down (92 percent to 8 percent, no less). Conventions in other states were squeakers: New York passed it 30-27, Virginia 89-79 and Massachusetts 187-168.

Ratification occurred but it was anything but a landslide.

Americans cite with great comfort that our Constitution is a product of Judeo-Christian enlightenment. They point to the separation of church and state in our Constitution as a pillar of American governance.

Of course they are wrong.

Our carefully constructed and composed Constitution runs 4,400 words and not a solitary one of them is "God." And nowhere in the body or the amendments is there anything that resembles a statement about the separation of church and state. About the only thing the First Amendment says is that government cannot forbid the formation of a religion.

What most Americans hold dear is nowhere in the Constitution. And it is by design.

—A very intelligent design.

What makes the Constitution so durable is that so much is left out.

Our Constitution was written on the hides of an animal rather than the pulp of plants specifically so that it would stand the test of time. And sad to say, our proud charter of freedom is constantly misquoted.

It's time for the Radical Centrists to print a correction.

As Michael Lind headlined in *Salon*, "Let's stop pretending that the Constitution is Sacred." It is deliberately sparse on many religious and secular themes for which it is nonetheless used as sword and shield. And let's realize as we read it and cite it that much of what we discern from it is an interpretation. And let's agree while we are at it that there is religion throughout our political process and there always has been.

There are ample citations from the "one nation under God" school of religion in politics.

In 1790, George Washington (the first George W.) replied to a letter of praise from the warden of the Touro Synagogue in Newport, Rhode Island, the nation's largest Jewish community and first synagogue, which traced its presence to the arrival of fifteen Sephardic families in 1658.

Washington's passionate focus was on religious tolerance: ". . . happily, the government of the United States, which gives to bigotry no sanction, to persecution no assistance, requires only that they who live under its protection should demean themselves as good citizens in giving it on all occasions their effectual support."

In 1821, John Quincy Adams drew a finer connection: "The American Revolution connected in one indissoluble bond the principles of civil government with the principles of Christianity."

Or did he? There doesn't seem to be clear proof that Adams actually said the phrase.

Adams' words or non-words are used by the opposing factions against each other, depending.

James Madison is another convenient framer whose varying views on religion mean that opposing positions can each invoke him as their authority.

His "Detached Memoranda," written after his presidency, retreats from earlier positions like proclamation of national days of prayer, passage of a bill that supported mass distribution of the Bible, and payment of government chaplains as unconstitutional.

And it was Thomas Jefferson who wrote in 1802, thirteen years after the passage of the First Amendment, to the Baptists of Danbury, Connecticut that they should be reassured that the new government would not interfere with their denomination because there existed "a wall of separation between Church and State."

What Jefferson said was that government had no business interfering with a religion's right to be practiced. "Religion is a matter which lies solely between Man & his God." The government would stay out of the Baptists' affairs. He said nothing about vice versa.

Follow their behavior and a different picture emerges.

In 1776, Virginia issued its Declaration of Rights, article sixteen of which proposed "free exercise of religion." To liberals like Jefferson and dissenting Protestants, freedom of religion meant separating the Church of England from the proposed state—disestablishing it. The wall between church and state meant that individuals were free to worship as they pleased and also began the pattern of preventing church from interfering in politics.

Lincoln's Second Inaugural Address is probably the most religious speech ever given by an American president. Lincoln spoke only 732 words, referring to God more than a dozen times and quoting twice from the Bible. He decried that both sides of the great conflict felt God was on their side and invoked His name against the other. With Old Testament doom, Lincoln said that if it was God's will that the war continue until as much blood was spilled by the sword as had been drawn under the lash of slavery over the past two hundred and fifty years, so be it.

This was March 4. Lincoln would be assassinated on April 14.

Ironically many historians cite the role of the Civil War in dethroning religion from its primacy in the political discourse, so vexing was the religious balance between a slave-owning elite and the Book of Common Prayer.

Ralph Waldo Emerson wrote, "Men are better than their theology."

And no less than Mark Twain observed "Man is kind enough . . . when he is not excited by religion."

But religion would be back, if it ever went away.

John F. Kennedy shattered the stained glass ceiling when he became the first Catholic elected president. As a candidate, he was pursued by critics who said he'd have a hot line to the Vatican in the Oval Office with the pontiff declaring, "Remember me first." In his September 1960 address to the Greater Houston Ministerial Association he upheld the idea of separated church and state and warned against bigotry.

> *"For while this year it may be a Catholic against whom the finger of suspicion is pointed, in other years it has been and may someday be again, a Jew or a Quaker, or a Unitarian or . . . a Baptist . . . Today I may be the victim—but tomorrow it may be you—until the whole fabric of our harmonious society is ripped at a time of great national peril."*

THE COMING THEOCRACY?

Since Kennedy, we have seen concern from fundamentalist movements who in one way or another pose the proverbial fork-in-the-road question between a candidate's faith and the laws of the United States. Religion makes the kind of ultimate demands that resist compromise, and brings with it the threat of a higher divine law playing a role in matters of state.

Today, the same caricature as existed with Kennedy and the Pope emerges with politicians' supposed Internet links to Mormon Tabernacle Elders, the Knesset, or the good professors at Oral Roberts University.

But American voters are shrewd judges of character and even among devout Christians there are major divisions.

Jimmy Carter, America's first evangelical Christian president, has warned repeatedly of a coming split among Christians. In 2004, he told the *American Prospect,* "There are two principal things that starkly separate the ultra-right Christian community from the rest of the Christian world: Do we endorse and support peace and support the alleviation of suffering among the poor and the outcast?"

Elements of the Republican Party have been extremely effective in connecting religion and values to fighting terror abroad and to battles against gay rights, stem cells, and abortion. The Democrats, too, invoke spirituality with their compassion for the poor, in routing injustice and providing health care for those who cannot afford it.

Just as Lincoln anguished about North and South in his Second Inaugural Address "Both read the same Bible and pray to the same God, and each invokes His aid against the other."

Here is a fact. Religion does not exist on one side of the aisle only. Republicans claim a provenance with the Religious Right but the tradition of the church is found in every major progressive movement in our history.

The Civil Rights movement was deeply embedded in the churches. Those who would ban religion from the public square should avail themselves of the ultimate example of the same and watch Martin Luther King Jr.'s *"I Have a Dream"* speech.

One of the clearest thinkers on this subject is E. J. Dionne who quite rightly points out in his book *Souled Out* that "The separation of Church and State is one thing and the separation from religion and politics is another."

The State and the Church have a long history of collaboration in providing social services, particularly in health and child care and in aid to the poor. So where to draw the line?

The answer is a bit of a lemon.

The sixteen words of the first amendment are sparse, and we know there were rejected drafts of language with more detail. Some say the intent was accommodation of religion, others see separatism.

The Supreme Court has been tasked with parsing through the wording and seeking intent. Justice Hugo Black's opinion in *Everson v. Board of Education of Ewing Township* (1947) creates a foundation: "Neither a state nor the Federal Government can . . . pass laws which aid one religion, aid all religions, or prefer one religion over another. . . . No tax in any amount . . . can be levied to support any religious activities or institutions. . . ."

But the real basis for much of the separatist thinking today comes from *Lemon v. Kurtsman* (1971), which created the lemon test and substantially limited government from offering any assistance to religion.

The lemon test in Chief Justice Warren Burger's majority opinion said government assistance only works if all three conditions are met: 1) It must be primarily secular in purpose; 2) It must have primarily a secular effect, and; 3) It must not create "excessive entanglement" between government and religion.

So are we suddenly a heartbeat away from a Christian Theocracy? The lemon says not so fast. Is Dominionism around the corner? The call in response is to leave the public square naked of religion, burning Christianity at the stake.

I say not so fast.

How has religious belief found its way into our daily governance? E. J. Dionne's confusing but providential comment captures it. The separation of church and state does not mean that politics and religion can't mix. They do every day.

At least 15 percent of the U.S. electorate align themselves with the Christian Right. The Religious Right was a label once claimed with fervor by the Reverend Jimmy Falwell. Today, a bleached and blander handle seems to wear more comfortably: "socially conservative evangelicals." By any other name they smell as sweet.

There is a narrative arc to the blossoming of the Christian right. Home base of the movement was in Greenville, South Carolina, the buckle of the Bible and textile belts. It was there in 1947 that Bob Jones University, late of the Florida Panhandle and Cleveland, Tennessee, opened its doors. Its mission was serving white men in the teachings of Christian Ministries and other subjects. Who could have suspected the swirling events around its leafy quadrangles would cause such a ruckus?

The 1960s saw a gravitational shift in the nation. The first signs of an exodus to the south and the west had commenced. Growing populations and wandering spirits of the far west were creating communities where churches played a centering role in society. At the same time, marches on Selma were raising a nation's consciousness about segregation and racial discrimination.

That perturbation culminated in the Civil Rights Act of 1964 and LBJ, the beleaguered president, conceded that the Southern Democrats would be lost to the party "forever." The alienation of the Dixiecrats was palpable and led zealots like Jesse Helms and Strom Thurmond to switch to the Republican Party. Americans switch more than their religions.

The GOP, still smarting from the landslide loss Barry Goldwater had wrought upon them, embraced what Nixon insiders would term "The Southern Strategy."

Both the execution and the goals were simple: Exploit the nation's anxiety on race and youth and religion and harness it to realign the South once and for all with the Republican Party. It was not painless but it was successful.

In these twin themes, the southern switch and the "drive to the west," lay the fertile opportunity for the Religious Right to flourish.

And in Greenville, South Carolina, while Bob Jones University was pressured to drop its whites-only policy, the school continued to refuse black enrollment until 1971, when only married blacks were accepted. Even when the school allowed unmarried black students to enroll in 1975 (in response to losing its tax-exempt status), it instituted rules against interracial marriage and dating, which were dropped only in 2000 in the midst of a media storm when candidate Bush spoke at the school.

It was during the early seventies that Jerry Falwell created the Moral Majority; Ed McAteer founded the Religious Roundtable Council; Pat Roberson begat the Christian Broadcasting Network; and Dr. James Dobson founded the Focus on the Family in Colorado Springs, a group that went on to create a lobbying arm, the Family Research Council.

Dr. Robert Grant created the American Christian Cause to advocate for Christian moral teachings in Southern California, by any definition a lofty ambition.

Paul Weyrich, a founder of the Heritage Foundation, also established the American Legislative Exchange Council (ALEC) to coordinate Religious Right state legislators as a counterweight to the liberal Think Tanks and foundations that were working the agendas at state governments.

ALEC took a fast-food approach to legislation, supplying thousands of pre-baked McBills to state lawmakers too overwhelmed to do the research or write the laws. This ghostwriting introduced over 3,000 bills during the period, of which 450 were signed into law.

Weyrich, Grant, and others went on to create the Christian Voice in 1978 to recruit, train and organize evangelicals to participate in elections and political persuasion. Jerry Falwell approached the line of scrimmage in a three-point stance: Not the Father, Son, and Holy Ghost but instead, get them saved, get them baptized, get them registered

Universities, carrying on in the tradition of Bob Jones University, were created to school Christian leaders. Jerry Falwell founded Liberty University in 1971. Liberty got an extreme makeover from its initial Lynchburg Baptist College baptismal name and its Law School was finally accredited in 2006. Similarly, Pat Robertson founded CBN University in Virginia Beach in 1978. It is now known as Regent University.

As a candidate, Reagan puckishly won religious conservatives over with a speech in front of 15,000 in Dallas in August 1980, when he announced, "Religious America is awakening . . ." The Southern Baptists and evangelicals were charmed. "I know you can't endorse me . . . but I want you to know that I endorse you and what you are doing." He made, as he had before and would again, his famous allusion that religion would make America again "That shining city upon a hill."

Unsurprisingly, the notion of Christian beliefs playing a stronger role in government gained currency during Reagan's Morning in America. As a platform for his 1988 presidential bid, Pat Robertson founded the Christian Coalition and hired a powerful spokesman, Ralph Reed, to run it.

During Robertson's campaign he claimed he "would only bring Christians and Jews into the government." He built support among his numerous media outlets, *The 700 Club*, and his Christian Broadcast Network. His early momentum was impressive. In 1988, Robertson beat the sitting Vice President George H. W. Bush in the Iowa Republican caucuses.

He did not win the mandate but he was successful at encouraging Christian activists to find their way quietly into leadership positions on a local level of the Republican Party. Robertson also considered the opportunity to triumph over voter apathy with fine-tuned organization.

Ralph Reed's Christian Coalition heeded the call. "Family Values Voter Guides" were his weapon of choice and the distribution outlets included over 100,000 churches across the United States. In the 1994 election, the Christian Coalition distributed 40 million guides: It was a watershed.

One cannot claim cause and effect, but a tide had certainly turned.

Before the 1994 election, the Republicans hadn't controlled Congress in 40 years. All that changed in '94. Until then, Democrats had strong majorities in both houses of most of the state legislatures. But in '94 the Republicans controlled 19 and the Democrats 18. By 2003 the Republicans controlled 21 state legislatures.

In the 2000 election, the apex of the Christian Coalition's influence, 75 million voter guides were handed out. By then, both Reed and Robertson were gone and in the 2002 election only a third as many guides were distributed.

But the slowing momentum in the Christian Coalition's fortunes belied the strong influence of the Religious Right. Ralph Reed joined the Bush/Cheney ticket as a senior advisor, and ran for Lieutenant Governor of Georgia before his campaign lost momentum due to allegations of linkages to Jack Abramoff.

The Christian Coalition lost its tax-exempt status but it continues to distribute millions of voter guides through America's churches. Christian crusader truth is marching on.

Periodic flare-ups give clear clues to the power and the passions that persist under the surface. In 2001 Roy Moore, the Chief Justice of the Alabama Supreme Court, installed a 2.6-ton granite monument to the Ten Commandments in the rotunda of the Judicial Building in Montgomery. After defying another judge's order to remove it, Moore was stripped of his position in 2003, a martyrdom that turned him into a conservative folk hero. (At his ethics hearing, Moore contended, "Without God there can be no ethics.")

In the Great Smoky Mountains of North Carolina, at the East Waynesville Baptist Church, Pastor Chan Chandler told congregants that anyone who supported John Kerry for president in his 2004 bid should leave the church or repent. Nine members, including at least one deacon, left the church. In the aftermath, many more protested, the nine returned, and Chandler lost his flock.

Today, battles brew in Texas over a rethinking of the fundamentals in history textbooks. Texas social studies curriculum board members are looking through the past darkly. Board member, suburban dentist, and self-proclaimed Christian fundamentalist Don McLeroy has been reviewing the degree to which the founding fathers were committed to purely secular government. McLeroy told the *New York Times* he believes the Earth was created in six days less than 10,000 years ago.

McLeroy and his committee have discerned that Thomas Jefferson, who brought you the "wall of separation" between church and state, should be deemed less crucial in Texas textbooks. The good dentist said "somebody's got to stand up to the experts." Check out ten changes the Texas board made in "Texas Cooks the Textbooks" by Barrett Sheridan in the *Daily Beast*. Texan kids should study painter Thomas Kinkade, the Moral Majority, and the NRA; rehabilitate Joseph McCarthy and differentiate European "imperialism" and Soviet "aggression" from American "expansionism."

With four million school children, Texas constitutes the country's second largest educational market. Many textbook producers use Texas as the model for books in other states. So when a tree falls in Texas, children across the United States hear it.

"Those who control the past control the future," said George Orwell.

"Those who control the present control the past," said William Federer, compiler of *America's God and Country*.

"I'm a dentist, not a historian," said Don McLeroy.

RUMORS OF GOD'S DEATH ARE WILDLY EXAGGERATED

THESE VENOMOUS DEBATES ON RELIGION'S role in politics must always return to The Great Irony of American Religion. (We want our leaders to be religious even if many of us aren't.)

A 2011 report by the Pew Forum on Religion and Public Life on the religious composition of our current 112th Congress explains part of the dramatic dissonance.

The report finds that the unaffiliated (atheists, agnostics, the unchurched, uncommitted, and selected college sophomores), at 16.1 percent of the population, comprise the largest religious group without representation in Congress. Only six members (about 1 percent) did not specify a religious category.

Let's put unaffiliated Americans into context: Their size equals the Baptists, is more than twice the Methodists, and is more than nine times the combined Mormons, Episcopalians, and Jews.

Why the underrepresentation?

Because being an unaffiliated candidate is un-American. Another Pew Forum survey said 72 percent agree that the president should have strong religious beliefs.

Can you imagine the following exchange occurring here?

Nick Clegg, the U.K. Liberal Democrats' new leader and current deputy Prime Minister, was asked by a BBC *Radio 5* interviewer in 2007: "Do you believe in God?"

"No," said Clegg.

Since entering a coalition with the Conservatives, Clegg has trumpeted Christian values and shown up in church, offering yet another testament to conservatism as the road to salvation.

But no serious American politician would have denied his maker even once before the cock crowed.

Noises can be made about the dissolute ways of atheists, and agnostics' failure to mingle, but there is a more obvious answer. We all know the 112th Congress is a pious bunch.

A study by the Interfaith Alliance dives deeper: A majority of Republicans believe the clergy should have some influence on government, versus 38 percent of Democrats.

How does that square with a 2009 American Religious Identification survey that concludes that the number of Americans who claim no religious affiliation has doubled since 1990 to over 15 percent? The study goes on to say that Christians are a declining *percentage* of the American population even as their numbers increase. Protestants are heading for a minority after many generations of supermajority.

Still, as Twain might have said, rumors of Christianity's death are wildly exaggerated. This is not a post-Christian narrative, but it is a profound trend. Donations to churches as a percentage of charity are dropping, though they are still enormous sources of income. According to a 2010 *Newsweek* poll 68 percent of the public believe religion is losing influence and only 19 percent feel it is on the rise.

Why then does religion feel like it has gotten more important in spite of the shifting sands of Christianity?

Two reasons: Religion is more important because certain people want it that way—"Their will be done. . . ."

Also, because religion in America fits into a decidedly un-heavenly stencil—the bell curve with strength in the extremes: fervor on one hand and non-belief on the other.

But non-believers have no caucus.

In the 1980s, a series of court decisions like *Roe v. Wade* pitted the Right to Life movement against what they called abortion by judicial fiat. Another troubling decision for evangelicals was termination of prayer in public schools.

There was a broader cultural hostility that spurred evangelical Christians to create the Religious Right.

Any student of Buckley saw this marriage coming. The Tea Party is a rhetorically different crusade focused on lower taxes and smaller government. Those two lynch pins carry with them a broader platform that is a reincarnation of long-held conservative views fighting redistribution and entitlement.

The Religious Right is a different movement, but it marches on a parallel path. The joining together of these two movements was blessed by Brookings research that confirmed majority overlap in membership.

There is so much commotion today over the linkage between the Tea Party and the Evangelicals. Michelle Bachmann was heartily endorsed by Ralph Reed.

For the Radical Centrists these shifting sands still leave clear directives.

It is almost impossible for a believer to completely separate religious convictions from political ones. Just like keeping religion totally out of politics doesn't have a prayer.

It is imperative that you fully understand a candidate's religious beliefs, even if they will not be practiced in office. But it is very troublesome when we put candidates to religious "tests." Are they Catholic or Christian enough? Are they too religious?

The American people have gotten more comfortable that leaders will choose their constituents over their creed, their law over their dogma when they encounter a fork in the road. Just examine the difference between the two JFK campaigns. Kennedy was put through the wringer on his Catholicism, and Kerry got more questions about his windsurfing.

It is also a problem when people argue positions solely on religious grounds. In a plural society, politicians must make their case to people irrespective of whether or not they share their religious views. Religious arguments alone cannot suffice in a secular democratic republic.

In a very real sense, atheism is a good thing both for the people of faith and for the republic. Forcing lawmakers to defend a law or a position on its secular merits means the religious cannot steamroll the process.

Religion invoked to inspire intolerance of another denomination is a dangerous manipulation of religion's intent. The trouble with constantly shifting moves between religions is that self-reinforcing clusters form. And with no balancing voices, these clusters can tilt toward fanaticism.

On one level, I can sympathize with the Religious Right because for so long they have been isolated by the left. Liberals who take a stand against intolerance should extend those courtesies even to the extent of religious views to which they object.

Religion that declares war on science also constitutes a danger. Most often scientists should be allowed to do their work unfettered in the laboratory. Thoughtful regulation with a moral eye to dangers is an acceptable form of monitoring. But when scientists become demonized or apocalyptic visions accompany every development, then religion has crossed the line.

In all things there is a need for balance. But let's face it: the meaning of life is basically nonnegotiable. We keep returning to the battle between infallibility and never being wrong.

Whether it is stem cells, abortion, or any other religion-versus-science debate it is very hard to find middle ground. It's striking how often two polar opposites, whether it is Lincoln's North and South or Islamic terrorists versus our brave troops, find comfort in the prayer "God is great."

Radical Centrists must remember the proportion of Americans who think religion can "answer all or most of today's problems" is at a historic low of 48 percent.

"All men," Homer once wrote, "need the Gods," but we have demonstrated our ability to cope with the ebb and flow of religious fervor in governing our nation.

Sometimes majority simply has to rule.

The Ground Zero mosque and Obama's religious affiliation are simplified, eye-catching topics. The Radical Centrist sees past these conveniences. They ignore the righteous stir caused when an American Christian preacher threatens to burn the Koran; or when Mitt Romney is castigated for his "weirdness" (meaning: He's a Mormon!).

We must move the debate beyond the cramped terms we have inherited. Religion has always been a part of political life. Jimmy Carter was a highly observant Christian and religion infused all of his conduct. George W. Bush went even further, declaring, "God is not neutral."

THE TEXAS CURRICULUM DEBATES ARE merely the tip of the iceberg. The wrangling over creationism and intelligent design versus evolution continues. The latest providential flanking maneuver demands to "teach the controversy" by reviewing alternatives to evolutionary theory; some call this "un-schooling."

The Lemon test has a role to play here. It enabled the Supreme Court to strike down state legislation that would have required teaching creationism versus evolution (*Edwards v. Aguilard,*1987) and avoiding the trap of "moments of silence" in public schools (*Wallace v. Jaffree,* 1985). The test also explains why religious leaders are so keen to have influence on the portrait of the high court.

Religious fervor finds its way into all societal regulation: Marriage, right to life, sex education, lifestyle choices, abortion, euthanasia, bioethics, pornography, and prostitution. Religious activists pray for change and they are very, very organized.

Religion is a factor in our foreign policy as well. The role Jihad played in 9/11 and the way that the U.S. has dealt with the Muslim world is less a matter of our religious fervor and more of our collective ignorance of Islam. But like it or not, the world evaluates us for toppling three Muslim regimes, whatever our motivations.

Our crusading foreign policy, our need to protect our access to energy resources, and our preexistent relationships in the Middle East govern more of our thinking internationally than Messianic zeal. We have embraced the Arab Spring, but from the days of Nasser we have felt Egypt was the key to peaceful relations between Israel and the Arab world. And every year we have spent billions to support our claim. Israel figures centrally in our Middle East psyche, but it is statism that shepherds us.

So what role does religion have in the center of things? We lose sight of everything if we let one dogma or another completely define us. The notion of fairness and balance can be found in texts and holy writ of every religion. Speak with an Imam and he will tell you that Islam has been a peaceful religion and that Jihad has been perverted. Speak to Christians and they preach tolerance.

But religion can simmer dangerously, waiting to blow. "Allah" crossed the lips of murderers as they piloted innocents to their doom. Tony Blair recently told me he plans to spend the rest of his life building better dialogue between the great religions to avoid volcanic eruptions.

We need storm chasers here at home too. Speak to an activist reviewing textbooks for the Texas school system and you will hear, in even the most balanced commentary, an angry political agenda. Try facing a circle of wheelchair-bound stem cell supporters against embryo defenders. We are back in front of that Vermont open mike, in minutes veins are popping.

Unlike politics, religion breaks before it bends.

History is full of monarchs and governing souls who used religion to fortify wobbling political ramparts the way a flying buttress props a cathedral. When both the architecture and the rhetoric start soaring, Radical Centrists are obliged to calm things down.

Whether it's a faith we understand well or one that is alien and troubling to us, we must acknowledge that fervor can hijack the dialogue and divert our common path. Tread lightly with religion in matters of human behavior. The belief in a higher power is a tie that binds so many of us, but without some sense of boundary, the history of the great nations, like the history of the great religions, strains to excess. And those excesses can freeze a country's destiny.

A nation infused with religious fervor is blessed, but when religions collide, more than souls are lost. And when infallibility meets never wrong, Radical Centrists must lead everyone back to every religion's first premise—Love one another.

FACTOR FIVE

It's My Party: The Hijacking of the Two-Party System

GEORGE WASHINGTON CLICKED HIS ROTTING *teeth and shuffled the drafted papers of his Farewell Address on the desk in front of him. His mouth was in agony again; his last aching tooth was accompanied by a phalanx of hippo ivory dentures. Ten thousand people were marching daily through the streets of the capitol city of Philadelphia, calling for an upheaval of the new government. Satirical cartoons lampooned Washington's refusal to join the French Revolution, depicting him with his head in the guillotine.*

It was September 1796, and for Washington it was déjà vu all over again. Four years earlier, a similar draft and a similar fatigued feeling had overtaken him. Back then his erstwhile Treasury Secretary, Alexander Hamilton, and his Secretary of State and fellow Virginian, Thomas Jefferson, had persuaded him to lead for a second term. It was a guilt trip more or less. About the only thing Jefferson and his Republicans and Hamilton and his Federalists could agree upon was that Washington was the only man to guide them. They told him he had to be Chief Executive for another term lest the growing divisions between the newly formed Federalist and Democratic-Republican Parties and the current state of foreign affairs tear the new republic apart.

This time his mind was made up.

Washington had firmly decided after forty-five years of service to the nation that there would be no third term. He was tired and wanted to retire to Mount Vernon. The exhausted patriot would not live three years after he left the presidency.

Washington amended and polished the earlier work on the address with the help of Hamilton, but in the final version the words and the sentiments were his and his alone. He would make a farewell address in the form of an open letter to every citizen, and the matters he covered would be those he felt vital to the prosperity of these newly United States. It was his valedictory after all he had given to the nation, and it came from the deepest regions of his heart.

"Let me . . . warn you in the most solemn manner," he wrote, "against the baneful affects of the Spirit of Party, generally.

"This Spirit, unfortunately, is inseparable from our nature having its root in the strongest passions of the human mind. It exists under different shapes in all governments . . . and is truly their worst enemy.

"The alternate dominance of one faction over another, sharpened by the spirit of revenge, natural to party dissension . . . is in itself a frightful despotism.

"There is an opinion, that parties in free countries are useful checks upon the Administration of the Government . . . This within certain limits is probably true—and in Governments of a Monarchical cast, Patriotism may look with indulgence . . . upon the spirit of party. But . . . in Governments purely elective, it is a spirit not to be encouraged . . . there being a constant danger of excess . . . A fire not to be quenched; it demands a uniform vigilance to prevent its bursting into flame, lest, instead of warming, it should consume."

THE BIRTH OF POLITICS AS USUAL, PART I

WITHIN MONTHS THE NATION WAS ablaze, and the elections of 1796 and 1800 would forever alter the face of our democracy.

First, in 1796 came a whole new election experience for America. The prior two presidential processes had been foregone conclusions: Everyone loved George. But no sooner had Washington refused to run than a new stage was set: Federalists versus Anti-Federalists. The former believed in a strong central government, supported by a ratification of the Constitution, a national bank, and infrastructure investment for the emerging industrialism that was building the economies of Europe.

The Anti-Federalists were states' rightists opposed to a national bank. They favored farming over manufacturing and as such opposed government funding of the roadways necessary for industrial expansion. As a harbinger, they called themselves the Democratic-Republican Party.

Battle lines were drawn. John Adams, the incumbent vice president, was the Federalists' favorite, while the Democratic-Republican Party heavily championed Thomas Jefferson. Each side wasted little time in trying out their new party's venom. The Federalists accused their opponents of mass hysteria and of supporting the French Revolution while the Democratic-Republicans invoked in their Federalist opponents images of the European monarchs and aristocracy.

Since the notion of a ticket with a candidate and a running mate had yet to be introduced, the winner of the electoral votes became president, the runner-up vice president regardless of party affiliations. So when John Adams narrowly won the presidency, his adversary Jefferson became vice president, setting the stage for what was to become the birth of the political dogfight: the election of 1800.

That's when the trouble really started.

For the first and last time in American history, a president found himself running against his vice president in the national election. Sparks flew fast. Though moderate and restrained by today's standards, this was the first time presidential candidates really campaigned. The Federalist contenders were John Adams and Charles Pinckney for president and vice president, and for the Democratic-Republicans, Jefferson and Aaron Burr.

In our Nation's first-ever campaign swings, Adams visited Virginia, Maryland, and Pennsylvania trying to drum up support. Aaron Burr traveled to towns throughout New England.

We also endured our inaugural smear campaigns. Jefferson took it upon himself to engage the services of a bottom-feeding journalist named James Callender as his hatchet man. Thus did Jefferson's camp call Adams a "hideous and hermaphroditical character which has neither the force and firmness of a man nor the gentleness and sensibility of a woman."

Today, he might just be called a Liberal.

In return, Adams' men famously called Jefferson "a mean spirited and low lived fellow, the son of a half breed Indian squaw, sired by a Virginia mulatto father." Martha Washington was even drawn into the fray, telling a clergyman that Jefferson was "one of the most detestable of mankind." George was rolling in his grave.

Callender was a radical Democrat with Calvinist tendencies and any politician who fell short of his rigorous moral standards risked being skewered by his favorite weapon, a well-researched accusation of sexual impropriety. Before the election Jefferson had witnessed his handiwork—this man was not an unknown quantity.

Callender had set his sights on Treasury Secretary Alexander Hamilton, in exposing a torrid affair with a married woman, Maria Reynolds. Congress had become aware of payments made between the Treasury Secretary and Reynolds' husband James. To clear his name, Hamilton confessed to the marital indiscretion, claiming James Reynolds had been blackmailing him.

Adams was an easy target for Callender. His Alien and Sedition Acts were tantamount to a monarchical overturn of freedom of the press. Besides, when Callender warmed to his subject, accuracy suffered under the weight of his predetermined agenda. Callender convinced many Americans that Adams was hell-bent on attacking France. It was an unpopular idea and Callender capitalized on those fears.

There were only two problems with Callender's handiwork: First, it wasn't true—Adams held no such view and nothing existed in writing to substantiate the claims other than under Callender's determined hand. And second, though Callender was persuasive, he was not quite persuasive enough.

The election ended in a tie.

Jefferson and his vice president, Aaron Burr, tied with 73 electoral votes apiece. John Adams got 65 votes and Pinckney 64. These results uncovered a serious flaw in the Constitution, whose original wording did not distinguish between electoral votes for president and vice president, which led to this highly problematic outcome.

The tie had to be decided in the House of Representatives in its new

Capitol building in Washington, D.C. The voting went on for days and there was no clear consensus. Beneath the surface, Hamilton's enmity for Burr simmered. Despite horse-trading and 35 ballots, there was still no resolution. Stalemate.

Hamilton's secret campaigning caused a shift on the 36th try and Jefferson won in a squeaker, Burr was delivered to the Vice Presidency, and Adams returned empty-handed to Massachusetts, the first incumbent in our history to lose his reelection bid.

But the battles were far from over. Too much acrimony and poison ink had been spilled. Burr and Hamilton continued their epic feud, culminating in a duel in Weehawken, New Jersey in July 1804. Burr shot Hamilton, who reportedly fired his shot harmlessly in the air. The stricken Hamilton was rowed across the Hudson to New York, where he died the next day. Though indicted for murder in New York, Burr enjoyed immunity from prosecution.

Figuring the murder indictment might be a political liability, Jefferson dropped Burr from the ticket in the following election. The man who had been a single vote from the presidency died broken and penniless in 1836.

Callender served jail time for his slanderous assaults. When he emerged from prison in 1801, naturally he felt that Jefferson owed him, but Jefferson did little to appease the now discredited Callender—a mistake with a very long shadow.

The following year, James Callender broke the story in a Richmond newspaper that Jefferson "kept as his concubine one of his own slaves. Her name is Sally." A series of articles went on to provide full form and detail to rumors that had been murmured about the president, that he had lived with Hemmings in Paris and that she had borne him five children.

The president made no statement about the articles, hoping that his silence would cause the inquiry and the subject to be closed, but the story plagued him for the rest of his life.

All political party activism in our nation draws from the notorious campaign of 1800, our first truly contested election. Political parties have grown vastly larger and more sophisticated but they are no less nasty.

THE BIRTH OF POLITICS AS USUAL, THE SEQUEL

BY THE 1820S THE DEMOCRATIC-REPUBLICANS had broken into two factions: The National Republicans and the Democrats. These were the seedlings of the parties that dominate the landscape today.

The Democratic Party of populist renown was born out of bitter personal feuds in the 1824 and '28 elections between Andrew Jackson, southwestern bumpkin, and John Quincy Adams, patrician New Englander. In '24, Jackson won the newly-installed popular vote but lost the election in the House of Representatives. Jackson rebelled against the eastern elite he thought had stolen the election, formed a new party, and celebrated his "jackass" moniker by choosing the donkey as its symbol

Considered by many to be the meanest election in our history, the '28 race had a sad casualty. Jackson's wife, Rachel, an earnest slip of a woman, had been divorced many years earlier. An administrative hitch in that proceeding gave Adams' henchman ammunition and he unleashed a fusillade of articles calling her a bigamist and a presidential whore. Offering an early lesson in political comebacks, the Party of Jacksonian Democrats swept its leader to the presidency. But Rachel died just before the electoral ball for the new president. He never forgave his adversaries.

The Democratic Party has held the presidency 14 times since, but their power in the Congress has been even more extraordinary. The Democrats controlled both houses of Congress from 1955 to 1981, an incredible feat in our modern democracy.

The Republican Party was born of the same fiery passion that created the Democrats. In the 1850s perhaps the most potent political divide was over the expansion of slavery into the new western territories. The Kansas-Nebraska Act allowed people in those territories to decide whether they would be a slave state or a free state—a clear repudiation of the decades-long Missouri Compromise which prohibited slavery north of 36 degrees 30'. Removal of that line on the map proved an adage that still carries today: Sometimes a capricious line in the dirt keeps peace better than opening up a debate.

Thus, in 1854, a group comprised of former Free Soil Party members, an anti-slavery ticket, plus like-minded Democrats and Whigs, gathered their collective objections to the Kansas-Nebraska Act, professed to be the true descendants from Thomas Jefferson's Democratic-Republican Party, and set up their own party.

Dubbed "Republicans" by newsman Horace Greeley, the new party named John C. Frémont as their first presidential candidate in 1856. Though James Buchanan soundly defeated him and the pro-slavery Southern Democrats gave Frémont just one percent of their vote, he made a respectable showing in the North and the first-time party won seats in Congress. Two years later, incredibly, Republicans took control of the House.

In 1858 a young lawyer with a staggering penchant for losing elections and a remarkable ability to turn a tale found himself running in this nascent Republican Party for the U.S. Senate in Illinois. A series of debates with a diminutive and polished statesman, held over seven sessions in Illinois, would etch the Republican Party forevermore into the politics of our nation.

Physically, Abraham Lincoln and Stephen Douglas could not have been more different, yet each was a potent orator. Lincoln, in his questioning, set a perplexing trap. He asked Douglas a simple but challenging question: Would he support the ability of new territories to block slavery?

Douglas answered in the affirmative. His statement appeased the Northern Democrats of Illinois and assured his election to the Senate. But as Lincoln predicted, his answer so angered Southern Democratic leaders that it virtually doomed Douglas's presidential bid in 1860.

Lincoln's simple question tore the Democratic Party in two. Yet Lincoln was hardly a presidential contender. Early in 1860, a list of 21 presidential candidates was published in New York and Lincoln's name wasn't on it. In Philadelphia, Lincoln's name was absent from a list of 35 names of best candidates. After he gave a major speech at Cooper Union, the *New York Evening Post* mentioned Lincoln among others as a potential president. It was the only instance in the East in which his name surfaced.

Douglas duly won his Senate seat but two years later, when the Democratic Convention met in Charleston, the first purpose of the Southern

Leaders was to defeat Douglas, despite his presumptive leadership status. For all his support he was not able to carry the two-thirds vote.

After 57 increasingly tense ballots, the Southern delegates withdrew from the convention and set up one of their own in Richmond.

With that first step, the journey of secession had begun.

Douglas was duly nominated by the remainder party, the Northern Democrats, but the nascent Republican Party, in Chicago holding just its second convention, dared to dream of the presidency. Presumptive nominee, New Yorker Charles Seward, packed the hall with boisterous and voluble supporters. Lincoln had less of a sense of the moment.

Each man made a brief speech, Lincoln focusing on the moral hazards of slavery for our nation. When balloting began, Lincoln returned to Springfield, so uncertain was he of winning. Only one day later a young messenger boy approached him with a telegraph clutched in his hand. "You are nominated!" the youth exclaimed.

Little did Lincoln know that this new party of Republicans was about to experience not one, but two paradoxes.

First, it dawned on Lincoln that the split Democratic Party made his Republican nomination the equivalent of a presidential victory. All he had to do was stay the course. The second paradox was that the success of the Republican Party, which would win both the presidency and control of the House, would be used by the disaffected Southern Democrats as the trigger to precipitate war.

All that stood in between was the lame duck remainder of James Buchanan's presidency.

Sadly, Buchanan's genius was for, in the words of Lincoln biographer Henry Ketcham, doing the most unwise thing. His annual message to Congress in December 1860 recommended slavery be extended to the territories, a puzzling request since it was the very thing the American people had just voted should not be done.

From the outset, the political parties had been crafted not to solve the nation's problems but to reflect an inability to come to terms.

By Lincoln's inauguration, there was little consoling the secessionists.

The Democratic Party of the south had become synonymous with slavery just as the baptism of fire the Republicans faced carried with it the acrid portent of war.

Generations after hard-won Emancipation, Republicans turned Lincoln's portrait to the wall, losing allegiance with crucial African American voters.

The Democratic Party's kinship with the Confederacy left the powerful organization in shambles. Post-Civil War Republicans enjoyed a period of national dominance that ran mostly uninterrupted for 70 years. Republicans have held the White House for 84 years with 18 presidents. In recent years, Republicans have focused more carefully on holding more governorships, state legislatures, and benches in their sway.

From these fierce oppositions came the birth of two mighty enterprises: The Democratic and Republican Parties. Understanding the passions behind their founding highlights the legacy of vituperation between the two. Even as power typically passes in waves from one party to the other, the parties persevere.

Something in me tightens when I hear the dewy-eyed describe how divided we are today without historical context of the battles we've fought. We find our stalemates faster today, and we have settled our differences in the last few generations without the loss of hundreds of thousands of lives in bloody civil wars and riots.

Our generation did not invent partisanship; we simply practice it in a bit less bloody fashion—but only a bit. Still, I can imagine a few politicians I would prefer to see dueling on the fields of Weehawken rather than across the studio desks of Fox and MSNBC. Some traditions are missed.

Understanding the history also gives you another signal about the two major parties: Don't expect too much.

In our terms, the parties were born frozen. They weren't created to solve problems, to lead, or to govern. Parties were created because we couldn't solve problems. How much political enmity can be traced to Jackson hating Adams, or Douglas being trapped into appearing anti-slavery? The political parties became a symptom rather than a cure, symbolizing our inability as a nation to find the common ground.

POLITICS BY NUMBERS

SO HOW ARE OUR POLITICAL parties different than in those formative and bloody years at the adolescence of the republic? Two principal answers cover it: Money and Organization.

What was the cost of the last three presidential cycles? In 2000 it was $3.1 billion. Four years later it was $4.1 billion and in 2008, $5.3 billion. That's $12.5 billion to elect two presidents, one twice.

For the last 20 years, the Republican Party has had a huge advantage over Democrats in raising hard money contributions ("soft" money was more or less eliminated with the various campaign reform initiatives of the last eight years). Despite the vast direct mail juggernaut Republicans possess, Democrats have staged a remarkable surge. In part because they won back control of Congress in 2006 and in part because of the advance in the role of the Internet, which favors the Democrats and their youth appeal.

How big are the election dollars getting to be? Staggeringly big:

The first year that the presidential candidates raised over a billion dollars was 2008—Obama brought in an astonishing $745 million and McCain raised $368 million. For 2012, Obama plans to defend his incumbency with a billion-dollar chest of his own.

Certain hotly contested congressional races produced some pretty fancy numbers. Al Franken's 312-vote victory over Norm Coleman in Minnesota cost the two combatants $50 million, factoring in legal expenses after the election. The price of the Kentucky horse race was $32 million and North Carolina's was $28 million. In the House, New York District 20 spent $11.5 million and two Illinois districts, 14 and 10, each spent over $9 million. The stakes have become huge.

If your PAC gave $2 million to federal candidates in 2007–2008 you wouldn't rank in the top 25 PACs. And if your company or organization gave $2 million to federal candidates in the 2008 election cycle you would rank 80th.

As always, drill deeper to find where the geological pressure originates. Bills get drafted, debated, and revised in committees and subcommittees.

Ask new panel members what happens to their campaign war chest once they are appointed to a banking, tax writing, or commerce initiative. Even in the halls of Congress they call such committee appointments "lucrative." It's pure Jerry Maguire.

Powerful candidates in key positions become money magnets. To begin with, they have a huge advantage in the reelection campaigns. The American electorate is too cynical to be bought. But the financial requirements of mounting a campaign are intimidating. Any candidate who starts the process with serious bread is a daunting adversary.

Is my thesis that possessing money makes our political process anti-democratic? Not so fast. Today, any candidate for a major office needs serious money from somewhere. If they aren't a self-feeder, then a lot of palms-outstretched meetings are a requirement for winning, and that's where promises get made.

Clearing these high hurdles requires vastly more funding than even the most endowed party can muster. Particularly on a state level, candidates are on their own. That's why so many Senate and House candidates rely so heavily on out-of-state donations. When Republican Scott Brown faced Martha Coakley for Ted Kennedy's Senate seat, the "out of nowhere" candidate found his coffers swelling by more than a million dollars a day once it appeared he might win.

Trust me, that money wasn't coming from Williamstown, Pittsfield, or Worcester, Mass. Nationally, Republicans smelled blood and money chased the opportunity.

The second big difference from the parties of yore is organization. Ask any old ward boss and they will tell you that parties used to work when the grass roots met the central command and no fights broke out.

Today, Democrats and Republicans have similar approaches to national design. The National Committees focus on the campaign strategy, fundraising and the convention.

The conventions have become less smoke-filled room and more show-biz. Delegates are pretty well-baked and the caucuses and primaries make the event more of a fait accompli than in the bad old days when the networks roamed the floor hanging on every word and decisions were actually made. Do yourself a favor: At least once, get yourself on the convention floor. You won't be impressed. Everyone knows who the candidates are, and the running mate cat is usually long out of the bag by the big night. The parties do throw some really great soirees and the delegates are a pun on themselves.

These national committees are supported by Senate and House Campaign Committees, which more than anything else are your chance to hear from your Representative and your Senator. For most of us, the only time we hear from our elected officials is when they are asking for money.

Chasing money occupies a significant percentage of politicians' waking hours. And when they aren't lining their own war chests or PACs, or getting their campaign debts paid down, then they are asked to do their part to raise money for the Senate and House Campaign Committees.

Other national party organizations bring their own fundraising initiatives to the effort: Republican organizations, for example, include the College Republican National Committee, the National Federation of Republican Women, and the Young Republicans.

There are many state and local organizations: Freedom Works, which fights to reduce the size and reach of government and to lower taxes (keep up the good work, gang), GoPAC, which aims to prepare a new generation of Republicans, and the Republican Governors Conference. Every state has its own Republican State Committee with county leadership, district leadership, precinct captains, and volunteers down to the neighborhood level.

A review of the Democratic structure offers much the same construct. There are also Democratic clubs in many communities, young Democrats organizations, and some women's Democratic groups.

There is a larger point here. Each party is organized this way because of the existence of the other party. The system favors two parties beating each other over the head, slaloming in and out of power, undoing, if they can, what the other party just did—or being tied up in knots with one party controlling the legislature and the other the executive.

The increases in money required to feed both the campaigns and the parties is symptomatic as much as it is causal. Do we have a system that can effectively deal with the major challenges our nation faces? Or is the duopoly self-preserving in such a way that horizons are too short, laws are too compromised, and problems are simply postponed?

With all of this organization, money, and energy, you'd expect well-run machinery, but that is often not the case. In some smaller states like Rhode Island, most of the funding of the state and local initiatives comes from the national organization—money that could pay for the executive officers of the party apparatus. In some states only rarely does the local party actually do fundraising for the party itself. Most candidates and party members are focused on their own fundraising rather than party building.

Declaration of Independents

What has emerged is a catch-22 party structure, and this may provide the opening for a third party, or more.

Here is the dilemma: In many states the party doesn't provide the level of resources that candidates desire so the candidates don't do much fundraising for the party. The parties must fend for themselves. As funding requirements rise for each campaign, candidates are forced to cast ever wider nets for money, threatening party unity.

And both the Democrat and the Republican parties are dealing with splinter groups, conservative and progressive wings. This is most noticeable on state and local levels.

Early signs of general testiness are emerging. The battle between proactive media and fundraising grassroots party structure, which mobilizes young activists on the one hand and the entrenched leaders on the other, is good for democracy but bad for the party. The youthful enthusiasm that Internet fundraising brings is often at odds with a rigid and entrenched party structure that prefers status quo.

Young party activists believe the party needs to do more than issue press releases complaining about leaders of the other party. They want action.

Party leadership prefers glacial change. The resulting infighting leads some to seek an independent course.

What happens when a party splits? Often they lose. The Civil War decimated the Democrats by splitting their party into Northern and Southern factions. In 1912 Teddy Roosevelt challenged the 300-pound incumbent, William Howard Taft, to be his party's standard-bearer. Failing to win the nomination, Teddy bolted from the Republicans and ran as a Progressive Party candidate. Split by Teddy's Bull Moose, the Republicans lost decisively to the tamer Woodrow Wilson.

Third parties in history provide a dramatic irony I call friendly fire. They often split and harm the party to which they bear the strongest resemblance. So Teddy Roosevelt cries bully and leads his former party to defeat while Wilson, a Democrat who wins on an anti-war platform, proceeds to hand the Republicans back control of the Congress by committing the country to World War I.

By that time Teddy's damage was done.

There have been many other third-party candidates, and for generations they have been more likely to spoil than to win. Thus has been the role of the alternative player.

Only two senators have won as Independents in the last 20 years and Joe Lieberman and Bernie Sanders are the only Independents who hold major office. There are no governors or members of the House from an Independent Party as 2012 begins, though in the nineties there were three: Jesse "The Body" Ventura in Minnesota, Lowell Weicker of Connecticut, and Angus King of Maine.

The only president who was an Independent was Andrew Johnson, who assumed the presidency after Lincoln's assassination. He was impeached but survived by a single vote. Later in life he served as a Democratic senator from his home state of Tennessee, so select history books refer to him as a Democratic president. Not so. He came to the party later in life, tiring of the uphill slog that comes with being a man without a party.

Since reconstruction there have been 31 senators, 111 representatives, and 22 governors that weren't affiliated with a major party. Over the 130-

year period, that constitutes barely one victory a year. Winning outside the party structure is very difficult, even as the legions of Independent voters grow, yet there is something in the American spirit that keeps Independents running despite their mixed record of success.

What is the status of third parties today?

There are three alternative parties that perennially run candidates for president: The Constitution Party, who are socially and fiscally conservative (everybody loses); the Green Party, which is socially progressive and fiscally liberal (an expensive combination); and the Libertarian Party, who are socially liberal and fiscally conservative (but have a hard time balancing a checkbook).

As you scan the nation there are some very interesting regional parties, none more successful than the Vermont Progressive Party. That group counts among its members five state representatives, two state senators, and the mayor of Burlington.

Then there is the emerging Tea Party, which proves that "Independent" is not code for Centrist. They have generated a lot of noise, and they have been a force to be reckoned with in the Republican House. But the jury is still out on what their contribution will be long term.

Here's a little secret: The system is pretty well rigged against third-party candidates. To begin with, we have based almost all our elections on horse racing—the first past the post wins.

That means winner takes all. Plurality wins in local elections, even if a majority isn't achieved. And splinter groups can usually point to undermining one of the major parties—ironically, often the party most closely associated with the splinter group platform.

In presidential elections there is a majority requirement, but even in the presidency there is a two-party tilt because failure to achieve a majority of electoral votes means the victor is elected by the House of Representatives. Since the earliest days the two parties have alternated dominating that chamber, with little room for a third party.

But the Tea Party has proven that there is room for a powerful alternative voice in the chamber.

And whatever your opinion of the Tea Party's positions, it is a great thing for our democracy that they have appeared on the scene.

Think for a moment about the two-party hegemony. In every facet of our lives we have seen choice replace the prix fixe menu. In broadcasting we have gone from three dominant players to a growing variety of cable choices. Internet proliferation has turned our news and information gathering into a highly customized self-directed exercise.

Books are published by the millions; digital mobility allows us to work from places of convenience, not requirement. In virtually every aspect of our lives we are presented with options, choices, mobility, and flexibility. In corporations once notorious for silo thinking and stiff refusal to accommodate customer demand, variety and options have become the watchwords.

Yet when I recently met with folks involved in Obama's reelection campaign, the strategy was pretty pedestrian for a president who has a reputation for out-of-the-box thinking.

The dilemma the two parties face is symptomatic of a new fragmentation and customer segmentation society.

Americans don't do duopoly anymore.

But don't expect the ice to crack just yet. The history of duopolies is that the players self-protect, and barriers to third-party success range from obvious to invisible.

Take ballot access. Each state sets its own rules, often based on a percentage of those voting for each party in the last election. Both Ross Perot and Pat Buchanan appeared on all 50 state ballots, though Perot paved the way for Pat Buchanan by opening voters' minds to the value of a serious third-party candidate. If nothing else, it gave his people the template.

Sometimes, ballot access can go to the extreme, as with the vaunted 2003 California recall which voted Gray Davis out of the governor's office. A month after reelection Davis had forecast a deficit of $35 billion, nearly double what he had just projected election night, and bigger than those of the other 49 states combined.

Recall supporters collected more than 1.36 million certified signatures (they needed 900,000) to force an election. To assure voters full access, only 65 signatures and a token fee were required to run for Governor of California. With 140 signatures you were credible enough that no fee was required.

With a scheduled October dual vote (one yes-or-no for recall; one for who should be governor), by late August the list of candidates had swollen to 135, not one of whom was a registered Democrat. Fears of a plurality meltdown threatened the proceedings.

Imagine that 47 percent (a plurality but a minority) supported dumping Davis and one candidate achieved a 20 percent plurality vote, which meant victory. A double minority could lead to a massive shakeup.

As October approached, a semblance of reason returned. Democrats figured having at least one candidate would not offend a doomed Davis and would provide a fig leaf for the party. Many Republicans, like Bill Simon, gallantly stepped off the ballot so that their lead horse, Arnold Schwarzenegger, might enjoy clearer riding. The Austrian muscled his way through the recall with 48 percent of the vote, disproving the fears of plurality meltdown and proving that celebrity sells in "Caleeforneeya."

Another barrier for Independents is the inaptly labeled presidential debates, which aren't really debates and are rarely presidential. Again, the system is rigged in favor of two parties. The first presidential debates were held between Richard Nixon and John F. Kennedy in 1960, though the Lincoln/Douglas debates of 1858 were a true precedent.

Kennedy's youth and vigor so profoundly impacted the 1960 televised debates that no presidential candidate risked treading in front of TV cameras for another 16 years. People who heard the debates on radio concluded Nixon had won handily, but on TV, viewers could see badly-shaven Nixon flop sweat while tan, athletic Kennedy looked cool and . . . presidential by comparison. In 1976 Ford and Carter debated three times, again with telling result. Though Carter trailed going into the debates, Ford's assertion in the second get-together in San Francisco that "There is no Soviet domination in Eastern Europe and there never will be under a Ford administration" cost him the election.

Four years later, Carter held a narrow lead but was no match for the telegenic communication skills Reagan had honed over a lifetime. Reagan trounced Carter in the debates and went on to win by a landslide.

It wasn't until 1992 that the first third-party candidate, billionaire Ross Perot, participated in the debates when he appeared with President George H. W. Bush and Governor Bill Clinton. (Reagan had gamely agreed to debate Independent candidate John Anderson in 1988, but Carter refused.) The idiosyncratic Perot held his own, particularly in matters of domestic policy. In his quirky way he was mesmerizing; and he, unlike the others, had a weapon. He was truly enjoying himself and it showed.

The real battle over the debates took place behind the scenes.

It was decided that the nonpartisan League of Women Voters should manage the presidential debates. Accordingly, they ran the show in the 1976, 1980, and 1984 elections. By 1987, debate preparations and negotiations grew increasingly intense and partisan. In October of 1988, just before the elections, the league issued a scathing press release withdrawing from the debates because, "the demands of the two campaign organizations would perpetrate a fraud on the American voter. The League has no intention of becoming an accessory to the hoodwinking of the American public."

With that, the LWV had left the building.

The two-party monopoly assumed control of the presidential debates through a private corporation: The Commission on Presidential Debates (CPD). The Commission has been headed since its inception by former chairs of the Democratic and Republican National Committees. Unless a candidate has at least 15 percent popular support in opinion polls he or she is excluded from participating.

Ross Perot would have been disqualified under the 15 percent hurdle since his support in the opinion polls ran in the high single digits, though his performance helped him earn 19 percent of the popular vote in the election. Despite his strong showing in the prior election, Perot was excluded from the 1996 debates.

In 2004, the Citizens Debate Commission was formed with the mission of returning control to an Independent nonpartisan body but in both the elections of 2004 and 2008 their pleas fell on deaf ears.

Another hurdle is that the news media rarely spends much energy or airtime pursuing the Independent candidates. Perot was able to purchase enough airtime to refuse to be ignored, and his first time out, he was both topical and original. Voters found him authentic so he attracted the attention of the fourth estate. Perot was press-worthy and he was rich.

The majority of Independent candidates suffer from the tree falling in the woods syndrome. Campaign funding reimbursements kick in when hurdles of five percent or more of the popular vote are cleared—a rare circumstance for the unaffiliated.

The money ball element of today's politics makes running without a party a pretty neat parlor trick if you can pull it off. Mayor Michael Bloomberg was chided for spending $102 million on his third mayoral term, shattering the previous record held by . . . Mayor Bloomberg. The mayor responded, "If I could have done it any cheaper, I would have . . . believe me."

Bloomberg has something special—true CEO quality. Unlike most politicians he has actually run something. He is a shrewd judge of character and situations and, oh yes, carries with him a net worth of $17 billion or so. Even the parties would have to be very wary if Bloomberg were to enter the race.

Seventeen billion dollars will clear a lot of hurdles.

Here's the greatest threat to any Independent, including those on the list worth less than $17 billion: The most powerful deterrent to the third-party candidates is the campaign trick called Vampire Neutralism.

Whenever a new group garners strong support it invariably comes principally at the expense of one party. Vampire Neutralism is the propensity to pounce like a squid sticking its blood pole into the heart of the new campaign. (As Bob Hope might have said to Mr. Taibi, "Thanks for the allegories.") Sometimes the vampire comes from the party most closely akin to the third party, other times from the party furthest away. Whoever does it, the concept is always the same: If there's a fresh and successful third candidate out there, steal their ideas.

Nature abhors an independent, and the vampire always comes and they don't stop when drinking 'til the body has run dry.

When George Wallace garnered ten million votes and 13 percent of the popular vote in the 1968 election with his American Independent Party, Nixon and his campaign strategists took notice. Nixon adopted his Southern Strategy specifically to court disaffected Southern Democrats who were frustrated by the march of civil rights through the Democratic platform.

By the 1968 passage of the Civil Rights Act, a great many of these Democrats, whose forebears had recused themselves and moved their convention to Richmond, were looking for a new home. LBJ and his fellow supporters of the landmark bill saw Southern Democrats drifting to the open arms of the Republican Party.

Nixon had neutralized his opponents. True Blood.

In 1992 Ross Perot had eviscerated both the Democrats and Republicans with his charts and tables which chronicled the vast waste and inefficiencies in government spending. Far more than his foreign policies, which were pure Sam Houston, it was Perot's sensible, businesslike domestic agenda and road map to greater efficiency that helped a relative unknown gather almost 20 percent of the popular vote.

He was fresh, he was colorful, but most dangerous of all, he was right.

The reigning parties did not stand idly by. Perot had taken voters out of both of their hides so there was only one course of action in '96, and each of the big parties pursued it in their own way. Both parties stole Perot's deficit reduction thunder and claimed it as their own.

In a whoosh of MBA jargon and best practices, Perot's campaign promises were eviscerated. The parties drank their fill and left the Texan spent, colorless, and without his defining edge. Perot was neutralized, his unique edge gone, and his campaign failed to attract the same army of supporters as it had in '92.

RUMBLING ROOTS

FOR ALL THE MONEY AND the momentum, the parties have the tired feeling of a legacy in decay. The mighty standard-bearers have the same kind of weary dominance of the broadcast TV networks: They continue to lead but there are ominous signs of generational change and the trend is pointedly against them, even as their coffers grow.

Change is afoot and, like most empires, the parties have been clumsy in embracing it.

The rising tide of voter independence is perhaps the most marked trend in politics over the last two decades. The ominous clouds signal dark days for the entrenched ways of party dominance.

In the year of my birth nearly 21 percent of voters considered themselves Independent. Today, 45 percent of voters between the ages of 25 and 40 describe themselves as Independent, according to Pew Research.

Independent voters, long derided as the fringe, are now the largest and fastest growing segment of the American electorate. Books have been written calling the surge in Independents a myth, suggesting that they tilt Democratic or Republican when the curtain closes. But such behavior studies carry with them too much accuracy for their own good. What they miss is the latency buried in all this disaffection.

I believe disaffected Americans are Independents-in-waiting, prospective voters who cannot be evaluated in classic party terms. Independents cut a very broad swath and there is little that unites them. Some are passionate joiners who cannot find the right pew, others are disconnected, and others completely apathetic. But they are growing steadily and they typically favor sentiment over organization.

Therein lies their power. They are fluid, and when they shift sides they can tip the boat.

What we are experiencing here is a tectonic plate shift as powerful as the fractionation of cable and Internet channels. And as flat-footed as the networks have been, so, too, the political parties have failed to find the right way to address the Independent incursion.

Politics as usual has been their playbook . . . so far, so good. But will there be a point when the boat tips too far?

In six key swing states Independent voters now outnumber Democrats and Republicans (Colorado, Iowa, New Hampshire, New Jersey, Connecticut, and Massachusetts). In 2008 there were a million Independent voters in key states where the battle is won or lost, places like Pennsylvania, Ohio, and Virginia.

In the sun states, which are enjoying powerful in-migration, (California, Florida, and Nevada) the number of Independent voters has more than tripled since 1990 while Democratic and Republican registration has flatlined.

THE TEA POT TEMPEST

SOMETHING PROFOUND IS HAPPENING ON the most grassroots level. Americans are shying away from the tired old polarized party approach. They are even more frustrated by candidates who claim to be conciliators, then jog to their corner once elected. There are rarely true bipartisan leaders.

The troops are assembling. Some are wearing three-sided hats. And they are spilling tea into the harbor.

The Tea Party movement is perhaps the most controversial and misunderstood group of Independents who are rattling their sabers today.

But history once again provides a clue. When Reagan was president he privately expressed admiration for activists who made it uncomfortable for the "weak sisters" in the Republican Party who didn't back his agenda. Bear that in mind as we examine the Tea Party movement.

To explain the Tea Party, it is almost easier to explain what it isn't. The revolution will not be organized. The movement prides itself on being leaderless. There are no central talking points or detailed national agenda. There is no e-mail list of millions or national party infrastructure. The trend is to act locally and network nationally. They resist the idea of a centralized platform on principle and their political targets are all over the map, which may be worse for Republicans and better for Democrats than meets the eye.

A growing number of Tea Party activists have launched their own Independent PACs , like Eric Odom's First Liberty, with a decided anti-Washington and anti-incumbent leaning.

Scott Brown's victory in Massachusetts proved a few things: That fundraising streams from Independents are there to be tapped by candidates who channel the Tea Party spirit, and that no seat is unthreatened no matter how long it has enjoyed the pedigree of a party or a family, or both. Rather than Republican victory, this was an anti-incumbency vote targeted well south of area code 617. It was a 202 shot across Obama's bow.

The Tea Party provides Republicans with both an opportunity and a problem.

Who are the Tea Party members? Well, they claim about 18 percent of the population. They are overwhelmingly white, male, Republican, and over 45. They are your Uncle Joe. Most describe themselves as both very conservative overall and more conservative than their Republican brethren. Though there is no central platform, there are some common denominators. They claim a fierce animosity towards Washington, which should alarm all incumbents, not just Democrats.

But their harshest criticism is of President Obama and his overall direction for the nation. They believe with powerful consistency that his administration favors the poor over the middle class, and that taxation as well as size and influence of government are wrongfully increasing. They consider out of control spending a symptom of an overreaching authority, and they have a passionate aversion to federal government interference in their lives.

What is hard to capture in a census, or the numerous surveys that have been conducted, are two characteristics that strike me as highly differentiating: The first is that many Tea Party members are first-time political activists who have not yet given any or even slight sums to fund a political movement and second, they behave as if their way of life and our national soul are threatened.

Combined, these may make for a forceful, if temporary, political movement. Their general lack of affiliation, centralization, and core platform adds one more imponderable to the mix: Volatility.

The Tea Party is also anti-cap and trade, which increases the government's role as it reduces carbon emissions. But health care trumps carbon for pure emotion every time. If The Tea Party loses ObamaCare as a dragon, will they keep their edge?

Some say the Tea Partiers need to move beyond the protests and create a more formal structure. The Nationwide Tea Party Coalition has drafted 28 local activists to form a National Leadership Team spearheaded by Michael Patrick Leahy, a former Republican delegate and Romney supporter. But the movement's spontaneous character remains its greatest strength; though its loose network leaves the movement open to fringe elements, including some who believe the 9/11 attacks were planned by the U.S. government.

They also got hijacked from their premises by the birthers until Donald Trump took up that tattered banner. The Internet coalitions and local groups tie many different niche groups together like ResistNet (which, along with the Patriot Action Network, was created by Grassfire.org, a conservative group that opposes what they call "the Obama-led socialist agenda"). The result is a polyglot network that is pretty tough to corral.

They do better with preaching fiscal restraint. That's a theme that binds. Tea Partiers need more glue than the anti-establishment anger at Obama-Care and creeping socialism. They need to focus on fighting big government, spending, and tax issues, and keep building their power in legislative elections.

Oppositional momentum can wane. Obama has staked his presidency on whether an economic turnaround can obliterate the discomfiture of his health-care plan. The midterm watershed which swept Republicans into House control should not be confused with a true groundswell of support for Republicans. It was a vote for changing the change.

The biggest risk facing Republicans is that voters want to change the change changers in the next cycle. So is the Tea Party friend or foe?

It is far too early to assess the impact of the Tea Party's aggressive spending-cut rhetoric on the Republican House majority. Democrats smell an opportunity to win back voters who thought they wanted change until it meant change for them.

Remember that the Tea Party is a passion play on the move. And if their gaze has turned to overspending by the federal government, that show, as they say on Broadway, has got legs.

Will Tea Party activists be able to forge some sort of pragmatic allegiance, to foreswear their splinter politics and join hands with the Republican Party? If Republicans can't make peace, at least in the form of a VP slot on the ticket, beware the Bull Moose.

Here's the quandary—moderate Republicans may have lost their taste for blood.

The Tea Party will be friendly fire to moderate Republicans and cause one of two reactions: either the moderates skew right and take their chances with the electorate or they will stay moderate like Reagan's "weak sisters" and take their chances in the primary. It is a very tough choice.

The practice of vampire stealing of potent new ideas is a problem for moderate Republicans because for many of them, the Tea Party blood is tainted. Skewing right to win the primary is simply too distasteful, so they will not drink their fill.

Or worse—in the general election, Medicare reform will be the third rail and may electrocute a few moderates. The fringe group is gaining traction and Republicans ignore it at their peril.

Yet Republican leadership will have real difficulty controlling the Tea Partiers because they do not want to be controlled. That is their DNA.

As for the Charlie Crist Independent option, it will occur on the margin because without a war chest and a name, such a battle is not winnable. And lest the Democrats think the moderate GOPers will get all the heat, the bell tolls for them as well.

This is where the rambling and random nature of the Tea Party is at its most powerful. In local elections different groups will target different candidates. Can a Southern-style strategy draw disaffected Democrats to the Tea Party point of view? Such a strategy worked for Nixon over civil rights, but ObamaCare and sweeping socialism may not be such a poison pill for disaffected Democrats. Job losses certainly could be.

With the splintering of the Republican Party and Democratic uneasiness with their incumbent, the Independents hold the keys to the house on Pennsylvania Avenue.

The appearance of the Tea Party is a good thing—it is the next best thing to having a new political party.

What good has the Tea Party done?

It has forced the debate within the Republican Party like no period in recent memory. It has provided a template for considering meaningful change. It has brought deadlines and metrics and a bit of harsh sunlight to a process which has been cloaked in too much party dogma.

Who knows whether Occupy Wall Street is a directional indicator or early warning system for Democrats the way the early Tea Party gatherings featured more three-cornered hats than policy debates? People who deride the occupiers' inability to articulate much more than their perception that the current system favors the top one percent at the expense of the other ninety-nine fail to recollect American history. Time after time change declares itself like an infant at first, mewling and puking. But with time comes maturity and articulation and persuasive force. So too will OWS. It is a peregrine circling overhead. Dismissing it does not contain it. Negative energy lifts the movement like thermals for a soaring falcon. Ignoring the occupiers is a risky strategy.

These splintering initiatives mean that votes won't necessarily follow party lines. Whatever your party, outlier voices must be considered.

A once predictable duopoly, like the old comic *Spy versus Spy,* has been turned on its head. And that is a good thing.

The restless political middle between Democrats and Republicans has attracted an iconic Internet effort called Americans Elect, which plans its own version of smoke-filled chat rooms. Just 800,000 signatures shy of the three million required to place a candidate on the ballot in all 50 states, Americans Elect has two bold and simple goals: to provide an alternative to stale choices, and to push a presidential candidate without a political party.

Anyone joining can nominate a candidate, and after a winnowing process, Americans Elect will hold an Internet Convention in June 2012 to declare their nominee. As a crowner that candidate must select a running mate from another political party besides his or her own.

I've spent time reviewing the business plan, the backers, and the sound financing of Americans Elect. Don't rule this start-up out.

Wags who dismiss it as the child of "one percenters" should recognize that the seed financing is meant to be a bridge. Ultimately the plan is to reduce the largest single investment anyone has made in the organization to a maximum of $10,000.

But these funding elements aren't what give me confidence in the managers of Americas Elect. Their secret is far from well kept.

They are focused on a yawning gap between the political parties and the people. By capitalizing on historic disapproval ratings and making the barriers to join very low, Americans Elect might just be the sidebar story of the 2012 election—particularly if the two lead candidates fail to inspire the voters.

We have been locked into a battle in which polarization leads to slow-moving responses, ill-considered regulations, and even some bad laws. The immovable two party system prevents nimbleness in confronting major problems. Splintering means a wide range of solutions are debated. And some courageous legislators are looking at horizons beyond their next reelection

I have met few voters on any side of the aisle who argue we are spending too little. But the notion of bigger, more intrusive government versus a more spare, less involved government which provides more individual liberties should be debated.

The Tea Party broadens the list of outcomes, multiplies the options and choices we have to make. It causes further splintering and makes the process messier. But the net result will be the consideration of a wider array of outcomes, the provision of more choices to the American people . . . and best of all, vitality to the republic.

No matter where you come out on the spectrum or which choices you make, having more wide-ranging debate and more options will lead in the end to more problem-solving and better lawmaking. Splintering is how we will thaw.

And that should be the life of any party.

TEN CATASTROPHES WE MUST AVOID

CHALLENGE ONE
China: A Co-dependency That Is Decoupling

"BEWARE WHEN CHINA AWAKENS." —NAPOLEON BONAPARTE

1919. A FEW HUNDRED CHINESE *teenagers milled around the wharf in the old port of Shanghai. The French packet ship, Andre Lyon, bound for Marseilles, bobbed dockside. For the young people facing months in steerage, their time in France would be marked by grueling labor only occasionally punctuated by the studies they hoped to pursue.*

Of the excited Chinese teens, the youngest and perhaps the quietest was diminutive Deng Xian Sheng, the first-born son of a Hakka (hill people) land-owner. Young Deng had big ideas.

The voyage was agonizingly slow, and soon after finally making landfall, the pent-up hopes of the travelers were crushed. Europe was recovering slowly from the ravages of the just-ended Great War. Those Chinese students fortunate enough to find work were paid half the wages of their French counterparts. Sixteen-year-old Deng worked constantly—doing odd jobs at a steel plant, working as a fitter at a Renault factory, as a train fireman, at a rubber plant, and as a kitchen helper—and had little time to study. But there was no alternative as Deng's family could no longer afford to send him money.

In France, Deng developed a lifelong taste for croissants and brandy at the behest of fellow student, Ho Chi Minh. He roomed with Zhou Enlai, a country-man six years his senior, a man whom Deng referred to as "elder brother," a role he continued to play in Deng's life in the decades to come.

Thanks to the October Revolution in Russia, workers' Marxist and social-ist movements in France gained momentum. Everything about Deng's experi-

ence was driving him towards Communism, especially the brandy. Under the tutelage of Zhou Enlai, Deng joined the Communist Party of Chinese Youth in Europe. During his five years in Paris, Deng went from being a patriotic Chinese boy to a passionate Marxist . . . the first eager steps of a revolutionary career. Deng became co-editor of the Socialist Youth League's newsletter, The Red Light. After France, he studied in Moscow like any good CIT (Communist in Training).

In 1927, he arrived home as most wanderers do, forever changed. His name changed too. For the rest of his days he was Deng Xiaoping or "small peace" . . . what an irony. During his career he earned two nicknames: "the living encyclopedia" for his wide-ranging intellect and, more colorfully, the "little cannon," acquired during his time as an officer in the United National Army for his fierce flashes of temper.

After the founding of the People's Republic in 1949, Deng held a number of military and civilian posts and helped to consolidate Communist power in Tibet and areas of Southwestern China. Those battle-hardened military relationships would never fail him. Deng formed opinions as strong as his army bonds and gained a circle of philosophical admirers.

But Deng and another rising star of the Party, Mao Zedong, clashed over the disastrous failure of the Great Leap Forward of 1957 and 1958 to convert China from a rural agrarian economy to a modern industrialized and collectivized Communist powerhouse. Collectivization, which outlawed private farming, caused massive grain shortages, widespread starvation, and a death toll of over twenty million. It was a catastrophic miscalculation

The Cultural Revolution that followed caused a further break between the two men: Mao more leftist and committed to collectivism and Deng more pragmatic, favoring private property and industrialization. In spite of the growing enmity between the two men, Deng believed Mao would never turn on him.

But turn he did.

One remarkable thing about Deng is that his life changed "forever" at least four times.

By 1966 he was a target. Prosecuted by the Red Guards, he lost all of his

positions and was sent into internal exile. In the ultimate irony he was ban-
ished to work as a common laborer as a fitter in a tractor factory—a job for
which Renault had trained him well. But the deprivations did not end there.
His son was arrested, tortured, beaten, and thrown from the fourth floor of a
prison in an attempted "escape" and rendered paraplegic.

Deng went to his grindingly dull job and connected with his army bud-
dies as best he could. Time and the weather have a way of eroding the hardest
edges.

In 1973, prodded by Zhou Enlai, Mao decided that Deng was "rehabili-
tated." In only a year, Deng gingerly re-entered the Politburo and consolidated
a power base. But he was not strong enough to oppose Mao's wife, Jiang Qing,
and the radical leftist Gang of Four who gained power in the latter stages of
the Cultural Revolution.

When cancer took the life of the popular Zhou, Deng lost his last line of
defense against Mao's wife and her cronies. Using the public display of mourn-
ing for Zhou in Tiananmen Square as a pretext, Deng was purged once again.

He maintained his relationships in exile. Deng was schooled in the impor-
tance of guanxi (connections and relationships) but in China, not all guanxi
are created equal. The army was a powerful base. He waited. The slow choking
of economic prosperity that cramped the Cultural Revolution sowed seeds that
Deng would harvest later.

On Mao's death, his wobbly designee, Hua Guofeng, was named premier.
In the vacuum, change came swiftly—the Gang of Four was toppled in a coup
d'état a mere month after Mao's passing. Once again Deng espied an opening
and grabbed hold. He ousted Hua bloodlessly and with restraint, establishing a
modern precedent. He was also measured in his condemnation of Mao and the
Cultural Revolution excesses: "Mao was seven parts bad and three parts good."

Deng secured his base and moved swiftly to open relations with the West
and to modernize the economy. He began by taking the unheard of step of let-
ting Capitalists join the Communist Party. He was deliberate in downgrading
Mao's lasting authority and systematically eliminated Mao's followers. In 1980,
the Gang of Four, including Mao's widow, went on public trial.

Deng was a pragmatist who believed China's greatness lay in moderniza-

tion and outreach to the West. In 1979 he signed a Treaty of Peace and Friendship with Japan. That same year Deng obtained recognition of China by the United States and visited President Carter in Washington.

This was not your father's Communism, but Deng's liberalism in no way signaled the end of massive central control and corruption. He always wielded a firm hand.

No matter how firm the grip on the tiller, it's hard to fight the winds of change. During Mikhail Gorbachev's 1989 state visit to Beijing, student demonstrations formed the other parentheses of Deng's Tiananmen Square irony— in 1976 Deng was purged for his role in a demonstration there; now students were protesting against him. Over 100,000 protesters gathered to mourn the death of former Secretary General Hu Yaoban and to express widespread impatience with the pace of change.

In response, disastrous decisions were made. The Tiananmen Square massacre of 3,000 protesters is called the June Fourth Movement or simply 6/4 by the Chinese. To the world it is burned into memory by a single searing image of a man facing a tank. That photograph was Deng's undoing. He ceased to play a public role in Chinese politics for the rest of his days.

He'd been banished before.

Once again, Deng methodically kept his network and influence. And once again, he was rehabilitated. Deng came to be canonized by his people as the architect of the prosperity China enjoys today. In his autumn years he was the subject of posters and promotion all floridly praising him in verse and in art.

The little cannon was an appealing character—playful, a commendable bridge player, and an ardent swimmer. He was quotable: "Let some people get rich fast." "Poverty is not socialism." "To get rich is glorious." And, "When our thousands of Chinese students abroad return home, you will see how China will transform itself."

Perhaps he was telling his own story . . . or China's . . . or ours.

IF YOU DON'T UNDERSTAND MUCH about China, I can promise you, China understands us very well. For the past 30 years we have been in a *pas de deux,* and a vast tectonic plate is shifting under our feet.

In the seventies with Nixon, Chinese leadership warily toyed with western style capitalism. The Forbidden City opened its elm wood doors just slightly to let some foreign trade and investment slip through the crack. Until 1989, when that iconic image of a man confronting a tank in Tiananmen Square signaled populace defiance, the grand experiment in capitalism halted as certainly, and as temporarily, as that tank.

In that tableau was the ultimate symbolism: a moment where China faced off with the world, its apparatus frozen in its tracks, spewing out choking exhaust, idling with a throaty grumble. As the world watched, China waited.

All around, Communism was in peril. One after another, like a reverse of the domino theory of a generation before, Communist and near-Communist nations of the Warsaw Pact saw their governments tumble.

By 1991, the die was cast for the Soviet empire. It, too, fell, less like a relic of a failed ideology than like a poorly constructed and maintained house finally giving way. The Chinese sought object lessons in the collapse of European Communism. There was no scarcity of teachable moments, but there was a single clear theme that carried through each regime's disintegration.

That lesson was simple, powerful, and not lost on the Chinese: every government must have as its ultimate goal the steady and unmistakable rise in the quality of life of its people.

Economists possess a bewildering array of tools to measure a nation's progress. Standard of living improvements take many forms, but they must always carry along the bulk of the populace. History reminds us that forward propulsion by the few to the exclusion of all others promotes a cynicism with one predictable outcome: Failure.

Stung by the world's reaction to Tiananmen Square, Beijing hard-liners stoked fires of paranoia about renewing the capitalist experiment. Even in a centralized place like China, a new style of Communist regime would be required. The USSR had taught them as much.

Rather than some impetuous youth, it took an 88-year-old man to bring

Beijing Spring to his country.

Deng never held office as the head of state, head of the government, General Secretary, or Secretary of the Communist Party—all positions of ultimate authority in China. Nevertheless, he was the Paramount Leader of the People's Republic from 1978 to the early nineties. It was Deng who breathed life into market reforms stifled by Mao's Cultural Revolution.

From the nineties, Deng's successor, Jiang Zemin, picked up the tempo.

And it was America they chose to be their dancing partner. Now it appears China is anxious to lead but at least we're still dancing; the music hasn't stopped; and there's still time.

Having lived and worked throughout the region, I can assure you that nothing in Asia is predetermined. Becoming China's bitch is not a foregone conclusion.

The Snake Venom Diet

IN THE LATE SEVENTIES, I moved to Tokyo as Director of Asian Business Development for American media conglomerate Capital Cities Communications. No matter how lofty the title sounded, it meant traveling solo to countries like Korea, Hong Kong, Taiwan, and China in the hopes of peddling trade news to emerging Asian nations.

The seventies were heady times in Asia. President Nixon made his historic visit to the People's Republic of China in 1972. Since the Republic's 1949 founding, the only kind of relations the two nations had enjoyed were frosty. Each viewed the other as aggressor. We considered China a Communist bloc nation; they saw our participation in Vietnam as another example of American aggression.

Nixon's visit and subsequent embrace of China had the fingerprints of his National Security Advisor, Henry Kissinger, all over them. Kissinger advocated recognition for two reasons: First, relations with the Chinese were a necessary ingredient in American withdrawal from Vietnam. But more characteristically, Kissinger saw unique advantage in playing the China card in the Cold War, perhaps further destabilizing the Soviet Union and threatening Sino-Soviet relations.

Mao trumped with his own Cold War card. The presence of American troops just off the Chinese coast on the island of Taiwan (then the Republic of China) was never far from his mind.

Withdrawing Republic of China recognition became a requirement for assimilation with the People's Republic. President Carter blinked, the troops were brought home, and recognition was withdrawn for the ROC. Carter's decisions went down poorly with the Republican-controlled Congress, a group notoriously wary of mainland China. Congress concocted a "nonrecognition" recognition plan, The Taiwan Relations Act (1979), a document only a legislator could love.

A few months later, I made my first visit to the Republic of China. I had already experienced the People's Republic on the mainland, entering as many did in those days via the New Territories through Kowloon. Traveling along peaceful countryside, the bustle and din of Hong Kong gave way to duck farms and villages. Hakka women, hill people like Deng, labored in broad hats and pajama-like garb.

Then, you traveled by East Rail train to the boundary of the forbidden land. For a small stipend you could get a border tour and a trip inside, but deep within, the cities of Shanghai and Beijing and other unpermitted mysteries beckoned.

I remember vividly seeing tables and chairs arrayed under a string of street lights along a roadway. My traveling companions explained that local villages had no electricity and that street lights had meaningfully altered the social mores of the town. Under the lamps each evening people gathered, sharing stories, smoking, playing mahjong, living their lives with free electricity.

Sixteen years later I remember approaching China from the other direction by bicycle. It was 1995 and riding through Mongolia was like traveling through a land that time forgot. Approaching China from the Asian periphery helped me frame my view of the Chinese nation and to make my own judgment of the country's vastness and power.

During the seventies, as with many directors of business development in Asia back then, most of my work was done on my own. I would check into the Lotte Hotel in Seoul, or the Mandarin in Hong Kong, or the Les Suites Taipei and I would be the only Cap Cities employee for thousands of miles. Self-reliance was a job requirement. And I learned the value of curiosity . . . especially when dealing in Asia.

One day in the ROC, after a series of disastrous meetings in Taipei, I consoled myself at the resplendent Buddhist Longshan Temple. I was blessed back then with a mop of blonde hair and a crowd of youngsters was captivated by it. A hundred children swarmed, all reaching out to touch me, pat my head, and occasionally yank at my hair. The bronze dragons on the right and left pillars of the main hall did little to protect me. Despite being outnumbered, I never felt threatened.

It was like swimming in a sea of warm Asian faces, benevolent and curious, not aggressive—a stark contrast to my abortive attempts at Chinese commerce that week. It dawned on me wading through those children that my innate lack of curiosity was to blame. In the end my lack of understanding had been an insult.

Those dozens of Chinese young people were more interested in me than I was in them. My whole approach to experiencing Asia changed in that moment.

Just a short stroll from Longshan is the notorious Snake Alley. It was a Friday evening, and everything was wriggling. To prove that I was Chi-curious I downed shots of snake venom, bile, and blood.

If you want to understand China, drink the venom.

Take Beijing. Inhabited by cave dwellers 500,000 years ago and rebuilt by Kublai Khan in 1215, Beijing sits high in the North China Plain, ringed on three sides by mountains. In the capital, modern and ancient coexist. The Imperial Chinese Garden of the Summer Palace captures the past just as Rem Koolhaas' monolithic CCTV skyscraper that houses the country's only broadcaster points to the future. To the north and west, the Great Wall snakes into the mountains, where on clear days the view and the air are sweet. However, on any given day a ghostly gray cloud of modern pollution can choke your enthusiasm and obscure the Beijing skyline.

Everywhere old and new seek a balance.

To the east on the Yangtze delta, the modern and beautiful port city of Shanghai is surrounded by vast wetlands. For centuries these marshlands held water towns where enterprising Chinese built Venice-like communities like Zhu Jia Jiao. These towns stand in stark contrast to the Houston-like modernity of the Oriental Pearl Tower and the sparkling night skyline.

Even in an overwhelmingly new metropolis like Shanghai, the old is never very far from the new . . . you just have to look a little more closely.

If you really want to drink the venom, take a bamboo boat down the Li River near Guilin. The scenery of jagged mountains, steep cliffs, and verdant river plain is an artist's dream. If you sail to Daxu, you will visit a town built in the Qin Dynasty over 2000 years ago. Travel the winding stone lanes among well-preserved traditional buildings and you experience the contrasts that form China.

For centuries China has been a slumbering giant with a multi-thousand-year-old culture. Once they were the famed Middle Kingdom, the center of the world.

But unlike the pathways that meander through the village of Daxu, nothing in Asia is set in stone.

In 1988, Clyde V. Prestowitz opined in *Trading Places* that an unstoppable Japan was destined to become the dominant world economy. Prestowitz, who worked in Reagan's Commerce Department, argued that Japan's web of protected cartels combined with a dynamic and inaccessible home market made it an economic powerhouse. In an oft-told story, Prestowitz recounted the lament of a senior policy advisor that captured the seeming inevitability of fortress Japan: "They'll sell us cars and we'll sell them poetry." Later as the story gained momentum, the word "semiconductors" was swapped with "cars," but the meaning was clear—Japan could not be denied.

I recall meeting Sony Founder Akio Morita at the Tokyo Press Club in the eighties. He was the silver-maned eminence of Japan's technological ascension. His prestige then bore a striking resemblance to Steve Jobs' status at the end of his life. (Remember the Walkman?) Morita calmly spoke of the certainty that Japan's economy would overtake the United States as number one. He said so like a doctor making a clinical assessment, not with any chest pounding. It seemed to him like a fait nearly accompli.

Afterward I privately asked Morita what gave him such confidence. He told me Japan had a secret weapon. Japan's advantage was its ability to focus its economy and develop technological products at a huge discount in comparison to U.S. costs. Then he leaned closer to share his secret recipe: their fundamental difference in outlook. America's short-term obsession with results versus Japanese long-term patience in achieving the goal would lead one economy to surpass another. It was simply a matter of time.

Morita's guaranteed result missed the mark. Many things caused Japan to lose momentum. A bursting real estate bubble and a conservative view of protecting and preserving wealth meant that Japan lost its edge in the digital revolution. The Japanese didn't double down in the dark days.

In the end many of Japan's strengths upended its progress. The near-inviolate conjoining of business and government meant that the economic tsars were flat-footed and not nearly nimble enough to deal with economic stagnation. Their unwillingness to stimulate meant a tepid response to a stalled economy, and an historical opportunity missed, perhaps for centuries to come.

China today looks a lot like Morita's heir-apparent Japan, only scarier. But Japan proved one thing: a lot can happen between announcing one's destiny and realizing it.

Ignoring China's national obsession will not make it go away. We can influence the course of history or we can let events wash over us.

The China's Bitch Syndrome

IF YOU MENTION CHINA TO most semiconscious voters they'll shake their heads and say, "Oh, China . . ." And nothing more. They'll sound serious and concerned. If pressed they might say that China is becoming too powerful or that it has so many people. A growing number will have a more cogent response, recognizing that China is our greatest export source and also the holder of the most U.S. debt (the co-dependency called "exports for finance") . . . which sounds bad.

And it is. Because there is a possibility that the U.S. might fall behind China in the economic race to the top, and that we might be dependent on China—because they hold our purse strings.

Becoming China's bitch is not inevitable. Our economic rapport with China can be cooperative rather than adversarial, but it will take work and a dose of ancient Chinese medicine we typically abhor: *long-term perspective.*

The bottom line on something as vast and complex as China's ascendancy is this: There is no way for America to dominate the economic landscape without specific and thoughtful strategies for dealing with China. Every American must wander into Snake Alley and take a shot of the venom. Democrats and Republicans need more intense curiosity about the very folks who are curious about them. We should know about their leaders. What do you know about Hu Jintao? We should know his story, and Deng's.

Deng: immigrant, radical, factory worker, communist, leader, exile, survivor, capitalist. It's such a different path from those our leaders take now, if anything, more like an eighteenth-century U.S. president than a twentieth. But we have to know them.

Any other view of the Chinese will harm the American Dream.

In my youth, we were a nation obsessed with the Soviet Union. We analyzed every move they made and dedicated our finest minds to it: Henry Kissinger, George F. Kennan, Zbigniew Brzezinski, and many others were our sentinels. The arms race and the advancing Soviet jackboot made for both healthy and unhealthy paranoia about the Russians.

Where is our paranoia about China, healthy or otherwise?

Here is the haunting clue to anyone who doubts this position: the Chinese have already come to the same conclusion about us. The American view must be that China is both a bigger threat and a more marvelous opportunity than the U.S.S.R. ever was.

The Chinese determined some years ago that their national coffers couldn't develop a manufacturing base to serve their own home markets on any reasonable timetable; and that they had a huge preindustrial workforce with the latent power to learn and grow. They also had Deng's pragmatism coursing through their Communist veins.

Then the Chinese figured out one more simple thing: they needed a partner.

They found us.

In us China found a comrade who could succeed where European Communists had failed, because we could drive the quality of life improvements that Communism miscarried.

Together, the U.S., European Union, and Japan bankrolled China's expanding economy by transforming it into an export powerhouse. Thus began a growing co-dependency. The United States, Europe, and Japan bought increasingly larger volumes of Chinese exports, and the three trading partners sought greater and greater levels of foreign investment and borrowings from China.

Chinese capitalism evolved thanks to American money and ingenuity, leading China up the value chain from cheap goods to increasingly more sophisticated products.

At the same time, America found in China a ready lender to finance its own expansion. But the rapport went far deeper than Sam Walton importing cheap goods to stock his shelves in exchange for China financing the U.S. government. Beware the bilateral "exports for debt" simplification of our relationship with China. You should accept as gospel that everything about China's relations with the United States is more complicated than it appears.

So, how best to think about China?

Chi-merica

IT'S A HORSERACE: ON THE rail is the largest economy, and coming on the outside is the largest population with the fastest- growing economy. On one level, China has already ended America's economic supremacy—we don't dominate like we used to. If you cannot appreciate that simple economic reality, you are in denial. Economies turn over the course of generations, and the coming decades will have China accreting and America ceding economic might. The only question is where our paths cross.

Staying on top overall while losing on some measures is the focus of this chapter.

Most Americans miss the old world order when China, the perennial sleeping giant with four times our population, hadn't entered the automotive age. I liked the old world order too. But this century is China's and we better be prepared. We need to understand its "through the looking glass" economic model—especially its defensive approach to currency and reserves.

The "exports for finance" dynamic sets up the economic equivalent of the Cold War, with some profound differences.

"Exports for finance" is shorthand for co-dependency. Walmart's slogan is "Save Money, Live Better." So too goes our nation.

We need cheap imported goods to deliver on Sam's promise. Target and other discounters have cottoned on to the same notion. Americans will abandon almost any retail relationship if they can consistently save money on quality goods. China has come quite a long way to deliver on the promise of inexpensive quality.

Now this penchant for cheap goods has a parallel philosophy embedded in it. Americans have had to borrow in order to sustain their prosperity, security, and well-being.

No one borrows like we do. We are the largest and the most consistent borrowers on the planet, and we go to China for our cheddar.

China has been willing to lend to us for a few reasons: 1) We are reliable repayers . . . so far; 2) We are by far their biggest customer and they need to keep us liquid . . . up to a point; and 3) By funding our ever-expanding consumer, government, and defense spending, the Chinese win the daily double. We reinforce their growing export machinery and at the same time we are so opiated by our own consumption, military buildup, and prosecution of conflicts around the globe that we don't focus on what China is becoming.

Funding America preserves and protects the Chinese export monster, but only until that monster chooses to stop exporting and begins serving China's home market.

Nobody ever said co-dependency was forever.

As one of the world's great autocratic states, China has seen its GDP grow at just under 10 percent annually since 1980. China emerged from the global recession stronger than ever. Some years, China's exports have grown by an extraordinary 50 percent, while in "weaker" years 25 percent growth has had to suffice.

As the number-one trading partner, the U.S. has maintained extremely large trade deficits (nearly $300 billion) every year. That means we bring in nearly $800 million a day more than we export back to China.

You don't need to be on the Council of Economic Advisers to know that long-term imbalances like that have consequences.

So how is a Radical Centrist supposed to know when enough is enough?

Bear down on two topics: how China's currency reacts, and the reserves the Chinese keep. I know. Could there be a duller way to monitor threats to U.S. economic might?

We are bored by currency and trade.

Trust me, China loves our indifference.

No one listens to currency experts. And let's face it, whenever currency is in the center ring, it doesn't even get an Andy Warholian 15 minutes of fame. Economists are too doctrinaire and political scientists too paranoid. Sometimes they switch. There's little basic understanding about how currency and reserves interact in a dynamic market because they are economic concepts that must also be considered in a political light.

You don't need to be Fed Chairman to show people the way. If you pan back the lens, reasonable solutions tumble right out.

The enterprise of China has extraordinary spread. With over 1.3 billion people, the country has seen the rise of its cities lift over 300 million people out of poverty—more than any country in the history of man. Still, troubled by the structural economic divide between the major urban centers and the vast rural expanses, China has moved on two fronts: one, to create industrial cities, satellite production centers, and regional wealth throughout its heartland; and two, it has begun developing a massive internal market subsidized by its export prowess.

The consumer market China envisions is four to five times bigger than our own. This newly endowed Chinese consumer represents China's next great economic station.

To accomplish that lofty goal, China will need to become the largest, most powerful economy in the world. If they manage such a marvel, the Renminbi (yuan) will become a super currency rivaling the dollar. A big "however" is that massive structural impediments currently prevent China from scaling the precipice.

Why am I so certain the Chinese will make the difficult decisions necessary to take the next step? Because China understands the most important single lesson in developing world economics: No country can depend indefinitely on low-cost labor.

There is always a nation hungrier for revenue, more willing to subjugate its citizenry, more willing to take chances on quality, more willing to pollute itself, more willing to use cheaper or outdated materials, more disinterested in moving up the value chain—even hungrier than China. Cheap goods are bankrolling China's journey to a higher plain, where technology transfer, reverse engineering, and intellectual property rule the food chain. Like an immigrant scrubbing floors to fund their child's college degree, China has shrewdly partnered and apprenticed with the most advanced companies on earth. Studying, copying, and slowly but surely innovating, China is advancing on the G7 with a single goal: number one.

Exponential growth has drawbacks: inflation overheats economies—and vice versa. Lately, property value escalation has dwarfed Japan's real estate bubble. China has other challenges. Expansion of manufacturing and production to higher value-added products has been accompanied by increased corruption, pollution, and waste disposal as well as a lack of quality controls—serious problems for Chinese manufacturers.

There is another big "however." Contrast corporate soul-searching and disciplinary actions when American companies ship bad products with corresponding reactions when Chinese companies make the same mistake.

China's river of communist capitalism simply swirls around the offending entity. Investigations are announced, managers are fired, and perhaps a regulator who was paid to look the other way resigns in disgrace. Then the river rolls on.

Chinese indifference to quality, particularly in consumer products like baby food and paint, where American consumers are mortally offended, will limit China's runaway growth in the intermediate term. Only when we punish vigorously will China get serious about quality.

Chinese central command has challenges too. Powerful regional authorities have emerged despite its centralized and planned economy. Even China must balance the power of local bosses with strong national policies.

More impediments exist. State-run enterprises are riddled with internal subsidies and structural inefficiencies. Beyond enterprise reform, the notion of intellectual property as a proprietary asset is beyond the ken of many Chinese executives. Piracy plagues content providers dealing in China, whether it's bootleg software or DVDs.

Freedom of expression and social welfare, items we regard as commodities here at home, are rare gems in Chinese business.

Just Google it and you will see what the search engine folk have experienced in their Eastern encounters. On human rights and intolerance, China stands in a league all its own.

(Hint: If your native Nobel Peace Prize winner is incarcerated and can't receive his medal, try the Lennon treatment and give peace a chance.)

Some pretty sharp operators believe China will get old before it gets rich. There is a huge savings rate in China, in part because there is no meaningful social safety net. By some estimates, in 2018 nearly 250 million people will be over 60. These elderly will become users rather than suppliers of economic resources. China's average age will continue to rise, unabetted by restrictions on real or perceived birth rates. Marry that with China's falling mortality rate and you are guaranteed a rapidly rising average age.

This age wave will certainly affect the trajectory of China's GDP. The costs of coping with hundreds of millions of aging Chinese will stymie economic expansion. By contrast, India's average age of approximately 25 means they will have to spend less on medical care and social safety nets than China.

Despite these significant obstacles to becoming a true superpower, China has a well-established interim plan.

China's power derives from its willingness to serve as the world's workbench. By keeping its currency weak, and manufacturing and labor costs low, China has prospered making items no one else wants to make. But there is increasing agitation over China's weak currency and the harm it does to America. At home, questions roll in waves. Listen out for them:

- *"How can we tolerate an artificially weak yuan and an artificially strong dollar?"*
- *"Why must we buy from China at subsidized prices that are so cheap when we have 10 percent unemployment and they have a 10 percent growth rate?"*
- *"Why must we tolerate piracy and economic espionage from our number-one trading partner?"*
- *"When we were looking the other way, China stole our factories and our jobs by cheating in trade and manipulating their currency; why do we let those tricky Asians copy our products?"*
- *"Why don't we force them to let their currency float freely and fairly?"*
- *"Are we slaves to the Chinese because they own all our debt?"*

Questions clog airwaves and blogs. We beg for simple solutions, but there are none.

To arm you, let's look at four subjects you need to understand about China. Ninety percent of the idiocy you hear from pundits and errant senators involves one of these easy-to-understand subjects. When something sounds outlandish, it is almost always because the person misses the point. Radical Centrists know better by understanding these four topics cold:

- *Trade and Reserves*
- *Currency*

- *Energy and Pollution*
- *Human Rights and Corruption*

TRADE AND RESERVES

THE TRADE DYNAMIC BETWEEN CHINA and America is the business story of our time.

Deng's successors detected that Americans were huge spenders. China gambled that our entire retail market would reward cheap prices if quality was reasonable. They wagered the American economy was powerful enough to sustain many years of current account deficits. But China could never have guessed how far we would push the envelope. (Current account deficits mean that we buy far more from China than we sell to them.)

Americans are heavy consumers with savings rates well below industrialized national averages: even after recent turmoil, Americans' personal savings rate is under five percent. (The rate of gross domestic savings in China has surged since 2000, climbing to over 50 percent of GDP in 2007).

On the most micro level, savings by the urban households in China which earn about two-thirds of the national income is about 30 percent—six times America's recent peak.

Self-insurance drives increased personal saving in China. Declining public provision of education and health and housing services is bestowing Chinese households with plenty of incentives for saving. Younger households save for future education expenditures and older households save for uncertain and lumpy health-care bills.

Through it all, we just keep spending.

China watched American consumers buy more and more, financing their consumption by borrowing against the steady rise in their principle asset: real estate . . . until the music stopped.

With obliterated property values, Americans have become more bargain-conscious than ever, reinforcing our thirst for inexpensive goods.

Our government is a co-conspirator, vastly overspending its current income and requiring prodigious borrowing. How bad is it? In the 2010 U.S. budget, 42 percent of what we spent had to be borrowed, and nothing about our trajectory has changed since.

Having decanted domestic resources for borrowing, the U.S. Treasury and government agencies, naturally, went abroad. In the last decade, foreign investors lent us about half of the federal debt. China and Japan accounted for almost 44 percent of that sum, with Britain and Europe following a distance behind.

In 2010, China's foreign reserves surged to $2.3 trillion, about two thirds of which are American securities, making it the world's largest holder of dollars besides the U.S.A.

Besides us, no one is a bigger investor in America's future than China. That worries a lot of people who believe dependence on cheap China imports to sustain our standard of living has been traded for a choke hold on our currency and our ongoing ability to borrow.

It should. No less prodigious an intellect than Larry Summers termed this situation, "The balance of financial terror." Even the Chinese have commented: Premier Wen Jiabao expressed growing nervousness about his country's massive exposure to America's financial well-being.

But let's recall the words of John Maynard Keynes: "If you owe your bank manager one thousand pounds you are at his mercy, but if you owe him one million pounds he is at your mercy."

Let's also review the facts, to the extent they can be known.

First, there is a lot of debate about the actual amount of Chinese holdings. The government entity that purchases foreign bonds, oddly enough called SAFE (State Administrator for Foreign Exchange), has what you might call "an aversion to transparency." So it is pretty hard to be precise about Chinese holdings and their trading strategies.

In addition, some believe China is purchasing U.S. securities through intermediaries. The result is that the reported $800 billion figure of U.S. Treasury holdings is probably over a trillion, or about 15 percent of U.S. public net debt. (While the numbers are doubtless huge, it is worth recalling

Bush Treasury Secretary Hank Paulson's admonition that China's holding equates to a few days' trading volume in treasuries.)

Why hoard all those reserves?

Accumulating dollar reserves became more pronounced after the 1997 Asian Financial Crisis. In that panic, currency speculators hastened a balance of payments crisis in Thailand, Indonesia, and South Korea by demanding dollars for local currency. Their actions caused a run on reserve dollars held by the central banks of those countries.

The Thai Baht collapsed under the weight of the panic and took many emerging market currencies with it.

Okay then, what about China's trade policies?

As a leading exporter, China runs a major trade surplus: more goods going out than coming in. Its dependence on exports to America was reaching unsustainable levels. China's U.S. trade surplus constituted over 98 percent of its overall trade surplus in 2007.

This surplus dropped to 90 percent in 2008 but the following year leapt to an imponderable 115 percent of China's total trade surplus. How can that happen? In 2009 the Chinese ran a trade deficit with the rest of the world and a surplus with the U.S.

So from every perspective dollars gush into China. Perhaps they need our bonds to invest in nearly as much as we need them to lend to us.

Here is an economic reality: China relies on exporting to the U.S. market for millions of its best jobs. So is China a prisoner to the Dollar? If Keynes is right, then the U.S. debt is a tether.

China's dependence on the U.S. export market is particularly acute in the Guangdong province in the south, and specifically in the massive industrial metropolis of Dongguan. There, factories belch pollution and churn out all manner of goods—toys, shoes, clothing, car and machine parts.

When we spiraled downward in 2008 and global recession followed, thousands of factories in Guangdong closed or cut production. And hundreds of thousands of workers from other provinces returned home. Across China millions of workers were unemployed by the western meltdown. Undaunted, China soldiered on and its economy continued to grow.

But something about their relationship with us had changed.

China's economic resilience during our travails emboldened their state capitalist system versus our free market-style capitalism. America may have run a trade imbalance, but as an offset, the Chinese had an imbalance of confidence. Not anymore. Could a decoupling be far behind?

Trouble is, China has no sensible way to boldly decouple from us. What options do they really have?

As a first choice, they can reduce their purchases of U.S. debt.

Treasury holdings being what they are, is the euro zone with the PIIGS nation difficulties (Portugal, Italy, Ireland, Greece, and Spain) able to provide the investment relief China seeks? Only with high-risk purchases like rumored Italian government bond investments.

Japan's economy is solid, if stalled, but with Japanese government 10-year bonds carrying an interest rate at a paltry 1.2 percent and a lackluster calendar of issuance, there simply aren't enough Japanese government bonds (JGBs) to fill the void. Can Yen satisfy their yen? Marginally.

Until China breaks its dependence on the dollar it will be compelled to buy American bonds. As China shifts from exports to greater domestic consumption, the need to purchase dollars will lessen and much of the extra cash will flow into commodities (though many are quoted and dealt with in dollars). China has been stockpiling commodities both as a tactical investment and a strategic imperative. (Companies can borrow against the stockpile.) Chinese purchases of copper, gold, and other commodities suggest the country never wants to be beholden to other nations for supply.

When China turns its manufacturing towards feeding its home market, where will America look to finance its mounting debts?

It is important to remember: debt freezes destinies.

China slowed its debt purchases in 2010, though it is too early to call it a trend. But whether your ideology is Confucian or Keynesian, having 90 percent of your trade with a single party who depends on you for more and more debt is an unwise economic model. And long term, unwise economic models either change or fail.

Can serious financial imbalances become weapons of mass destruction?

Having our largest trading partner as our largest lender is a threat to national security.

As a second choice, the Chinese can sell securities.

The fact is they do, but not too aggressively. Why? American companies might temporarily benefit from a weaker dollar, but among those hurt by bold selling are holders of dollar assets, the largest in the world being the Chinese, through SAFE. Aggressively selling U.S. bonds would cause Chinese assets to diminish and would strengthen their currency against the dollar—something, like Br'er Rabbit, we dearly want. And they don't.

If SAFE, the largest holder, is selling boldly and incurring losses, who would be willing to buy U.S. assets in significant size as the market price was falling?

In this case, better SAFE than sorry.

Punishing America by selling dollar assets, something China considered when our Taiwan policy upset some generals, would be equivalent to shooting a Zhu-Rong pistol in their own foot. China is in a dollar trap. They have checked in, but it isn't so easy to check out.

A snide officer in the Chinese Academy of Social Sciences chided that the dollar's reserve currency status is dependent on China's goodwill as America's lender. Many take umbrage at the fact that China is "America's Banker." Don't get exasperated. Whoever enjoys the tilt today in the balance-of-power needs to know that in any Cold War symmetry, subtlety rules. Blowhards, whatever side they come from, risk upsetting a delicate balance.

There is another option. Get ready, because there will be blood. The other choice is for China to discontinue its massive intervention in the yuan.

CURRENCY

THERE IS NO AREA OF SINO-AMERICAN relations where there is greater heat and less light than currency. When someone who has not seen the dark side of a dollar cross-trade holds forth like a latter-day George Soros, hold on to your laptop—you are about to get "garbage out." Currency is both an asset to be traded and a highly political medium of exchange. Take care whenever someone confuses the two.

There is plenty of evidence that the yuan is undervalued. There is even more evidence that the Chinese government is keeping that currency "stable" . . . daily. But as Barney Frank notoriously asked, "Could it be stable but a little higher?" We will debate valuation, but please resist the urge to leap to the conclusions that you hear from economists and would-be currency mavens about the outcomes of revaluation.

Currency manipulation is the mother of unintended consequences. With currency, always think "delicacy." Outcomes of revaluations are not knowable with certainty, except the certainty of being dead wrong.

What is the essence of the debate? A major yuan appreciation means: Chinese goods become more expensive, our dependence on Chinese exports will shift to goods made here, creating more jobs at home, Chinese and foreign consumers will buy more "cheap" American products, the balance of payments for the U.S. will come into equilibrium. China's growth will slow and we will "export" our unemployment because the demand for products made in China will revert back to the U.S. producers, who will hire in droves to meet the surge in demand.

To consider this passionate point, let's check the lens of history.

The first yuan (also *Renminbi,* or RMB) was introduced in 1948, about a year before the People's Republic of China was formed. The intent was to replace many of the Communist paper currencies floating around. Later, the new regime intended the notes to help cope with hyperinflation.

By hyper I mean warp-speed inflation.

The note size had to keep rising, so a 10,000 yuan and a 50,000 yuan note were created. By 1955, a revaluation was necessary and one new yuan was equal to 10,000 old yuan.

Just keep making bigger bills and then like in *The Sound of Music,* head right back to *do*—or dough, as the case may be. Replacing a 10,000 yuan note with a fresh bill called "1 yuan" is a rapturous way to cure hyperinflation—literally paper over your problems with a reset and move on as if all is well.

But that is precisely how China handled it.

In the late 1970s when Mainland China "opened" its markets ever so slightly, the RMB was usable only domestically; foreigners had to contend with awkward and unavailable foreign exchange certificates. The rules were so restrictive and the value so disadvantageous that their existence virtually created an entrepreneur's currency—otherwise known as black market.

About this time, the RMB was pegged to the U.S. dollar at 2.46 yuan. The Chinese currency appreciated to 1.50 yuan to the dollar in the 1980s. (Remember, the smaller the number of yuan to the dollar, the stronger the Chinese currency is. The greater the number of yuan to the dollar, the weaker the Chinese currency is.)

As its market opened up in slightly greater earnest, the Chinese government massively devalued its currency so that dollar trades in 1994 brought the holder 8.6 yuan. (On New Year's Day alone, the Chinese devalued their currency by 50 percent). Since that walloping devaluation, which obviously priced Chinese goods extremely cheap for dollar-based trade, the yuan has appreciated by 20 percent—but at a glacial pace.

Today, the yuan trades at about 6.50 per dollar, slowly but steadily strengthening against the greenback.

People are howling for a revaluation, some for a one-time 20 percent–plus markup of the yuan. But Vice Commerce Minister, Zhong Shan, warned that profit margins on many Chinese export goods are two percent or less, so major revaluations are not affordable.

I imagine a shared moment of Chinese candor with the minister. I might get him to agree that a weaker yuan keeps Chinese exports competitive, its factories humming, and its people employed and productive.

He might even admit we have never really had free trade with China. They intervene daily to cheapen their currency and protect their workers. Steps taken since that 1994 revaluation have helped China, Inc., create well over 10 million manufacturing jobs, even as U.S. manufacturing has dwindled by over half that amount. You can tie the steady crumbling of our manufacturing sector almost to the very day of devaluation.

But clear truthful conversations like that can only happen between you and me.

So we should all be calling for a major valuation upward of the yuan, right? Not so fast. It might be that yuan revaluation would work wonders, but here are a few thoughts to the contrary:

Even if you change the exchange rate by 20 percent–plus, it may not help the trade deficit because the U.S. is addicted to bargain prices. Rather than forgo cheap products, people may prefer to buy from other low-cost manufacturing countries besides China—and it won't do U.S. manufacturers any good if we replace from fresh exporters at an equal rate.

If American consumers can't find cheap replacement goods, blocking Chinese products would cause inflation and upward cost pressures on the American economy. We can't turn on cheap manufacturing here at home on a moment's notice. Many of the goods in which China dominates haven't been made in the U.S. for a decade or more.

And remember, nothing about Chinese trade is as simple as we would like.

I think it's important to consider the role outsourcing and subassembly play in the equation. As much as half of the goods we bring in from China are merely the offshore production of U.S. companies for their home U.S. market.

U.S. companies produce in China not merely because of the exchange rate. Other hurdles send producers abroad like labor rates, union work rules, construction costs and delays, regulatory costs and procedures, taxes, pollution and waste control abatement, retirement and worker protection, medical requirements, shipping regulations, and a host of other harassments that are all far less intrusive when manufacturing in China.

Currency hawks ignore unintended consequences like these because they oversimplify.

My question to the hawks on forcing a major yuan revaluation is: How much would China have to revalue its currency in order to meet the economic indifference point of American manufacturers and consumers (and still beat the many advantages Chinese manufacturing provides)?

The number is simply not knowable.

It is far from a foregone conclusion that a one-time 20 percent–plus revaluation would renew a robust export of U.S. goods to China, reducing our domestic unemployment.

Particularly in the one-off Band-Aid ripping style, the outcome might be an immediate slowing of the Chinese economy and a slowing of their export base, perhaps even a major blow. Maybe John Maynard Keynes was right after all. Is it any wonder that the Chinese leadership prefers "stability?"

So before we find a solution, where else can China go? Is there another currency China can hold to support their trade? If you look at all foreign reserves around the globe, the dollar is the majority, something like 60 percent, (admittedly on a decline). The next currency, at about 30 percent, is the euro, followed far behind by the pound sterling (once the dominant currency of trade before the dollar brushed by) and the yuan.

Europe's PIIGS form a sort of Club Med no one wants to join and pretty well eliminate the euro's chances of replacing the dollar in the foreseeable future. China might consider bailing out Europe for trade benefits and hefty returns. But don't confuse vulture capital with currency policy.

More important, in my judgment, is a structural fault with the euro. There is no common sovereign euro debt market (they will have to create one), and the ability to print money and control the money supply is spread over a handful of Feds, in contrast to America's single Fed.

Germany's Chancellor Merkel and France's President Sarkozy face a narrowing political range of motion but without a shock and awe solution of shared sacrifice, the Greeks will keep on bearing gifts.

For all its shortcomings, the dollar remains the most liquid currency. Its long- and short-term debt is still the most freely traded in the world. Many major commodities, like oil and gold, are quoted worldwide in dollars. (Though Russia and others are trying to create their own contracts.) Roughly 88 percent of all foreign exchange trades around the world involve dollars.

And China is in the process of discovering its greatest economic flaw: they can't decouple just yet.

China cannot create a massive consumer market simply by throwing on a switch. Home-market consumers need to ratchet up at their own pace. For the time being, China must pin its economic hopes on continued American spending. Chinese consumers aren't ready to spend like Westerners yet.

There is just one problem with this inspired plan. We are fading like a wheezing racehorse in the stretch.

It has been a marvelous Mardis Gras "Laissez le bon temps roulez." But the endless American upward real estate climb which funded it all has disappeared like an apparition. And the good times won't roulez anytime soon.

That is our problem, but it's also China's mistake—which signals that the time is ripe to negotiate firmly with them. We are flagging, but our currency still dominates, and China can't replace us with another trading partner (including themselves), much as they would like to. Where else will they invest in the necessary size besides in commodities?

We all know that China is a daily currency manipulator. We know, too, that we exported a lot of jobs—simply gave them away to the Chinese miracle.

But we have to negotiate with the realization that those manufacturing jobs may not return in the numbers we hope. We cannot engage in currency intervention battles, or worse, trade wars. P.S. I am not certain we would win if we did.

Remember there is no economic excellence for America that doesn't meaningfully involve China; selfishly we have to find a middle ground.

Our best solution is to negotiate unilaterally with China to create a Free Market Distortion Treaty. All the major trade regimes and regulatory bodies—including the grandpappy, the World Trade Organization—would allow it, maybe even welcome it.

The treaty should have a general statement about how trade imbalances exceeding 50 percent are to be considered unstable long term. A formula should replace a one-time ripping reset, which is too much like pulling a pin on an economic grenade.

Instead let's push for what I call "Five over Five"—a five percent per year revaluation over five years, depending on certain agreed to measures of trade imbalance and comparable unemployment and GDP growth rates. I prefer an annual review to a one-time increase because it will promote ongoing dialogue and review, it is measured, and the Chinese just might find it palatable. Besides, whatever Keynes said, just how hard can you beat up your banker?

For free-trade weepers and laissez-faire types, China has been a bully. Taking massive steps to continually keep their currency weak when they enjoy GDP growth much higher and unemployment much lower than their trading partners—that is the exact opposite of free trade.

So a reasonable interpretation is that China is violating the multilateral rules set up by the IMF and the World Trade Organization. Why have we not filed formal complaints, perhaps with a coalition of the willing who also feel impugned by China's currency manipulations?

What is the point of creating paths for complaint on the moral high ground if we simply ignore them? It's time to go to court.

A popular technique for sending up flairs is using countervailing duties (CVDs), which were a centerpiece of recent trade legislation proposed as a part of the Senate-defeated Ryan Bill. Tariffs talk loudly and carry a small stick. They sound great from a podium, as Richard Nixon found, but they are the opposite of the moral high ground.

Tariffs are the land mines of trade wars. Years after hostilities cease, they still linger under the surface, latent, simmering, ready to be detonated by an innocent.

Despite China's failure to play fair, I think simultaneously threatening surcharges while upholding NAFTA-style free trade agreements elsewhere would test even a politician's two faces . . . not to mention our nation's. We should be tough, take the high road, and negotiate now.

Besides, deep down, I think China really wants to belong.

Here's a long-term bet—a little dodgy but interesting to imagine: Waiting in the wings like an ingénue is the yuan, dying to be a true leading world-currency star. But it needs an extreme makeover.

Zhu Min, Deputy Governor of China's Central Bank, serves as a Special Adviser to the International Monetary Fund. The IMF has historically been led by a European but quietly dominated by the U.S. Involving China at such a senior level indicates to me a willingness to create a greater role for China in the world currency panoply.

Before any major revaluation and free floating makes sense for China, the nation must push through some very difficult economic and structural reforms: land reform, energy, state-owned enterprise reforms, social welfare, internal government subsidies (a biggie), and structural inefficiencies.

If China can address these daunting issues in the next 20 to 30 years, then the worm may turn. But recall the straight line planning of those who foresaw Japan as the leading world economy. These structural issues, the graying of the Chinese population, and others make the uncontested surge of China unlikely. Unless they make changes, the Chinese will stagger and wheeze into the lead. But under any outcome they are a force with which Americans must contend.

It may be that our children will inhabit a world where the Renminbi is the dominant currency of world trade. But that is far-off speculation and in the meantime, China's unrelenting growth brings more dark clouds to our horizon today. They want something we also desperately need.

China has developed a vampire's taste for the elixir of our economy.

ENERGY AND POLLUTION

THE CHINESE EXPORT-MANUFACTURING DYNAMO has propelled China to the top ranks of oil, coal, and energy consumption. A sobering reality is that China's need for energy is projected to double by 2020.

China's role as our competitor for imported energy will be covered fully in the Crude Awakening chapter, but a little refining of the diplomatic issues is relevant to this discussion as well.

Like the United States, China's proven reserves are small in relation to its unquenchable thirst. But the parallels end there. China has pulled up to a marvelous intersection. Just as affordable cheap cars are available to import, China enters the automotive age.

There is little doubt that China will have the largest number of autos within 20 years. Chinese gas prices, by the way, rank among the cheapest in the world.

So long, bicycles and mass transit; grasshoppers, start your engines!

We now have a growing competitor for oil on the world energy scene.

And we are both dependent on others for this mother's milk. Confrontation is unavoidable, even if it's restricted to the boardroom.

Right now, China is the only member of the UN Security Council that has refused to consent to further sanctions against Iran. Was Treasury Secretary Geithner's decision to postpone its "official report" on China's currency (code for revaluation study) a diplomatic reprieve?

Could a stay of execution be U.S. trade bait to press for sanctions on Iran?

Today well over half of China's oil imports come from the Middle East. China's energy security, much like our own, comes from the same source.

A day of reckoning is coming, particularly as U.S. foreign policy seems focused on maintaining a strong presence in the Middle East. Long term, it will not be in China's strategic interest for America to be the dominant player in determining the direction of the Middle East. Chinese leadership will maintain a strong economic and diplomatic influence in the region.

Beijing, we have a problem.

No country on earth can rival China for the production of greenhouse gasses yet ironically the Chinese have identified new energy technology as a massive area of focus for their economy.

President Hu Jintao, a political heir of Deng Xiaoping, wants to create a new green China. For anyone who's ever visited, that is beyond a hyperbolic goal. On the flip side, research and development expenditures have grown faster in China than any other big country, to $70 billion last year.

If you take every dollar of research and development spent around the globe last year and put it together, 25 percent of the total were spent in China. This year, the United States will graduate about 40,000 engineers from its colleges and universities; China will top 400,000. Research and development expenditures by China on energy grew more than 50-fold in the last 16 years. The world's biggest polluter wants to be the greenest nation too. Fancy that.

The list of vexations of U.S.-China relations is growing, as is their willingness to confront us head on. At the December 2009 climate change summit in Copenhagen, China took a comfortable position as principal objector to western proposed limits on carbon emissions.

Nowhere is a special handling of China more critical than in energy and petrochemical matters—it is no stretch to see an emerging carbon cold war. Will you be at the post?

HUMAN RIGHTS AND CORRUPTION

IT'S OBVIOUS. THE COMMUNIST PARTY in China has a deep distrust of any civil, political, or religious group. Not to mention any Internet search engine outside its direct control. Congregations praying outside the state-controlled churches have been repressed and some, like the Falun Gong spiritual movement, have been simply outlawed.

The United States recently began its 15th round of the human rights talks which it instigated two decades ago. (All talks were suspended between 2006 and 2008).

As China has matured, central control has been sustained. Growing numbers of civil rights activists have been put in prison, or under house arrest or surveillance. Harassment is common and death penalty statistics are something of a state secret.

Two years ago, the Supreme People's Court stipulated that first offender non-death penalty cases be held in open courts. However, death penalty trials are still held behind closed doors. "Reeducation through labor" is the manner in which hundreds of thousands of people in punitive detention are processed without the benefit of a trial. Basic rights, such as freedom of expression, are routinely squashed by the vigilant central authority that is Chinese justice.

Tibet continues to draw the world's attention, as China increasingly settles that country. Tibetans face growing disaffection and there is a significant economic divide in the tiny state between Tibetans and their Chinese neighbors. Tibetans have been reduced to an insignificant minority and their distinctive cultural heritage is fading away. At this stage the Dalai Lama's last line of defense is trying to preserve Tibetan culture and spirituality. Everything else has been commandeered.

China isn't afraid to capitalize on American squeamishness about human rights. We've caved.

At the other extreme from Tibetan spirituality is a culture of corruption. But has it harmed China?

Measuring corruption in an enterprise as vast and complex as China is an impossibility. But that doesn't keep some watchdog groups, or the Chinese government for that matter, from trying. The Chinese Communist Party makes a great show of huge numbers and grave disciplining of corrupt party members and officials. The party's anti-corruption agency, the Central Discipline and Inspection Commission, punishes 150,000 party members a year, though most get off with just a warning.

What causes such a culture of corruption? The temptation is to list one or two things, but there are many. Lacking a free press or a political party process with the give and take, the intrigue, the inquiry, members in the Chinese bureaucracy seek street economics.

Graft happens.

There is a surprising amount of debate about whether corruption is an impediment to China's ascendancy. Widespread corruption doesn't appear to have done it any harm. China's East Asian neighbors South Korea, Japan, and Taiwan all had serious issues with corruption during their most pitched periods on the growth curve, apparently suffering no lasting consequences. There is even a school of thought which describes graft as the grease for the wheels of an otherwise inert bureaucracy—enabling economic productivity.

These cynical claims won't stand the test of time. Everyday corruption does not cause revolutions, but there is a staging, like a revolutionary's barricade, built in bursts without an architect's eye, and composed of jumbled logs and timber. When a revolution comes, as it inevitably does, corrupt ruling elites pay dearly for their misrule: Marcos in the Philippines, Suharto in Indonesia, Baby Doc in Haiti, Idi Amin in Uganda, and maybe someday Mugabe in Zimbabwe, are all scoundrels whose corruption sealed their fate. Mubarak the looter will likely pay dearly for enriching himself while his people suffered.

But China brings a zeal to its corruption that causes the jaded to wince. It has no villainous peer.

One study, by the Carnegie Endowment, estimates $86 billion as the cost of Chinese corruption for 2003—that's more than IBM's revenue. Corruption in China is centered in areas with extensive state involvement. In June 2011, The Bank of China published a report quoting the Chinese Academy of Social Sciences which concluded that nearly 18,000 officials and state-owned enterprise managers have fled China in the last 20 years, taking with them an estimated $120 billion. For that kind of money, you could buy Intel, PepsiCo, or Disney—take your pick.

Commissioners keep track of "naked officials," so called because they typically send their families overseas while remaining alone in China . . . that is until they, too, disappear. By the way, China does not have extradition treaties with most major "destinations."

What's striking is how new incentives and opportunities created by policy reform also point the way for new forms of corruption. Two-track pricing systems invite operators to buy commodities at low planned prices and then sell them at a huge profit in the "open" market.

In the countryside, policies grant local functionaries new leverage over farmers and villagers. In provincial cities, officials have broadened discretion. With new powers come rent-seeking opportunities for local bureaucrats. In these outposts, removed from the watchful eye of central investigatory and regulatory bodies, corruption has found root.

New policies redefining family businesses versus collectives have led to an active trade in "favorable certifications." In the same vein, export restrictions increase the dependence of smaller firms on official exporting organizations—a magnet for graft.

Exploding land prices are also a beacon for corruption. According to the head of the Regulatory Enforcement Bureau at the Ministry of Land Resources, the government uncovered more than a million cases of illegal acquisition of land between 1999 and 2005. The sheer magnitude would leave Capone blushing like a schoolgirl. Half of the provincial transportation chiefs in China have been sentenced to jail terms and some even executed for corruption.

Why so corrupt?

Certainly the absence of a competitive and contrary political process that encourages dialogue and debate, the lack of a discerning and free press, incomplete reforms with widely inconsistent application of regulations and tax policies, and a poorly organized system of banking and payments are all major contributors.

Party disciplinary bodies and prosecutorial agencies and a hostage press do produce some mighty impressive statistics and an occasional headline worthy of a scold. But few Chinese really believe that a systematic and sustained anti-corruption program is underway.

When you ask them, they shrug. It is the way of things for now. Culturally, there is a practice of buying and selling appointments in the government called *maiguan maiguan*. Particularly in less developed regions, selling appointments creates a culture of abuse.

If I were to pick a single overarching reason for such massive corruption it is China's hybrid economy, which is more typical of a smaller emerging nation than an economic superpower.

The state and business are partners in grime . . . dirty even when they act clean. Today, the state sector accounts for a staggering array of assets and influence, representing about 35 percent of the country's GDP, and controlling the largest corporations, banking, power generation, and natural resources.

By a tight corset of regulation, the state controls currencies, interest rates, and land prices while at the same time controlling real estate development, infrastructure, and construction permits. That's like controlling the NYSE and the SEC as well as owning Goldman, Morgan, and Merrill.

It is a story of moral bondage as much as a tale of economic necessity— and what corruption has joined together . . .

Is there an effect on us? Many bury their head in the sand and write it off to cultural differences a million miles away. But can we ignore the fact that Chinese competitors are buying favorable terms or rates or prices? Is it worthy of the United States to decry, then weaken on Chinese human rights and corruption as Presidents Clinton, Bush, and Obama each have in turn?

In real life, most companies and individuals turn a blind eye. Often it is consultants or agents who pay what needs to be paid, outside the watchful eye of Sergeant Schultz ("I see nothing!"). But we compete with China on the global field of commercial battle, where their purchase of advantage comes at our direct disadvantage.

In a nutshell, it is an economic fallacy that we can simply continue by saying, "It's there, it's huge, but it doesn't impact me."

Not when corruption is a coin of the realm.

MORE BAD NEWS

PARANOIA IS APPROPRIATE FOR US in relation to China. They have many ways to impact us: our debt, our dollars, our energy, and our source of cheap goods. But their planned economy and their expansionism should give us pause too.

Here are a few examples:

Rare earths. Just the name tells you they're not plentiful. Rare earths are key in both computer and wireless technologies and in many activities of clean energy technology. Rare earth metals are found in iPods, BlackBerries, laptops, and plasma TVs. They are utilized in many goods because they are an efficient and compactible metal. What some purveyors have told me is that they are a key ingredient, even strategic, without easy substitute.

Sounds like the start of some bad news.

The good news, in the 1970s and 1980s, was that we dominated in developing and mining rare earths. Today, however, China provides nearly 97 percent of the world's supply. Worse, the country is cutting its exports to feed its home markets. Governments may challenge the legality of Chinese export policies, and firms may look to move production to China to get around export restrictions.

If you go back to the words of Deng Xiaoping in 1992, "The Middle East has oil; we have rare earths." How concerned should we be? China abhors the spot market. Whether it's dealing with thuggish governments to buy access to commodities, or hoarding, stockpiling, and restricting access to rare earths, China has demonstrated one thing: They never want to be starved for want of a nail.

What about batteries? Are we shifting from oil dependence to battery dependence? Again, there is reason for paranoia. Batteries are technological innovations. They are minerals from the mind—intellectual property, not natural resources. Even if we innovated the technology, the U.S. can fall behind an empowered China—who plans to dominate batteries.

How about food? You are what you eat, depending on who sells it to you. China supplies about 80 percent of the world's vitamin C and one third of its vitamin A. Because of weak border inspection, lead-contaminated vitamins from China showed up in the U.S.—some bound for baby food before the pabulum producer caught it.

China has become the provider of choice for teas and other foodstuffs. We know by reputation that environmental controls and quality standards are lax in China, even if the goods are due for export.

So we can rely on the FDA, right? Not so fast. The FDA food inspectors review about half of one percent of all food imports. The Agency has 650 food inspectors covering about 418 ports of entry—they are also responsible for policing about 60,000 domestic food producers. In 2011 the Agency plans to close about half of its 13 food testing labs.

Here are the facts: U.S. food companies are responsible for food safety. Forget looking to the government to protect our food quality, U.S. food companies are our last line of defense against contamination. This past year, the FDA examined contaminated toothpaste and cough syrup for a chemical used in antifreeze—that's my definition of bad breath.

THE CHALLENGE FOR AMERICA

WHAT WE ARE FACING IS nothing less than a test of American independence. We have a co-dependency with China for goods, services, and production, and we need to set boundaries. China is also back to double-digit defense spending increases exceeding $90 billion for 2011. These expenditures mask a much higher number estimated by the U.S. Department of Defense at double the highly publicized figure.

Make no mistake: China intends to be a world military power and it spends like one.

We need a sentinel for tainted goods, and we need something more. Every Radical Centrist will recognize the call: We need a plan.

The challenge is not that China is investing in the U.S. On a relative basis we are investing far more heavily in their companies than they are in ours. The challenge is that we must find a way to deal with China.

In spite of China's pollution, corruption, and record on human rights, our addiction to their cheap goods, and their appetite for our debt, we must find a way to maximize our national interest. Hotheads on the right or left want to treat with blunt instruments that which should be dealt with surgically. They are to diplomacy what carpet bombing is to combat. Suggestions of punitive regulation or debate about tire, steel, and honey tariffs belie the real issue.

We need a global strategy for dealing with China.

If we can't join 'em, beat 'em.

There are nations like India who could play a useful role. Our European and British colleagues can help here too. In part it is about deciding what strategic assets we wish to provide ourselves, or finding and developing alternative sources beyond China.

We will need to invest in order to defend our independence. Rare earths are a good example. We should not panic, but should we abnegate our supply entirely to China?

In a phrase, China plans their economy and we negotiate ours.

Who has their eye on what China has planned? In fact, who even knows what they are doing?

China will happily engage with our moral opposites. They will supply our needed financing and stock our Walmart shelves. They will continue to shelter their currency and their home markets. They will pollute and cut corners on manufacturing even as they supply us more food, pharmaceuticals, and over-the-counter medicines. They will plague us on the human rights front and, step by step, their economy will grow—not in a straight line by any means, but nevertheless, steadily over time. And with their billion-plus consumers, their economy will likely become larger than our own.

We simply cannot reduce such a complex and vital relationship to economic slurs and broad-brush harsh penalties. Both are dangerous and will serve us poorly. We need to think more strategically. We need balance and sophistication. Hard-liners will do more harm than good. We need a Centrist dance, not a dueling dictatorship of wills or China, with the benefit of central control, will out maneuver us.

We must understand China at least as well as they understand us.

And we must acknowledge without blinders China's unrelenting and imperfect drive to win.

If China does become the world's largest economy, they will do so with the largest population of the poor, the elderly, and the sick, the most pronounced culture of corruption, and the worst pollution of any dominant economic superpower in modern history.

We have so many talents and weapons (still) at our disposal.

Remember, becoming China's bitch is not inevitable. Nothing is historically ordained until inaction makes sure that it is. Anchoring in the snug and safe harbor of "debt for exports co-dependency" is one certain way to ensure a catastrophic outcome in our relations with China.

They are the ancient Middle Kingdom after all, the undisputed senior civilization for centuries—other cultures simply revolved around their perimeter. Ironically it is their young people who have tired of the world's decision to accord China second-class status. It is the young, not the old, who are insisting that China retake its natural place as world leader. China is preparing many different kinds of weaponry, not limited to defense armaments. Our response has been to send a couple thousand Marines to northern Australia, guaranteed to be a stone in China's shoe until they depart.

These anemic reactions belie a powerful truth. America's greatest weakness is our failure to grasp the most basic weapon of all: understanding.

Never confuse understanding with appeasement.

Understanding removes us from the frozen state of misaligned inertia that has us watching as China blows by. Remain in the dark and the Chinese will certainly reclaim their transient glory.

But in the harsh spotlight of the dance floor, Americans can still circle and twirl. Both parties have a passion to lead the dance, and each has its own rhythm. So let us dance warily, thoughtfully, and with leonine grace.

For this is a power tango and it's far from predetermined who in the circle will hold the rose in their teeth.

CHALLENGE TWO
The Silver Surge: The Aging of America

A TSUNAMI IS HEADING TOWARD US.

When a tsunami builds as a result of underwater seismic action its initial signs are slight, imperceptible. Many times a huge and devastating tsunami raises the water only a matter of inches in the open sea. At depth, a murderous and devastating wave raises boats by just the length of your hand. In monstrous circumstances the elevation is less than a foot.

Because the wave length is so long, often as much as 120 miles, it takes 20 or 30 minutes for a wave to pass, even when traveling at its typical speed of 500 miles per hour. Ships at sea rarely notice when a huge tsunami passes beneath them.

It is only when the wave meets shallower waters that shoaling occurs, and the speed slows to, say, 50 miles per hour and forms something that looks like a cresting wave. Because of its enormous length it usually takes several minutes to reach its full height. In all but the very largest tsunamis, the wave does not break but instead resembles a tidal roller.

In many cases the whole wave is disguised by what scientists call a drawback. A tectonic plate sinks far out at sea, and water rushes to fill in the space. The onshore experience is a major retreat of the waterline well past the usual tidal lines, often exposing parts of the sea invisible under normal circumstances. The drawback has a magnetic appeal. As with a magic trick, people focus on exactly the wrong things.

It is a cruel irony that people have an alarming tendency to follow the drawback farther and farther out to sea. Depending on the wavelength and the shape of the ground, these retreats can last so long that people can be drawn far out into what will soon be a powerful surge. The mesmerizing power of the drawback entices you to go precisely where you should not go. Like rolling thunder, the wave bears down on you, coming toward you like a wall with enormous momentum. Even slowed by 90 percent, the tsunami still has the speed and the crushing power of a thousand freight trains bolted together and hurtling down on you.

When a tsunami hits the shore, having built up the momentum for often hundreds of miles, it leaves a wake of devastation and death.

A wave is coming.

WHEREVER YOU ARE IN AMERICA, wherever you stand, whatever you do, this wave is going to dramatically affect your life. Unlike a tsunami, which rolls on through with perhaps an aftershock or two, what is about to happen to our nation is a shift so significant that the change will be permanent. And many people in power are chasing the drawback, looking at the wrong thing, and taking us exactly where we should not be going.

People have theorized about it. Economists, God help us, have already recommended solutions.

Unlike with a tsunami, I can tell you the exact moment the wave hit, because the deluge has started. And for at least 100 years, it is never going to stop.

When did the roller make land? A second after midnight, December 31, 2010.

For generations it will be a ceaseless sea change. Whether you are right or left, I can assure you the changes will be more profound and more intense than the people who have been watching the wave will ever tell you. Trust me.

What is the wave that is rolling over us?

Right now it is in the inches-high phase, but the first signs of shoaling are occurring. What's happening is that the first group of postwar babies, the baby boomers, born in 1946, are turning 65. The trailblazer was a woman named Kathy Casey-Kirschling, who was born in Philadelphia one second into January 1, 1946, and who turned 65 one second into January 1, 2011, at home in Maryland.

So what, you say? Imagine you are on a ship and the gunnels just lifted a hand length or two. That's what just happened—so *that's* what!

Let me translate with specifics. The number of Americans 55 and older will nearly double in the next 19 years from 60 million today (21 percent of the population) to 108 million (31 percent of the population). By 2050, 40 percent of the American population will be over 50 and nearly a third will be over 65. And 40 percent of those 65'ers are projected to live to 90 years of age. In 1960 about 14 percent of 60-year-olds could survive to age 90. By 2010 the number was up to 25 percent. We are surviving better.

What this means is, by 2030 you will see a lot more walkers than strollers. And by 2050 everything about our society will have to change.

There were about 80 million American babies born in the boom period of population growth from 1946 to 1964.

It was the most prolific time of population growth in our nation's recorded history. So profound was its impact that 20 years later a second boomlet, or echo, occurred because the children of baby boomers started having their own children.

This human wave, now underway, will create a permanent change in the age structure of our nation. The implications of what happens as this large generation hits retirement age are vast.

Both the benefits and the costs of a population with a permanently inverted age pyramid will be greater than official forecasts indicate. But in essence, there will be far more old people in the United States. Everything in our society, from education to family structure to health care to workforce management to volunteerism, was built to cope with a society with a fundamentally different age distribution than we will experience in very short order. All will have to be reconsidered. And, needless to say, there is no plan.

Both Europe and Japan have aged before us. Each has had the same basic trends, with two notable exceptions: The American total fertility rate

(TFR) has been hovering at about 2.1, which is about equal to our death rate, so we are replacing ourselves. Official immigration into the U.S., apart from last year, has been running around a million people a year. These two factors mean the U.S. is experiencing net population growth, unlike Russia, for example, which is projected to fall in size from 143 million in 2011 to 111 million in 2050—fewer and older rather than more and older.

In Japan, the fertility rate has been dropping steadily for 40 years and is below 1.3 per woman. Italy, a predominantly Catholic country, is at 1.2 babies per woman. As for immigration, Europe is diminished and Japan is xenophobic.

So these two theaters have already inverted their age pyramids.

But these were more orderly processions; we have a wave hitting us.

The trouble is that we are going to age faster and more intensely than either Europe or Japan. The principal reason is demographic. We effectively diluted the elderly and kept our aging average down because we had this generation of baby boomers and their 20-year echoes to keep the pyramid small side up.

As the boomers gray, all of that changes. The pyramid isn't shifting so slowly that demographers barely notice it, it's a full-speed spin. So hang on. The boomers will now accelerate us into the inversion, and our numbers will change more starkly and will carry on for longer. Shoaling has occurred.

Again, so what? A simpleton's view is that this shift is just about getting and protecting our Social Security and Medicare checks.

It goes way, way, way beyond that.

We are going to have to reengineer many of our most core assumptions and institutions. Leaning across the fence to see how Europe and Japan coped won't help because we have to get there faster and it's not as though they have found the silver bullet—or better, the gray bullet.

Biomedical advances have assisted in creating a surging effect in two ways: First, the disease-specific model has had far less success with cures but fared better in lowering fatality rates and longevity of living with disease.

As someone who has been deeply involved with a disease-related charity, I can say with authority that there is equal emphasis on care as on cure, and the payoff is living longer and more comfortably with an affliction. Whether for cancer or diabetes or HIV/ AIDS, we have developed cocktails of pharmaceuticals and sustaining therapies which prolong life. A second, but growing, area of biomedicine which will also amplify the age wave is a series of interventions that actually slow the advancement of the aging process. Far from disease therapies, these interventions, which range from hormone therapy to preventative evaluation, have a singular impact: they tend to prolong life. And judging by the sales and market research, if you build an anti-aging regimen, they will come.

Life expectancy in 1900 was about 46 years. Today it is about 76 years. According to even the more conservative assessments of life expectancy of the Social Security Administration, the number of citizens over 85 will double by 2030.

The MacArthur Research Foundation has a Network on Aging in Society chaired by a former Chris Reeve Foundation board member, Dr. John Rowe. Their findings suggest that current government projections may underestimate life expectancy by three to eight years.

Every year difference in life expectancy brings a meaningful difference in age-related expenditures. Using the Network's figures in comparison to those of the Census Bureau and the Social Security folks shows that there will be 164-240 million extra person years lived between now and 2050. Tying those years to government programs for the elderly, cumulative outlays for Medicare and Social Security would currently be underestimated by $3-$4.7 trillion.

Whatever way you look at it, for the first time in our history, seniors will outnumber children and young people.

Dr. Rowe told me: "By the middle of the next decade, the United States will become an aging society with those over age 60 outnumbering those under age 15." And the whole notion of family will change.

With an aging population, five- and maybe six-generation families will exist. If we're talking about a fifty-year-old couple, that will mean them, their kids, their grandkids, and some grandparents in their seventies and maybe great-grandma going strong at 97. Another family may manage an extra generation at the young end. Where will they live? How will they live? Noted psychologist Laura Carstensen of Stanford says, "Families used to be vertical and biological, now they will be horizontal and voluntary."

It won't merely be a matter of plural generations choosing to co-habitate. Many will have no choice. The more telling current scenario is grown adults going back to live with their aging parents because they can't afford housing.

There will be social upheaval, much of it for the better. Baby boomers have always been the center of attention, and initially that should continue as the 55-plus age group controls more than 75 percent of the nation's wealth. But here's the rub: they won't have nearly the disposable income they thought. Living longer will require working longer, and for many parents and grandparents, supporting longer. That nest egg will simply have to last longer and feed more.

What is going to happen to transfers? As people live longer, their consumption based on their dwindling resources means that they will have less to leave to their children. Individuals who were relying on inheritances for their own retirements will be forced to rework the numbers as one or both parents live thirty or forty years beyond 65.

Health-care spending will rise dramatically. Presently, health-care expenditures for those 65 or older account for 60 percent of all health-care payments, 35 percent of hospital discharges, and 45 percent of hospital days. Medicare expenditures for hospital costs alone are expected to rise from 1.5 percent to 2.75 percent of GDP by 2030. As people live far beyond their wage-earning years, often their ability to pay for care themselves is seriously degraded.

To really get the scope of the problem, you have to peer under the hood. First, if we are living longer, are we healthier? Not necessarily.

Recent studies by the RAND Institute and the University of Michigan have examined the rates of disability. What's clear when you evaluate different generations, boomers and busters and boomer echoes, etc., is that each group carries different frailty, mortality, and disability risks and characteristics.

True economics suggests looking at frailty and disability rates as well;

we may live longer but we may be frailer. Though we are living longer as boomers, the current 55- to 64-year-old age group has significantly higher frailty and disability than those in retirement aged 63-74 today.

Dr. Jay Olshansky, professor of public health at University of Illinois, worries that the growing significance of childhood obesity adds a greater risk of coronary heart disease and diabetes for the following generation. What's clear is that the steady march of the morbidity tables, which is the chief star by which most Age Wave ships guide their boats, is an insufficient measure.

Education and racial background play a major role in thinking the issue through. Among those who did not attend college and are age 60, 75 percent are not physically fit. If you went to college you are 60 percent likely to be physically fit—almost a mirror opposite.

Older racial and ethnic minorities in the United States are on average in poorer health, less educated, and have fewer financial resources than the norm among whites. There are some who view immigration as a natural way to maintain the age pyramid and counteract the falling birthrates, both in the U.S. and abroad.

Here is a fact that the economists seem to have overlooked: Immigrants age too.

In fact, racial and ethnic minorities are the fastest growing segment of the older population in the United States. The number of older minorities is expected to increase five-fold from 6.4 million in 2003 to 34.7 million in 2050. Currently, minorities account for 18 percent of the over-65 population and by 2050 they will represent 40 percent of the over-65 demographic (Asians and Hispanics will experience the sharpest growth).

So what does the Institute of Medicine say about the quality of health this fast-growing and aging demographic enjoy? A few big-picture items will help guide you to the answer.

Most of the 45 million uninsured Americans are ethnic and racial minorities. In 2005, one out of three Hispanics were uninsured, as were one out of five African Americans. This compares to a one out of 10 proportion for whites. According to Medicare reports, roughly one in five of its beneficiaries are members of a racial or ethnic minority group, and that proportion is expected to jump to one in three by 2030.

Older minorities cannot afford preventative treatments such as vaccinations and cancer screenings, with obvious results. The Institute of Medicine concludes that minority groups have higher rates of illness, injury, and premature death and less access to health care, and receive lower quality care than their white counterparts.

We have a very large, growing, and aging population of poor in our country, and they are desperate for support.

A report conducted by the Population Resource Center concludes that since many older minorities lack additional economic resources, such as pensions or income-producing assets, they, on average, rely more on Social Security. Almost half of black and Hispanic beneficiaries rely on Social Security for 90 percent or more of their retirement incomes.

OLDER, LONGER

SO WHAT DO WE DO about the inverted pyramid? First, because we haven't done anything to prepare ourselves for something we've seen coming for decades, we have to start acting now.

We must react as a nation with real solutions when developments this profound occur. There have been attempts to make this a political issue and drown it in the polarized nausea of who gets what today.

Well, today is just an hors d'oeuvre, and supper's on the table. This is not a political meal. It is a reality, which is either the longevity curse or the longevity dividend. Yet for most leaders it is a matter of political voice.

It isn't. It is evidence based, and is neither right nor left. It is reality. And our government has not embraced this reality, even as the wave is getting set to crash on the shore.

Economists have been great at figuring out the trends, but there have been some pretty lame ideas from that group in attempting to resolve the issue.

In Italy, a group of economists concluded that the obvious solution was to elevate the birthrate by convincing women to have more babies for the good of society. Berlusconi may have come up with that one.

In the industrialized world there are four major reasons that birthrates are declining: available birth control, more career opportunities for women, the costs of having children are rising, and the transition from an agrarian society to an industrialized and information society is largely complete in the developed world.

Ciao! Va bene . . . but the birthrate isn't going up anytime soon. There will be no baby boom 2.0.

Other economists are focused on immigration as a solution. Clearly, in countries of modest immigration, the pyramid can be sustained a bit longer. But the river's direction is already determined; the current is too strong.

Watching what has happened in the United States suggests that since immigrants age, too, the likelihood is that countries that use immigration as a salve will wind up just like ours. The U.S. will have an aging population with a large, high-growth proportion of minorities who are undernourished, less well-attended to in matters of health, and less supported by their own financial resources.

This age shift is the ultimate eventualism. It is done, even if it has not happened yet. In fact, someone calculated what would have to happen to U.S. immigration if the combination of aging immigrants, birthrates, and life span were all factored in. For a number of years immigration could increase by 1,000 percent and we would still not maintain the age pyramid.

One thing is certain. When the fastest growing segment of your population is in the over-85 age group, you need to adjust. We haven't. Let's look at Social Security.

SOCIAL INSECURITY

I HAVE SEEN ACTUARIAL STUDIES that say even though our return on investment is in the very low single digits and worse some years, Social Security can meet its obligations.

There have been studies, too, that say the plummeting ratio of workers to retirees, with the resulting fewer workers to support the public outlays, pose no threat to Social Security's ability to pay.

There are people who reassure that the payroll tax per retiree ratio that is being paid by today's workers is going down, but that Medicare will be able to meet its hospital insurance obligations.

To all of those most learned economists, I say baloney. You should too.

Compounding and simple math tells the story. Actuarial acrobatics cannot defy the very basic law of gravity. We have to develop a core set of policies, incentives, and institutional approaches to the 100-year shift in age dynamics.

We are in denial. And every day that passes, you are moving squarely into the affected zone. We need to find actuarial balance for Social Security and Medicare.

First, there are only three ways to make Social Security capable of meeting its obligations and be in "actuarial balance": Increase the return on investments, increase the payroll taxes paid into the fund, and reduce the outlays.

Contrary to what Meatloaf sings—"Two out of three ain't bad"—we need all three.

The events of the last two years will have a pulverizing effect on the risk tolerance of the Social Security Administration. No four-legged swaps or derivatives. And the impact on IRAs and Roth Accounts across the land means individual accounts for Social Security are sleeping with the fishes.

Government alone can't goose returns. I recommend a ten-year experiment: outsourcing five percent to investors who can achieve strong returns. As people gain more comfort, the allocation could be increased. With Social Security, modesty is the best policy.

Individual risk is an ogre. I believe equity markets long term will outperform treasuries. But having a huge group of financially unsophisticated investors managing their thirty-plus-year retirement risk is a disaster. With one panic, even the most independent-minded will demand bailout. Crafting a people's TARP bailout is no solution because the whole reason to design an individual Social Security program is to create a shared responsibility—not another federal program. But is there wisdom in offering a 15-20 percent privatization program for those who want to manage a piece of their liability with something that looks and feels like an IRA?

Radical Centrists know that single overarching federal solutions never solve massive problems. Tying 20 percent of our future obligation to individual responsibility makes Americans partners in the solution. Social Security cannot manage the entire burden alone, nor can our current workers.

There are two remaining solutions. Both will be necessary and blisteringly unpopular. One, payroll taxes will have to increase. Period. More people, needing more money, for more years, funded by fewer people working, for fewer years is an unsolvable equation without an intervention.

Sadly, even a huge increase in payroll taxes won't be sufficient. We have made some pretty ambitious promises, and we won't keep them all.

Which means, two: A reduction in outlays is inevitable. (See the healthcare chapter for an explanation as to why Medicare's predicament is even more dire.) I said this in a public forum recently and the high earning attendees went crazy. My reply: "I guess that's why these are called 'entitlements.' I hate to break it to you, but somebody has to. The money's not there; it's time to get over it." (Sometimes, I face a situation where it's clear why I wasn't cut out to seek elected office.) There is something kind of disgusting about rich people in denial.

Upper income folks will be the first to see major reductions of coverage. Social Security payments via payroll tax are exactly that: a sunk cost, a tax you paid from which you are apt to get modest recovery.

In that respect the well-to-do are no different than autoworkers that got dream retirement packages at age 48 and are just now learning dreams don't come true. So the rich may get angry, but they will not get as much Social Security as they planned.

RETIREMENT REDUX

IF WE CANNOT PROLONG THE working life of Americans, my opinion is that everyone will be paid less in Social Security. In 2010, France raised its retirement age to 62 from 60, and the age from which full benefits could be enjoyed from 65 to 67. In this country, we must get financial incentives aligned to extend both work life and benefits as France did. There's no easy way for Americans to face this music. How many politicians have the courage to push such a program? Yet this problem gets worse by the day.

To put a number on it: Retirement age should go to 67, and full benefits the same.

I can hear it now. I am the merchant of death. So shoot the messenger if you want, but it won't make the problem go away. This trend is inevitable.

The Urban Planning Institute has done some great work around "Retooling the Workforce" to cope with the wave of cotton tops approaching.

Time is a-wasting and these decisions are not getting any easier. Every six seconds someone else turns 50. The poll power of the seniors is growing, and necessary change of the type I am describing will get harder when the majority of Americans are late 40s and older, and that day is coming soon. An equally strong counterpoint is emerging from the young.

Will a youth population with large numbers of Hispanics, African Americans, and Asians be willing to support an ever-growing number of mostly white seniors?

What is very clear is that this is not a seniors' issue but a whole society issue. David Wise of Harvard University has done interesting work to show that higher senior employment rolls means higher job statistics for youth as well. In an age-inverted pyramid, it seems a rising tide truly does lift all boats. But the place to start is improving the lot of seniors, often by extending their ability to work.

A result of the 2008 crash is that people are lingering longer in the workforce, reversing a recent trend of earlier access to Social Security. That reversal must be permanent; we need older workers, even if we have to find them something to do.

There are ways to accomplish this besides just extending the retirement age. We need a council on age redeployment. Have seniors work longer by giving them training jobs to share their skills with younger workers. Look to seniors to provide day-care, child-care, and elder-care services. Work with corporations to create flex-time and half-time jobs which keep seniors gainfully engaged and employed, even if it is for reduced hours.

What I am describing is a reengineering of many of our core institutions and incentives. For example, low-paid seniors could be incentivized to leave the workforce because Social Security will constitute a larger proportion of their retirement income. Another extremely unpopular solution is extending the time it takes for an employee to get retirement benefits. In a unionized workforce this will be a battle worth winning.

Asset managers like Fidelity and Merrill Lynch will have to reconsider what retirement looks like. Customers will require Wall Street to design a new way forward. Seniors I know in their 60s and 70s have already begun to redefine retirement.

We also need to rethink elder care. The number of vibrant, healthy 65+ year-olds engaged in the life of the nation will certainly increase. However, some beneficiaries of life extension will be frail, and it will be expensive to provide them care.

New volunteerism models will refashion the existing safety net for seniors. One new concept is paid home care—if caregivers were paid even a little it would keep many people out of the hospitals. Health-care providers and government alone simply cannot do the job. We'll need to leverage our senior population.

Immigration laws will have to be reconsidered since we will need a workforce to support the aging population. Will we be able to find people to do the jobs we need done?

We will need to reimagine our cities. The World Health Organization is working on a large-scale project to review the Healthy Aging Cities of the World. New York City is one under consideration.

The MacArthur Foundation has engaged former HUD Secretary Henry Cisneros to craft a network study on Housing and Community Design—but it is more than urban planning that is required. We need a serious dose of true economics. Many political leaders can't tell the difference between a bad policy and a savings today which will cost triple tomorrow.

The State of Massachusetts recently cut home-care services for disabled seniors, a basic program of such services costing $8.76 a day. If a senior cannot get aid and has to enter a nursing home as a Medicaid recipient, the cost to the state is $158 per day—a clear-cut case of true economics gone bad.

Another sign of wrong way policy is the trend in the number of certified geriatricians—down 25 percent since 2000. An Institute of Medicine report blamed the trend on relatively low pay versus other specialties like radiologists, surgeons, and dermatologists.

For sure, we will have a lot more folks worried about aging than about zits in the next dozen years, so we need to rethink our entire approach to the graying of America. Remember, don't be seduced into following the drawback when polar platitudes are taking us out to sea.

Unions are dithering over defined benefit versus defined contribution while ignoring a more basic problem: It's not that we cannot afford what we want; we cannot afford what we have.

Can we extend the usefulness of seniors? In my opinion, they are a longevity dividend and not a curse.

Seniors are getting more educated. Today, less than a third of adults aged 70 to 74 have at least some college education. By 2015 that number should increase to over 50 percent. And when the over-50 crowd is 40 percent–plus of the population in 2030, over 60 percent should have some college in them. That is a brain trust trifecta with education, experience, and poll power. We are fools not to harness that energy. If extracting that intellectual power must be done differently, then we should get on it now. Don't toss redundant 45 year-olds on the scrap heap. As a nation we need a mid-course correction to capture the true value of a 45-year-old boasting another 25 years' contribution.

Retraining may mean reimagining a school into more of a community center for learning so that buildings are designed to enrich the minds of seniors as well as schoolchildren. Is there a "retraining night" usage of buildings that are typically dormant in the evenings?

Can we extend retirement, boost volunteerism, and solve numerous social ills at once? One creative plan I read involves building schools next to assisted living facilities. In Connecticut, near my hometown, the Westport Senior Center moved into an unused wing of the Staples High School a decade ago. Proximity has given seniors there access to an indoor track, indoor pool, and all manner of gym and exercise facilities.

Let's return society's elders to roles they once played in villages all over the world—volunteering, instructing, and guiding our youth. We need to rethink education from an intergenerational perspective. These kinds of co-locations are predictive of harnessing the longevity bonus.

Can corporations capture the longevity bonus in a way that helps society? The CEOs of America are not as dumb as you might think. The more financial resources that seniors possess for the longer period of time, the more likely they can care for themselves and prevent becoming wards of the state.

Marketers have always focused on the baby boomers for the simple reason that there are so many of them. I predict more senior products: watch doorknobs fade and handles replace them. I see newer lifestyles, real estate developments, and city planning.

Older Americans have more financial resources than in prior generations. Seniors spend over $30 billion on travel annually, and they are a boon to pharmaceutical and health-care businesses.

Older folks are rediscovering religion. I heard of a plan to take some big-box retailer's abandoned store's "Ghost Boxes," and convert them to megachurches for the seniors who are attending services in droves.

Plans are hatching in American boardrooms to extend retirement by allowing seniors to work and volunteer on a reduced pay scale. Corporations must take the lead in employing seniors. Government should create incentives for right-to-longer-work opportunities.

Imagine adopting a renewed attitude toward youth—a Boomer notion, made popular by Bob Dylan, that we are "Forever Young." The temptation to refer to ourselves by our activities rather than our age belies a nation of "amortals." (Amortal is a word Catherine Mayer coined in *Time* magazine in 2009. It refers to people who refuse to let age define them or what activities they pursue.)

Our youth culture will blossom into one of amortality, where age is viewed as a gathering of wisdom rather than of dust.

Boomers already believe in amortality. Now we have to reflect it in our laws and our core institutions—because the truest thing about the phrase "Forever Young" is the "Forever" part. (As for Dylan, he turned 70 May 24, 2011, and he's touring like a rolling stone.)

There is a cruel reality here affecting no less than the American Dream. As a nation we have been weaned on the notion that progress assures each generation a higher quality of life and greater wealth than the one that preceded. Perhaps it's because we are a nation of immigrants, but Horatio Alger courses through our national DNA.

Here's the rub, having nothing to do with overspending or national debt. Hold all that to the side for a moment and let's look at the boomlet of the boomers' kids. Whatever they earn, even if it is more than their parents, they are likely to have a fundamental problem. This tsunami has already hit and the silver surge is barely a part of the dialogue. And when it is discussed it is only in the most tactical and superficial way.

We simply are not facing the problem.

Let's suppose it takes five more years for our leaders to face the music. We haven't just kicked the can down the road; we have kicked that can into our children's teeth.

Boomers' kids will bear a lot of the burden of caring for their long-lived parents. By delaying, we virtually assure that our children will be less well-off than we were.

If that generation is the first to be worse off than its predecessors, I forecast a political backlash that could be very divisive.

Faced squarely the longevity bonus can harness a huge demographic wave of wise seniors. It is time to chart a new course, because this change is as certain as the tides.

The tsunami is upon us; we are all aging, and the silver surf is up.

CHALLENGE THREE
Labor Pains: The Devolution of the Labor Movement

I︎T WAS A BALMY SATURDAY *afternoon in late March, well past the winter chill that had gripped New York City six weeks before.*

Like many people enjoying the fading Saturday afternoon, Doctor Ralph Fralick was walking across Washington Square Park in Greenwich Village, heading toward his home on Waverly Place. A block away, Charles T. Kremer and Elias Kanter were finishing up a class at NYU Law School. Between these three thus-far unrelated New Yorkers was a ten-story structure in which 500 workers on the top three floors were getting into their street clothes.

It was 4:40 P.M.; nearly five hours after all other workers toiling in the building had been dismissed for the day. But Max Blanck and Isaac Harris had a shipment deadline to meet and they, along with Mr. Blanck's children and governess, were wrapping up the day's business in their tenth-floor office.

Within ten minutes the entire building would be empty. And everyone winding down their workday in those top three stories had Sunday on their mind.

In a flash, the quiet erupted into madness.

A small spark exploded the top three floors of the building into flame. Within fifteen minutes, four alarms had been sounded. Before the first trucks arrived, five young girls had already leaped from the windows to their death. Doctor Fralick had broken into a sprint by then.

A throng from Washington Square Park and Broadway rushed to the corner of Greene Street and Washington Place. What they saw transfixed them.

The first girl was a tiny nervous creature. She carefully climbed out the window onto the ledge and stared nine stories to the street below. After a moment or two she jumped, crashing through a plate glass overhang that extended over the sidewalk below.

Messers Harris and Blanck, Blanck's children, and their governess escaped from the roof to an adjoining building.

Inside the building was pandemonium. The 500 workers inside were mostly young women ages 16 to 23. Most could barely speak English, and almost all were the main support of their families. One of the two elevators was out of service. Firefighters would later find more than 30 bodies clogged in the open elevator shaft, piled layer upon layer like sedimentary rock.

There was one fire escape in the entire building, an internal one. A few girls were able to squeak through the wall of fire, but within minutes the stairway was consumed in flames and collapsed. Each step was choked with bodies piled high upon the next, as if they had compressed themselves as they expired.

On the street below, girls' bodies blocked firemen from setting up their equipment. Even as the trucks approached, young girls spinning end over end came crashing down around them. Witnesses recount how five stood bravely at a window and held their place as they watched a fire ladder inch steadily toward them. When at last it stopped at full extension two stories below them, they stepped out on the balcony and leaped together, clinging to each other, fire streaming back from their hair and their dresses.

The jump nets firemen set up did nothing to stop ten stories of momentum as the young ladies rained down. One pretty young girl deliberately removed her hat and gingerly placed it on the outside ledge away from the flames before plunging to her death.

Meanwhile, on the roof, the NYU law students led a hundred more volunteers in lifting 150 workers to safety. The law building was a full story taller, but the enterprising students had commandeered two small ladders. Another fifty escaped by jumping a half a story to the roof of the adjoining building.

In thirty minutes, it was all over. By the time the fire was extinguished, so were the lives of 148 employees at the Triangle Shirtwaist Factory.

The building itself was fireproof; it showed hardly any signs of the disaster *that had overtaken it. Nothing in the Asch Building was the worse from the fire except furnishings, equipment, and inventory—and the lives of 148 girls and men who worked in the upper three stories.*

What had burned the afternoon of March 25, 1911 was what the employers had put there. Shirtwaists—popular womens' garments of the time—by the thousands hung on lines above the heads of the workers; sewing machines placed so close together that a slender girl could hardly pass between them and the floor littered and piled deep with wisps of shirtwaist trimmings, scattered thread, and acres of cuttings. Poor ventilation ensured a gauzy air of dust and debris, making it difficult to breath.

It was a perfect tinderbox, housed in a fireproof enclosure.

The Asch had experienced four recent fires on lower floors and had been reported to the Building Department by the Fire Department as unsafe due to "insufficiency of exits."

New York Fire Chief Croker, a man witness to many such scenes, was described as quivering when he emerged from examining the premises. Over whelmed firemen left a heap of corpses on the sidewalk for over an hour.

Only seven of the girls lived long enough to make it to Saint Vincent's Hospital. All lost their battle within hours.

The fire sparked a spontaneous walkout of workers at the building and a storm of protest around the world—extraordinary for the day.

At a historic meeting at the Cooper Union, thousands of garment workers from all over the city gathered to hear Samuel Gompers, President of the powerful American Federation of Labor. "I have never declared a strike in all my life," he said." I have done my share to prevent strikes, but there comes a time when not to strike is but to rivet the chains of slavery upon our wrists."

OTHER MOMENTS IN HISTORY MIGHT claim to be the birth of the labor movement, but those haunting 30 minutes at the Triangle Shirtwaist Factory on a quiet Saturday served as the rallying point for a new development in the emerging industrial revolution.

Labor had gained two things: its own voice, and popular support independent of the workers themselves.

Eighty years later, the march of labor had moved steadily onward. But a specter still lurked in the shadows.

It was a steaming hot day deep in L.A. County, smack at the end of the Santa Fe Trail, in a city of 120,000 souls named El Monte. When you enter the 228th largest town in the country you are greeted by a signature sign, "Welcome to Friendly El Monte."

It's generally a quiet town, though the American Legion Stadium in El Monte was the scene of some raucous rock 'n' roll concerts by Johnny Otis, Dick Dale and the Del Tones, and Johnny Guitar Watson back in the day.

Back then, rock 'n' roll was the Devil's music. As far as folks in El Monte figured, that was the last time he had visited.

They were proven wrong one August 1995 afternoon when police arrested eight operators of a clandestine garment sweatshop.

Police freed 72 illegal Thai immigrants who had been held in captivity, claiming they were paid $1.60 an hour for up to 17 hours' work a day, forced to pay for their food and the cost of their transport to the country, and confined to dingy rooms in the razor wire-enclosed compound, some for four years or more. They were immigrant slaves for greedy producers and their dreams had been preyed upon for profit.

Plus ça change . . . Labor is a movie that plays over and over—at its center, a pendulum swinging side to side.

The 80-plus years separating these stories explain why the story of labor is such a hard one to tell. Greed left unchecked knows no limits and holds no conscience. Anyone claiming greed is good has never been to a sweatshop.

Greed rapes. And it never tires.

Labor Rising!

LABOR STRIFE IS NEARLY AS old as the republic, as is the scourge of the broken promise whenever the economy falters. Radical Centrists should recognize that the consequences of breaking down de facto or de jure pacts among government, business, and the workforce are always serious. Pressure from these fault lines is building in unemployment, social security, wages, and workers' rights.

Left unattended, these pressures cause earthquakes and social upheaval.

In 1825, there was a strike for the ten-hour workday in Boston. Ten years later the children employed in the silk mills of Paterson, New Jersey, went on strike for the 11-hour workday, six-day workweek. In 1827, a mechanics union of trade organizations was formed in Philadelphia—the country's first labor organization.

Before the 1840s, a worker's income was based on price, often of a commodity they produced or a craft item they built. The introduction of machines created a separation of labor into component parts, and that separation created wages. The lure of wages without ties to prices but rather to output, together with the roar of industrialization, led young and old alike away from their farms and into the major cities. By the 1860s nearly five million workers were wage earners.

For unskilled laborers, earning wages was a pact with the Devil, and he rarely got the short end.

In 1882 the Knights of Labor and their charismatic leader Terence Powderly held a parade in New York City to coincide with their national conference. The parade was repeated on the first Monday in September in 1884 and designated Labor Day. The Knights bore the same passion as the early labor unions, but with more organization, greater inclusion, and a naïveté which would ultimately sink them.

In 1885, the Knights led the rail workers of Jay Gould's Southern Railway to victory. But the canny Gould sensed an entirely different division of labor when he famously observed: "I can hire one half of the working class to kill the other half."

Labor relations were still determined by the cracked skull.

Less than a year later, police action at a demonstration outside the McCormick Reaper Plant in Chicago left four unionists dead and scores more wounded. Outraged, a group of anarchists, led by August Spies and Albert

Parsons, tried to organize an even larger demonstration in Haymarket Square. A disappointing crowd of ranging estimates gathered. Chicago has always understood policing, and the constables were prepared.

The evening proceeded more or less without incident until an individual, whose identity has never been confirmed, threw a bomb that killed seven policemen and injured 67 others.

All hell broke loose.

Powderly's measured message of inclusion was garbled in the fury that was unleashed. Hysteria is contagious, and Chicago in 1886 was not immune. The city rounded up eight anarchists, tried them with scant evidence, and sentenced them to death. Four, including Parsons and Spies, were executed. They died for their words, which up until that time could not constitute a capital offense.

Labor had lost its innocence and the Knights were finished.

In their place, the American Federation of Labor (AFL), led by Samuel Gompers, created the business union movement with a focus on organizing millions of skilled craftsmen. When the federal government granted statutory rights for collective bargaining to Gompers' federation, the modern labor union was born.

By 1904 there were nearly two million members of the AFL.

As World War I approached, unions became the grudging partner of government. Woodrow Wilson strongly encouraged union growth as a way to energize the working class behind the war effort, and union worker ranks rose to over 4.25 million. AFL officers were appointed to most of the war boards organized by the government.

But Labor did not speak with a single voice. As Gompers organized skilled workers, John L. Lewis, the autocratic President of the United Mine Workers (UMW) from 1920 to 1960, fought tirelessly to organize the mass production industries and created the industrial union movement, unionizing unskilled workers.

After the war, labor's alliance with government was broken. Labor's opponents used a fear of Communism and workers' revolts to drive a wedge between the once comfortable bedfellows. Red Scare tactics were used to break up union gatherings, and a clever legal interpretation of the Clayton Anti-Trust Act of 1914 meant that injunctions rained down on union organizers.

BROKEN PROMISE

UNDER THE BANNER "WELFARE CAPITALISM" (taking care of your workers), corporate experts in industrial relations began the prudent course of competing with the unions for workers' allegiance.

Unions experienced stagnation and decline. Major industries, particularly the fast-growing ones, improved worker productivity and support.

Business had learned the lessons of industrial relations in the hardest of ways. Unionism persisted in many declining and slow-growth industries. But despite best efforts to organize, there was diminishing appetite for union dues as a way to settle industrial grievance.

Labor unions might have ended there—a necessary and temporary bridge across the Industrial Revolution's adolescence. But even as industrial welfare gurus spread their "don't beat 'em, join 'em" philosophy, storm clouds were brewing—the kind that try a nation's very soul.

The Great Depression was a terrible swift sword.

Not a person among the unionists hoping for an end to their stagnation could have speculated that in three years, 25 percent of the civilian labor force would be without a job. Unemployment, which had been hovering below two million in 1929, exploded to 13 million within 36 months.

Welfare capitalism meant standing behind your workers, compensating them, and keeping them employed in times of stress. Smoothing economic imbalances obviated the need for a unionist's intervention. Corporations were preaching a new canon to workers that unions were once necessary bridges that had outlived their usefulness.

That dogma had a fatal flaw.

Throughout the corporate sphere, workers learned the same hard lesson: when the pie shrinks to nothing, labor relations become a zero sum game. Anything workers win, employers, shareholders, or creditors lose.

Without a working contract, there was no legal recourse, only the highly variable outcome as to whether the employers cared. Many cared but simply could not afford to keep their promises.

Bankruptcy code at the time contained no broken-promises clause.

Reaction to the huge broken promise, both in the United States and abroad, in the wake of economic collapse is a matter for every Radical Centrist to burn into their brain.

We must all recall what happened next.

American and European voters abandoned centrist political parties and vigorously embraced extremists of both the right and the left. Throughout the world there was a rejection of anything that businesses had to say about solving the problem. Broken promises shattered corporate credibility. In Germany, Nazism—National Socialism—was a devastating critique of capitalism; in Russia, Marxism-Leninism rejected the existing model just as forcefully.

In country after country there was an impulse to take public control over the economy. Why? Free market, invisible hand capitalism and the orthodox finance practiced on Wall Street, and in bourses throughout the capitalist world, had led to disaster. Unemployment rose to over 15 percent in Great Britain, Germany, Canada, and Austria. Politically, people headed for the poles.

The Nazis became the largest party in the German federal election. Popular Front governments uniting Communists and Socialists with bourgeois liberals assumed power in countries like Sweden, France, and Spain. The latter government was overthrown by a Fascist rebellion culminating in the decades-long dictatorship of Francisco Franco.

Standing virtually alone was the former Soviet Union, which relied on the total control it exerted domestically to spare itself the scourge of economic collapse. Its day would come later.

The object lesson is too glaring to ignore. Today we sit in the midst of an economic conflagration of global proportions, and we are married to the same reaction to spin far right and left, to reject centrism, and to over-regulate where we under-regulated before, as if erecting a barricade to keep out a monster that has already dined and moved on.

What happens to unions after an economic collapse? In this country in 2010, nearly a million union members left their unions, either because they lost their jobs, their companies failed, or they withheld their dues for necessities closer to home.

Union Dues, Union Don'ts

INITIALLY, THE SAME HELD TRUE in the Great Depression, until it didn't. Five years after the depths of unemployment in 1933, union rolls surged. As always, the tension between the craft unions of the AFL and the enthusiasms of the unskilled mass producers' unions were never very far from the surface.

In the mid-1930s, John L. Lewis bolted from the AFL and created the Congress of Industrial Organizations (CIO). Using the resources of the UMW, Lewis established the United Steel Workers of America—a natural move because steel companies owned many captive mines. Lewis's genius was in reading the industrial rationale, the connectivity between one industry and another.

The CIO also enjoyed significant state support. New Dealers passed The Wagner Act in 1935, protecting unions and promoting collective bargaining through the National Labor Relations Board, which by 1945 had supervised over 24,000 union elections involving some 6,000,000 workers.

Lewis pulled his beloved UMW out of the CIO early in World War II. Then in 1943, during the most challenging part of the war, when most of labor was observing a policy against industrial action, Lewis led half a million mine workers on a 12-day strike for higher wages. Lewis was the most hated man in America and for many, a symbol of all that was wrong with the labor movement; but his workers got their pay.

Public outcry was palpable. Lewis had provided potent seeds to congressional conservatives. At the war's close they were waiting. Unions had gained ground by avoiding strike actions. During the war, union membership soared as workers, including a significant number of women, were automatically enrolled.

Post-war labor aggression woke Congress from its slumber. Walter Reuther took control of the United Auto Workers and led them in a major strike in 1946. A steel strike followed. A crippling rail strike that year was prevented when the government stepped in. In 1945, five million American workers went on strike, and the following year the number approached six million. Reaction was guaranteed.

Unions had quite simply pushed too far. Congress passed the Taft Hartley Act in 1947 as an undisguised attempt to reign in mounting union influence. Though Truman called it "a slave labor bill" when he vetoed it, Congress overrode his objections.

Earlier in 1935 FDR had signed the National Labor Relations Act to delineate unfair union practices and set new rules of the road for unions, collective bargaining, and strikes. The bill also created the oft maligned "right to work" laws. These targeted the "closed shop," where new employees must join a union when they are hired, and if these employees fail to pay dues, or for any reason they lose their union status, they must be fired by the company.

Unions had become too coercive.

Taft-Hartley had teeth.

Currently, all of the deep southern states, a number of the traditionally Republican states in the Midwest, plains, and far west have right to work laws restricting unions. The provision authorizing the President to intervene in strikes that create a national emergency was a direct reaction to John L. Lewis's coal walkout in the midst of the largest war in our history.

Similarly, Walter Reuther's brilliant negotiations on behalf of the United Auto Workers achieved high wages and benefits for workers at the Big Three. But his winning formula proved to be a bitter pill when the Germans and the Japanese started exporting more cheaply made cars into the U.S. in the 1970s.

In 1955 the AFL and the CIO merged to create a labor colossus representing about 35 percent of the non-agricultural labor force in the nation.

The merger worked in part because the AFL had twice as many members, and was successfully organizing white-collar workers, like clerks. George Meany ran the combined union until 1976, an extraordinary achievement given the complexity and tension between the two organizations. At the same time, in the public sector, less than 10 percent were union members versus the 35 percent in the private.

Unions became powerful political forces away from the bargaining table. Often aligned with the Democratic Party, unions represented a key constituency for much of the social legislation enacted, from FDR's New Deal to Kennedy and Johnson's social programs.

Corruption was still a profound problem for the unions, especially at the peak of their power. Meany was a good leader with a strong record of fighting corruption in New York and was openly critical of the highly corrupt Teamsters Union.

In the early '60s, firebrand Attorney General Robert F. Kennedy brought Teamster corruption to national attention in highly visible Senate hearings. For many in the union family it felt like friendly fire since Kennedy's position as Attorney General derived in no small measure from union support. Kennedy's target was Jimmy Hoffa, who led the Teamsters from 1957 until he was imprisoned in 1964. The McClellan Hearings transformed Hoffa into a national symbol of corruption. And Kennedy was cracking the whip.

GOLDEN RULE

DESPITE THE INTENSE SCRUTINY, THE period of the late '50s to the mid-70s has been described as the Golden Age of the union. Even among the most recalcitrant major employers, unions found a secure place at the bargaining table with corporate leadership. The mantra among the business cognoscenti was: negotiate hard but make the deal.

Union workers benefited both in the 20 percent differential they enjoyed on average over non-union workers, and in the steady two percent per annum improvement in their wages.

Use of the giant strike steadily diminished. It was enough to *have* the club, and less necessary to *use* it. Work stoppages involving a thousand or more employees had been in the thousands after World War II. By 1975, work stoppages involving a thousand or more employees plummeted to 235. By 1995, the number was 31.

The period also saw an ever-expanding list of benefit programs find their way to the bargaining tables. Unions had grown savvy, and shied away from the more "intrusive" subjects of capital allocation, pricing, and business direction that had plagued the discourse in decades before. Unions won medical and dental insurance benefits, as well as increased paid holidays, vacation days, and maternity leave. Generous pensions and supplemental unemployment and workman's compensation benefits were freely traded to satisfy union demands. Future entitlements were easier for management to trade than current cash, and unions drove brilliantly hard bargains. By the 1970s, union employees enjoyed a 60 percent benefit advantage over non-union employees.

THE OVERPLAYED HAND

IN 1970, AFTER A 67-DAY strike, GM allowed employees to retire after 30 years with full pension and health care. The 30 and out plan was first set at a minimum age of 58, but that minimum was later removed.

In 1976 UAW leaders were flabbergasted that 29 percent of the GM workers who retired were younger than 55. The liberalization of the retirement age meant huge cost increases, all pushed years into the future. Worse, when the world moved from defined benefit (a fixed retirement amount) to a defined contribution benefit (a fixed corporate contribution and no fixed benefit), the UAW held the line.

With the sweep of the pendulum, unions began to sow the seeds of a bitter harvest. There was a fatal flaw in the American union approach, particularly when they over-pressed their advantage.

What was the shortcoming? It was so obvious even a CEO could see it.

Excessive union success meant that some unionized companies stood at a competitive disadvantage. Corporations were encouraged to find shelter in the Deep South and in countries with low cost and more accommodating work rule environments.

At the same time, the U.S. economy began its inexorable shift to a post-industrial, knowledge worker job market. The combination of outsourcing American jobs to flags of convenience; worker replacement by robotics and technology; and the true birth of the low-cost, high-quality import all summed to one thing: trouble for the unions.

Mass immigration of both legal and illegal workers from outside the United States and the outsourcing to cheap labor nations effectively restructured the domestic workforce. Powerless to do anything about it, unions were smacked by Adam Smith's invisible hand.

Labor is a market like any other. And when costs become excessive, true economics tells us that alternatives naturally present themselves. This notion that a laborer's input is a competitive indice that can be measured against alternatives was missing from the calculus of labor negotiation.

For 50 years, labor negotiators had the luxury of knowing that employers' only alternative was scab labor. As foreign low-cost manufacturers achieved better quality standards, and computer and factory automation technologies improved, something profound had snuck in the back of the smoke-filled rooms: alternatives.

In the purifying renewal of bankruptcy and rebirth, companies that refused to avail themselves of the alternatives, or were prohibited from doing so by restrictive work rules and contracts, found themselves at a disadvantage. Companies failed and whole industries, like textile manufacturing, fled offshore.

Shifting consumer tastes also depreciated the unions. Customization, and the need to change and upgrade products frequently in response to constantly changing market demands, required employers to manage differently. Those who couldn't respond nimbly lost customers.

Classical top-down hierarchies no longer worked. Management came to rely instead on self-directed, localized, interdisciplinary teams. Employers facing low-wage foreign competition needed to vigilantly engineer costs out of every expense.

Retail developments also had impact. Big-box category-killer stores like Walmart focused on price, quantity, delivery, and flexibility. Aggressive markdowns meant there was little margin for error.

Young workers came to view unions as expensive anachronisms that restricted their independence. A growing tendency toward individual advancement and dissociating one's future from collective actions meant young people were making alternative choices to joining unions.

Union numbers steadily decreased in corporations across the nation. Only in sectors that function as near monopolies, like government, hospitals, police, correction, firefighting, local municipalities, the postal service, and public schools, where there were fewer, if any, "alternatives" did the unions continue to make gains.

PUSHBACK

EIGHT MONTHS INTO RONALD REAGAN'S first term, in the dog days of August 1981, some 13,000 members of PATCO—the Professional Air Traffic Controllers—rejected an FAA offer, pushed back from the table, and walked off the job. Laws against strikes by federal employees had been steadily strengthened, but the union looked at President Reagan, a former president of the Screen Actors Guild, as a union brother and likely supporter. They misjudged him.

Reagan's response was swift, and as it turned out, premeditated. He declared the strike illegal and ordered the strikers to return to work. Most did not.

In secret, Reagan had ordered his Transportation Secretary, Drew Lewis, to ready a large army of trained military replacements. Once they were in place, two days after the walkout, Reagan fired 11,000 strikers.

They were never rehired.

In many respects, this event was the bookend to the Triangle Shirt Factory disaster. Corporations were energized to continue their pattern of resistance and move more union jobs overseas. At the same time, the American worker's pyramid was upending. The ranks of retirees were growing at an alarming rate and pension and health-care costs were looming larger. Unfunded obligations cast doubt on companies' ability to pay. In many cases a few thousand employees were being asked to support multiple thousands of retirees.

The cost of post-retirement medical benefits in the American car business surpassed the cost of steel in the vehicle. UAW contracts, negotiated with such brilliance by union leaders decades before, were proving both uneconomic and unaffordable.

Had unions slaughtered their golden goose?

The unions were still powerful, make no mistake, but they were facing steady erosion. The proportion of unionized private sector employees in the 1950s was over 35 percent. By 2007, that number had dropped to 7.5 percent.

Intriguingly, the shift in the public sector was equally dramatic, but in the other direction.

In the 1950s, less than 10 percent of public sector employees were union members. In 2007 the number was over 36 percent— higher penetration than private sector unions ever enjoyed.

These trends are clearly mirror images of one another.

Age demographics tell an interesting story of their own. In 2007, among all workers aged 55 to 64, union members comprised 16.5 percent. Among workers aged 16 to 24 the number was 4.8 percent.

For all the declines, the absolute numbers continue to be enormous. The AFL-CIO still comprises 56 unions with 11.5 million members. Massive get-out-the-vote drives and cash donations support union-friendly candidates.

The recession of 2008 hit the private sector unions particularly hard. In 2009 alone, unions lost over 830,000 members. The UAW negotiated vigorously in the Chrysler and GM bailouts, becoming significant owners of Chrysler in the process. The UAW protected the health insurance and pensions of retired workers as best they could while agreeing to dramatic declines in the pay scale of workers and reduction of rigid work rules.

On every front, unions are still fighting. In the 2004 and 2006 election cycles, unions spent $560 million to elect their candidates, a 50 percent jump over what they spent in the previous two campaigns.

Unions remain a major force in the workings of our government. For the 2010 passage of health-care legislation, AFL members made more than four million phone calls. The AFL-CIO has created a new group called Working America, an ingenious product extension. The Federation was able to add 3 million more supporters to its 11.5 million members through this affiliate.

Working America unites the union with workers who don't have an AFL-CIO union, creating a new source of grassroots worker power.

In the 2005 gubernatorial election in Virginia, over 50,000 Virginians joined Working America to get out the vote, and they are credited with helping put Tim Kaine in the governor's mansion.

The AFL-CIO has worked closely with the National Caucus of State Legislators, a bipartisan network of union members and union-friendly state lawmakers.

Today, unions are spoiling for a new initiative called the Employee Free Choice Act. Two chief attributes of the proposal are attracting venomous debate. The first is "card check voting" in workplace union elections. The current system involves a lengthy process of certification culminating months later in a secret ballot election. Supporters argue that the current system leaves too much time for employers to cajole and pressure workers.

Clearly a system where a simple majority of workers could check a card in a single vote and unionize has advantages for organizers. Conservatives in Congress argue that card check can be a tactic for undermining an orderly process.

There is a second power provision in the Act. As written, if employers and workers cannot reach a contract within 120 days, a government arbitrator will intervene and set terms. Never in the history of labor would unions enjoy more flexibility to organize and would the government become more directly involved in resolving collective bargaining disputes.

DRY WELLS IN THE CAPITOLS

THE MARRIAGE OF THE UNIONS and the government is having sobering outcomes, and this proposal is but one indication.

Why has this betrothal become so pronounced?

As is often the case, wages tell the story. According to the Bureau of Labor Statistics, total employer compensation costs for private industry workers averaged $27.73 an hour in March 2010. By contrast, total employer compensation costs for state and local government workers averaged $39.81 per hour worked in the same period.

No wonder so many state budgets are in the red. Having a state capitol in your city is like having General Motors in your town. Except state governments never have a bad model or a bad year. They simply spend through problems.

Union power becomes pronounced when essential public employees are allowed to unionize and exert authority over their political managers. The 2010 award of a four-year, 19 percent pay raise to the Boston Fire Department is a perfect example of the asymmetry.

Imbalance defines a collective bargaining agreement in which unions negotiate with politicians over whose incumbency the former exercise control. Public sector negotiation has this profound difference. Private sector rank and file don't elect their bosses.

In the Golden State, the California Public Employees Retirement System (CalPERS) sharply increased benefits for state retirees in 1999. "CalPERS investment returns provide this historic opportunity," declared then board President William Crist—"without causing any additional taxpayer burden."

Since then the state's public employee pension outlays have ballooned by 2,000 percent while state revenues have increased only 24 percent. According to a recent report, some $3 billion has been diverted in 2010 from other state programs to pay pensions.

Just how far short are the nation's public pension funds? The answer depends in part on assumptions made about returns. At eight percent, which old hands like former SEC Commissioner Arthur Levitt consider entirely too high, the gap is estimated to be $500 billion.

The Pew Center calls the shortfall at least $1 trillion, adding that they believe they may be low. If the public pension plans were forced to use the same accounting standards as private pensions, the number would be considerably higher.

The other unmentionable is a pesky set of initials: "OPEB," for "other post-employment benefits." Public service unions have learned well from their private counterparts. The chief element of OPEB is health benefits for retirees, many of whom are in their 40s and 50s. The Congressional Office of Government Accountability called a conservative estimate of the underfunding of OPEB well north of $500 billion.

This is starting to add up.

Recall how GM and some major employers stayed with defined benefit plans when the whole world realized significant risks accompanied guaranteed coverage? You remember how those risks made our products uncompetitive and contributed to the bankruptcy of two of the top three automakers?

That same genius governed state pension plans. The irony of union history is that mean-spirited corporations ultimately disintermediated the union-worker relationship, and it was government that provided the most fertile field for the growth of unions.

In 2009, in a dramatic passage, the two arcs crossed: for the first time in our history there are more public employee unionists than there are in the ranks of private sector unions.

So, it should come as no surprise that New Jersey boosted its pension benefits by nine percent even as it was reducing required pension contributions from state employees.

The numbers should terrify you:

In 2000 only two percent of the cops and firefighters in New York State had six-figure pensions.

According to the Empire Center for New York State Policy, in 2010, 13 percent of the newly retired police and firefighters had pensions exceeding $100,000 a year.

Here's how it works:

Police and firefighters can meaningfully increase their pensions by collecting overtime; union contracts allow them to do that.

What is striking is that one of the top New York State pensioners is the former president of the Port Authority Benevolent Association. He was able to rack up tens of thousands of dollars of overtime even though his chief responsibility during his last 18 years was working for his union.

Here's another Empire State benefit: unlike workers in the private sector, retirees who worked for the state of New York are *exempt* from paying New York and municipal taxes.

In 2010, the *New York Times* listed a league table of public pensioners. The top six all worked in the school systems, and number one received $316,245 per annum. The number-four pensioner on this list is a former chief of the New York State Teachers' Retirement System who took home $261,132 a year, for life. At the same time he was also President of SUNY Albany, a $280,000 a year job with its own ample retirement benefits.

We shouldn't be surprised.

Included, of course, in an Empire Center database of 350,000 retired state and local governmental employees, are lawmakers convicted of felonies who can collect their pension even while in prison (totaling over $1 million every year).

New Jersey Governor Chris Christie told the following story to his State Legislature: One 49-year-old state retiree paid a total of $124,000 towards his pension and health benefits during his career. The state now owes him over $3 million in pension and about $500,000 in other benefits.

Let's use another Christie story to introduce an additional area of misalignment—the teacher's union.

The governor told a story to the assembly about a teacher who was due $1.4 million in pension payments even though her total payments towards pension were $62,000 while she was working.

Everywhere you look there are examples of labor's excess, even in places where the instigating work was necessary and sometimes brilliantly executed. But the pit and the pendulum describe a repeating pattern of reaction and overreaction, protection and greed. Real wages have not grown much in the last five years but union benefits keep marching on, even when the underlying math provides evidence that the promises will be broken.

What are the Radical Centrist prescriptions?

First, acknowledge that many of the municipal and state employees in the pension and finance function have absolutely no business making the commitments and arranging the financings they are doing. They so severely lack subject matter command that some sort of statewide panel must be created.

Another is that the Tower Amendment, a little known coda, prevents the SEC from regulating municipal finance the way it regulates corporations and their financing.

Recognize that the unions have found the ultimate imbalance when negotiating public pensions and other benefits. Voters in their rank and file indirectly pick their adversary; anyone too tough gets spit out in the political process.

Key safety and public well-being workers need to be governed by a set of tough new standards. The pension and benefit shortfall in my estimation is closer to three trillion than one trillion. (A trillion is a thousand billion, by the way.) No one is watching except the rare courageous treasurer like Gina Raimondo in Rhode Island.

Strict pension accounting standards that require private companies to disclose their short funding of pension and other retirement liabilities should be applied to public pensions—though seeing the gaps didn't stop GM from making unaffordable accommodations.

Beware the danger of big government administration with a huge union representation that protects turf and slows innovation. Beware any increase in benefits matched by a decrease in contributions. Abhor the fixed nature of defined benefit retirement plans; they are what killed the dinosaurs. Encourage government to outsource services done better by others.

We are creating our own PIIGs in the major state and city economies of our nation. Some are using pension bonds for which entities issue debt to ameliorate pension payments. But pension bonds are like a cold compress;

they help modestly and cool things down but are really just one debt substituted for another.

Beware the entitlements built into the system, and force states and municipalities to accurately measure their exposure. Distrust smoothing techniques—five-year averages—and lower your assumed rate of return below eight percent.

The state of California pension assets are something like 70 percent of what they were before the crash of 2008. What good does an eight percent return assumption do if you are that far underwater on your investments?

Abhor any program that enables people to retire with full pension and health care before they turn 60. It is flat-out unaffordable. We turn into Greece otherwise.

Any new workers have to be hired at a lower pension rate and higher retirement age. Perhaps a seven- to ten-year fade-in for the new retirement plans should be structured for all state and municipal employees. If you know at 50 what you can expect at 50 and 55 then you have been treated fairly.

And those states which exempt their pensioners from paying taxes need to reassess the total cost of the package.

Automatic cost-of-living adjustments in pensions for retirees are hidden costs that virtually guarantee the investment returns will fall far short of required funding. They are unaffordable. Beware OPEB (other pension employment benefits). Full health-care benefits for the retiree and their family, and other such surrounding benefits, were probably never affordable, but they are certainly unaffordable today. No defined benefits—only defined contributions.

Stop standing by while grossly irresponsible administrators trade away extraordinary future rewards for their current election or nomination to office. They may not bankrupt a state, but they will bleed it dry.

Look, things are better today than 30 years ago in terms of watching pension funding, but the compounding has caused the numbers to become gigantic.

Let's face it: there have been only three municipal defaults on general obligation bonds since 1970 and no state level defaults in that same period. The last state default was in 1933 when Arkansas had to restructure. California could well be next.

So the heart of the matter is that the unions are setting the priorities and state workers' benefits will cause severe bleeding elsewhere.

Whether you are right or left, you have to appreciate that these unions mean increased cost, less flexibility of public finances, and a misallocation of resources. Taking control of our nation means getting involved when someone else gives our future away.

That leaves it up to us. When workers have unionized jobs, they are protected against employer abuses that created disasters like the Triangle Shirtwaist fire. But industrialized union power has had its heyday and government has emerged as labor's growth industry. And trust me: they are getting brawny about their 36 percent penetration. Removing all collective bargaining rights from public employees is waving a red flag in front of a bull. That's why what worked in Wisconsin got gored in Ohio. Americans get exercised when their rights are trampled, even if their state can't pay the freight.

We are frozen by unionists' unwillingness to make accommodation. If your state has pension obligations you should begin the process of decoupling ambitions from your balance sheet. They simply don't match.

Unions have an impending problem. They are losing the moral high ground because public employees earn much higher wages and benefits than their corporate employee brethren—i.e., the voters. So unions must demonize those who abscond with their rights, or the earnest state treasurer trying to balance the books, or the upper one percent.

In the end, we will all have to face the very basic music.

It's not that we can't afford what we want.

We can't afford what we have.

__CHALLENGE FOUR__
The "M" Word: Same-Sex Marriage

I ADMIT IT. I CAME *full circle slowly.*

I first met Kevin in the coldest of forums. Buried in the bowels of a midtown New York law firm—not one accorded the white shoe label across the entire span of its partnership—was a stuffy windowless conference room. Florescent lights overhead hummed loudly enough to carry a tune. The pale beige walls and the Iroquois tan carpet were stained and marked.

Snuggled between a clutch of lawyers and associates, Kevin and I sat across the table from each other. The heartwarming scene was a real estate closing for an apartment building deal. Kevin was the seller and my investment company was the purchaser.

There could be no more inauspicious start to a relationship.

He was a gentleman even as he quibbled. He was forthright when he negotiated and gracious in compromise. I expected the half-life of our interaction to last only the morning, but I was wrong. He recommended a property manager he knew quite well and who, more importantly, knew the property even better.

Craig, whom I met that afternoon, was everything Kevin advertised: focused, intelligent, knowledgeable, and very service-oriented. Dealing with high-end New York City apartment rentals, I needed all of the above. He was hired. In retrospect, it was a fantastic decision and an even better recommendation, considering it came from the seller.

Little did I suspect how much these two gentlemen were to teach me.

Craig became a frequent presence, making monthly reports and numer-

ous visits to the premises. We talked about his two young children, the trials of raising a family in New York, and Craig's work with a local acting company.

One frigid February day during a President's Weekend from hell, a utilities-paying tenant in the basement decided to save a few pennies and rely on the rest of the building to heat his offices. For the well-being of his patients, I can only hope the good doctor paid closer attention during his psychology lectures than he did during the "warm air rising" high school science labs.

Three days of sub-zero tundra tripped the good doctor's money saving strategy. The pipes that fed the sprinkler system, and also ran through his ceiling, burst like the great flood. In a matter of an hour we were thigh deep and floating. And in far less time than that, Craig and Kevin were there.

There is nothing romantic about a basement flood; but a few hours thrashing around in the freezing filthy water left me with a clear impression that I probably should have surmised long before.

MY KIDS TELL ME I am clueless and that I was blind to the obvious fact that Kevin and Craig enjoyed more than a working relationship.

They were, by every measure you might imagine, a couple.

I confess right here to two things: I had never known an adult gay couple before and I was struck by how comfortable it was to watch a hardworking duo who cared very much for each other contend with the stresses of careers, raising children, and finding balance in New York City.

I'm not sure what I was expecting.

To be completely honest, it was striking how normal their family life was; when the kids quarreled, the parents settled them down. Kevin and Craig were no different from any parents—they wanted the same things for their children and they were prepared to slave away at their respective careers in order to help fund the warm and happy life they enjoyed.

As I got to know them, I found myself coming full circle. It became clear to me that the gay marriage issue goes far beyond spousal insurance and tax treatment. The day-to-day nausea of family administration gets too much attention.

But it really isn't the point.

According to the Government Accountability Office, more than 1,138 rights and protections are conferred to U.S. citizens upon marriage by the federal government. After 30 years of marriage I honestly don't feel I have that many. The administration of a marriage does bring many legal questions with it: What rights do I enjoy? How can I participate in a health plan? Are my children eligible for tax credits? Can we have rights of survivorship in life insurance or estate matters?

This flood of questions drowns us in the legality and practice of a union in the eyes of the state; and if you've ever raised a child or been married you will acknowledge how crucial these recognitions can be in managing your life.

But they ignore an even more fundamental truth. If you have every single one of the 1,138 items in your portfolio, are you then married in every sense of the word? Is marriage in our nation no more than a bucket of rights and protections? Because if you can answer that fundamental question, then everything else in the same-sex marriage debate is about a simpler concept: parity.

Absolutists on both sides mis-frame the argument. The gay marriage debate is certainly a civil rights issue but it is much more than that; it is about the true meaning of marriage, beyond the contract and administrative points like hospital visitation rights.

In fact, I believe no piece of paper or legislation, no matter how brilliantly conceived and written, can ever replicate a societal construct like marriage any more than a written treaty can truly be a sustainer of peace between belligerent nations. The piece of paper serves to legally bind a couple that is already entwined in all the more important ways that human beings can experience with each other. The couple is, for better and worse, in love.

The debate on marriage cannot be saved by a carefully structured civil unions clause, because when we love one another there are no insignificant others. Civil unions are a cop-out.

It's not simply a lack of parity, nor of appropriate genitalia. It's not fair to characterize the debate as identical to the rights denied to African Americans, or women or immigrants of innumerable types and stripes. Those groups denied in our history could be justifiably annoyed by the comparison. Every battle for inclusion is different . . . and the same. Certainly there are common elements—as with any Venn diagram in high school discourse, there is overlap. We shouldn't be interested in ranking rights; we should be interested in doing the right thing.

There is another layer to be pulled back, because what we have is a government searching for a definition and relying on a religious concept of marriage to define citizens' rights.

Religious leaders are saying, "No, you can't get married in our church but you can't get married anywhere else either, whether we are involved in it or not. And you can't have all of the 1,138 rights either." It is one thing to rule on the connubial bed, but the joint tax return?

Is nothing sacred?

But is there a more central question we should be asking?

"Why?"

WHY ASK WHY?

WITH THE SAME-SEX MARRIAGE DEBATE there is a stark religious overtone which calls to mind the interracial marriage prohibitions buried in Jim Crow laws. Perhaps it's time to reprise "Guess Who's Coming to Dinner?" with a "la Cage" twist.

My message to everyone who opposes same-sex marriage on the basis of religious fervor is that this isn't about civil rights or about your religion.

It's about your family.

Civil rights throughout our history always involved categorization, putting people in tidy little boxes organized by race, creed, color, birthplace. By assuming commonalities within the target audience, almost any crazy idea could be pressed into service, and was.

Here's a wrinkle: gay people can't be characterized by race or creed or color or background. They are your mother, your brother, your aunt, or your son. They are every one of us. You can't use a W-2 or a zip code to find them (that is unless you include Chelsea or P'town, but you get the point).

Here's another difference: gay activists have the power to surprise. You never know when one might turn up. No gay-dar is good enough to sense who is in favor, because many of those most in support are still in their own sort of closet. And sexual preference has less and less to do with it. Sometimes you support something because it is about your family, not your lifestyle.

(Some of my best friends are heterosexual supporters of same-sex marriage. . . . Not that there's anything wrong with that.)

This debate is about the rapid pace of change in our society. It's about the true acceptance of homosexuals as individuals and as equals. In the coming months and years it will also be about something so basic that almost everyone in the argument tends to overlook it: Who gets to decide?

The framers of Proposition 8, the California law that revoked and banned same-sex marriage, even as it left standing the domestic partner program I like to call "marriage light," say it's the voters who should choose. The will of the majority in California should make the decision, which, on its face, seems far from a crazy assertion.

Others with passionate rhetoric call same-sex marriage a civil rights issue and therefore it belongs squarely in the wheelhouse of the Supreme Court. The Supremes have always had the final say in protecting the rights of the minority.

Before we get to the painful truth, let's review the state of play in same-sex marriage. Don't cry for me, Argentina, but the United States has become a gay mapmaker's nightmare. Today, six states—New York, Connecticut, Iowa, Massachusetts, New Hampshire, and Vermont—currently allow same-sex marriage, along with the District of Columbia—and more are about to. California is kind of bi-curious on the matter. First they allowed it, and then they stopped; but they now still accept the same-sex marriages performed in the Golden State while it was legal for four months. About

18,000 couples made the cut, which gives new meaning to the phrase "get me to the church on time."

With Prop 8, it's back to civil unions. Ah . . . the good old days.

Now, if you have the urge to merge in Oregon, it appears the Coquille Indian Nation will marry a couple of braves. I cannot give you any details on the ceremony, so use your imagination. Maryland and Rhode Island are in the "don't ask don't tell" category. They recognize same-sex marriages, but they won't perform them.

So imagine a drive around D.C. some spring afternoon. If you cross any bridge from the District into Old Virginny, your gay marriage suddenly dissolves due to a state constitutional ban on "any" recognition. So much for "Virginia Is for Lovers."

Take the Beltway back just a couple of miles to Chevy Chase and, like magic, your marriage is recognized again. Just be sure and turn back before the Pennsylvania border because State Senator Joseph Eichelberger wants a belt and suspenders approach (PA passed a law in 2006 which defined marriage as a union between a man and a woman), but is worried that's not definitive enough. He wants the Liberty State to have a constitutional ban on same-sex marriage so that the courts cannot overturn it. Thirty states have such constitutional bans.

It's too long a drive to get to the reservation in Oregon, but you get my point. We have a mad quilt of rules begging for rationalization. Thus far, the federal government is resisting temptation.

Unlike medical marijuana, which wafted out of California, same-sex marriage was kind of a New England initiative (Connecticut, Massachusetts, New Hampshire, and Vermont).

It's a very Yankee subject after all.

Things ran a bit chilly in Maine when the initiative came up for review. Maine had a bit of a John Kerry moment—it was for gay marriage in May of 2009 but then the people voted against it in a referendum six months later. Let's face it: the waters don't get swimmable up there until August anyway. They'll be back once they thaw out.

In a portent of the coming jousting match, two states of the five that support gay marriage were granted the right by a vote of the legislature, and three were a result of a court ruling.

For hundreds of years, the federal government has had the good judgment not to interfere in someone's marriage. The law of the land was basically that the federal government recognized any state marriage, but the states made their own rules.

The feds didn't get too fussed when the states didn't agree. The last time there was this kind of hue and cry was when interracial marriage was banned by a handful of states in the 60s and early 70s. Inside the Beltway, they just whispered words of wisdom and let it be.

All that, of course, changed in 1996 when the federal government passed the Defense of Marriage Act. My guess is they thought marriage needed defending. The federal government decided it was theirs to determine and they ruled that marriage must be defined as a union of a man and a woman. That's when the trouble really started.

The DOMA, as it is called by the cognoscenti, poses a bit of a problem for the four New Englanders, New York, and Iowa, and is even trickier for the District. Truth be told, there are only a few places where a same-sex marriage is recognized and only one of those is anywhere involving the federal government. You don't even need to go for a spring drive to be confused in D.C. Are you legit or not? It really depends which office building you are visiting.

So what do the advocates and the dissenters do?

Going for marriage parity by the legislative process feels like the Bataan March or at least a dance around the Maypole. Once Maine held the referendum that defeated its 2006 legislative initiative, a grand total of 31 states had voted against same-sex marriages. That's 31 defeats in a row when same-sex marriage has been put to the voters.

Ten states have created civil unions with varying subsets on the rights and privileges married couples enjoy. Many, if not all, of those 1,138 protections might exist in a civil union, but it ain't a marriage. Iowa's law was put through by a unanimous vote of the Supreme Court. In one very real respect, the battle lines over who will get to decide have been drawn.

EVENTUALISM

SO FAR, SO BAD.

We're in a holding pattern but I believe it's clear what will eventually happen three, thirteen, or thirty years down the road: same-sex marriage will be legalized in the United States. That's called eventualism.

A Gallup poll released in Spring 2011 found that a majority of Americans believe same-sex marriage should be legal. In 1996, a scant fifteen years previously, Gallup found that only 27 percent of Americans supported gay marriage. Opponents rightly point out that opinion polls in Maine and California showed majority support for gay marriage in those states right before voters rejected gay marriage. Clearly what goes on behind the polling booth curtains is as hard to fathom as what happens in the boudoir but the trend is obvious and inevitable.

History assures us that the two curves will cross and the American alchemy that turns a minority into a majority will come to pass. That has always been our genius. America eventually gets it right . . . always.

As the bumper sticker says . . . approximately . . . "Eventualism Happens."

I think back to the adolescence of our nation, of our inner psyche that was apparently so established by the time of Madison's presidency that in 1817, Adams put his quill down, considering the story already told. Our national character had already been determined.

We are inclusive by birthright, and many of our earliest colonies were formed because our congregations were not welcomed elsewhere. That religious freedom, as well as other freedoms, are a part of our DNA. But lately we have lost touch with that common characteristic.

This leads me to the central thesis of the entire debate:

Same-sex marriage may be a way to rediscover our national soul.

If gay marriage is inevitable, do we wait or do we take a stand and force the issue more urgently? Do we still possess the American genius, or have the generations dulled our sense of inclusion and made second-class citizenry an acceptable state of affairs?

Do we pass the test or do we fail?

I know there are hurdles—if nothing else an entrenched, if shrinking, minority.

In America, nothing is more intractable.

In May of 2011 the Rhode Island lawmakers pondered a proposal to allow civil unions, hardly an earth-shattering piece of news. But on closer examination the legislation arose as a compromise position after it became clear there weren't enough votes to aim higher and get a marriage bill through the process. Illinois, Hawaii, and Delaware enacted civil unions in 2011 for much the same reason.

I say they fail the test of their soul even if they pass on sobriety.

Because you can call a civil union partner anything you want, but you can't call her or him your wife. Not really.

In a sign of desperation, Minnesota accepted the 30th constitutional prohibition on gay marriage on the 2012 ballot. Activists tell me it is their battering ram strategy. Bang away until one state finally breaks the losing streak. Smart money is betting the Twin Cities will lead the way. Eventually.

So, the argument runs, why not sit this one out and wait? The Supreme Court has the powerful responsibility to protect the rights of individuals, but the Court must recognize its own limitations and refrain from overruling the choices of the American people.

We all know that civil rights don't automatically trump majority preferences. Edicts and mandates from the Supreme Court are sometimes a way to spark a dialogue, but they rarely provide the ideal solution to a nagging and intractable problem.

Civil rights are vitally important, but so is judicial modesty. Gay marriage divides so neatly along these battle lines and after that there is nothing tidy about it. Hard-liners say the Supreme Court's job is defining civil rights and protecting them. Period.

The Proposition 8 framers and, by proxy, the states' rights advocates, say that gay marriage is neither a marriage nor a civil right and the Court oversteps its bounds to assert that it is. They say, put it to a vote state by state. Let Americans decide, they claim. Majority rules. Or does it?

What should the Radical Centrist view be here?

My own view is that Americans of the same sex will, and should be able to, marry. They can, either in five states or in numerous foreign countries including Canada. Some allow clear anomalies. A handful of states recognize foreign marriages and, bizarrely, New York State used to recognize marriages conducted in other states but wouldn't conduct them itself.

But that is not really what drives my view. If you are married and reading this, imagine you traveled a few miles from your home and your union was no longer blessed or recognized. Imagine that the federal government considered your marriage a sham. Or worse, picture that the neighboring state to which you must move for work considers your marriage illegal.

America's haphazard distribution of same-sex marriage rights creates something we have tried to avoid since we assembled in 1776 as a stew of second-class citizens and outcasts: the countryman of lesser rank.

America doesn't abide second-class citizenship. It harms our national soul not to fix it.

But is it a catastrophe if two lesbians can't tie the knot or two gents can't be husband and husband? Where are the catastrophic losses of life and limb? It's a moral catastrophe that leaves no external markings or scars. But damage is done. State-sanctioned denial of rights is catastrophic when it creates second-class citizenry.

Think how foolish we look through the prism of history. Women were accorded the right to vote in 1920. African Americans were extended full citizenship benefits only in the 1960s. Our children will look back in disdain at how long we tolerated yet another embarrassing anomaly until early in the twenty-first century.

We as a nation are being asked to respect the 31 states in a row that have spoken by voting against the provision for same-sex marriage. I have read chapter and verse about how the elections were rigged. Even so, there is a buzz in the heartland, and the proponents of same-sex marriage have to acknowledge the fact that they have not yet made an overwhelmingly compelling case. Thus far in the Democratic Darwinism, the protagonists keep slipping back into the primordial ooze. We are told we must trust in the

American process. And I do believe that patience will be rewarded. Eventually.

But some seven million Californians voted to ban same-sex marriages. The real problem at the moment is that Americans at large don't appear ready to vote in favor of something that seems entirely consistent with what we stand for as a nation.

Some will say that to fight the entrenched diehards who oppose the inevitable is basically a wasted effort. Better to respond with patience and doggedness. Whether it is same-sex marriage, or stem cell research, our national genius is finding ways to defeat those who exclude any citizens from the promise of America.

But if it's going to happen . . . eventually . . . why are we sitting by and allowing the forces of reaction to put up more barricades?

We shouldn't, because a degraded citizen is not really a citizen at all.

People who fall in love with people with the same genitals are not a carbuncle affixed to American society—they are your family. They are connected to every one of us, which gives them something not available to your basic "huddled masses yearning" . . . access.

Rather than relent and move on to more dire issues, the response of opposition hard-liners is to fight with every fiber of their being. It's the Tripoli siege mentality—fight until the last dog dies. Obstructives have figured out that money and fear can block anyone's rights—at least they can right now.

Americans have fought since our earliest days for our rights. It's as if every new group must fight their own Democratic Darwinism, every disenfranchised group is forced to struggle for their slice of Apple Pie. It is wasteful, frustrating, and at times heartless. But it is our process.

So why not help them, why not extend a hand to family now?

Just because we believe it will happen eventually doesn't mean it should wait. It's a measure of our ability as a nation to see the way forward, past the patchwork of contradictory and demeaning rules held together with bailing wire. All you need to do is light a match to a fuse.

Here's how it will happen: Either the states in favor will propagate with New York and a few of the biggies leading the way, or if the states dither then the courts will feel compelled to join the fray. The instigation won't happen in the Supreme Court, but in the United States District Court. Some state law will be targeted as illegal and appealed. The scene of the action will be in the Federal District Court. You watch.

After that showdown, next stop is the Supreme Court and the end of the debate. This decision will be challenged via the Supremes issuing a writ of certiorari to precede the review. It will take time, it will be painful, and if I were manning the bridge I would forget the slow and arduous trail of dealing with voters across the country. I would respect the prudence of jurisprudence and fight it out in the courts.

A Radical Centrist knows what is going to happen, just as Gretzky knows where the puck is going to be.

And what's going to happen, in my opinion, is that the Supreme Court is going to wait until it can wait no longer, a flurry of states will pass laws that come close, but activists will not be satisfied—and the court will push the agenda more effectively than the long slog of voting wars won inch by inch and town by town.

For the sake of efficiency and pushing through reforms that are way past due, the Supreme Court will rule positively in favor of gay marriage and overturn the structure of Proposition 8 and all its kissing cousin "pilot fish" laws across the land.

Eventualism happens, and in time, gays will be happily married in our nation. Watch Elena Kagan finesse this. The Supremes will rule long after they should have, but they will rule despite powerful dissent from the conservative court. Not to worry.

It may be as simple as the passing of a generation. Younger Americans of all political and lifestyle persuasions say they are more tolerant of homosexuality than older generations of Americans. But the time will come, we can make sure of it.

Let's seize the golden opportunity to reclaim our national soul. Then gays will marry, we can finally relax, and we'll all stock up on confetti.

THE BLONDE STRIPPER TUGGED HARD *on her cigarette, picked at her nails, and played endlessly with a rubber band. She was the kind of stripper you prefer remain fully clothed. She had a story to tell, and it was a whopper.*

The parable was about a man she had been living with for a few months. It had the basic elements: girl meets boy. Their relationship was forged over the counter at the pizza restaurant where she worked when she wasn't on stage. She, comely but covered in flour, her blonde American looks a magnet for the foreigner.

Girl likes boy. There were the everyday things that endeared him to her. The fact that he liked pork chops and the Beastie Boys, and the grin he wore as he skillfully piloted the snappy red convertible he drove.

But, after they moved in together at the Sandpiper Apartments in Venice, Florida, she came to see the other side.

Girl dumps boy. He was always drinking, snorting coke whenever he could, wearing expensive jewelry, and dancing that head-snapping disco dance like, I mean like Will Ferrell in A Night at the Roxbury, *like.*

It was the latter, not any of the former, that caused the relationship to collapse, which tells you a lot about the woman in question. She broke up with him because he was dancing on a speaker in a nightclub doing that neck-jarring head bob; and besides there was someone cuter on the dance floor. Isn't there always?

End of romance . . . but not of the relationship.

He told her that night that she would regret dumping him so unceremoniously. In a time-honored tradition, she left his suitcases by the door and barred his reentry. Such was the daily drama at the Sandpiper; out with the old and in with the new . . . like the tides. But ours was a hurt and determined young man, with a score to settle. He was forgotten but not gone.

When she returned from work (it's not clear whether this was her pizza job or her striptease sideline), she found the peace of her household had been disturbed—someone had broken in to her apartment. Worse, someone had disemboweled her cat, dismembered her kittens, and strewn the remains all over the flat.

It was a message from a madman. And it was then she began to appreciate that her ex-boyfriend was a disturbed individual.

Not even as keen an intellect as hers could have predicted what would happen next.

In a matter of months, her former lover had decamped the Gulf Coast and found himself at the opposite end of the meteorological spectrum, on the granite shores of Maine.

One morning, he booked a flight south, returned a rental car before departure, caught a connecting flight, commandeered the pilot's seat, and flew the Boeing 767 headlong into a looming tower.

Her boyfriend was Mohammed Atta. Such was her claim. He, like fourteen of the nineteen men who hijacked planes on 9/11, had spent time living in Florida—a choice made even more curious when you consider the facts at hand.

Gulf Coast Florida is one of those low-key but high-heeled places where time moves pretty slowly. By one report, the town of Venice has the second oldest population in the country; the median age is sixty-nine.

This is just the place you would imagine a nice Muslim boy would meet a spiky pink-haired girl to prepare him for the parade of virgins in the hereafter.

Isn't it?

I watched with great interest the twenty-five-minute video interview the woman in question conducted at an undisclosed location. No one reviewing her slowly told tale would consider Amanda Keller particularly bright.

That might explain one of two things. It either explains why she thought nothing of a licensed unemployed pilot from a country of ambiguous origin taking flight lessons with a seemingly endless stream of funds, cocaine, and alcohol suddenly landing at an apartment complex in geriatric-ville. Or it might explain something far more profound: how, after claiming to be Atta's bedmate and party pal, Amanda Keller suddenly denied everything to the FBI. "It was my bad for lying." She told the Sarasota Herald Tribune.

OUR STORY PROBABLY NEVER HAPPENED.

One might ask, why would Amanda Keller fabricate a tale in such intricate detail? Whatever her veracity, the story doesn't end.

Now it's a bizarre footnote, yet another myth in an endlessly painful story. Worst of all, it's a story that seems to hold as its central premise a war without end.

THE QUESTION WHY

THREE THINGS BURNED INTO MY memory that horrible day:

First was the crystal clear and cool September perfection of the morning. It was a flawless counterpoint to the horrors that followed.

Second was the assault of smells that poisoned the air around the World Trade Center. The stench of electrical fire, vaporized cement, and death wafted down the canyons of Wall Street, drifting like a cloud of depression through the neighborhoods of upper Manhattan and across the bay into New Jersey. It smelled like Guernica and Hades and the end of days.

But my most lasting recollection on September 11th and the days that followed was the endless variation of questions which flooded our consciousness, all beginning with the same word: Why?

Why did they do it? Why do they hate us so much? Why are we always the target when we do so much good in the world?

The why's buzzed around the streets of Manhattan, across the Internet and the broadcast booths, in the churches and the schools, and included this one: Why were we caught so unaware?

We now know that many in government had a strong sense of trouble brewing. And as with every bridge collapse and market crash there were seers who saw what was coming, who for whatever reason were just not heard.

Even President Bush's August 6, 2001, daily briefing contained an item entitled "Bin Laden Determined to Strike in the U.S." We also know that a fateful struggle among intelligence agencies, most notably the FBI and the CIA, suggests the 9/11 terrorists were known to be threats and known to be in the United States. Reports of a meeting where the CIA dangled photos in front of FBI agents of at least two 9/11 terrorists whom they refused to identify indicate a tantalizing target for inquiry: the acrimonious adjacencies between government agencies bound to protect us from terror.

Here is the apparent truth: we knew that 9/11 leader Mohammed Atta was a bad guy. We knew he was in the United States. Some ordinary (and now guilt-ridden) citizens had dealings with him but weren't suspicious enough to report him to the authorities. Articles in both the *Miami Herald* and the *Dallas Star Telegram* claim the National Security Agency monitored conversations between Khalid Sheik Mohammed and Atta before 9/11. "Apparently NSA analysts didn't recognize the significance. . . . " Some claim that the CIA was watching the flight schools but the denials have let that trail go cold. Whatever those who knew were doing, they weren't telling and they especially weren't telling the FBI, which is the agency with jurisdiction over would-be terrorists operating in the United States.

The age-old internecine warfare between intelligence branches of our government is no longer a charming but tolerable anachronism. The time has passed where we should indulge defensive turf watching.

There's real turf the agencies need to be protecting, and it's not their own.

Do you remember the last line of the 9/11 Commission Report? I'm a big fan of reading the last line of reports—the good ones always hold the baton forward, ready for someone to grab it and run ahead. In this case, it was:

"A question remains: 'Who is in charge of Intelligence?'"

The tragedy of course is that the question is rhetorical, and as such an embarrassment to the memory of those who perished.

That query is an administrative indictment too.

But Radical Centrists need to address a far more profound and damning point.

Most Americans that morning, myself included, had no idea what the central motivation was behind the attack. Most of us lacked even a working hypothesis, which means that neither our sentinels nor we the citizenry had sufficient knowledge to self-protect.

Many of us had always presumed we were the good guys. Then a miserable bunch of assassins comes to tell us they think otherwise.

In more ways than one, what Israeli P.M. Benjamin Netanyahu told Tom Brokaw two days after 9/11 was right: "This is your wake-up call from hell."

In the days that followed, we were so desperate to make sense of what had happened that the story of an unevenly endowed stripper assumed major significance.

Frankly, it could be that she was telling the truth before "My bad . . ." and the FBI silenced her. More likely, she was looking for a payday and her 15 minutes. As near as I can tell, she got neither. What we got was the perverse ability to castigate a murdering scoundrel with the ultimate ad hominem: he was an unobservant Muslim. Take that, Atta.

Folks, it ain't the pork chops or the Beasties or the pasties that matter. Freaking out about Atta's profligate lifestyle as some form of indictment of Islam misses the point entirely. I don't care if he chased tail or drank Bud Light or vice versa. He murdered thousands of innocents in a bid for holy war. That morning as I trudged through the lunar landscape of my place of work for 30 years and breathed the fetid air, I constantly returned to my burning question:

Why?

GLOBAL JIHAD

THE GLOBAL SALAFI JIHAD IS the kind of movement many religions have sprouted, particularly the great ones like Christianity and Judaism. It is a revivalist movement. Like all revivals it carries with it a reenergizing spirit, a new force that animates all discussions, all writings, all preaching.

What was the essence of this revival?

Let's start by describing jihad. Muslims tell me that jihad is akin to striving. Its root is unassuming but it can be a dangerous word depending on who is interpreting it—jihad translates to the individual's non-violent struggle to live a good Muslim life, simply an unassuming urge to do right by your religion.

Islam is as full of divisions and contentious issues as any other religion. There are interpreters of jihad that expand its meaning to consider offensive and defensive jihad. Muslims face persecution in some societies, as do Christians, Buddhists, Jews, and so on. And even among good Muslims there are trials. In some cases, the very direction of modern society runs counter to the basic daily struggle to be a good Muslim.

Religions under attack adopt a similar balance of prayer, observance, and obedience to leadership. It's not always clear if this is offense or defense.

The role of defense in the nation of Islam inspires another word: fatwa. In its simplest form, fatwa is a legal opinion, an individual obligation to take part in a defensive jihad to protect the faith.

When the Soviet Union invaded Afghanistan in the last days of 1979, several Muslim religious leaders issued fatwas with a single compulsion—they asked good Muslims to repel the infidels. Few of us could have argued, and we went a step further ourselves and helped them defeat the Soviets. Charlie Wilson saw to that.

One of the first Arabs to join the jihad against the Soviets was Palestinian-born academic Sheik Abdallah Azzam (1941-1989). His worldwide fatwa, issued in 1979, promoted the notion of a defensive battle, and as a result many young people traveled to Peshawar in Pakistan, joining Azzam and the jihadists.

The fight grew bigger and became part of a broader, global notion of Salafi jihad. The Salafists had in mind the creation of a great Islamist state stretching from Morocco to the Philippines, eliminating national boundaries. The Sheik's message called for more than a reclaiming of Afghanistan from the Soviets, it called for reclamation of formerly Muslim lands lost to non-Muslim governments.

It was only a short leap from there to call for defeat of the Western powers, which were preventing the establishment of an Islamist state. The Salafi movement and the Tablighi movement—a pan-Islamic organization founded in India in the twenties—went on to form a dense global network. With al-Qaeda at the vanguard, these movements became the major force in twentieth-century Muslim revivalism. Here began a perversion of the notion of being a good Muslim. So many bad ideas start out as good ones.

Zealots who joined the jihad with one concept in mind quickly found themselves redirected.

With its headquarters in Lahore, Pakistan, al-Qaeda had its recruits obtain visas for Pakistanis to study in Tablighi schools, while in reality they were training in Afghan terror camps. These camps were a key link in the dark metamorphosis that turned jihadists into terrorists.

The defensive fatwa drew aggressors with broader agendas—but knowing who these jihadists really were explains why the transition took time to evolve. Contrary to many writings on terrorism and terrorists, a more informed and surprising understanding emerges.

Members of the global Salafi jihad were generally middle class, educated young men from caring and religious families who were raised with spirituality and community concern. The majority of them were married and most had children. Except for the Maghreb Arabs, who engaged in petty crimes, there is scant evidence that the terrorists were hardened criminals no matter what the press would have you believe.

Obviously there were notorious leaders, but many rank-and-file jihadists did not display the pathology, paranoia, and hatred that pervaded press accounts.

Even when you read some of Osama's early speeches—and I write this with care and sensitivity—they possess a thin gauze of reason stretched over slow-simmering hate. In them, he called for a boycott of Western goods—nothing more.

So what accounted for the deepening fervor? There are a variety of theories, and none is the silver bullet explanation. What drove these jihadists to madness?

Some derive great comfort in the inconsistency of the 9/11 hijackers' behavior and their devotion. Topless bars and drinking binges are evidence, but they do not disprove devotion, even among the Religious Right. The proof of their misplaced devotion is demonstrated by their final act of slaughtering innocents for their "holy" cause.

Some claim it is the slow agony of waiting when held in suspense in a terrorist cell, some claim it was the hijackers' dramatic underemployment and deprivation vis-à-vis their skills. But for none of these does there seem to be much evidence of the deep pathological hatred necessary to kill thousands of innocent people.

Perhaps it is all of the above. But I see a mad genius in the work of the surgeon Ayman al-Zawahiri, Osama bin Laden's ultimate successor, who practiced gradual radicalization. His jihad began reasonably and was built in increments into the perversion of Islamist terrorism we live with today. Al-Zawahiri was a shrewd talent collector and is said to have favored recruiting former military officers. These activists could be called into action, often abruptly, after long periods of waiting.

No matter how they cloak their rhetoric in religious fervor, these mujahideen (Arabic for people on a jihad) were enthusiastic murderers, and it was the intention of theocratic amateurs like Osama bin Laden and his predecessors to turn Muslim radicals into cold-blooded killers.

How did they do it?

There are examples of both short-term and longer-term planning, so no absolute definition like brainwashing will work. The U.S. Embassy bombings in 1998 in Dar es Salaam and Nairobi, when the name bin Laden first came to prominence, were at least five years in the planning. Yet the assassination of Anwar Sadat in 1981 was hatched as an unanticipated opportunity just days before the operation.

The Tanzim al Jihad, which carried out the attack, was created by the merger of two clusters of Islamic groups, both spoiling with rage over the Sadat-driven peace initiative with Israel. But unlike with the painfully deliberate planning of the World Trade Center attack, many of the attacks in a given year are crimes of the moment.

But what turns a jihadist into a cold-blooded terrorist? Answering the question "How could they do it?" helps us grope towards an answer to the question, "Why?"

Among hundreds of terrorist organizations spanning many geographies and tribes there are endless differences, and yet a few common denominators provide part of the answer.

One that deserves mention is the conversion of an individual to religious fanaticism. In any movement there are literalists who believe the teachings of their mullah implicitly. So fierce is their allegiance that they become willing instruments of their holy men. Prompted and protected by the invocations of their clerics, the malleable become lethal.

Beyond a holy call to do unholy things, there are other reasons cited by experts throughout terrorist literature. Some of them will surprise you.

SOCIAL AFFILIATION

THIS IS THE MOST PROVOCATIVE reason, and in many ways the most useful. Study the National Counter Terrorism Center's (NCTC) reports, and you will be baffled by the mapmaker's nightmare that is worldwide terror. These are linked and unlinked cells, and an ever-changing chain of hundreds of groups and organizations. Among the links that exist are powerful charismatics and social connectors, men of skill in energizing their colleagues and friends.

A network of terror needs passions to power it. The social joining and the mutual acceptance of men on a mission create their own sorts of principalities. These are stateless enterprises and there are shrewd individuals who play a major role in providing the glue. These leaders search for willing zealots longing for approval and acceptance. It's too simple a psychology to call it religious fervor. It is about disaffected people belonging to something that includes them.

TURNING UP THE IDEOLOGICAL HEAT

BRING SOMEONE INTO THE FOLD and then progressively expose them to more intense levels of belief. For the global Salafi jihad two elements support the steady escalation of ideology: the first uses the teachings of the Koran, and the second is deemed holy as well—the words and deeds of the prophet as told in stories (this is called the Hadith).

Purists live within the words and deeds of Mohammed. Other leaders weave hawkish Islamic scholars into interpretations not found in the Koran or Hadith. Inciting hatred through these religious teachings and innovative interpretations is a greenhouse for extremism.

GANG AFFILIATION

FINALLY, THERE IS THE FORMAL acceptance into the jihad through an encounter or action which binds one to the group. In many respects, this is tribal and patterns itself on any gang activity, despite the religious overtones. We are all Crips or Bloods in our own way.

LEADERSHIP

THE PATHWAY TO RADICALISM CAN be traced to specific leaders, many with far more credibility than Osama.

Tracing through bin Laden's history, there is little to indicate that an unexceptional, rich Saudi boy with a penchant for throwing up before battle would lead a revolutionary initiative across the Muslim world. Even among the most reverential reports on Osama, a cloud of lingering questions follows him. That portends less tribulation for al-Qaeda in the wake of his killing. There was dancing in the streets in the United States, but many considered bin Laden a peripheral player by the time Seal Team 6 burst through his bedroom door.

It is far more likely that the original impetus for worldwide jihad came from a frail Egyptian scholar, whose fundamentalist views made him the most powerful personality of the Muslim world in the last half of the twentieth century.

He is without doubt the most famous person you never heard of.

The scholar Sayyid Qutb (1906-1966) spent a few years in the United States, including studying at Colorado State College of Education in Greeley in the forties. Qutb was the chief developer of the doctrines that legitimize Islamic Holy War as we know it today.

So dissatisfied was Qutb with America's shameless sexuality and modernity that he joined the fundamentalist Muslim Brotherhood immediately upon his return to Egypt. His seminal work, *In the Shadow of the Koran*, a 30-volume commentary, was followed by an equally well researched, but strident, *Milestones*.

Qutb deduced that all Christians are bound for Hell and in his latter work railed against Jews and Western convention. But his fiercest polemics were reserved for Muslims, particularly those leading in Muslim countries with a Western tilt to their way of life.

His writings sparked a striking pattern which has been oft repeated and yet is largely ignored by Western media and punditry—jihadists' most energizing rhetoric and most pointed assaults are directed at their fellow Muslims. So before we tar with a single brush or a broad slur, consider this: Muslims have chastised and killed more Muslims than they have Western infidels.

We have much to learn about our enemy.

Qutb called for the implementation of Sharia, or religious law. But neither Egypt, under Nasser, nor Saudi Arabia, under the monarchy, did as he commanded. Qutb responded with his writings. He knew firsthand how to harness anger among his jihadists. Both Qutb and bin Laden recognized the untapped power of the disenfranchised, who were both angry and powerless in their own countries. They knew what drives many Islamic extremists: poverty, hunger, and lack of opportunity are powerful motivators.

Egyptian and Saudi indifference to their people sowed the seeds of terrorism. It wasn't just American imperialism and profligate ways.

Qutb proselytized that territories of Islam were governed by corrupt, Westernized, and modernized dictators and princes. He wrote elaborate rationalizations for killing non-Muslims that tapped into Islamic militancy and anger.

There is probably no greater influence over al-Qaeda than Qutb. He became an outspoken critic of the secular nationalism of the Nasser regime, which was so incompatible with the requirements of the Islamic Brotherhood they even refused to ban alcohol.

His writing became self-fulfilling prophesy.

A botched assassination attempt on Nasser brought a crackdown on the Islamic Brotherhood. Qutb was imprisoned for ten years, and shortly after his 1964 release, he was imprisoned again. His thinly disguised contempt and his calls for radical solutions left the government with no option. He was hanged as an enemy of the state in 1966—ensuring his martyrdom.

Qutb knew that an effective writer can influence eternity if succeeding generations take his words to heart. In the absence of a truly holy terrorist leader, Qutb played just such a role long after the twisted rope wrapped around his neck. It was never Osama bin Laden. He was, quite literally, the base's beard.

UNINTENDED CONSEQUENCES

NO MATTER WHERE YOU COME out on the need to topple Saddam Hussein and to bomb the Afghan poppies to kingdom come, you have to conclude that our actions in Iraq encouraged strong reactions from world-wide jihad.

Our U.S. intervention in Iraq changed the Middle Eastern landscape by making the United States a more visibly direct participant in the region's politics. Toppling three Muslim regimes, no matter how unpopular they might be, gets you noticed. Rescuer or not, liberator or occupier, we have altered the calculus of terror by acts of our commission.

Clearly having bases in Saudi Arabia, the land of the holiest sites in Islam, is inconsistent with the wishes of mujahideen like Osama, al Zawahiri, and their henchmen. The United States is viewed as an occupying force and it's a simple calculus: U.S. troops in Iraq and Afghanistan will build volunteers for jihad.

The Iraqi conflict also sets up a very difficult equation for America: succeed and the U.S. undermines jihad, but fail or withdraw before stability is achieved and jihad is strengthened. In the Bush Doctrine there was great opportunity but equally great danger.

President Obama's Cairo speech early in his presidency called for an entirely new approach to the Muslim world. But closer analysis shows little difference in approach for the first two years of his presidency from the Neocon Bush Doctrine, except Obama uses far more predator drone strikes. Even as we withdraw from Iraq and, later, Afghanistan, the question remains, are we better soldiers than nation builders?

Some believe America's direct and indirect toppling of two Muslim regimes was the catalyst for the Arab Spring that led to our involvement in getting rid of a third (in Libya). Post-9/11, the $1.5 trillion prosecution of these wars certainly marked a new doctrine of preventative maintenance and a reassertion of U.S. military power. Bombings we are conducting in Somalia, Pakistan, and other nations where we are waging undeclared wars will have their own impact on our position in the Middle East.

Let's not forget that the killing of Osama bin Laden and the systematic targeting of al-Qaeda leadership has also caused passions to stir.

A crucial element of the Arab Spring is that revolutions happened throughout the region without the United States or Israel serving as flash points (even if you think we were the catalyst). Fair enough that the U.S. supported Mubarak for decades to the tune of billions in aid. But for the first time the people of these nations sought to overthrow their dictators on their own.

Until we began bombing Libya, the United States and Israel were basically bit players in the unfolding drama of the Arab Spring. Here we have the most epic convulsion in the twenty-first century, affecting over 300 million people who live in the region. And in country after country, the people took matters into their own hands.

Cheers for the spread of democracy may be premature. Be careful what you wish for. We saw in Palestine how democracy fomented the election of Hamas, a known terrorist organization. If you know Egypt, you know democracy is a long way off.

Democracy is far from easy. Will the imbalances created by the people's uprisings in Syria, Tunisia, Libya, and Egypt lead to greater volatility and a bigger stage for the dark forces that drive extremists to terrorism?

Volatility in the region is about the only certainty. And whether it is the Muslim Brotherhood, or a fully separate initiative, let us move with great caution, for our actions in Libya, just like our inactions in Syria, will have unintended consequences. If we helped in getting rid of Gaddafi, don't expect too much gratitude. Throughout the region there are hundreds of organizations still seething with hatred for the United States and looking for ways to do us injury and harm.

In a strange way it all ties back to that stripper and 9/11. Our reaction to that morning creates a powerful irony we will puzzle for generations in the ongoing chess game with terrorist forces.

It raises a question most people dare not ask but Radical Centrists face head-on:

Did bin Laden strike us on 9/11 we would react predictably with a trillion-dollar recoil?

Were we so opiated by our revenge impulse and by the threat of losing our precious oil that we focused our treasury and young people's lives on shock and awe in the Middle East? Did we play into bin Laden's hands by ignoring the giant Far East panda that seized the moment of our distraction to dare to become the world's dominant economy?

Could the terrorists have been so diabolical to plot that our economic standing could fall just as easily as the towers? Wars bankrupt countries, even the victors—look at Great Britain after World War I.

HOW WE RESPOND: THE NEW FACE OF WAR

AS STEVE JOBS SAID, WE have to "Think Different."

A different army means a different war. This enemy is so different that we should consider whether describing our battle as a "War on Terror" actually glorifies the profane. Are we making the illegitimate orthodox?

The earliest wars were tribal. Gathered by community, natives protected their land, their hunting grounds, and, in time, their store of grain. Tribes joined in regional compacts, and nations became the vehicles for conducting war. There were ongoing examples of tribal uprising writ large as the Goths took down the widely expansive Holy Roman Empire.

There were also religious crusades, which both transcended and ignored national boundaries. These were meant to be wars of moral philosophy but the trappings of victory had a consistent way of polluting ideals and expanding national boundaries.

These warring nations were often monarchies with feudal lords and mandarins who traded favors, intermarriage, titles, and land to create allegiances. These interwoven partnerships found support even in those nations where monarchy gave way to rule by the governed. Weaker nations sought refuge in league with more powerful partners.

An assassination of the Serbian Archduke Franz Ferdinand, hardly a Big Dipper in the constellation of European monarchy, had the direct impact of pulling on one string connected to another and another and another. We plunged into World War I.

Then a madman's expansive need for empire drove another set of allies into World War II and an attack by an emboldened Japan brought a sleeping giant into the fray. Once again, massive armies of allied forces brought nation after nation into the conflict.

Wars turned into massive global enterprises with the consequence of millions of deaths; the vast majority of the lives lost were noncombatants. Genocide has a nasty habit of skewing the numbers toward the slaughter of innocents.

A new model for fighting arose after World War II. For fifty years, two competing philosophies fought a Cold War characterized by massive build-ups of armaments with thousands of nuclear weapons creating "mutual assured destruction" and a fearsome stalemate.

Rather than risk obliteration, the opposing superpowers instead fought wars by proxy—global conflicts fought on intermediate ground far from either protagonist's or antagonist's home soil.

Vietnam and Afghanistan are two examples. One involved full-disclosure battles, albeit without a clear battle plan; the other a war fought through funding subterfuges off the backs of Afghan freedom fighters armed with Stinger missiles. Each used the technology and elements of old-style fighting. Each caused the competing philosophy to invest heavily to win the local contest. As a result, both Vietnam and the Afghan conflicts punched ahead of their weight. And in the end each result was unsatisfactory.

Today, we have reverted even further. Worldwide allegiances are incapable of stopping genocide.

Even when the UN or NATO condemn, they do little to change the course of "tribal" murder. Consider Darfur, Rwanda, and Bosnia. After nearly two years, the Clinton administration intervened in Bosnia while we avoided involvement in the other two countries.

The problem of course is we have created baffling rules of engagement.

The trade-off, as with President Obama's intervention in Libya, means deciding that intercession is necessary on humanitarian terms despite little national interest or benefit.

There simply aren't enough U.S. resources to wage war on every dictator who threatens annihilation of his people. So we have gone from wars by proxy to wars where we pick our spots. Gaddafi's legacy of intransigence legitimizes our attack on Libyan soil, whereas Syria warrants nothing more toxic than sanctions.

Our episodic involvement stirs terrorists into a frenzy of anti-Western fever when we act. When you're an activist superpower, you can't win.

Like an errant bacteria, terrorism has adapted from a subordinate role in nation-state conflicts to a prominent international influence in its own right. In modern war, terrorist cells are the new enemy, ignoring national boundaries, fighting on multiple fronts, confusing governments versed for centuries in opposing other nations in combat.

While the terror cell is a necessary thing to monitor, it's practically impossible to do so. Cells have no direct contact with leadership. They thrive on anonymous communications through disposable cell phones, long-distance phone cards, and Internet jihad communications. Numerous recent arrests have been made of jihadists radicalized by materials and training received on the Web.

Thanks to technology and the linkage of Islam, terrorism is both tribal and global—the worst of both worlds.

How We Respond: Knowing the Enemy

WHO ARE THESE SUPRANATIONAL ENEMIES? One trouble with a "war on terror" concept is that you must first figure out who you are fighting other than some all-encompassing noun (such as "The War on Drugs").

The Taliban, for example, is not a uniform group. In Afghanistan, the Taliban was a sort of nationalist movement. But the Taliban is a number of different factions. The Afghan Taliban's one-eyed leader, Mullah Omar, is now based in Pakistan. He follows Deobandi Islam, which experts tell me is close in ideology to al-Qaeda. In the late 90s Omar was quoted as saying, "All Taliban are moderate." After the 9/11 attacks, he told the BBC: "The real matter is the extinction of America."

If he is a moderate, I would hate to encounter an extremist.

The Taliban has other factions: The Haqqani Network, led by the popular warlord Jalaluddin Haqqani and the Quetta Council. (In World War II, everyone knew we were fighting Germany, Japan, Italy. Now we're up against the Haqqani Network, which sounds like a marginal cable channel no one ever watches.)

Pakistan has its own Taliban, a dark amalgamation formed a few years ago when a dozen or more militant groups realized that Pakistan had become a rented state. Imagine the Pakistan borders of India and Afghanistan. The landscape is like a crumpled piece of paper. Foreboding, hard to access and traverse, the lunar surface is un-policeable.

While much of the antiterrorism focus has been on the Federally Administered Tribal Areas, or FATA, near the border, Taliban and al-Qaeda leaders have been killed and captured in cities like the metropolis of Karachi, the parliamentary city of Islamabad, and Lahore, in the center of the Punjab state.

In Pakistan's tribal territories a number of small independent militant groups started networking and the Tehrik-i-Taliban Pakistan (TTP) was formed, naming a crafty cat with nine lives, Baitallah Mehsud, as their leader. The Pakistani Taliban developed its own identity independent from the Afghan Taliban of Mullah Omar.

Mehsud, as his name suggests, belonged to the Mehsud Tribe in Pakistan's troubled South Waziristan region. After waging a guerilla campaign from 2006 against the Pakistani Army, and a wave of suicide bombings, Mehsud and his lieutenant Qari Hussain ruled the region as a personal fiefdom.

In an astonishing 2007 al-Jazeera TV interview, Mehsud said his ultimate aim was to attack New York City and London. In the closing days of 2008 Mehsud stepped out of the shadows of the tribal areas and masterminded the December 27 assassination of Benazir Bhutto, plunging the nation into days of mourning and setting off riots around the country. Mehsud later denied CIA accusations of involvement in the plot, but few in Pakistan believed him.

Mehsud was the most notorious militant in Pakistan, commanding as many as 20,000 Taliban fighters—and clearly more active than Osama, who was holed up in Abbottabad watching videos of himself.

After purportedly being killed in a farmhouse drone strike in January 2009, Mehsud was spotted near the Afghan border. But in August, a CIA drone fired two Hellfire missiles at a remote farmhouse where Mehsud and his second wife were sheltering. Ever notice when a bad cat encounters the dreaded tenth life, it is rarely in the company of the first wife?

The objectives of the TTP are to rid Pakistan of NATO forces, to fight the Pakistani Army, and to enforce Sharia law across the land. And yet, there have been recent signs of ambitions to incite well beyond their borders. It appears that the TTP has forged links with both al-Qaeda and the Afghanistan Taliban.

According to the Combating Terrorism Center at West Point, al-Qaeda has assumed the role of mediator and coalition builder among the Pakistani militant groups. ISI, the premier intelligence agency in Pakistan, sees al-Qaeda in the same light.

I think there is an additional businessman's explanation for the development of these syndicates. Al Qaeda is feeling the pinch, and its greatest strength may no longer be its operational capability, but rather its skill at co-opting other militant groups for their operating capabilities. It's a variation on the outsourcing theme.

We have impeded the growth of al-Qaeda by successfully interdicting cash smuggled out of the Gulf Region into Pakistan and Afghanistan. Crunching down the flow of illicit finance has harmed, but not killed, the al Qaeda network. Much of bin Laden's support came from Saudi Arabia, and there is evidence that al-Qaeda used to directly fund operations from Afghanistan. Wealthy individuals may still fund offshoots, but there are ongoing fundraising and cash-strapped pleas throughout the Webosphere.

Ayman al Zawahiri was quoted as saying, "Many of the lines have been cut off." I have read reports in which jihadists are grumbling about having to pay for their rifles and training at the camps. Al-Qaeda ain't broke, but it needs to count on the economic assistance of strange bedfellows; hence it turns to affiliate groups.

Naturally, these developments lead to a few questions.

Is al-Qaeda the driving force behind the expanding jihad of the Pakistan Taliban? Here is a group whose mission was entirely focused inside its own borders, now training young mujahideen to go and set off bombs in Times Square. Much of the Afghan Taliban leadership is holed up in the badlands of the border zone. Can Obama's plan to clear Afghanistan succeed if it ignores the criminal nexus of Taliban and al-Qaeda, which appears to operate with impunity in the "rented state" of Pakistan?

If the Taliban returns to Afghanistan, it will have a strategic rear guard of TTP and al-Qaeda in Pakistan. Afghanistan, particularly in the south, holds the great promise of the drug trade—an irresistible intoxicant to terrorist group leaders and other junkies.

Here is the Radical Centrists' informed query on how to peel apart the al-Qaeda issue in Afghanistan: Can you selectively resolve the al-Qaeda problem while ignoring the larger jihadist sea in which al-Qaeda swims?

That strategy has failed in the past and will fail in the future. You cannot possibly resolve Afghanistan without dealing with the Pakistani Taliban and al-Qaeda issue. It simply cannot be done. We have barely begun dealing with the Taliban in Pakistan.

Media Darlings

SOME BELIEVE MEDIA COVERAGE ENABLES terror. That argument sounds right until tested by the facts. The Trade Center attacks were impactful, I know. Like many of you I lost dozens of friends and colleagues that day. But when confronting a vicious and different enemy, let facts rather than emotions (however appropriate those emotions may be), drive your battle plan.

Even counting the numbers of attacks is a challenge. On the morning of August 17, 2005, there were 450 or so small bomb attacks in Bangladesh. The NCTC counts these as a single attack, while other groups count each blast. By a conservative NCTC count, there were nearly 12,000 terrorist attacks in 2008 resulting in at least 54,000 deaths, injuries, and kidnappings. The Western media missed the majority of these. After all, most happened outside the West.

In 2010, the NCTC tracked over 11,500 terrorist attacks in 72 countries with again over 50,000 victims and over 13,200 deaths. The number of attacks rose by more than five percent from 2009 but the number of deaths declined for the third consecutive year.

More than 75 percent of the world's terrorist attacks and deaths took place in South Asia and the Near East in 2010. The fewest incidents in 2010 were reported in the Western Hemisphere.

It's even tougher to monitor attackers. In 2008, for instance, over 60 percent of the terrorist attacks had unknown perpetrators. That means there were 7,000 times we could not identify or find in open source information who did the misdeed. At best, we can infer who the perps might be. But it is dead reckoning.

In 2010, Sunni Extremists committed most of all worldwide terrorist attacks and significantly increased their death toll to almost 70 percent of all terrorism related deaths.

So how can the media be complicit if it neither covers the attacks nor knows which groups are culpable? Of the remaining thousands of incidents where there is some identification, more than 150 subnational groups, some of them well-known terrorist organizations, some clandestine agents, some small subgroups not well known, are deemed to be the perpetrators.

You can rest assured, among the people not "on top" of the world of terrorists, is the Western media.

We have to be intelligent about our adversary. There are so many groups and most Americans see only one.

Try any list of terrorist organizations and it runs page after page after page, single-spaced. They are sometimes linked, sometimes not. The designations often used to describe these groups, like "Sunni extremist," conjure either the answer "who cares?" or "no shit!" It is the opposite of too much information.

Sheer numbers do little to help. A pipe bomb that explodes, killing no one, carries the same statistical weight as one with an awful body count. Some cells may fall off the stats one year but that doesn't mean they have been successfully policed. It may mean that the cells are dormant waiting for the next Atta or the next opportunistic moment where an Anwar Sadat will be exposed.

The standard rules of engagement do not apply. Repeat ten times.

And for those who simplify the battle against terrorism as another proxy for "Islam against the rest of us," consider this fact: Well over 50 percent of the victims killed and injured in terrorist attacks in 2008 were Muslim. In 2010 Muslims continued to bear the brunt of terrorism because most terrorist attacks occur in predominantly Muslim countries. Many attacks are on Muslims *by design.*

The demographics of terrorist victims yield other fascinations: At least two-thirds are believed to be civilians rather than combatants or military. And most shocking of all, children remain disproportionately affected by terrorism. Terrorists specialize in hurting innocent Muslim kids. So much for the holy war against the infidels.

Are there trends in terrorism worth noting? One general trend is for vehicle-borne over person-borne suicide bombs—though in Iraq, Western military forces thwarted these attacks by targeting factories making the car-borne devices. So terrorists shifted their insurgency to person-borne devices.

Repeat this too: Terrorists adapt.

Another trend is the increasing use of women as suicide bombers. Women have been able to hide behind cultural restrictions on physical contact to circumvent security procedures. A more disturbing trend is the growth of high-fatality attacks. The media and even the public have developed attention immunity to the small, highly targeted, unclaimed attack.

How We Respond: Adapt or Die

AROUND THE WORLD TERRORISTS ARE upping the ante and we need to redouble our efforts. Terrorists are more linked by clan or creed than by country. Attacking a nation state is the old model and may simply mean the cockroaches move to another flag of convenience.

The need for precision bombs, stealth operations, and the ultimate killer app—the unmanned air vehicle, the predator drone—suggests that our time-honored method of fighting one state in defense of another won't work. We need the opposite of a Star Wars Missile Defense, constructed to combat an evil empire. In World War I, the cavalry charged the tanks and lost. Now we're back fighting the cavalry but our tanks don't work against them. We have to think more like tribal chieftains going after one another: nimble, mobile, and fast.

Note our military response to 9/11. The national mood meant it was impossible in practical terms for President Bush not to authorize a major military response. Someone was going to get invaded. We went into Afghanistan to look for al-Qaeda and we hunted for bin Laden at Tora Bora with 15,000-pound Daisy Cutters, a sledgehammer to crack a nut if ever there was one. A second, more questionable, response was to invade Iraq, another sovereign state, this time with no established links to 9/11.

These were the anachronistic responses of a major power, understandable perhaps, because we were attacked in a way unlike anything we had ever experienced. But establishing vast military front lines thousands of miles from home has been costly: 4,474 servicemen and women dead in Iraq; 1,646 in Afghanistan, with tens of thousands wounded. Civilian casualties are horrific.

Radical Centrists should be enthusiastic proponents of what has become known as the Powell Doctrine, after General Colin Powell. The doctrine includes, but is not confined to, the idea of an articulated exit strategy that permits U.S. forces to leave an engagement as quickly as possible. It is linked to another branch of the doctrine: a clear and reasonable objective. I believe we lack each of these in all three major engagements we are undertaking currently. What is our mission in each case?

Bin Laden was taken ten years later, following a painstaking intelligence effort, by Navy SEALs in two helicopters. In doing this mission, we had adapted. We invaded the airspace of our ally Pakistan and got our man. The massive military presence on the ground really hadn't been a factor. We have become a warrior to be feared in a different way than shock and awe.

The last two major terrorist incidents in the U.S., an aborted airline attack on Christmas Day and the 2010 Times Square attempt, are sobering cases in point. Count them as terror research and development. Like 9/11, these attacks threaten us at home. "We are all on the front lines" blared an advertisement in the New York papers to commemorate the tenth anniversary of 9/11 as if to both scare and warn us.

Was our wake-up call from hell so exquisitely timed to coincide with the apex of American economic and military superiority? Every time we are exhorted to "stay alert and stay alive" by law enforcement are we forced to surrender just a bit more of our precious freedom?

Travel in the Middle East and Israel and such self-protection and security measures are a matter of routine. Those nations long ago surrendered to the tyranny of fear that accompanies anyone in the crosshairs of global jihad.

Our open society makes us great and makes us vulnerable: Mass gatherings like rock concerts, ball games of every type and stripe, political conventions and caucuses, religious worship in large groups, shopping malls, movie theaters, superstores . . . all are grist for suicide bombing. I shudder to think how we as a nation will manage if the suicide bomber technology catches up with us.

Because it has really been a long time since we have all been on the front line.

How We Respond: Follow the Money

TERROR FINANCE 101: FOUR BOMBS, four knapsacks, some train tickets, a few phone calls, and some petrol. Cost: under $2,000. Impact from a terrorist's perspective: priceless. Such is the cost-benefit of a terror plot that bombed a few sites in London on 7/7 in 2005.

The range of cost estimates for the 9/11 attacks ran from $500,000 to nearly a million dollars. The resultant impact on the American economy was at least $150 billion.

When you compare the impact versus that of conventional warfare, you can appreciate the dark economic appeal to the twisted minds of terrorism.

There is an old proverb, which seems to drive the economics of terrorism in an age of heightened alert and media-centric masterminds: Kill one . . . frighten 10,000.

Unfortunately, the costs are but one indication of the added complexity of fighting a terror network.

The true economics, of course, tell a different story. The financial support these groups require goes far beyond the paltry sums spent on specific attacks, whether they are around the corner or around the world.

Terrorists require two things to maintain their reign: sustained funding, and lots of it. Between attacks, they need resources to support their operatives and their kin. They must also provide funding for recruitment, training, travel, indoctrination, and of course, the occasional bribe to get across a border or forge papers. A river of money flows through many tributaries.

There are always two key elements, like the positive and negative charges of a detonator, at work in even the smallest, most clandestine cells. Terrorism is the connection of sinister hands and money. Cut either or both, and the cell will die, or at least transmute to another place.

As we have seen with al-Qaeda, pinching the money flow works.

But how is terrorism financed? Though charity begins at home, terrorism in the modern age has taken on a potent new aspect. Terror's tradition is within its own borders with militants focused on dismembering a home regime. But the jihadists have reconceived it as an export product, and that means money must not only change hands, but also cross borders.

To the discerning eye that means one thing: a money trail.

Following terrorist funds is much harder today than even a few years ago. Many obvious institutional sources have been identified and corralled by the Patriot Act and other money laundering initiatives like the Financial Action Task Force (FATF) in Paris and Money Val, a body set up by the Council of Europe.

Throughout the world, charity is required of all good Muslims through a system called zakat: an Islamic tithe specifying at least 2.5 percent of one's earnings every year. Many of the tens of thousands of charities have connected to networks so that funds flow freely, particularly as the diaspora of Islam takes its followers far from their native lands. The PLO, al-Qaeda, and Hezbollah have also established their own international network of charities.

But there are more sophisticated networks even as charities multiply, and selected mosques provide cover for illegal cash shipments. Some are honest mosques with Imams who dishonor their well-intentioned donors. Others hide behind an air of respectability, threatening lawsuits to cause writers and publishers to cower even as they dispense the funds. These charities are funding sources, but many complain bitterly about being singled out. Having a black mark virtually assures serious loss of donations.

Once upon a time, donations from individuals and charities were the largest source of funding for terrorism. Some sources claim only a few hundred of the tens of thousands of Islamist charities are providing support to known terrorist organizations; and the charities themselves have gotten pretty nimble. Nevertheless, hundreds of millions of dollars have been frozen.

Just as terrorist cells morph, so has terrorist finance evolved.

Enter the Hawala, an informal exchange that is extremely effective at moving money but very hard to trace. Particularly when the Hawala requires no social security number and no account number, and leaves no trail since the money never leaves the United States, this becomes an almost invisible river of dough. Most of these exchanges are benign, but they take place in the shadows and are tailored for terror.

Here's how a Hawala works. It is so simple it's frightening. Say you wanted to get $5,000 to a buddy in Lahore or Kabul. Since you or another member of the Hawala conduct business in both places, someone gives your friend $5,000 in Lahore and you pay $5,000 here. Money has been moved without changing hands in a traceable way; there is no official record and no official border crossing, so no money trail.

Now super-Hawalas have been created where peer-to-peer transactions are capable of being executed in anonymity.

Many other accounts are paid through a vast network of men and women sending money orders for under $10,000 from the U.S. back home. In that size, transactions are not reported and are hidden amidst millions of clean transactions where folks are "sending money home to support their families."

The U.S. Treasury is trying. About seven years ago, they set up the Executive Office of Terrorist Financing and Financial Crimes. They also created Operation Green Quest, a multiagency terrorist financing task force. The Treasury has even gone so far as to work with the Afghan Central Bank to license and track Hawalas. Let's hope the "multi" in multiagency is acting in greater concert than elsewhere in our government.

Another source of cash is narco-terrorism finance. Remember that Afghanistan is the Google of heroin production, accounting for over 80 percent of what is sold in Europe, and over 70 percent of what's sold worldwide. Terrorist propinquity to the poppy is as addicting as the drug itself. Terrorists have gone from shielding the heroin trade to partaking in it. Heroin is a multibillion-dollar cash business, which already attracts the worst people in the world.

Is this a party the terrorists can afford to miss?

Reports of al-Qaeda involvement in the Afghan poppy trade come from every part of the countryside, particularly in southern Afghanistan. Another cash crop of choice for the terrorist coffers is the production of methamphetamine.

Akin to narco support are illicit operations around the globe. They range from the darkest—extortion, kidnapping, smuggling, and prostitution—to the less sinister, but still lucrative world of counterfeit, video piracy, credit card, and ID theft. These activities signal a new development in terror: self-financing.

Once, a cadre of mysterious donors and "fund managers" for al-Qaeda managed major funding across borders. Now, terror has franchised itself, creating its own funds flow from an array of petty and serious crime practiced on a local level. Dealing with tiny unidentified cash transactions makes these local franchisees even harder to trace.

Endless mutation, like some financial biology, helps terror elude capture. It is a ceaseless and nimble enterprise—imagine Apple on steroids—with a singular mission: avoiding discovery.

Another source of terrorist funding is the states we know and others we suspect. Iran and Syria support terror, and many have suspicions about Saudi Arabia. Some of these states use terror as a political weapon to achieve their goals and exert influence at home. Some, such as Pakistan, host training camps and other activities while turning a blind eye. Sometimes the Pakistani blind eye is turned just blocks from its most prestigious military institute.

Afghanistan provided an extraordinary petri dish for expansion of terrorism during the period commencing in the 1990s when the Taliban exerted its control. Radical Islamic groups like al-Qaeda used the country as their operational and training base.

Iraq is an interesting study. The U.S.-led invasion of Iraq caused a focus of terrorist activities from terror groups around the world. Accusations abound that Iran is supporting terrorist activities in Iraq. Other areas of support are unregulated commodity markets like precious stones. There is a vast market of illegal trade in these portable commodities.

As an extension, we are finding increasing examples of legitimate businesses operating as fronts for sinister work. The cleansing of money through legitimate and illegitimate means calls to mind a rare apt comment from Paul Wolfowitz: "Al-Qaeda is not a snake you kill by lopping off its head but a disease that has spread to many infected parts of a healthy body."

How We Respond: Drone Wars

BEHEADING THE SNAKE VERSUS FIGHTING a disease leads to a sensitive subject: The Predator Drone.

In both Bush terms, fewer than 45 drone strikes were ordered in the FATA and Obama surpassed 200 in Pakistan alone in his first two-and-a-half years. Drone strikes raise the issue of civilian casualties, and of secret targeted assassination.

The United Nations senior official for extrajudicial executions, Philip Alston, in July 2010, called for the United States to explain the legal rationale for what he characterized as a "vaguely defined license to kill" in the CIA's campaign of drone strikes in northwest Pakistan, a country with whom we are not actually at war.

The drones have claimed a number of victims including civilians and Mustafa Abu al Yazid, an Egyptian founding member of al-Qaeda who served as the group's number three. Also at the receiving end of a drone missile that May 2010 morning in North Waziristan were Yazid's wife, three daughters, and a grandchild. These civilian casualties provided Alston and others both inside and beyond the Pakistani borders with ammunition against the strikes.

In Yemen September 2011, a CIA drone killed American citizens Anwar al Awlaki and Samir Khan, two al-Qaeda operatives. Their death reenergized debate on drones and killing U.S. citizens.

The gild on the lily is that we are killing a higher proportion of bad guys and fewer civilians than in targeted combat, but anyone calling drones a surgical strike is misleading themselves. Drones are personal attacks, they are directed, they are targeted, but they are not hand-to-hand. Collateral loss of lives is a virtual certainty. These attacks occur in the targets' home, office, car, or social gathering place.

But they are an effective way to kill terrorist leaders if you can stomach the excess loss of life necessary to prosecute these missions. Criticisms leveled at the Obama administration, the CIA, the drone manufacturers, and the desktop operators of the unmanned equipment, all have a basic emotional appeal, but they ignore a powerful counterpoint.

There are men, women, and sadly but increasingly, children who are arming themselves and training themselves to kill us. Chief among their targets are innocents, or noncombatants. Traditional acts of war cannot work in allaying or removing these enemies from their positions to harm us.

Drones kill with precision relative to conventional combat, especially nonprecision bombing, but they are rarely solo killers. It should go without saying, but neither the Pakistani government, nor their intelligence apparatus, nor even parts of their army have been blocking the stepped-up American use of the unmanned attack. There are moral questions and practical ones, too, when evaluating the execution of this new style of war.

But there is an even more important overarching question regarding the strategy of targeted attacks on terror leaders: Are they effective?

How We Respond: Beheading the Snake

LET'S BACK UP AND LOOK at the bigger picture first: Can the systematic killing of an organization's leadership cause the collapse of a sinister enterprise?

Ariel Sharon had a similar plan to dismantle Hamas command by selective pruning and assassination. Forget the killing of so many rank-and-file Hamas members, and follow the pattern of attacks on the leaders. In July of 2002, the house of Hamas military leader, Salah Shehade, was bombed by an Israeli missile, killing him and 14 others. The loss of civilian lives was condemned by Ari Fleischer in the United States and by the UN.

In short order, Mohammad Deif took Shehade's post as military leader. In a September Israeli air strike, he was badly injured, but he recovered. In August of 2003 Ismail Abu Shanab, the public face of Hamas, was killed in a targeted air strike. Tens of thousands of Palestinians took to the streets to protest.

In March of 2004, Sheik Ahmad Yassin, the spiritual leader of Hamas, was killed by an Israeli missile aimed at his passing car; protests broke out everywhere in Gaza City. The very next day Abdel Aziz Rantisi was named his successor. A month later, he and his 27-year-old son, Mohammad, were killed by an Israeli missile attack. The combative Dr. Rantisi spent most of his four weeks as Hamas leader in hiding before he was blown to pieces in his car by an Apache helicopter. Again, there was a powerful Palestinian response. Reports had youths plastering Dr. Rantisi's martyr poster on every flat wall in Gaza.

On September 26 of that same year, a senior Hamas military leader, Izz Eldine Subhi Sheik Khalil, was car bombed in a plot later ascribed to Israeli Intelligence.

There were soldiers and civilian supporters who died by the thousands during Sharon's deliberative parallel process to eliminate its leadership. But something profoundly ironic was occurring: each Israeli killing of a Hamas leader only seems to have enhanced the street popularity of Hamas in Gaza.

There was something more compelling that drew the Palestinians to Hamas. The militant group ran a large network of social programs including schools and medical clinics. For many Israelis, these charitable initiatives were a detestable sham. But to a more important audience it was a defining characteristic and it signaled the fundamental flaw in Sharon's approach.

Social welfare propositions bolstered Hamas in the eyes of many Palestinians. Particularly in Gaza where the people were poor, hungry, and lacking much hope, Hamas built itself to a central and supportive role in their lives, or so they claimed.

Not surprisingly, and wisely, when the next leader of Hamas was selected, his name remained secret because the office carried very little job security.

In September of 2005, with some reluctance, Israel withdrew from Gaza. The following January, Hamas won a majority of seats in the Palestinian parliamentary elections. But for all the home-fired support, their prime minister, Ismail Haniya, has only governed the Gaza Strip since 2007.

You cannot behead a movement, only an organization.

Playing-card targets may fire up an army, but the strategy may have precisely the opposite impact of what was intended. Hamas is obviously different than the Taliban and al-Qaeda, but the central point remains: the efficacy of the killing of leaders of a terrorist movement is far less if that group is bonded to the local population.

If it is an embedded movement with strong ties to the local population, like the Taliban in Afghanistan, the drones can strike each leader, with successors popping into the next slot like PEZ. There can be massive casualties among the rank and file, but your outcome will be doubtful.

In fact, the strategy may be precisely wrong even if each assassination brings on the euphoria of revenge. Smart Centrists are results- and not revenge-oriented.

If it's a disconnected organization like the al-Qaeda in Pakistan, which is a collaborator, and let's just say less than venerated by the Pashtuns, the strategy might work. A systematic drone war may be a crucial part of a selective dismemberment of a functioning organization with "mixed" relations with the population.

History has many examples that social movements as opposed to organizations are particularly difficult to decapitate.

Terrorist sands are constantly shifting. The TTP and its affiliated groups are doing some of al-Qaeda's bidding. And the selective assaults may be the only way to drive a wedge between the parties. Particularly if we can starve al-Qaeda finances, our new war may succeed even as it alienates the UN and other parties with its nonsurgical (with civilian collateral deaths) strikes.

How We Respond: The 16-Agency, 100-Committee Front Line

SO IF TERRORIST GROUPS ARE our mortal and lasting enemies, how have we armed ourselves to do battle? Let me answer a question with two more questions: Do you know who Dennis C. Blair is? Does it matter to you that he resigned/was forced out of his position in May of 2010? His job, by the way, was one of the key recommendations of the 9/11 Commission, calling for a new director of national intelligence to "connect the dots."

Like a tree falling in the woods, Admiral Dennis C. Blair, the nation's Director of National Intelligence, responsible for the 16-plus agencies of the intelligence community—our intelligence czar—was put out, a casualty of administrative war, bureau-terrorism, and turf battles. His replacement was Lieutenant General James Clapper, former head of the Defense Intelligence Agency (DIA) and the Geospatial Intelligence Agency. The latter manages the nation's spy satellite products and output.

Are we surprised?

Clapper has run two of the 16 intelligence agencies and has enormous experience, but he is the fourth DNI in the six and a half years since the job was created (the fifth if you include Acting DCI Gompert in the summer of 2010).

All three of Clapper's predecessors are bright and experienced and, before their dismissal as head of DNI, extremely productive leaders. Sometimes, if three outstanding professionals cannot make the job work in a five-year period, it's because someone upstairs isn't looking.

Obviously we are in very good hands . . . a lot of them. You can relax—even if the executive branch is not watching, Congress is at the post. In fact, there are over 100 committees that claim some jurisdiction over the intelligence effort.

Actually, we have a very simple problem for which there is no easy or even very hard solution.

The problem is that there is no agency that considers itself responsible for tracking and identifying all terrorist threats, which is an interesting way to conduct a "war on terror." (Small mercy, but thank God we've grown shrewd enough not to call it that anymore.)

To be fair, there was a National Counter Terrorism Center set up following the 9/11 attacks with the goal of analyzing and integrating all of the terrorism information the government has. Thankfully, we had a test run on Christmas Day 2009, when Umar Farouk Abdul Mutallab was allowed to board Northwest flight 253 to Detroit and light his pants on fire. Happily, a citizen was able to prevent what our intelligence apparatus could not.

I am not sure it was the fact of the aborted homicide bombing attempt (I prefer the term to the suicide bombing moniker because it amplifies the criminality) or the following statement that lost Blair his job: "Institutional and technological barriers prevent seamless sharing of information." Essentially he told the truth, which is why he was forced out.

A Senate Intelligence Committee report, and follow-up reports citing Democratic Senator Dianne Feinstein and ranking Republican Kit Bond said, ". . . there were systemic failures across the intelligence community that failed to detect the threat. . . ." There is a glaring issue and we have not solved it. Tom Kean, former co-chair of the 9/11 Commission, shared his exasperation with me. Publicly he has been no less measured: "If we don't get our act together, we're going to be in serious trouble."

Let's face it. People were unharmed in recent terrorist attacks mostly because the perpetrators were total incompetents. Counting on continued inept terrorists is a bad strategy.

We have been in possession of the 9/11 Commission recommendations since 2004 and Congress has done nothing meaningful on intelligence reform. So, ladies and gentlemen of the Congress, the executive branch, and the Intelligence services, I have a simple question: What is more important to protect, your country or your turf?

The role of the Director of National Intelligence is a key position, but needs a bit of airing out. So let's open the window and let some sunlight and truth in. Some people want a Spook Daddy; a superstrong boss who through sheer force of personality and some authentic Presidential backing can order folks around and change things.

Let's get real on a few points. With respect to Presidential support, it just has not been there. President Obama consistently sided with his CIA chief, Leon Panetta (until he made him Defense Secretary), and his Deputy National Security Adviser, John Brennan. Blair was often the last to know about CIA predator attacks and other direct action programs. Often he was not informed until after the strikes had taken place.

The historical circle of covert action ordered or sanctioned by the president and carried out by the CIA remains unbroken.

Here are two problems implicit in leaving CIA covert authorities intact: First, Congress created the office of DNI with certain license, which is being ignored. Second, there is no ability to pre-evaluate the wisdom of an attack or, more important, to assess the effectiveness of the actions of the CIA.

Sharon's step-by-step surgical dismantling of Hamas leadership had exactly the opposite outcome than was intended, and yet there was little mechanism for anyone to assess the effectiveness of Arik's plan.

Gelding the DNI means we botched a reorganization of the Intelligence community.

How We Respond: Empower the DNI

SOME GREAT STRIDES WERE MADE shortly after 9/11. But just as terrorists adapt, so, too, does the protective instinct of the Intelligence community. Hindrances have a pesky way of creeping back if left unchecked, and they have. No less an expert than Homeland Security Committee Chairman Joe Lieberman warned: "Perceived ambiguities regarding the DNI's authorities must be resolved."

Even with presidential support there is the simple reality to consider: No Spook Daddy will ever get 16 Intelligence agencies to bend to his unilateral will. Virtually none of the leaders actually work for the DNI. They all have their own bosses and their own chain of command, so a little business management sensibility must be brought to the task.

The role of the DNI is merely a coordinator unless there is a meaningful budget.

Any effective DNI must have at least four things:

1. The president must be a staunch supporter and view the role as a valuable part of the entire process, which means no shadow DNI among his team (this means you, John B.).

2. An excellent rapport with the CIA director (this means you, General Petraeus). The CIA has always been the head of the Intelligence community, but this DNI construct was designed to change that imbalance of power. Nevertheless, the CIA director remains the gorilla.

3. The ability to know the Intelligence community but also to step away and make critical evaluations without feeling treasonous to his clan.

(This means you, Defense Department with eight separate intelligence units: Army, Navy, Air Force, Marines, National Geospatial, National Reconnaissance, National Security, and of course, DIA.)

And you, Homeland Security with two units: Coast Guard Intelligence and Office Of Intelligence and Analysis.

And you, too, State Department and Bureau of Intelligence. It means you, Department of Justice with the FBI and the DEA.

It means you, the Department of Energy with the Office of Intelligence and Counter Intelligence.

And finally, it means you, Treasury Department with the Office of Terrorism and Financial Intelligence.

The CIA is the only independent agency of the government. The others are offices and bureaus within vast executive departments of the federal government, which naturally leads to the final requirement.

4. The DNI needs an extremely artful management style since he is an influencer without sufficient heft to enjoy the privilege of command. The key to the DNI is not that the office be a micromanager of intelligence—with its far-flung mandate, it quite simply can't. And whether it sits near the President in the West Wing or within BlackBerry range in an outpost in Tyson's Corner, the DNI must conduct evaluation. It must have a voice in the overall direction and prosecution of this battle.

The DNI must create a system of teamwork, of collectors, of information across various silos and departments within the disciplines: Signal intelligence, human intelligence, geo-spatial intelligence, financial intelligence, and narco-intelligence. You get the picture.

The FBI and DEA cannot hold out on Defense.

When fellow agencies ask to withhold the passport of a man flying on Christmas Day and the State Department refuses to do so for its own agenda, who breaks the tie?

Adjudicating disputes is a key part of winning in the war between ourselves. There must be a passion to follow a stream of threat to its conclusion, even when it crosses the boundaries and adjacencies of other departments.

In his defense, General Clapper has reimagined the DNI job. Like his mentor, former Defense Secretary Bob Gates, Clapper has demonstrated a willingness to cut waste in his office. He trimmed the roster of deputy directors for national intelligence from four to one. He created an integration effort in a new team of National Intelligence Managers (NIMs) who drive collection and analysis in 17 subject areas.

These NIMs combine the supervision of collection and analysis, but without power they won't be able to deliver the goods.

Another key recommendation of the 9/11 Commission was for Congress to create an oversight of the 100 or so committees that monitor the nation's intelligence effort. Rather than consolidate the authorization and appropriation in the House and Senate Intelligence Committees, as the Commission recommended, the two activities remain separate.

And if you wanted something as simple as the answer to the question "What is the makeup of our intelligence budget?" the answer lies buried deep inside the separate budgets for the Defense, Treasury, State, Homeland Security, and other departments.

Which means the answer is not available in detail even though the unified national intelligence budget is a matter of public record. The Senate Intelligence Committee apparently recommended moving to a single intelligence appropriation for 2010, but the idea failed on the floor.

Unsurprisingly, with the creation of such a huge department as Homeland Security, there have been pork, waste, and senseless anomalies. A *Denver Post* article in September 2011 noted that while Colorado had received $354 million in Homeland Security money in the ten years since 9/11, it can't account for what much of it was used for. The paper did note that $11,250 was spent on terror-busting fridge magnets and $54,000 on a trailer that sat unused for four years and is now occupied occasionally by deputies patrolling elk and deer hunters.

Such idiocy obscures the fact that the state as a whole is better prepared for a major disaster, terrorist-inspired or otherwise. Still, within the state, more money was spent per capita protecting far-flung rural areas than Colorado Springs, home to four military bases and the Air Force Academy. And Wyoming in recent years has received twice as much money per head as New York and six times as much as New Jersey.

Looking over the Commission's major recommendations for Congress ten years after the assault on my home city, I see that nothing major has been adopted.

Congress preserves and protects Congress. So we can all rest easy.

How We Respond: Twenty-first Century Solutions

BY MANY YARDSTICKS WE HAVE caused injury to al-Qaeda and other terrorist groups. We have hurt their purse and thwarted many of their leaders, but they are an adaptive breed. Though al-Qaeda has yet to execute any operation on the scale and scope of 9/11, they are far from a one-hit wonder. Al-Qaeda has launched far more attacks since 9/11 than prior.

They are doing their best to collaborate and outsource in the face of diminished resources.

There is still a dark shadow chasing us. These people write with glee about executing us, and dream rapturously of shedding our blood. They are a mortal and hidden enemy who spend every waking moment imagining ways to kill us. Al-Qaeda is willing to compromise, be flexible, and adapt in order to harm us.

Are we willing to be as flexible and nimble to protect ourselves?

Take terror threads. The analytics and records that lead to identifying and tracking terrorists must be seamless. The Terrorist Identities Datamart Environment (TIDE) must be accessible. The way we are tracking individuals does us a disservice.

The UN's 1267 List is comprised of roughly 370 individuals and entities associated with al-Qaeda. These folks are subject to asset freezes and travel restrictions. Let's face it: this is a black list. Maybe it's the way we have to go, but the task is to keep track and follow, and sometimes not to let on that we know who they are.

Lists of names lack that level of sophistication. Congress must reassess its polyglot empire. Too many cooks and too many committees make change an impossibility.

There is another absolute need, which is appalling because we have the ability, but neither the will nor the near-term funds to fix it: we are plagued by disparate and disconnected information and communication systems. When you realize that each of these 16 intelligence "elements" has its own official seal, then you can begin to appreciate the intractability of their data mining and storage.

Yet technology will help us win this battle. The traditional industrial approach to espionage and war won't prosper in fighting terror. We are not in need of a battlefield solution, at least not in tracking terrorists. The War on Terror, which the Obama administration has taken pains to leave behind, is an outdated model. Terrorism is vanquished by ever-vigilant policing, tracking, intelligence monitoring, and arrest—and sometimes direct attack.

We should combine U.S. military presence with a collaborative local military—a light footprint rather than a massive battlefield solution.

But Libya and Pakistan may be more of the future model for combating terrorism. Obviously in Iraq and Afghanistan that has not been our approach. In Libya time will tell whether our role in toppling Gaddafi will really translate into good relations with the emerging government. And Pakistan's dance between its occasional U.S. ally and its domestic jihadist keeps switching from a samba to a tango—and with all that shuffling back and forth, more than just a few toes are trampled upon.

Perhaps Libya and Pakistan will be exemplars for future Middle East allies of the United States—they, not quite ours, and we, not quite theirs, either.

It's time to upgrade our phones too. Central to the policing and arrest model, and even to the drone approach, is world-class communications and effective, flexible technology. Legacy systems, which do not permit peer-to-peer interaction, reaffirm the old industrial silo approach to prosecuting an intelligence operation.

We are fighting a whole new enemy and we have to guard against looking like the 1776 British, draped in their crimson easy-to-target finery, kneeling in row after succeeding row of effortlessly targetable lines.

One avenue that we still leave wide open is cyber terror. We know that our grid of electrical production is exposed. We know, too, that terrorists have shut down electricity in cities in Brazil. But companies in private industry are outside the vision of our defense forces. What are the safeguards on our 2,400 drinking water and waste treatment plants? Chlorine gasses and other highly toxic industrial ingredients are owned by companies whose compliance with Homeland Security is entirely voluntary.

Congressman Jim Langevin chairs a committee of the House, which reviews the matter and considers the electricity suppliers beyond lax in protecting our citizenry. He freely acknowledges that he has caught major companies lying to Congress about their degree of preparedness and protection. He told me: "Their priorities are simply different than my priorities for Homeland Security."

We need leaders who wrestle with these vexing problems. We need a public-private partnership to fix these glaring holes in our shield of defense. The trouble with fighting terrorists is that much of their most devious work is conducted in the quiet of places only accessible by drone technology. Their leaders don't engage on the field of battle. House-to-house searches are like hunting with beaters: the tigers always hear the clanging and escape.

We know that terrorists prefer to strike noncombatants and that the USS *Cole* incident in 2000 was a rarity. We need to clearly assess our vulnerabilities and protect them. We never considered a commercial airliner a weapon of mass destruction until it was. So, too, a chemical or consumer products company that uses vast amounts of chlorine gas, or an electric utility, or a water treatment facility has not been considered weaponry in our lexicon. But in the language of our enemies, these are implements for destruction.

Our understanding of the language of war must be as fluent as theirs. At the moment we are behaving like illiterates and it's time to get hooked on the new phonics.

Radical Centrists must reject the orthodoxy of both parties. Start by following the potent and appropriate recommendations of the 9/11 Commission. We have tolerated dysfunction and petty bickering for too long. Looking to Congress to react with prudence and decisiveness is like waiting for Godot only with less point. The right and the left are frozen in process.

When your mortal enemies change faster than you change your defenses, you're dead.

The passage of an uneventful decade since an empowered handful of terrorists briefly brought us to our knees is cold comfort. You can argue that we've been lucky rather than good. Despite its $80 billion budget, there were about 25,000 security breaches at airports from 2001 to 2011—prohibited items or people getting past the TSA.

Since we all serve on the front lines we need to focus on twin adversaries: those who wish us harm, and an intractable bureaucracy of those charged with protecting us. Both will require courage.

We are locked in a non-war against a non-army fighting a non-strategy. The enemy never sleeps and our defense should never rest. Everything we expect from a combatant has been stripped away, like a cake with no ingredients. Yet for all its nihilism and nothingness, terrorism is a lethal foe.

Both political parties have been "soft on terror" because they have allowed complacency to displace courage.

They have resisted change and strangled common sense with bureaucratic process. They have authorized the spending of more than a trillion dollars as if motion alone is enough. They have allowed federally mandated departments to run roughshod over the natural need for efficiency and they have sent thousands of our finest to their death without making the necessary changes at home.

The right and the left may lay claim to the weapons and the armaments, they may boast the appropriation and the budgetary authority. They may even claim to have the support of the people.

But they lack the common sense to win a war against a nimble enemy. All the jawboning and deal cutting in the world won't trump a common sense solution.

You have to become part of the mission—move antiterror security issues to the forefront. Jihadis don't target military personnel. They target you, your family, and your employees. What have you done about it? What is your local threat exposure? Don't be one of the ones who asks the right questions too late—that automatically makes them the wrong questions. You have to boldly inquire about your drinking water, your electricity, your local nuclear plant. If you don't, it likely won't be done.

Have the courage to protect you and yours and do not trust your government to get it right. There will be push-back. You will hear a litany of "There, there's." But self-defense is a non-delegable act.

And that is why the Center may turn out to be the home of the brave.

CHALLENGE SIX
Political Hack: Tobacco Road to Ruin

THE WOMAN WHO LOVED ME *more than any person, until I met my wife, lay still as dawn surrounded by her seven children. Every 30 seconds or so, the absolute stillness was disturbed by a single drawn breath, like the opposite of a sigh.*

Pachelbel's Canon in D wafted in from another room, providing a melodic sentence which the twice-a-minute wheeze sharply punctuated. It was as if her air was interrupted. She was home and loved and prayed for with every fervent wish with which a young adult might hope to save their mother.

Our prayers would not be answered.

Ravaged to a double-digit weight, robbed of the sweeping mane of gray glamor that once framed her now angular face, reduced beyond effectiveness of stray tissue and contaminated flesh, shunted and shot through with poison cures and toxins, seared by radiography, scarred inside across the fading heaves of her lungs and choked by the cancer that would take her at any moment, lay the woman who had birthed and nursed me across a thousand childhood terrors. I have never felt more useless.

She was at peace and I, underneath the placid moment, was yet again at war.

Drawn together with our spouses and siblings, the seven of us formed a handheld circle and prepared ourselves for the inevitable.

It did not come with a thunderclap, or any sound and fury.

When it was over, the 30-second gasps grew shallower, and then the space between them went to a minute, then two . . . and then forever.

No matter how old you are, when you become an orphan, your history dies.
And beloved as I have been by the most adoring wife and children, when
my mother's spark expired, something inside of me expired too.

I SHOULD TELL YOU WHAT you may well have surmised already: My
mother came of age in a postwar generation that glamorized and encouraged smoking. I remember my grandmother, a writer long before that was
a common profession for women. In her book, *Common Sense for Mothers*,
she opined that nothing could be more glamorous or alluring on a woman
than, "a well-smoked cigarette . . ."

We have come a long way, baby.

As I compared the image of each cool and languorous drag, each careful
tug on a lipstick-stained Lucky with the gasping death rattle that coursed
through my mom in those endless minutes of waiting, it was like hearing a
music box turn with a tune until its exhausted coil left the last solitary note
hovering in the air.

I know this like I know my name: Cigarettes killed my mother.

I recollect Sunday trips to Mass in a wood-paneled station wagon, all
seven of us, each a variation on the same facial theme, all dressed in some
sort of parallel manner against the winter chill. The windows were rolled up
and frosted. There, way in the front of the endless expanse of 1960s automobile, were both my parents puffing away with the windows shut. We sat there
hermetically sealed against the elements, repurposing my parents' exhalant
as if it were God's fresh air.

It's no wonder when the time came for sprouting, I squinted my eyes
against the Marlboro light and drew on a borrowed Winston with the practiced expertise of a washed-up prize-fighter.

From age 16 to my late 20s, but for occasions of athletic endeavor, I was
never far from a Camel, my father's bone of choice.

It took my loving wife and a page from *Lysistrata* to get me to at long last
quit in our honeymoon year. I was addicted like I never imagined, both with

a killer craving that ached through my bones when I first went without, and with something more. Cigarettes hooked me as a nervous silence-filler and tough-guy accessory, right down to my first morning hack and expectorant.

I was a Marlboro Man all right, and everywhere was Marlboro Country.

Today, 18 years after my mom's last note played, I can say with certainty that there is no single consumer product I can think of which causes damage and shortens life every single time we use it—in moderation or not—except cigarettes.

The Smoking Gun

WHATEVER YOU THINK YOU KNOW about cigarette smoking, you do not know the facts. You have been professionally, expertly, and fiendishly misled.

Today, the number of smokers hovers at around 20 percent of our nation's population. A more interesting subset is the eight million people who are sick and disabled as a result of tobacco use. Smoking kills about a person every minute in America.

It looks as though things have improved. Smokers used to puff on a pack a day on average in the early 60s and today they consume about 13 cigarettes daily. That trend sounds like an improvement—perhaps.

In 1995, about 35 percent of high school students smoked, long after health warnings and widespread understanding of cancer statistics was promulgated. Today, about 20 percent of high schoolers still smoke, and that decline has stalled.

One third of those high schoolers will die prematurely of tobacco-related disease, according to the CDC.

Gone is leather-jacketed Joe Camel, the cartoon dromedary with the penis-shaped nose. But there is little to stop the $12 billion per annum tobacco marketers spend on peddling their product.

Antismoking campaigns have faded into the background like 33-rpm record albums.

Not that it's easy to be a smoker these days. Half of the U.S. population lives in places where smoking is banned in workplaces, bars, and restaurants, and that noose is tightening. In 2011, New York City banned smoking in its parks, and Los Angeles and Chicago have similar restrictions underway. What's more, a recent survey said 70 percent of Americans don't allow smoking in their homes, including many current smokers.

This sounds like we have turned smokers into pariahs: picked on, singled out, another group of decent Americans deprived of their life and liberty. A few inquiries raise more questions than they answer.

Several government studies show that 70 percent of the nation's 46 million smokers say they want to quit and about 40 percent try every year.

How do they fare? Not too well. Monkeys like it on your back. Those same surveys say only about 2.5 percent kick the habit.

Decades ago, tobacco companies responded to rising popular awareness about what havoc their products brought on our bodies by introducing so-called "light" cigarettes. Following on the strength of light beer, it seemed natural that consumers would sooner take less than give up altogether.

And take less they did. In one of the most dramatic shifts in consumer product history, light cigarettes captured 90 percent of the U.S. market. Never before was one product so hungrily adopted to replace another.

There was just one problem. It was total bullshit.

Study after survey after study has shown that among the many reasons for the overwhelming shift was consumer belief that light cigarettes were safer. The National Cancer Institute of the NIH said design changes made to "light" cigarettes didn't make them less likely to cause disease. The manufacturers made a fuss about lower tar levels and yes, a smoking machine measured less tar from a light cigarette than from a regular cigarette. But as the NCI noted, "People don't smoke cigarettes like a machine," and tar levels rise "if the smoker takes long, deep, or frequent puffs." Smoking machines don't have nic fits.

The FDA finally figured out what everyone already knew: the light cigarette bonanza was predicated on a very basic falsehood. And the FDA took decisive action sure, swift, and certain to change a 90 percent market share product in a niche serving a scant 46 million nicotine addicts.

What was their Gideon's trumpet? What Vulcan sword struck big tobacco injustice?

As of the summer of 2010—are you ready for this?—the word "light" and its descriptive stepbrothers "mild" and "low" were banned from the labeler's lexicon.

Happily for those hugely infringed-upon consumers, the silver, pale green, or sky-blue packaging evocative of all that is light and breezy, and inextricably coded and linked in many smokers' minds with the mistaken belief in healthier cigarettes, gets to remain.

Never let it be said that the FDA pulled a punch when it came to tobacco regulation. I sleep better knowing they are at the post. I want them on that wall; I need them on that wall. And at cocktail parties I can't wait to talk about how boldly and bravely the new regulators of tobacco products have protected me and mine.

Now, it's worth taking a moment to review the facts, because whenever so many are claiming victory there is a chance that the real losers are covering up. Or as Warren Buffett famously advises, if after ten minutes at the poker table you don't know who the sucker is, then the sucker is you.

We hear both big tobacco and antismoking advocates crowing that they have cut the percentage of smokers from 42 percent of adults in 1965 (which is staggering when you think about it) to 20 percent in 2008—a clear victory, right?

Not so fast.

In 1965 about 50 million Americans smoked, and today the number has fallen to only . . . well, in 48 years we have reduced the number of smokers by only seven or eight percent because there are just that many more adults in the U.S. today.

That's right. Since the Mustang was introduced, only four million fewer people smoke. Their smoking volume may be down, but more than 70 percent of American smokers smoke every goddamn day.

If you subscribe, like the leadership of the CDC, to the notion that a very low rate of cigarette ingestion drastically increases the likelihood of heart attack or stroke, then dropping four million smokers in 50 years feels like not much real progress has been made, even if those remaining smokers ingest far fewer than the pack a day that their parents did.

So, from a public health perspective—pay attention, all you victory lappers—we are not really that much better off after 50 years.

How could that be? Isn't the rate of smoking dropping like a stone? Again, not so fast.

Do the math, and pay no attention to the CEO behind the curtain. It's simple: About 1,300 people die every day from cigarettes in our country, and about double that number quit daily. The offset, of course, is new smokers taking up the habit. Studies suggest about 3,600 people between the ages of 12 and 17 pick up smoking every day and new adults and failed quitters make up the difference.

That's how one of the biggest misdirections in history has been perpetrated on the American people. In report after report, I read with disgust how smoking in our country has fallen precipitously. It's pure baloney.

Volumes are way down, but the number of smokers, not so much. The youth and young adult replacement market has been crucial in keeping the number of puffers remarkably stable over a 50-year period. It's like the trenches in France in the First World War—behind the serried ranks of the fallen are more volunteers marching, however reluctantly, into the breach.

Bottom line, we still have 46 million folks who are deliberately doing something we know shortens their lives. They know it, too, and most say they want to quit.

The Dean of Michigan's School of Public Health, Kenneth E. Warner, and his colleague Dr. Steven Schroeder, went further in the *New England Journal of Medicine:* "Cigarette smoking remains by far the most common cause of preventable death and disability in the United States."

Against these numbers and a virtual scientific certainty, our FDA's response, newly empowered as they have been by no less than the President and Congress, is to ban the use of the word "mild."

Thank God they are not defending our borders.

Again, underneath all of the supposed good news is more cause for concern.

The poorer you are, the more likely you are to smoke. One third of people living below the poverty line are smokers.

Here's a news flash: in a very real way, you are paying for that.

Among military veterans in the care of the Veterans Affairs health-care system, the number of smokers is 43 percent higher than in the general population.

In case you don't know it, you are paying for that too.

According to the *New England Journal of Medicine,* there is a powerful correlation between smoking and mental illness. Smoking rates exceed 80 percent among persons suffering from schizophrenia, 50 percent plus among depression sufferers, and well over 50 percent among alcoholics.

Yep, you are paying for that as well.

We can't get people to quit smoking even when they know it might be killing them. Worse, we can't even eradicate smoking when it kills loved ones too. The National Cancer Institute says that the collateral damage from coffin nails in the form of lung cancer kills 3,000 adult nonsmokers a year in the United States, and in the form of heart disease up to 46,000 people, and causes increased risk of SIDS, pneumonia, asthma, and bronchitis, and stunts lung growth in children.

If a parent gave a kid a drug cocktail of cyanide, arsenic, benzene, carbon monoxide, and ammonia washed down with a heavy metal chaser they might face legal sanction—unless they are smoking it themselves and breathing it on the rug rats.

Thanks to the tobacco industry you are running up quite a tab. But not to worry, big tobacco has a theory that says they are actually saving you money.

That's just the kind of people they are. How can they be saving you money? Here's their rationale:

When there is such a massive participation in a life-limiting activity, it is hard not to trip over the theories of British economist Thomas Malthus who, two hundred years ago, observed that plants and animals produce far more offspring than can survive, and that man, too, is capable of overproducing if left unchecked. Malthus concluded that unless family size was regulated, famine was a certainty.

How does Malthusian math affect you?

Assessments vary when I ask the simple question: How much does smoking cost our country every year? But every measure puts the annual cost in a range of $76 billion to over $100 billion for the health-care costs alone.

So creating a cessation plan for smokers should save us a bundle right? Wrong.

Here is the ghoul calculus: smokers tend to live at least a decade less than nonsmokers. The simple math is that the costs of supporting longer-lived Americans may well outstrip the costs of smoking care.

(It says something about the nature of the debate when premature death in a large segment of the population is seen as a positive outcome.)

But even if you give big tobacco its due—which I suggest you don't—should we let the tobacco machinery hum?

Here's the Radical Centrist's answer:

So this smoking initiative may not pass the math test. Who cares? We should try and eradicate smoking for a higher purpose, because it is the right thing to do. Period.

You see, smoking is easy, and it's hard. The math you have been using is flawed and people have been profiting off your largesse.

Take a marvelous piece of business called, grandly, The Master Settlement Agreement of 1998. In it, big tobacco agreed to spend $206 billion to compensate the states for their additional health-care costs over 25 years. It's interesting to compare the present value of such a payment stream (well under a hundred billion) to our annual costs for smoking—it means the companies paid for about a year of health-care costs.

You wuz robbed. Done in by large numbers that sound good but don't stand up to inspection. It reminds me of the Million Dollar New Jersey Lottery: A dollar a year for a million years.

That's where smoking is hard. You have to force yourself to look behind the curtain, and doubt the numbers. To understand smoking in America you have to ignore the words and follow the deeds of the big dog.

ALTRIA-ISM

MICHAEL SZYMANCZYK (2010 COMPENSATION $24 million) is living proof that smoking does not stunt your growth. At 6'8," the towering former Indiana hoopster cut his teeth in consumer marketing at the premier boot camp on the planet for packaged goods, Proctor & Gamble.

P&G is the 82nd Airborne of the consumer packaged goods world. Starting there means you are drilled in the details of consumer buying, marketing communications, branding, packaging, distribution, pricing, and promotion—the entirety of the marketing mix. No one is better prepared than a multiyear P&G exec, and Szymanczyk learned his lessons well.

He was a natural at managing Philip Morris's cigarette business and he rose steadily. Just before the Master Settlement Agreement was announced with great fanfare, Szymanczyk was named head of the cigarette maker's U.S. operation.

It was the ultimate marketer's challenge. Philip Morris's reputation was in tatters even though the cash machine spewed out dollars like confetti at a wedding. His company's fall from grace would have been hard to imagine eight years prior when he joined as sales chief in 1990. Back then, Philip Morris was number two on *Fortune*'s list of most admired companies.

It would take cleverness and guile to fix what was so apparently broken. His first assignment was to embrace the reality that tobacco was harmful. The courts had already done that job for him. Nevertheless, the company did begin acknowledging that smoking kind of killed you. That charm offensive was supported by increasing moves to practice what they described as "good corporate citizenry."

And most important, the company was now a stand-alone entity separated from its corporate parent. Kraft had dexterously spun off its smoking subsidiary; the whole organization was repositioned, rebranded, and renamed. It was a new day.

It was like a corporate witness protection program. Philip Morris was living in another place with a different handle. The result was a company with an alias that sounded like a cross between that great human attribute, altruism, and an STD: Altria.

Things were definitely tough for Altria. Many avenues where Szymanczyk had learned to use his considerable marketing muscle were closed to trafficking. TV and radio had long been blocked. But now, billboards, hats, T-shirts, and a host of other mass marketing channels of communication were also foreclosed to him.

Undaunted, and confident that 75 percent of smokers continued to smoke every day, Altria soldiered on. They had a secret weapon in their marketing arsenal: customer loyalty.

I define customer loyalty as using a product even when you know it is killing you.

Skillfully using mass mailings, in-store signage, shelf positioning, product placement in movies, and a host of other clever marketing strategies, Altria was able to do something few thought possible. They made the company grow.

There are no crowds that I know of demanding to see smoking scenes in movies. But Altria has been canny about finding that same glamor in smoking that so captured my grandmother. Even when the smoking is laughably incongruous, Hollywood makes it work with the script.

Since the blistering settlement talks, how has Altria fared? Bans on indoor smoking and punishingly high federal state and excise taxes (cigarettes in New York City retail for up to $14.50 per pack) have accelerated a sectoral decline in the volume of domestic cigarette sales.

But Altria's profits are growing and the company expects to sell nearly $15 billion of cigarettes this year. It controls about 50 percent of the U.S. cigarette market. Make no mistake—Altria is the gorilla.

Which leads to the question: How in the heck can they be growing?

Two prime engines of growth are squarely on the minds of cigarette manufacturers. They have to sell more smokes to your kids, and they have to sell more overseas. And worldwide cigarette sales are rising at least two percent each year.

Philip Morris International was spun out of Altria in 2008 so that it could be free to aggressively pursue the global cigarette opportunity. This year PMI sued the government of Uruguay, calling its tobacco regulations "excessive."

What were some of Uruguay's unfair tactics? First, health warnings cover at least 80 percent of the package. Even more dastardly, the South American nation limits each brand to a single package design; no lites, ultra lites and other such falsely packaged artful dodges which might lead someone to conclude that those cigarettes are more benign than the others.

Just to be clear, the GDP of Uruguay will probably be just $30 billion this year and Altria's market value in 2011 exceeded $60 billion. That's a big gorilla happy to confront a much smaller entity—a sovereign nation.

Another company spending huge sums to clear the way for more foreign trade is British American Tobacco. If you want to howl with laughter, go to their Web site and check out the video "Who's in Control?" in the Consumers and Trade section. In it, black-garbed dealers in illegal cigarettes play tough in their Eastern European Bad Boy accents.

The video suggests that changing tobacco regulation will lead to child prostitution, terrorism, drug abuse, and death. Not since Boris and Natasha have "nogoodniks" been so amusing.

As mentioned above, another requirement for big tobacco's health is that they hook your kids on nicotine. In Indonesia, the fifth largest cigarette market, minimal regulation means that tobacco companies can appeal to children by sponsoring concerts and selling packages with cartoon characters. There is no other way to say it: if tobacco companies are not regulated they will do almost anything to reach the kids' market. They want to turn your kid into Casper.

Long gone are the days and ways that it was easy to market smoking to American minors and those just over the line. But Altria devised another marketing strategy: nicotine addiction.

The FDA and regulators have spent precious little time on the real problem—on the real reason why, since I was 16 years old, only four million fewer Americans are smoking.

That is the Radical Center of the matter. Cigarettes are nothing but one thing: a delivery system for an addictive drug. The solution whenever you face a regulatory roadblock is to search for another gateway.

Why has the FDA not aimed at eliminating the addiction rather than simply taxing and settling with the tobacco companies?

Altria figured out what every pusher knows: if you build an addiction, they will come . . . and come . . . and come. Faced with scattered but persistent resistance on the smoking front, Altria did the shrewd thing to keep in front of the youth market. It was one of the only moves left, and they executed it brilliantly.

YOU SNUS, YOU LOSE

THEY WENT SMOKELESS. THE SMOKELESS story began with a home brew of Marlboro snuff. The company figured its branding prowess was such that Marlboro had permission to go anywhere nicotine led. Unfortunately for them, only a few pinches made it into the cheeks of American youth.

Then the boys in the lab got excited by a product that first found fame long ago in nineteenth-century Sweden—the Holy Grail if you like—a smokeless *and* spit-less tobacco called snus.

Europeans first experienced tobacco when Columbus landed in Haiti in 1492. As his men beached, the locals bearing gifts bestowed dried tobacco leaves which held great value for them. (I don't believe it was payback for subjugation.)

Later Columbus's men watched Indian priests inhale powder through a tube into their noses. Whether that powder was tobacco or not, the practice of snuffing through one's nose influenced the Europeans when the plant was brought home by Spanish and Portuguese sailors.

Ironically tobacco was quickly adopted by doctors who believed the herb could cure cancer and a range of other maladies.

The French ambassador in Lisbon, Jean Nicot, was so enchanted by the product that he brought it back to help the French queen, Catherine de Medici, ease her clanging headaches. On Nicot's advice she crumbled the leaves, inhaled the powder through her nose, and the headaches disappeared. Suddenly snuff was all the rage in Paris.

The ambassador was memorialized when the plant was classified as *Nicotiana tabacum* in Latin—and fits and fiends have taken his name as their legacy ever since.

In the eighteenth century snus was a must with ladies and gentlemen of upper-class Europe—especially Sweden—and snuff apparatus became symbols of refinement and elegance. The cans became one of the most popular gifts among the monied, often executed in silver and gold with precious stones.

In the 1800s, Swedish farmers found smoking or snuffing difficult when tending the fields, and soon just a pinch made its way between the cheek and gum way, way before Nascar took off.

The first portion-packed snus was launched in 1970, which opened the door for snus use by baseball pitchers and college sophomores. It came in a little pouch and the Swedes placed it under their upper lip during those long winter months inside where spitting on the floor had a way of putting people off.

Enter Marlboro SNUS, which when said without a pouch in your mouth rhymes with papoose. Targeting adult smokers, especially those adults mature enough to not be circumspect about putting a pouch in their mouth, Altria chose the tagline, "When smoking isn't an option, reach for Marlboro SNUS."

They were clearly targeting an adult market in America.

Like, when you're in class, dude, and the teacher, like, won't let you smoke. Or like in the football stands, like, when you might get busted for lighting up. Or on the baseball field. Or, like, anytime . . . Of course what they really meant was using SNUS during a board meeting, when the other members of the Audit and Finance Committee might object to your spitting, you could simply take a pouch and very quietly put it in your mouth and get your nic fix without suffering dilution of earnings per share. Or perhaps during surgery when stepping out for a gasper is simply out of the question.

That's probably what they meant. They probably wanted the busy business professional or the life-saving surgeon as their target audience. Sure they did.

There really hasn't been a huge new product in the tobacco world since Skoal Bandits in a pouch in 1983. Snus's Scandinavian roots impart a noticeable legacy on today's American brands. Skoal of course refers to the inter-linguistic term which in Norwegian, Danish, and Swedish roughly translates to "Cheers" or "gum disease."

Many millions have been spent on the holiest of holies: the smokeless cigarette. But after years of testing, making a healthy cigarette has eluded the great minds of science. A Chinese scientist named Hon Lik invented the "electronic" cigarette in 2003. His first company, Golden Dragon, changed its name to Ruyan, meaning "to resemble smoking," or "why is that man sucking on a ballpoint pen till his eyes bulge out?"

There is just one problem with the electronic cigarette—it replaces smoke and nicotine with mist and nicotine.

As even Bill Clinton knows, sooner or later, the customer always inhales.

So in the darkest days of 2008, culminating that September when the world as we knew it ended and became the hook of an old R.E.M. song, Altria made a bold if maladroitly timed move. It purchased the market leader in smokeless tobacco, UST, for about $12 billion.

It has been a star-crossed deal, in part because Altria was swimming upstream against the financing tides. But the result when the marbles stopped spinning was impressive. Altria now controls over 50 percent of the U.S. cigarette business and over 55 percent of the admittedly smaller smokeless segment. Nevertheless they control both the drug market and the gateway drug market.

Altria has figured that it will pursue the same strategy that created the tidal wave of adoption into reduced harm alternatives like light cigarettes—and has requested permission from the FDA to do so.

Smokeless, Altria argues, is the reduced harm alternative for nicotine. (And by the way, far less regulated.) Though smokeless sales are a mere $1.2 billion for Altria, as the smoking alternative and cigarette proxy it represents another leg of growth for the big dog. And it's a highway on-ramp to the bigger market later on.

It will pay to watch the company's moves with the FDA, particularly now that mint and other smokeless flavors constitute the majority of Altria's smokeless sales. Flavors are another engine for growth. Kids love sweet flavors.

And no matter what your boys may tell you, they want Copenhagen Wintergreen between their cheek and gum.

Here is the especially hard part: nicotine is a drug of personal choice.

What in the hell can we do about smoking and still maintain every American's God-given right to ingest something we know for certain will shorten their life and likely kill them?

The Radical Center solution is no silver bullet, but rather a whole magazine of them, which can stop the menace. These techniques have extensibility beyond cigarette butts to big butts because obesity, in a caricature of itself, is ballooning in our country. Particularly among the youth and, in frightening ways, among impoverished inner-city youth.

You can see parallels between smoking and other dumb ingestions. There are similar patterns of corporations profiting off our willingness to pay for the cleanup.

ECONOMIC DRAG

SO HERE ARE A FEW recommendations.

First, the FDA has to go after the problem of nicotine as if it is fighting drug addiction. Because let's face it, it is. I cannot think of another product in America where nearly three-quarters of its consumers say they wished they could stop using it, but they just can't do it.

I've quit smoking many, many times. It's a real bitch. But remember this: ultimately everyone stops smoking.

Only sugar and alcohol appear to have the same hold on people that cigarettes do. But we all know that Ben and Jerry's in moderation, and a couple fingers of Jack Daniels, are not apt to ruin your health.

Okay, maybe they do too.

But for perspective, I read one study that said as few as three cigarettes may cause a radical shift in your health outcome.

We have to get the FDA to focus on reducing toxins in cigarettes, but more important, we have to earnestly reduce the number of smokers and the amount they smoke.

Outright prohibition won't work. We learned that the hard way with booze.

In 1919, a year before Prohibition went into effect, Cleveland had 1,200 legal bars. By 1923 the city had an estimated 3,000 illegal speakeasies along with 10,000 stills. An estimated 30,000 city residents sold liquor during Prohibition and at least 100,000 more made home brew and bathtub gin for themselves and friends.

Prohibition not only fostered widespread contempt for law enforcement, it did something far worse. It created a huge consumer market unmet by legitimate means. Organized and disorganized crime filled the vacuum created by the closure of the legal alcohol business. Worst of all, drinking during Prohibition generally increased, meaning the law did exactly the opposite of what the law intended to do.

But there are many other tools at the government's disposal.

We need to dispel the economic theory that says premature death due to smoking saves money in the long term. The Surgeon General said it best in his 2004 report: The goal of the U.S. health-care system is "prolonging disability-free life . . . thus any negative economic impacts from gains in longevity should not be emphasized in public health decisions."

The natural train of "logic" from the Malthusians who say "live and let die" to smokers is that anybody around age 65 showing any signs of sickness should be denied treatment since it is obviously the cheapest thing to do.

Another step I recommend will be exceedingly unpopular even as it is exceedingly fair.

In schoolyard parlance: "You choose . . . you lose."

If you choose to smoke, you should have to pay part of the extra cost to society. And the cost is not limited to health-care expenses.

In addition to the $100 billion health-care costs of smoking, there is a special employee bonus of another $100 billion or so in lost productivity. A study in the *American Journal of Health* of 2,500 postal employees found absentee rates for smokers were 33 percent higher than for nonsmokers.

A growing number of private and public employers are requiring employees who use tobacco to pay higher health insurance premiums. Put it this way, for every pack of cigarettes smoked, the nation has to pay $7 or more in medical care and lost productivity.

Frankly, charging smokers higher premiums will never cover the cost differential. We simply cannot charge them enough. But by adding an economic charge for the behavior, some may choose to quit. And if smokers don't pay, then we all will.

Calling a "partaking" penalty unfair and intrusive questions who we really are as a people.

As chairman of a hospital that provided millions in charity care for those who could not pay, I was always faced with trade-offs: When do you deny the care, when do the hospital's needs take precedence over the patients? These questions always came down to allocating scarce resources and to denying people who could not pay. Choosing was always tricky, but I found our caregivers naturally drawn to the patients who had a deep personal stake in getting well.

Among the many systems that should be part of tomorrow's health-care offerings, one that stands out is incentivizing health. Nothing incentivizes like an intrusive fine. And tough incentives are necessary when patients are addicted.

Many claim their right to smoke is a civil right and the government is wrong to make demands on where and how often they smoke.

Fair enough. Just pay your bar bill and be on your way.

But health-care administrators don't have to be the only heavies.

Employers can be asked to take a lead, both for their own benefit (reducing productivity loss) and for that of employees (reducing deaths). We can require employers to provide smoking cessation programs. Perhaps a combination of cessation meds with a reduction in premiums might offer an inducement.

Asking doctors to get more directly involved seems like a natural because, embarrassingly, it just ain't happening at the moment. A 2006 Robert Woods Johnson study is the most sobering of all. A survey of 1,120 primary care physicians found that only 10 percent referred patients to programs or experts to help them quit. It's time for primary care physicians to intervene.

By the way, doctors make nothing from smoking cessation plans.

We should change that too. Let's incentivize the doctors to get their patients to quit and stay quitted.

A cynic may ask why primary care docs need an incentive. Who knows? If you pay them, they might come . . . so to speak. Medicare allows eight counseling sessions over the course of a year, and cessation medicines are rarely covered. Let's pump up that process. Medicaid is the same story. About 38 states have some cessation coverage and the majority require patient cost sharing for medicines, which rules out low-income patients. It's natural to expect that states with resources such as quit lines and clinics should be a constructive force, but a closer look paints a troubling picture.

According to a Tobacco Free Kids report, no state in the union is funding tobacco prevention programs at levels recommended by the CDC. Only about nine are even at half the CDC recommendation.

Remember the Master Settlement? In theory anyway, a good portion of this $206 billion was meant to defray the costs of smoking-related sickness and to support antitobacco and smoking cessation programs.

Again, Tobacco Free Kids provides insight: "In the last ten years states have spent just 3.2 percent of their tobacco-generated revenue on tobacco prevention and cessation programs."

Let's face it—there were no guidelines, so the states did the obvious. Many sold the annuity for a "present value" sum and used the proceeds to plug one budgetary hole or another. That's right, a number of states have already spent all the money, earmarked to run to 2023.

States facing their own version of Europe's Greek tragedy will not spend settlement funds on fighting tobacco. Some states have used settlement funds to tackle diabetes and obesity, as bigger causes for concern, and not without some justification.

Sin Tax

THE STATES HAVE DEVELOPED AN addiction of their own: to smoking revenues. This year states will collect over $20 billion in cigarette taxes. In fact there are eight states which will clear more than a billion dollars apiece in cigarette taxes. Take a long drag on that, state legislators.

So what is a state to do? The least expensive and most effective "bang for the buck" thing an impecunious state or city can do is the smoking ban. In cities across the world, smoking bans have seen almost a corollary drop in cardiac hospitalizations of ten to 17 percent within a year of implementation.

So go ahead, tax like crazy. Manhattan's at about 75 cents a nail. What this country needs is a good $1 cigarette.

States need to be as creative as the companies and the consumers. Tax hikes are driving smokers to alternatives. Small cigar sales are skyrocketing, as are snuff and smokeless products. States need to be adept at taxing all tobacco products.

Watch the consumer, then tax.

States can also use high-tech tax stamps, monitor Internet sales, and watch for border crossings and sales outside of the tax net. New York State estimates it loses up to $200 million in annual revenues to Native American tribal sales. California implemented the new tech tax stamps and saw a $100 million increase in tax revenues inside of two years.

Rock on!

States also have to try and eliminate black market cigarettes. They exacerbate all the problems without anyone making any extra kwan . . . except of course for black marketers.

Jump from ingestion to digestion and states face a similar bellyache—obesity. In three years 40 percent of American adults will be obese. Forty years ago when I was a teen, about four percent of children were obese. Today close to 20 percent of kids qualify. Obesity in places like Harlem and Bed Stuy in New York is so bad that my friend Geoff Canada considers it one of the chief demons he is facing in his bold Harlem Children's Zone initiative.

Fatty food taxes and banning trans fats in restaurants help some people, but most just find a detour.

We should provide direct rewards to low-income Americans disproportionately affected by nutrition taxes. Combining domestic tariffs on offending products with shrewd rewards beats prohibition every time. Doing both decriminalizes soda pop, and rewards better choices.

We have been timid about charging companies rent for profiting from poor health choices Americans make. Commonwealth taxes on producers who profit by poisoning society are way past due.

If sinners pay sin tax, why not the Devil?

Big Tobacco's $206 billion over 25 years is not trivial, but it is just a tithe. Cigarette companies can afford to pay more than $8 billion a year. Powerful tobacco lobbyists spend over $100,000 every day Congress is in session to stop their clients from having to pay any more.

Foodies have their own agenda.

So, when Congressional lawmakers tabled a so-called Coke Tax on sugar-sweetened beverages, all they signaled is cowardice with respect to social reform. Their excuse that sin taxes don't work (they don't in isolation) means Congress didn't think globally enough.

In fact, why not get global? Joe Califano, founder and chairman of the National Center on Addiction and Substance Abuse (CASA) at Columbia University, has an even bigger idea.

His concept is simple and bold: "Mount an all fronts effort to reduce the cause of 30 per cent of sick care costs: smoking, excessive drinking and illegal and prescription drug abuse."

CASA ascribes an annual tab of $730 billion to the 72 diseases that abuse, addiction, and ingestion exacerbate.

Imagine the benefits to a strained Medicare system and the budget relief to the states attempting to support Medicaid to the poor. Huge portions of Medicare and Medicaid tabs are attributable to smoking, drinking, drug abuse, and obesity.

Empower Congress and national health authorities to mount a massive public health campaign, far beyond the timid efforts thus far, that addresses everything we do to ourselves that is unhealthy.

If a mortal enemy were systematically killing nearly half a million Americans a year, we would mobilize the armies of the night and let loose the dogs of war. Instead, we run TV advertisements claiming soda pop taxes harm consumers.

Pogo the iconic cartoon character said it long ago: "We have met the enemy . . . and it is us."

The time has come for serious steps.

We allow corporations to profit while they poison us. They are targeting your children. They mean to fill them with an endless aching need. They spend tens of millions to capture the health of your young adults. If you are hedonistic enough to be pleasured by life-shortening habits, so be it, but do you recoil when they target your teens? Just how close to your heart does their arrow have to fly before you cry foul?

Woody Allen once said, "If you smoke after sex . . . you are doing it entirely too fast." Nothing about the way we deal with cigarette smoking is happening too fast. The FDA has the ability to rule on packaging. Does anybody believe a bigger skull and crossbones stops addicts from smoking? Hell, I have seen cancer sufferers rationalize just one more soul-sucking drag. Do you think a nasty picture will get them to stop?

For my two cents, secondhand smoke will be exposed as a ruse for fighting firsthand smoking. As far as that goes I am pure Rhett Butler: "Frankly my dear, I don't give a damn."

Mayor Bloomberg used the convenient truth of secondhand smoke to at long last make restaurants smoke-free in NYC, which has been a fantastic development . . . unless you are a smoker. But something in me tightens when some overweight schlub sucking on his 35th cigarette of the day proclaims it's his God-given right to smoke—so long as Smokey the bear pays the freight cost of his ingestion to society.

Stupidity shouldn't be costless. Our biggest national addiction is to cost-free choice.

We need a complete rethink of the smoking phenomenon and how we are coping with it.

Our government has experimented before. Aiming to discourage illegal drinking during Prohibition, the U.S. government spiked industrial alcohol with deadly poisons. The "chemists' war of Prohibition" may have killed 10,000 or more Americans.

As drinkers started dying, public outcry mounted and the program was quietly and abruptly halted.

I am not suggesting we poison our citizenry. Smokers are doing a good job themselves. But they must compensate us.

I call for a reopening of the whole tobacco settlement talks. There should be a massive health tax charge to every shareholder, employee, and company engaged in tobacco production. Profit if you like, but pay a health dividend to a central authority.

Every pack of cigarettes, smokeless tobacco, and cigars should carry a health tax in addition to the myriad sin taxes levied. All marketing to minors of any kind should cease. Flavored products should only be available to adults.

The FDA should finally get some balls and regulate tobacco. All sports sponsorships, product placements in movies, and tobacco-related marketing should carry with it a health surcharge.

Why should tobacco be a hugely profitable cash-flow machine when so many citizens get stuck with the tab?

Health insurance for smokers should be significantly higher.

Cessation plans and abstinence bonuses should be incorporated into health plans.

Mayor Bloomberg's public park, beach, and outside smoking bans should be extended so that smoking is simply too inconvenient. Fines should be increased.

For the civil libertarians my answer is simple: Do whatever you choose, but if your choice costs society, then you and the enablers of your choice should pay.

CHALLENGE SEVEN
Sick and Tired: Today's Care, Tomorrow's Cure

DECADES OF LEADERSHIP IN HOSPITALS *and disease-related charities did not teach me what I should have known. I needed a wake-up call and I got one.*

It began at a Christmas party at a friend's house. My wife Eaddo wore a look of surprise as I stood up to leave the table once again.

Something was wrong.

On my fourth trip to the bathroom my effluent became a cheery holiday red.

The pain came in a searing blaze that felt as if someone was knifing me in the back. My first thought was, "not the hospital"—I had made it my business to avoid them as a customer for my 36 years.

But this time I knew my body had turned traitor.

One look at my drained face was all my seven-months' pregnant wife needed. Her well-developed maternal instincts took over as we made excuses and departed. It occurs to me now, we have never been invited back.

We must have made quite an impression, both of us shuffling along. But it was Saturday night just days before Christmas and I needed to head for the barn. My wife sensibly directed me to the hospital, but I was determined to sleep this minor irritation off in my own comfortable bed. I had the wheel, so it was home sweet homeward bound.

When I first stumbled into the kitchen it seemed I had made the right decision. Moments later, I felt like a fool.

Pain relaunched its sneak attack. For the first time in my life I was experiencing what felt like the absolute limits of my pain threshold.

Reached at his home in the wee hours, my doctor insisted I head to the local ER and get myself in the protective arms of the health-care system. My doc said he would phone ahead and check in on me the next morning.

Ho ho ho . . . to the hospital at high speed. My parking was imperfect and as we entered the emergency room with our peculiar gaits, the attending nurse's assistant took one look at us and rushed the wheelchair to my pregnant wife. English was not so comfortably within the assistant's command, and I eventually told my weary wife to just go with it.

We approached the front desk, me ambling and dancing, she wheeling. As fortune would have it, a young resident was busy chatting up an indifferent angel of mercy who manned the admissions desk like she was gauging who gets into Princeton. The resident's lightning-fast diagnosis was almost entirely on the basis of my inability to stand still. As I did my jig, the admitting angel showed no more interest in my charms than she did the resident's. But she did do me the honor of leading me through an exhaustive and endlessly detailed series of questions that were necessary to answer if I ever hoped to get beyond those magic automatic doors.

Frankly I wanted to get back there so badly I would have given my debit card PIN code and the title to my house just to get to "doctorland" on the other side. Every time I encountered another sneak attack, which came every three minutes, regular enough to time an egg, my wife insisted that the nurses move faster.

Ironically, the more we needed speed, the slower they seemed to go. It became clear the wisest course was to stop asking.

At long last, the gates swung open and a beaming nurse whisked me away in my own wheelchair. I bid my wife adieu and she returned home to our slumbering three daughters. We agreed to speak in the morning.

Once inside, I was wheeled to a gurney, and with little encouragement and no help, I climbed aboard. In the land of scrubs and whites I stood out like a Christmas tree in my flaming red socks and candy cane-striped tie. I was seasonally adjusted, but out of place.

And I didn't give a shit.

The pain was making me delirious. A new nurse came by, told me to hold on, and crisply snapped the curtain that rolled on a ceiling track. Swaddled in the fluorescent light I was alone in a loud and busy place. I retreated to my corner, and I waited.

In the next hour I boiled another 20 eggs. The sharp pains entered a whole new realm. Sometime in the wee hours, I was wheeled to a lab for some kind of test, an X-ray or something—frankly I was delirious and can't be sure what it was. The man who ran the test told me it looked like kidney stones, but I should wait for the doctor's confirmation.

I had been inside doctorland for hours, and I hoped to see one soon.

I was returned to my little corner and sealed off by my trusty curtain.

A night out of Fellini followed. I recall dragging my bag of bones to the toilet and getting violently sick all over myself just when I'd made it back to the gurney. Between bouts, I managed to sleep fitfully. There was pandemonium in the room a few times. I could make out shards of the broken conversation—a knife fight in a bar, screaming and angry words, then silence and more fitful sleep. I think a nurse came by to check on me. From somewhere a pillow appeared.

Sleep finally took me.

At dawn, I awoke with a start to the sound of a bellowing voice. My doctor had come by to find what room I had been sent to only to learn that no one seemed to know much about me. I heard someone offer that a test had been run and then my doctor screaming at the attending, "Where the hell is he?"

A quick search ensued and suddenly my curtain snapped open. At least a dozen faces peered in at the wondrous sight. My holiday finery was crusted with bloody vomit, and my face was as green as Christmas spruce. As I lay there stiff on the gurney with a bloated stomach, I moaned in operatic pain as the assembly looked on. I squinted against the light.

My doctor's face was like the painting The Scream. The young attendant muttered something unintelligible, the montage of faces started to swirl, and I blacked out.

IT WAS MY FIRST PERSONAL experience of being in a hospital when no one gave a damn.

Our health-care system is an odd series of contrasts and ironies, caring and disinterested, patient-focused and indifferent. And like me, most everyone secretly just prays for the stone to pass so we can escape the system's clutches.

We are surveys of one. We are detailed experts in our own tale. (Try asking someone about their recent dental work to pass an evening.) But our expertise hinders us from grasping the big picture. I believed ERs were chronically underfunded because I spent a night on a gurney in one.

The goal of this chapter is to make you one of those unique individuals who understands the broad sweep of health care. And to make you sage about the choices that confront us.

Let's start with a human irony. We are each unique, but if you chart our use of the health-care system, almost everyone looks the same: episodic use in blips along the way, then later in life a chronic problem or two or five, and then in the last months of life, a six-sigma spike—often most acute in our final days and hours. We go out with a bang. Much of our total life-care cost hits in a peak, as we and our families fight to remain on this mortal coil. Often the medical establishment takes over, and spends heavily, even in the face of unlikely odds.

Suggestions of economy in final days sound like the work of a ghoulish CPA. It's a matter of life and death with a huge tab.

The same goes for insurance. Different as we are, the flow of our lives is remarkably predictable yet health-care programs and insurance offerings are oddly dissociated, rippling along on their own course. Many Americans are uncovered when we could be; and untreated when we should be.

Addressing this mismatch is the first step in reorienting health care.

To get up to speed on health, let's start at the opposite end of your personal experience and look at the whole darn thing.

Health care is massive. Spending on U.S. health care is two and a half trillion dollars a year and it's growing between seven and ten percent every year.

Within the system, hundreds of regulatory regimes have blossomed without true central command and control. Some rules exactly contradict one another. And fresh rules in one area have impact elsewhere in the system in a thousand ways no regulator can imagine, so they don't try.

Almost no one grasps the big picture which is why it is so vital that you do.

The best way to think about health care is as a value chain. Imagine a continuum that begins with manufacturers of drugs and devices followed by distributors and testing services, then providers like hospitals, clinics, and nursing homes, then payers, health-plan sponsors, and finally you.

Another layer running parallel provides supporting and enabling services and technologies to each link in the value chain. Yet a third parallel track is the nontraditional players in the value chain who have cropped up in every link and category, like health clubs, corporate clinics, and retail testing kiosks, with new ones joining every month.

It's as if a massive pyramid is facing point down at you as you lie in your sickbed.

Where does the $2.5 trillion come from?

The biggest slice, $800 billion, comes from private insurance. Your employer provides it, or you buy into a plan, and that insurer pays a chunk of your health-care costs. It is an extremely difficult business and some insurers do the job exceedingly well. Many do not because of the over-profusion of regulations and a lack of incentive to do a really great job. Most are simply trying to make a buck.

Next biggest payers are the Medi's—Medicare (for the elderly) at $500 billion and Medicaid (for the poor) at $400 billion. These vast bureaucracies, established nearly 50 years ago, need an extreme makeover. You know what doctors recommend for 50-year-old men?

Annual proctology exams.

Because the Medi's serve the neediest, suggesting change in them unleashes storms of protest and chary visions of death panels. You already know this. No intelligent evaluation of our budget, our spending, and our health-care costs can be accomplished without these two programs bending over.

These systems can be designed to serve more people with better services if we open up Pandora's box. But we are too timid to look inside. Whether you are a Medicare recipient or not, waiting to tackle these programs is costing you personally.

The next biggest source of funds is $900 million of cash a day coming out of your pocket. Between deductibles, uncovered procedures or medicines and direct pay, you're spending over $300 billion.

Other third-party payers, who are chipping in $260 billion total, are work site health care, Indian Health Services, the Substance Abuse and Mental Health Services Administration, and school health. Another $100 billion comes from the Department of Defense and Veteran Affairs and special health insurance plans. Investment returns account for the remaining $156 billion.

We will soon spend 20 percent and more of our GDP on health care (currently we're running at 17 percent). That costs you personally even if you went through the past year with only a head cold. And it means any cuts have double impact because health care is such a huge part of the economy.

Without making a statement about ObamaCare in particular, what are the odds that Congress could effectively restructure something this huge and this complicated in a matter of six to eight months?

I'd say they are zero, particularly if coverage is more important than following life's flow. Because expanding coverage of a poorly run program is no prescription for health.

So let's go with the flow.

Have you heard there are 50 million uninsured Americans who have been tossed aside by society and cannot get coverage?

Let's test the thesis.

About 170 million are covered by their employers. Another 45 million apiece, roughly, are covered by Medicaid and Medicare. Obviously some of those numbers overlap. About 27 million of us purchase our own health insurance and another 12 million are covered by various military programs.

Who's left?

About 51 million Americans are without health insurance.

Their stories say a lot . . . and lawmakers aren't listening.

It turns out that health insurance in our nation has a basic flaw: It doesn't go with the flow. Imagine jogging through life and at each major transition you must leap over a stovepipe. Failure to clear the gap means you plunge inside. But these stovepipes make many people uninsured at a moment in time, but not permanently. Hmmm, that sounds fixable.

Stovepipe moments include college graduation, discharge from the armed services, retirement, job dismissal, divorce, and having a first child. The forks in the road are different but share one thing in common.

They can bump us out of eligibility for health insurance, even people who expect to be covered. The vast majority of these stovepipers are not indigent or even chronically uninsured. They are just uninsured right now.

Over a ten-year period, most of these 51 million uninsured will be covered; one out of five will suffer coverage gaps of a year or less; another fifth will suffer longer or repeated gaps for one to three years.

There are ten million (some say 15) who are permanently uninsured, a real problem that will cost us even if we completely ignore them. So let's make it our business not to. Developing plans to help the uninsured makes sense to even the hardest bitten accountants among us. Charity alone won't do the job and solutions will be extremely costly.

Very little of the latest health-care overhaul addresses the 50 million because people in power never took the time to ask the basic questions. The number 50 million was such a powerful and convenient rallying cry, why bother developing something tailored to meet their needs? We all know you get more news by screaming than by fixing the problem.

Before we can seamlessly cover the stovepipes, we have to be willing to face facts rather than hyperbole. So often facts indicate how to solve a problem.

We have seen the hint of the solution already in the evolution of retirement plans. But in order to heal ourselves, the individual is going to assume a larger and larger responsibility in picking their health-care course. Just as we have seen in retirement benefits, the philosophy will be to subsidize those who can't afford it and incentivize those who can.

In the future, we will have an individual account that follows you through life, not a model where you show up when you're sick and the system has to heal you and then send you a bill that someone else pays. I believe whether you are a Democrat or a Republican, health-care reform is heading inexorably to this place.

Remember that parallel developments didn't come swiftly to the world of retirement. We fought those changes every step of the way.

We began with a simple construct—the defined benefit.

After you retire, you and your family will get sick and we will heal you with little additional cost except if you hit single year or lifetime coverage limits. Next with some wailing and gnashing, we converted defined benefit to defined contribution—we know generally what you're going to get, but we want you to pay some and that number is predictable and is your "fair share" of the projected cost.

At the same time we set up IRAs, 401-k's, and Roth Accounts with investment and tax incentives to encourage participation. You were given the option of managing your retirement needs. In time we all came to accept responsibility for our retirements. And when bankruptcy provided sufficient cover for review, such as with GM or Chrysler, meaningful concessions for retirements and benefits were renegotiated.

But people still don't have sufficient explanation or coaching. Most Americans are relatively "over insured" on their auto policies and relatively underinsured on retirement and health insurance.

And health care has seen some recent innovation: The latest entrant into the IRA type family is the Health Savings Account.

As with IRAs you can invest and generate returns tax free. But HSAs are even more powerful. Here are the bare bones: You can take out up to $6150 *every year* from your income and get a deduction. These monies can be used to pay almost any medical expense you incur at any time in your life. So it is like an IRA from a tax perspective but there is no penalty for early withdrawal.

Here's the rub on HSAs. In order to get the various benefits you must join an approved plan which often carries a high deductible. However, that deductible can be offset by using your HSA.

These high deductible plans are very different from co-pay plans. Patients ration their care under high deductible approaches. The HSA drives you proactively to make the wisest medical choices about your care.

And unlike most individual plans with surprisingly low per-incident and lifetime limits, many of these high deductibility plans provide more coverage in the disaster scenario.

Not only are these HSAs the best deal if you can afford them, they also give a clear indication of where the world is headed—no matter which administration governs Washington.

If you want to know where I think the world of health-care benefits is heading, think of a one-word pneumonic device: **GLIDERS.**

G: *Guaranteed.* Like it or not, I believe the nation will be looking for some sort of assured coverage even under a Republican administration. It is only a matter of degree.

L: *Lifetime.* Even Congress will figure out that stovepipes cause more uninsured people than poverty. Congress will pick the low-hanging fruit. This is not a tough problem to solve.

I: *Individual/Insured.* Everyone will have their own account insured by some means.

D: *Distributed broadly.* Distribution of health coverage will be a real challenge now that new regulations require selected expenses to come down. The new law is that 85 percent of your premiums must be paid to get medical services. Translation, only 15 percent remains for the providers' administration and commission costs. Since most commissions exceeded 20 percent or more, it suddenly became a lot less lucrative to sell health policies. Distribution methods will have to change to more mass-style selling with less hand-holding, more self-service, and more efficiency. In periods of big change, laws limiting sales support are dumb.

E: *Evaluation of investment options and co-pay.* Watch for a lot more noise about the HSAs.

R: *Responsibility based.* It will be your health to insure, not simply a community good you can collect from like a public water fountain. There will be incentives for saving and for intelligent use of resources.

S: *Subsidized.* Yep, we are going to bail out those without health insurance. Get used to that idea too. It will cost a fortune. There is no end to the entitlement, just to its form and to who is eligible. Medicare, Medicaid, and other subsidies will continue to exist.

The Untouchables

YOU KNOW THE THREE BIGGIES—Social Security, Medicare, and Medicaid—are key to any health solution because the government will do anything to avoid facing them.

Social Security isn't strictly medical, but it involves seniors and defines the problem too.

All three are dramatically affected by the Silver Surge so delay by even a year only makes the problem worse.

Social Security, established in 1935, was designed when people lived a dozen years beyond retirement. Its pensions come from a 10.6 percent payroll tax split 60/40 with your employer. Benefits are paid by a formula based on two things: your average wage during your 35 highest income years, and an adjustment based on average wage growth (typically faster than inflation).

On average, about $15,000 is paid yearly to about 44 million retirees; and if you are like many folks, you will live long enough to take out more than you paid in.

The Silver Surge sweeps 77 million longer-lived boomers into the pool in the coming decades so we can realistically expect 88 million retirees by 2030, which is why Social Security will reliably go from four percent of our GDP to six percent by 2050.

We had a near miss with Social Security insolvency in 1983, so a Trust Fund (superseding and incorporating the Old Age and Survivors Insurance—OASI, and the Disability Insurance—DI) was established with the notion of having trillions in place when once again payroll taxes alone wouldn't suffice. You and I paid higher payroll taxes to build surpluses in the Trust Fund.

What happened to those surpluses? They are long gone. Congress spent them already.

Every year any excess over disbursements was lent to the general cash account and spent by the Congress.

So forget the Trust Fund. It is misnamed. It holds IOUs—special Treasury Bonds redeemable any time at par. Social Security is now really pay-as-you-go. Any shortfall beyond payroll taxes and disbursements, like the $49 billion in 2010 and the $46 billion projected for 2011, must be paid from one of two sources: taxes or fresh borrowing.

But what about the Trust Fund that I was taxed all those years to support? My advice is to get over it. The best line from the movie *Animal House* is when Otter chides a young pledge:

"Face it, you fucked up . . . you trusted us." Remember, this was Congress that we trusted.

But without a safety net other than general borrowing and taxing authority, change must come quickly. The money gap is growing fast. The retirement age will have to be boosted to 67 for starters, but if we wait too long, many waves of the Silver Surge will have washed into our billowing liability—you can't un-retire someone.

We will also need to do one or all of the following: means testing, making income adjustments to target needy seniors, and abandoning the absurd practice of using a wage hike inflator like a super COLA (a hyperactive Cost of Living Adjustment).

We also need to do one more thing: be fair to everyone under 30.

Right now the system is generationally unfair. Just like our payments into the trust fund have been spent, payments by our children will be sucked up by the needs of nearly 90 million retirees. They will be funding our growing gaps, some estimate by as much as $5 trillion by 2050, others say "only" a trillion or two. Either way, little will be left for them in their dotage.

The only generation-fair approach is to create an option for a part of the obligation where individuals create their own trust fund. Let the youngest among us split the payments between paying our unserviced obligations and prefunding their own. Seniors who squawk about the risks of such an approach are simply living off their young, and they should face reality and take responsibility for what the government has done, or failed to do, in their name.

The Supreme Court ruled that entitlement to Social Security is not a contractual right despite the tax being a legal obligation. Try telling that to a large audience of seniors. But change is inevitable, and fewer people must expect fewer dollars. And that is a real inconvenient truth.

MEDICARE

MEDICARE WAS CREATED IN 1965 for Americans 65 and older. About $9,500 is spent on average on each of 43 million seniors. Unlike Social Security, only one part of the program is a social insurance program where you earn the right to benefits with lifelong payroll taxes.

Medicare's vast construct has three major components relevant to our discussion here:

Part A – Hospital and Skilled Nursing—funded by a 2.7 percent payroll tax (split 50/50 with employer).

Part B – Physical and Outpatient care. This optional program requires a monthly payment of 25 percent of program costs and the government funds the 75 percent balance. Most seniors participate.

Part D – Set up in 2003 as the prescription drug benefit. Also funded from general tax revenues. Enrollees pick from competing private health plans and the government reimburses.

Parallels to Social Security abound. Yeah, that trust fund is gone too. Get over it, the sequel.

According to the Social Security Administration, the Medicare HI Trust Fund faces a more immediate funding shortfall than Social Security. Last year the fund's exhaustion was forecast by the SSA as 2029, this year it is 2024. Exhaustion is coming at us a lot faster than we are coming at it.

The conclusion of the 2010 SSA's Trustee report is harrowing and devoid of bureau-speak:

"Projected long-run costs for both Medicare and Social Security are not sustainable under currently scheduled financing and will require legislative corrections if disruptive consequences for beneficiaries and taxpayers are to be avoided."

Holy shit. That's the Social Security Administration Trustee calling a three-alarm fire.

—And the response? Congress isn't sliding down the pole.

To fix Medicare and Medicaid we need multiple scalpels, not a single sledgehammer.

Why not start by making changes everyone can agree upon before tackling the truly vexing issues of coverage?

Go after the bad guys.

The Government Accountability Office opines that one of every ten dollars Americans spend on health care is subject to fraud or suspicion. Numerous reports say Medicare fraud runs over a billion dollars a week.

How can this be?

Each year Medicare handles over a billion claims. Law requires that Medicare pay them between 15 and 30 days from billing. Marry high velocity payment requirements and dizzying volumes and you have a recipe for massive fraud.

FBI operatives say Medicare fraud has elbowed past cocaine in parts of the nation as the crook's biggest payday. In Los Angeles and South Florida where disproportionately high Medicare billing occurs, the warning signs are dire. The Cities of Angels Medical Center is accused of rounding up homeless to live and eat at the hospital so that tens of millions of Medicare bills could be submitted. In South Florida home medical suppliers increased by 20 percent in twenty months.

It is startlingly easy to get into the Medicare fraud business. The three-month medical company is all you need to get started in a life of crime. Find some real patient names and numbers stolen from a hospital or a doctor's office; rent a store front, secure an occupational license, and a compliant doctor or some forged prescription pads. Then bill your brains out for 90 days. Collect funds and on the 90th day, kill your company, leave town—lather, rinse, and repeat.

Recent high-profile stings covering a few hundred million dollars of billings are a drop in the bucket. We need MediCops to support the FBI. A tiny fraction of Medicare providers are even visited by anyone resembling an evaluative authority. Building an aggressive front-end approval process will help. So would requiring a surety bond or other capital as a prerequisite to becoming a provider.

One pharma services company suddenly began billing at six times the largest Walgreens in Florida. Invest in tracking systems to alert to likely fraud before paying that bill. Check surges in artificial limbs, electric wheelchairs, oxygen equipment, glucose monitors, the highest billed items with the most profit and a magnet for fraud. Check for the same names being used over and over by many different billers—sounds like someone sold a list.

Is $60 billion of fraud a year enough to warrant putting a few extra investigators on the payroll? Starving Medicare fraud is a fool's economics.

Massive frauds say nothing of errors and overpayments. A government-led initiative recovered nearly a billion dollars from 2005 to 2008. You know there are multiple billions more of waste and error. It's time for a bounty on recovery.

Electronic patient records are way past due. Requiring all-new tests when you travel from one city hospital to another city is a massive waste. Hundreds of thousands of doctors in small practices may be required to link up with larger groups in order to implement this technology. Too bad for them. There are many naysayers and doctor-patient confidentiality ostriches who have thus far stymied this sensible next step in the technology of care. And it is costing you.

We should start with a youth that is at ease with cloud computing and electronic record keeping and create a digital health record that follows a patient from provider to provider. Microsoft has created Health Vault and has a relationship with a small New Jersey company, Zweena, which offers concierge service to create a Personal Health Record.

And it's time to declassify performance.

Public reporting of performance measures creates transparency and motivates hospitals and doctors to improve quality and lower costs. Claims data can be bleached of patient identity and the public could compare health-care providers and doctors on cost and clinical results.

It's time for term limits too.

Setting up a health system which goes for 50 years without restructuring gets us where we are today.

The Untouchables (Social Security, Medicare, Medicaid) should be 20-year programs set up with five-year periodic reviews when expenses, costs, or systems are out of alignment. The notion that the Untouchables could go for decades without meaningful adjustment has lost all its charms.

Tougher ideas to implement include continuing the demand for lower payment rates to hospitals. Having chaired a hospital board I can tell you this approach has value, until it meets diminishing returns. You can only diet so much before structural change is necessary.

Reduce Parts B and D for upper income families, since those plans are really taxpayer subsidies and not social insurance. Fairness requires a testing of means—otherwise we are subsidizing upper income seniors in Parts B and D.

Distribution of Medicare benefits must be improved. We need tighter coordination between the doctors and the regulators. Medicare expenditures have shifted to greater reliance on ambulatory care. And increasingly, longer lived seniors are facing interrelated chronic conditions rather than discrete injuries. Medicare does not provide enough coordinated and preventative care for the 21 percent of its recipients who claim to have five or more chronic illnesses simultaneously. This group is approaching 70 percent of Medicare spending. It's past time to react.

Everybody hated the HMOs in the '90s but one thing they did was force an allocation of resources in an integrated context within a fixed budget. We need to bring that discipline to Medicare.

Every study that reviews Medicare claims chronic care needs a different, more integrated model. There is one program called PACE for selected elderly patients in both Medicaid and Medicare who are so frail they must live in extended care facilities. It should be radically expanded.

We need to avoid the "Doc Fix" problem. Each year for the last ten, the AMA has implored Congress not to inflict cuts to health-care providers, claiming the reductions would chase doctors from Medicare patients. Beginning in the '90s these cuts were postponed and the number is growing from five percent back then to nearly 27 percent today. These cuts cannot be postponed forever.

Another change is to introduce choice and competition into the equation. Medicare is going to have to move from defined benefit to having greater personal responsibility involved. Having some portion come through a defined contribution is a requirement.

The Federal Employees Health Benefit Program created a voucher program so employees can purchase coverage from competing health plans. Until the incentives are aligned and competition is really introduced, until personal responsibility and co-payment is involved, we will not dent the problem of Medicare.

Finally, if we engage the patient and give them choice, particularly at end of life, we can reduce many of the six-sigma expenditures. Encourage hospice, an extraordinary program, by allowing patients to go home and enjoy palliative care. Using the current strict per diem rate for hospice means that home care cannot provide comforting services, which are far more expensive to administer in a hospital setting.

Because the system is designed for acute illness, it tilts toward hospital stays rather than forms of community care. Too much incentive is placed on caring for the sick at the most expensive institutions, rather than in skilled nursing facilities or at home.

MEDICAID

ANOTHER 1965 PROGRAM, MEDICAID IS a federal/state partnership to aid low-income individuals. It currently serves over 46 million enrollees. Each state runs its own program but the federal government sets standards for eligibility and benefits. An important distinction from Medicare is that the federal government reimburses states for an average of 57 percent of all program costs.

About a third of Medicaid recipients are seniors because Medicare doesn't cover long-term care.

Like Medicare, Medicaid use is expected to more than double expenditures by 2050. The principal problem with Medicaid is that it is structured to incentivize states to spend more, since those 57 percent of the costs are covered by Uncle Sam.

So why not turn Medicaid into a true states' rights initiative by giving block grants of a fixed amount and eliminating incentives to overspend?

Allow states to design their own programs and police collections and fraud. Let the federal government stick with what it does best, administration and bureaucracy.

DRUG TSARS

ONE OF THE BIGGEST FACTORS in health care is also the biggest target—manufacturers.

They come in many guises: Big Pharma; generic manufacturers who make cheaper versions of drugs once patents have expired; biotech companies—start-ups hoping to create super drugs and become Amgen or Genentech; device manufacturers (an exploding category as we find more ways to become bionic); and durable medical equipment encompassing everything from wheelchairs and walkers to home hospital beds.

Almost universally despised, big drug companies in America face a nearly impossible challenge. We cannot achieve the longevity dividend within our grasp without their help.

Literally, we can't live without 'em.

In most foreign jurisdictions, the government is both regulator and support system.

Some countries pay to keep drug prices down. Other nations underwrite huge research grants. Some countries make approval very difficult for U.S. companies. Others provide no patent protection from generics.

By any comparison, U.S. drug manufacturers are flying solo.

The FDA maintains an excruciating regime of phased trials, safety studies, dosing studies, and packaging reviews. Each takes significant time and resources.

The year 2010 was a banner year for drugs approved: 21 (2009 was even better at 25), up from years in the 17 to 18 range. Why so few acceptances?

Ninety percent of the drugs fail to measure up and an increasing number of drugs are failing late in the game in Phase 3—a very expensive dry hole.

Industry people tell me the hurdles are more numerous and the bar gets raised every year. One former FDA officer told me the FDA has gone from the business of reviewing drugs, to the business of approving drugs—a total change in mindset. And if they approve Vioxx, which has serious negative outcomes for patients, the FDA takes as much heat as the drug company, maybe more.

So FDA risk has become asymmetric: little upside for speedy approval, and calamity if an approved drug kills someone.

Their mindset is focused on drugs with near-universal tolerance. Many drugs will fail in the process more often for trivialities, or tiny populations of negative outcomes, than because the drug kills people.

The FDA's dilemma is compounded for big Pharma.

New drugs are horrendously expensive. On average today, companies spend an estimated $1.25 billion on research and development for each approved drug or biologic when you factor in costs of drug failures—almost double of what it cost ten years ago.

Reimbursement rates have plummeted too.

Why should you care? Pharma expenditures on R&D have been significantly reduced over the past eight years. Reduced R&D means fewer applications to the FDA and fewer new therapies as a result.

What has happened here?

Pharma has taken a beating with high failure rates, the incursion of generics which crush paybacks, intensifying regulatory scrutiny, and lawsuits and settlements with big financial repercussions.

An exciting growth industry has been turned into a mature business.

For a while, biotechnology looked like the answer. These start-ups were more nimble without Big Pharma's huge compliance infrastructure, siloed operations, and hierarchical R&D.

Pundits called the biotech binge a fundamental shift in how drugs would be created. Big Pharma's massive balance sheets and marketing muscle could propel freshly acquired and licensed product. Biotech and biopharma would discover and develop drugs. Mergers became the new drug research, legitimizing Big Pharma cutbacks in R&D.

Here's how biotech funding worked: Angel investors and venture capitalists provided seed funding for early research. Revenues were generally impossible before FDA or regulatory approval, so other milestones tracked progress.

Typical yardsticks were incremental steps through the FDA maze, starting with safety studies—the Hippocratic Oath's first tenet is "Do no harm." Venture capitalists like to aim a bit higher.

Capital was raised at stepped up valuations tied to each milestone, usually in private transactions because public stock markets thrive on trivialities like earnings. Well-timed investments in great biotech companies could return 100 times your initial stake. Or not.

Outcomes were binary. If a biotech succeeded—tunes of glory. But if it failed, salvage was some office furniture and an unpaid office lease.

Biotech exploded once public shareholders were let past the velvet ropes. The more exclusive the club, the more overheated the valuation. It seemed for a while that everyone "Knows a guy who knows this company . . ."

Public offerings of biotech equity swelled in the '90s and 2000s. Thousands of companies attracted institutional shareholders and wealthy individuals. Earnings were nonexistent and often not within easy reach for years. But in a tale as old as time, the public shareholders were unswayed.

They came, they saw, they struck out.

Public shareholders were funding a reordering of medical markets.

Until they weren't.

Subprime fiascos were bad for our health as well as your 401-k. Biotech funding slowed to a creep. Valuations collapsed, and meeting your milestones had no impact on value, except to signal a coming financing.

Mergers happened at such depressed values they were called "take-unders."

Hundreds of companies, some with extraordinary prospects, starved to death, others sold for pennies on the development dollar to well-heeled pharmas.

THE VALLEY OF DEATH

THINK OF MEDICAL RESEARCH AS a torturous path.

As scientific discovery proceeds from a discoverer's first blush of genius, government funding plays a significant early role, with all eyes on uncovering the basic science. As researchers meander down the twisted and frustrating road to a cure, greater private funding enables the translation of basic science into a product or therapy. Government financial support fades as commercial funding opportunity looms and scientists leave behind the public domain and wander deeper into the proprietary world of private intellectual property.

By the time discovery makes it to the bedside it is typically owned by medical companies and venture capitalists keen for a return on their multi-year investments. Along the pathway, scientists encounter a dramatic financial irony.

The closer they get to approval and the risks theoretically diminish the costs of exploration skyrocket.

It's one thing to lose a few rats or a rhesus monkey (though many would say we are too cavalier about animal testing), but no one disagrees that human clinical trials must be conducted with meticulous safety monitoring.

And in between those two extremes is a wide-open desert of translational research—taking some fabulous discovery from the bench to the bedside.

That is the Valley of Death.

And that is where you are getting screwed. If you die from a disease that might be curable, it could be your cure has perished already in the Valley of Death.

We've become great procrastinators. We aren't curing so much as we are extending lives. Too much focus on living with cancer, not enough on curing—because the whole system is misdirected.

How many times has the media reported about some extraordinary breakthrough meant to cure some vexing disease?

And how many cures have been developed in our lifetime? Too few. But not for lack of spending.

The National Institute of Health (NIH) is the largest funder of basic medical research in history. Between 1995 and 2005 the NIH budget doubled to $31 billion.

We have a biomedical research and training infrastructure which does one thing superlatively—they make breakthrough discoveries in basic science.

But judging by another criterion—how many cures and treatments for disease has the hundreds of billions of dollars spent in the last decade brought?—this research and training are not so superlative. Many discoveries, but few cures. Are the incentives wrong? Are the motivations and systems governing scientists, teaching and research hospitals, and private companies driving us toward a collaborative game plan for finding cures?

Scientists primarily get their funds by submitting a detailed grant request to NIH or a major foundation. For years, I chaired the Christopher and Dana Reeve Foundation and our scientific advisory panel reviewed hundreds of applications for a handful of grants.

As with other foundations and NIH, few applications make it through the rigorous review process. But scientists are undaunted, because awards to conduct research are a virtual prerequisite for advancement at academic institutions and teaching hospitals.

Yet awards lead to work carried out in relative obscurity. Academic researchers are not incentivized to share their incremental triumphs. In fact they are encouraged to zealously guard any breakthrough until the wine is ready. Time, tenacity, and luck may result in a breakthrough which is published in a peer-reviewed journal. Again, publication is a prerequisite for advancement at most institutions.

Every year nearly a million professional articles are published.

In spite of some slowing of the growth in NIH budgets, basic research is very much alive and well in the United States.

Still there are warning signs.

The average age of a principal investigator getting their first grant has gone from 37 in 1980 to 42 in 2008. More to the point, the NIH is funding far more investigators over 70 than under 30.

Fewer and fewer new molecular entities (NMEs)—pre-drug molecules necessary to create a drug or therapy—are being filed and approved by the FDA, in spite of dramatic increases in federal, private, and nonprofit spending.

What has gone wrong?

Many discoveries perish in the Valley of Death—some because they were meant to, others because there simply wasn't enough money to fully explore their promise.

Even when promising discoveries get the attention of pharmaceutical developers, there is no rush to the altar. Companies and private funders are less enthused when someone else owns the intellectual property behind the discovery.

Michael Milken's foundation, FasterCures, the Michael J. Fox Foundation, and the Reeve Foundation are but a few that are funding some of this elusive translational research. For the nonprofits the good news is we care less about who profits—our mission is to heal the sick.

Foundations are not venture capitalists, but increasingly we are behaving like them. But we lack scope to invest in a thoughtful portfolio. If 5,000 compounds yield one approved drug by the FDA, then only a portfolio approach can work when searching for a winner.

Are a handful of nonprofits really the nation's answer to bridging the Valley?

Foundations are practicing venture capital without a license.

But what foundations do have is the freedom to break the mold.

At Reeve Foundation, we created a global consortium of paralysis researchers—"A laboratory without walls." Our open architecture means sharing breakthroughs, not jealously guarding them.

Our approach ran contrary to the status quo—joint research and co-publishing among principal investigators was required. To focus our scientists on patients, we held an annual meeting where researchers faced paralyzed patients and their caregivers in a town hall setting.

When people who are afflicted tell a scientist face to face that he is researching something they don't care about, change occurs.

And most important, unlike members of academic institutions, consortium members are not tenured. Scientists have to earn the right to participate. Failure to collaborate means dismissal.

Frankly Reeve, Michael J. Fox, and the handful of others leading the nonprofit foundations lack sufficient funds to play the translational research game. We need more billionaires to join the fray, to do for translational research what Bill Gates and Eli Broad are doing to transform education.

And we need the NIH to adapt—not simply with new money, but with a new mindset.

The only way through the Valley is with government money meeting private capital in a coordinated effort. Otherwise we will not cure disease as we should.

Change may be afoot. Thought leaders in pharma see translational research as a bridge to government funds and the key to renewed revenue growth. Pfizer will collaborate with the University of California, San Francisco, to tackle translational research.

A good friend to the Reeve Foundation, Senator Arlen Specter, created the Cures Acceleration Network within the NIH. CAN has at least $500 million this year to push biotech companies, academic researchers, and advocacy groups to help bring about promising discoveries across the Valley.

Five hundred million dollars is just the ante to a high-stakes poker game. It will take many times that amount every year if we are to bring discovery to our deathbeds.

We need the NIH, and biotech and Pharma to mount up with the giant universities and teaching hospitals, and we need large-scale incentives to vigorously embrace translational research. Universities and teaching hospitals have increased their commercial appetites out of necessity—they need greater access to IP (Intellectual Property) and the rewards it brings.

SADDLE UP

IT'S TIME FOR YOU TO stop engaging in citizens' malpractice. Yes, you are culpable. We all are.

We have collectively ignored the crushing obligations of entitlement, hoping against hope the music stops when the other guy shows up to be healed. For decades we have allowed a dysfunctional delivery system to tap our national resources in the misbegotten belief that someone else would work out a solution.

And we have spent tens of billions on basic science with no more interest in a cure for disease than a cure for Medicare's and Medicaid's ailments.

Every American needs to saddle their steed, speak to their legislators, and demand from their candidates a fresh approach to finding cures rather than elating at endless discoveries in basic biology. We need to change the discourse on health care from caring for me to caring for others. We will bankrupt our economy and deny our children the promise of our nation if we dither.

It's time to incent Pharma and the teaching hospitals to cure diseases and to embrace rather than flee from the discoveries just beyond our grasp. Healing is often a matter of money and institutional will.

So saddle up and ride with me into the Valley of Death. That's where we will connect today's care with tomorrow's cure.

Part II: Superman's Kryptonite—Stem Cells and Snowflakes

IT WAS A PARTY. THE *president was coming. The children in the room were special and excited (after all, what children aren't?). They were snowflake babies, born from the placement of fertilized eggs into the womb—the ultimate meshing of science and love. And you could feel it in the room.*

Yet for all of the joy there was a darkness . . . trace elements hidden just behind the strained smiles. The children made ideal decorative pieces—better than any tagline, but sadly no more persuasive. Those children were so beautiful it was easy to forget how many zealots had spewed horrible bile about "test tube" babies.

Back then, in vitro fertilized children were cast into ungodly darkness. Some of the same organizations celebrating the children at the party had been quickest to cast the first stone a few years back.

But now, those dark times had passed and the festive air and the president's arrival dispelled any dark clouds. President Bush was buoyant and defiant. He was going to fulfill a campaign promise. How often does a politician get to do that? He was about to be both honest and dishonest at precisely the same moment.

Bush was about to veto embryonic stem cell legislation as he had promised, and just as he had done once before. Despite overwhelming majorities in both the House and Senate and amongst the American people, the president had promised he would block any legislation involving federal funding for embryonic stem cell research. He had promises to keep. But in 2007 he did not have miles to go before he slept. His presidency was waning and he wanted to go out on a high note.

He viewed embryonic stem cells as latent children, just like the snowflake babies who surrounded him. He was protecting them as well as those faithful who had entrusted him with the high office of Protector in Chief. He was enjoying the moment. Anyone watching could tell.

In spite of overwhelming support for embryonic stem cell research across the nation, Bush held a press conference at the White House. In a room filled with snowflake babies, he implied that if you were pro embryonic stem cell, you were anti-baby. It was a false pretext and he knew it, and with that, he stroked his second veto.

WATCHING ON TELEVISION, CHRISTOPHER REEVE turned and said to me, "That guy just signed my death warrant."

Here's what didn't matter that day: Most Americans favored embryonic stem cell research (federal funding for which would have been provided by the Acts Bush vetoed in 2005 and 2007). Even more support it today. Nearly a dozen states enacted stem cell legislation in reaction to Bush's refusal to embrace the new technology.

A Reeve Foundation survey found over six million Americans who are paralyzed and more than 50 million seriously disabled. Think of every single person in our top 20 cities in a wheelchair and you get the picture.

Nearly $50 billion is spent annually by families providing care to paralyzed or seriously disabled loved ones. The scope of pain and suffering in our nation, considering technologies promoting longevity of life, is nothing short of biblical. Yet Bible Belters remain unmoved.

Stem cells come from many sources: adults, umbilical cords, and the skin of mice. Each source carries its own level of potency as well as research shortcomings. But the most adaptable and dynamic are believed by many scientists to come from fertilized human eggs found stored in fertility clinics and stem cell storage facilities. Embryonic stem cells are called pluripotent by those who prefer their adaptability and vigor to other stem cells. Doctors implant these fertilized eggs into the wombs of women wanting to nurture and give birth to a healthy child.

Without such implantation embryonic stem cells will not become babies, but because the process of in vitro fertilization is so unpredictable, most expectant families produce far more fertilized eggs than the three or so implanted in each attempt at creating a pregnancy. Embryonic stem cells can be frozen for years or disposed of once an egg begins to grow in the woman's womb.

The essence of the Bush Law upheld by his twin vetoes was that these cells could be flushed down the toilet but could not be used for federally funded research.

For many scientists pluripotent embryonic cells represent the best hope in advancing a new form of healing known as regenerative medicine. The promise of stem cell regeneration is still a ways off, but the impact of using your own cells to generate healthy tissue has the potential to transform medicine.

There is a vocal minority of Americans who believe using embryonic stem cells is immoral, and an important member of that minority happened to reside at 1600 Pennsylvania Avenue at the time. It was his party.

There are sophists who claim embryonic stem cells are unnecessary—that adult stem cells, or stem cells taken from umbilical cords, or stem cells derived from the skin of mice, are all we need to combat disease. Using these cells means no difficult decisions.

There are people who say embryonic stem cells can become babies, so experimenting on them is tantamount to murder. Yet every day embryonic stem cells are flushed down the proverbial toilet as a matter of routine.

Disposing of them like waste is certainly that: a waste.

Most Americans—68 percent in one poll—supported embryonic stem cell research the day Bush spoke. He knew it. Parents who created the stem cells in question were generally in favor of using them for potentially life-saving experiments.

A whole generation of potential was lost. Young scientists were choosing to ignore the promise of stem cell research because there was diminished funding and few jobs. For example, an all-star scientist we worked with through Chris Reeve's foundation is now developing a strain of seedless watermelons. Some day we hope a watermelon will walk.

After the stem-cell legislation passed in both houses, I was upbraided on a talk show by an advocate of the Religious Right who called the action a slap in the face of every God-fearing American.

To me this was an interesting take on victimization.

I had always labored under the misconception that the millions suffering from Alzheimer's, juvenile diabetes, Parkinson's, paralysis, and other excruciatingly painful diseases were the victims. My misunderstanding was that the families financially decimated by the burdens of supporting and caring for a loved one were the ones in pain. My error was thinking that the young children who were vigorous enough to survive but not enough to be cured of a diminishing and debilitating disease were the ones needing rescue.

Thank God I was set straight on that talk show and the scales fell from my eyes, and I saw that the minority of Americans who oppose stem cell research enjoy the most direct link to the Almighty.

But here is my shortcoming: my upbringing. I was taught as a young Irish Catholic by my parents, the priests, the nuns, and the community of the laity, that the God we pray to wants us each to do everything in our power to help the sick and the downtrodden.

My religion taught me to consider the nobility of the cause and the determination of the adversary. Well, there is no more noble cause than alleviating the suffering of the sick. None.

And there is no more vexing and determined adversary than cancer, or spinal cord injury, or Parkinson's. What kind of knucklehead would go into the ring to fight an adversary like that with one hand tied behind his back? (Here's a hint—he was at the party that day.)

That day of Bush's second veto was a crushing blow to the spirits of the sick and downtrodden. I was with them, consoling them. I know.

That afternoon, a promising light was once again extinguished. It was a triumph of political manipulation, yet another casualty of messianic zeal. I formed a new prayer that day: "God keep and protect us from our saviors, they know not what they do."

Bush's policy was an unsolution-solution. And he knew it.

That day the American people met the stone wall. George Bush created a short list of stem cell lines, most contaminated by mouse DNA, and mandated that these preexisting lines be the only ones that could be used in federally funded research.

IT WAS A CASE OF economic malpractice. Universities had to spend millions of dollars creating duplicate laboratories and elaborate legal, compliance, and accounting practices so that no federal dollars touched the wrong stem cell work in any fashion.

An unwitting monopoly was created among Bush's chosen lines because their owners charged money for their use. The fact that there were literally hundreds of pure uncontaminated stem cell lines available from some of the leading universities for free was completely overlooked by the president.

The head of NIH, the largest funder of research on the planet, told the president, who had appointed him, that the plan was unsound. Senator Tom Frist, an MD and influential Republican leader, called for a change. The majority of Americans called for a change, the majority of parents who created the embryos called for a change, and the House and Senate called for a change, twice, with clear majority votes. In the later stages of the Bush administration, virtually every presidential candidate in both parties called for a change.

But there was good news that afternoon. I found solace in real estate: The occupant of 1600 Pennsylvania Avenue is a renter. And as my sainted father used to tell me, "Sometimes you just have to outlive the bastards."

Obama was in office less than 100 days when he began to lift the ban, but unfortunately he didn't go nearly far enough.

The stem cell Kabuki dance was a case study in how forces of change can run headlong into forces blocking change—even to the point where a president can only buy his allies a few more months.

The chief lesson of the parable of the double veto was this: Our adversaries were far more organized than we were, and yet our beliefs propelled us to persevere and change the law.

The states played a pivotal role in winning the stem cell fight, particularly California's $3 billion commitment, called the California Institute for Regenerative Medicine.

The hidden persuaders were foundations and endowments that contin-ued funding to be sure the candle was not extinguished. Still, the country lost world-class scientific talent to foreign labs and teaching hospitals.

How can the U.S. deliberately turn its back on a leadership role in re-generative healing?

By almost any measure, the United States is the apex in the exacting and complex process of getting drugs, treatments, and therapies approved. There is no more stringent and demanding combination of federal, state, foundations, venture capitalists, pharma companies, and the constant eval-uation of the public market, than the world of American Pharma. Fraudu-lent findings, like those perpetrated by Korean scientists in 2006, are dealt with harshly. And the United States would be ruthless in prosecuting an even more dastardly development—stem-cell tourism—in which hopeful families are duped of their life savings by charlatans in foreign nations who inject false hopes and odd concoctions into their patients with the only guaranteed result of searing disappointment.

America is the gold standard for medical research and we have been benched.

Cell Block

LIFTING THE STEM CELL BAN is merely a first step. We have a timing mismatch. The two, four, or six-year preoccupations of our politicians make them myopic and timid.

There needs to be a Manhattan Project mentality with a twenty-year sweep towards building our talent in regeneration. We must decide that America is the best country to lead the world in regenerative medicine. It will cost hundreds of billions and will take decades. But the promise of cures could literally tilt the world's axis. And whenever so much is at stake, shouldn't the one superpower with a true conviction about rightness and fairness lead the way?

The Chinese government has already spent huge sums of money hoping to catapult itself to the forefront of this technology. I have spent time with their scientists and they have extraordinary motivation, and very deep pockets. Even as America makes promising strides, it has failed to respond with enough vigor and courage to ensure its rightful place at the head of the parade.

The presence of politics (and politically-slanted interpretation of the Scriptures) in the laboratory means we are not letting the scientists do their work. We have created a patchwork quilt of state laws to cope with short-sighted federal laws and regulations.

Silo thinking results. Diseases are highly prismatic problems with endless refractions of light. Collaboration and open architecture are the only ways such complex conundrums will be solved. The old-school mode of a lead scientist controlling a piece of real estate, hiring every person, and tightly controlling the outputs with a particular eye toward publication, or more cynically, toward awards, must be supplanted by an open architecture and cellular sharing of findings—shared discoveries beget other break-throughs.

Muddying up already complicated waters among and between laboratories because of the type of funding they receive, or the state of their domicile, makes life almost impossible for scientists. The result: cures come more slowly, and suffering persists.

As Americans and Radical Centrists, we need to fight entrenched bureaucracy in medical research, we need to support young scientists, we need a more effective and planned manner of supporting initiatives we deem important, and we need to keep the politicians and their soapboxes out of the laboratories.

In the same way that patients' rights transformed the dialogue among hospital administrators and patients, we can transform our approach to disease if we have a planned economic response to it just like we do with the prosecution of a war. We need a disease watch.

It's our darkest hour and our sentinels are dozing.

CHALLENGE EIGHT
In Stir with Love: Education Versus Incarceration

BREAKFAST WAS EATEN BUT NOT *nearly finished.*

Throughout the ballroom were 1990s Wall Street elite, at a time when such enclaves were titanic rather than Titanic as they are today. At the podium was a 21-year-old boy in a borrowed suit. He was street tough and nervous.

Both sides spent a silent moment sizing each other up. The titans had met their match.

Years later, captains of industry would recount the dreary December morning as the moment they realized we were in serious trouble.

The boy began:

All of us can probably point to . . . defining moments in our lives. Mine came when I was running across a rooftop with a gun pointed at my back. Something inside me snapped and I just knew I didn't want to be in this life.

I stopped running.

I grew up on the streets of South Jamaica, Queens. Each neighborhood has its culture and so did mine. Ours included playing skellie with your friends while your older brother is 20 feet away . . . selling crack or weed or heroin.

Do you know what hustling is in the ghetto?

It's simply the American Dream for us. You see we're not so different. We all want the same things. Everyone wants respect. Everyone wants a home for their family. Everyone wants to prove themselves—it's just that in New York's poor neighborhoods the only thing young people see that can get them ahead is hustling.

I watched my older brother and his friends climb the ladder of ghetto suc-

cess. First we saw them deal weed. Then . . . move up to crack. We saw people treat them with respect. We saw their expensive clothes and their hot cars. We saw them give people money when they needed it to survive. . . . This was our definition of a hero, and even if you heard something different at school, it didn't matter. It mattered what you saw. . . .

I started hustling at 16. After school . . . I would sell drugs. I did my homework before each class . . . and managed to slip by. A combination of luck, smarts, and being really fast on my feet kept me from being busted for two years. But then I made the decision to stop running across that rooftop, was arrested, and sentenced to six months at Rikers Island.

When I was at Rikers, my aunt and cousin both passed away. . . . Neither I nor my older brother Antwone, who was upstate after being busted, were there for my family. I sat in my bunk overwhelmed with shame and humiliation, imagining my mother in the funeral parlor having to answer the question, "Where are the boys?"

Around this time I met Clinton from Friends of Island Academy. He came to Rikers to talk to us about joining Friends' post-release service program. This guy was different. His warmth, integrity, and commitment seemed real. So I decided to give it a try and the day after getting out, I went to Friends.

Friends became my first functional family. . . . They helped me find a job as a janitor and they provided the support I needed to work for the minimum wage and then go home to my neighborhood and not be drawn into the life around me.

You see, the streets are always five seconds behind you.

Later, Friends helped me get a job at a clothing store, Paul Stuart no less, and they helped me apply to college. . . . I'll be earning my BA next week. But most of all, Clinton . . . showed me what real manhood is about.

My transition back into society has been all these things, but it has also been heartbreaking. Because . . . the streets are always five seconds behind you. It took a little while, but . . . I finally convinced my best friend, James, to join Friends and quit dealing. I waited for him the next morning . . . but he didn't show. . . . He had been murdered a few hours earlier.

James was killed in the same project where his dad was murdered, at the same age: 21. Next time you hear the phrase "break the cycle of poverty," think of James. Think of his father. Think of his son, Tyrek. Think of the "cycle of poverty" in human terms.

Eight months ago, our family suffered its greatest loss . . . Antwone was killed execution style in a drug-related robbery. This Christmas my brother will be in the cemetery and here I stand. . . .

Now if you've been listening to me and thinking, "Yeah but this kid's smart, he's different. . . ."

I have to tell you my brother was smart too. But he was also filled with the self-hatred that the street culture gives you, and that denied him the confidence to believe he could live outside the street culture.

Antwone left five children. James left two. Seven children that I want to be role model for. Seven children that represent tens of thousands more that need to see that there is life outside of this neighborhood prison.

An alienated person is a dangerous person. If they don't destroy themselves they will destroy others. We have to stop the isolation that overwhelms . . . young African American boys and girls in our worst neighborhoods.

I ask you the next time you find yourself in a bad area and you see a kid hanging out . . . please don't just be afraid for yourself, be afraid for him too. His chances are not good.

WALL STREET WAS RIGHT, FOR a change. We are in serious trouble.

There is an old African saying for when things turn upside down: "The sea has drowned the fish."

Every politician you have ever heard campaigns with the motto: "The greatest lasting investment we can make in our future is to educate our children."

Tell us something we didn't know.

Part of that commitment should be to keep Americans, and especially young Americans, out of jail. Improving K-12 education to reduce the prison population is not a goal that should make us proud but it's time for politicians to finish the sentence. These twin demons have avoided capture for too long because we deliberately ignore the dark umbilicus that connects them.

This year about 7,000 young people will go to college at Harvard, a fine school we use to indicate our unparalleled success in the world of academics. I suggest a more telling measurement: 7,000 is also how many American kids will drop out of high school *today*.

We have built ourselves a study in stark contrasts.

Our schools are slipping and our prisons are bursting at the seams.

Incarceration.com—America's Growth Industry

WE HAVE OVER 2.3 MILLION people behind bars (more than the population of our fourth-largest city, Houston, and about five percent of the world's entire prison population), which costs us more than a billion dollars every week. No other nation, including giants like China, has a higher proportion or even a higher absolute number of prisoners.

And if you include parole and probation, there are seven million Americans in the justice system. Over the course of any year more than 13 million people flow through jails and the justice system—that's equivalent to every man, woman, and child in Illinois.

Five states—Vermont, Michigan, Oregon, Connecticut, and Delaware—now spend more on corrections than they do on higher education. California's close. Former governor Arnold Schwarzenegger lamented, "What does it say about any state that focuses more on prison uniforms than on caps and gowns?"

And we don't do very well at keeping these folks out of prison. A 2005 study of California's system found that more than 66 percent of parolees had returned to prison within 1,000 days of release. Fully 40 percent of these rearrests were due to technical violations.

Everywhere you care to look, the statistics are appalling. Black males are incarcerated at a rate more than six times that of white, non-Hispanic males.

Last year, one out of every ten black males aged 25-29 was in prison—whites were closer to one in 65.

Our performance with our children is, if anything, even more alarming.

The juvenile court and criminal justice system in America incarcerates more of its youth than any other country in the world. About 500,000 youth are brought to detention centers every year. Some inmates are status offenders—children who commit acts not considered criminal for adults (truancy, curfew violations, drinking, running away, and chronic disobedience). Others do things that would make you cringe.

In recent years, 47 states have made it easier for young people to be tried as adults—moving away from the original, more protective, model for dealing with juvenile justice. By age 23 at least a quarter of all American youth are arrested at least once for something more serious than a traffic violation, according to a December 2011 University of North Carolina study.

We are stuck on this bad-news carousel. The nation's prison population increased by 80 percent between 1990 and 2000. Happily that rate of change has slowed dramatically. Perhaps we are running out of people to lock up. Whatever the reason, the truth is, we cannot afford our current incarceration rate, let alone any increase.

Paying more than we can bear for criminal justice has a parallel universe in education.

No one should ever accuse us of being stingy on public elementary and secondary school education. In 1960, we spent less than $400 per pupil on current expenditures; today it's over $10,000. (Halfway through the intervening 50 years, state administration expenditures were excluded so, apples-to-apples, it is well over ten grand per pupil.)

This year, the U.S. Department of Education has a budget of $31 billion. (For comparison, NASA's budget was $6 billion and the Department of Transportation's, $26 billion. And for yucks, note that the interest payments on our debt through April 30, 2011, totaled $244 billion.) Total spending on K-12 public education is over $550 billion—more than four percent of our GDP.

For both education and incarceration, an unvarnished truth has emerged. Simply increasing government spending is no longer a viable option for either federal or state policymakers. Increasing education spending does not appear to improve American students' academic achievement. We have plenty of hard data to prove this.

Similarly, spending increases alone do little to reduce recidivism and improve prisoner outcomes in the justice system. The time has come to make intelligent choices about what works and what doesn't in both arenas, because in a very real way they are related.

It's the diploma dividend.

Failure in the one system—education—often leads to the other: jail. One study showed that a 10 percent increase in male high-school graduation rates would reduce murder and arrest rates by 20 percent. The trick is to graduate the right males, not necessarily the easiest ones to teach.

A five percent graduation increase would benefit state government by about $8 billion per year. As it cost $47,000 a year to incarcerate a California youth in 2008-9, the formula for success is easy to spot—increase graduation and reduce incarceration—but very hard to execute.

Sure, we have had successes. Some pretty expensive ideas have produced measurable results—yet it easy to turn our backs on the prison population. It's such a temptation to feel hermetically sealed from their criminality. But especially with young offenders, there is a constantly revolving door. And ignoring the problem is like watching the spread of disease.

We are breeding carriers instead of cures.

Leaving Children Behind

IN EDUCATION THE LACTIC ACID is setting in and we're cramping up. We lack the stamina to drive expensive programs that work, and the resolve to jettison programs that do not.

Bizarrely, the school system is at its most vigorous when surging to squelch a new idea. In education the only thing more dangerous than a good idea is change.

Try shuttering a school in New York City that has been failing for decades by every objective measure. Attempt to alter a work rule, or worse, to reassign a teacher with years and years of complaints of incompetence in their file.

Pundits preach that all politics is local, and the same can be said when it comes to fixing your local schools. But there are common national themes—of fear of innovation, and of allowing bureaucracy, not educators, to point the way forward. There are constant debates around these issues, even to the extent of questioning whether our schools are failing or not.

Taking on education is like wrestling with a Jules Verne creature—part squid, part dragon, and part school marm—in a word, terrifying.

The education system in New York City, the one I know best, is choked by misaligned priorities and conflicting objectives. But I have served in leadership positions in grade schools, colleges, and graduate schools around the country—both private and public. And I have worked on nationwide research on charter schools and youth issues. Wrestling between local self-determination and national standards is a constant complicater.

As with everything in education, there is a ditch on both sides of the road. Ignoring a national standard will fail us, even as the local needs of New York's poorest children require a unique approach.

It is hard to argue against the fact that schools in high-income neighborhoods correlate well with excellence. But here is the dirty question our politicians won't answer: Are the kids from the poorest communities irredeemable?

I have been directly involved in schools that prove the contrary. But poor kids have a real problem. Public schools lost the people with the power and the voice many years ago. And the poorer the school district, the fainter the voice became.

It is the civic duty of every American of means to support their local schools, regardless of whether their children attend. Over the years the manifest destiny for your hometown school has been obliterated by a tax strategy which used local real estate levies as a proxy for school costs.

It was a flawed premise, and worse, it gave people of power and means the ability to feel they had paid their dues. And it starved the poorer neighborhood schools of cash.

Happily, change is in the air. All over the country, people of extraordinary means are supporting local schools, particularly in the poorest neighborhoods. And for others, the notion of expanding technology to rural towns where no such donor base exists has gained favor.

Warren Buffett, a huge benefactor of education, says, "A good public school is like virginity; it can be preserved but not restored."

We are in a race against time.

Are we in fact failing our kids? Is the U.S. education system broken? I would say it depends where you look. Defenders say that American students from well-funded schools who come from middle-class families outscore students in nearly all countries on international tests.

Others make excuses:

- Our averages are less than spectacular because, at 20 percent, the U.S. has the highest percentage of children in poverty of all industrialized countries versus perennial challenger Finland with just 4 percent.
- Many kids in Korea and Japan take single high-stakes tests and they cram like their lives depend on it (they do) versus Americans who are lackadaisical because no *one* test determines their fate.
- Japan has a whole second school system called jukus, which are "cram schools" that many students attend every day after school.
- Russia directed its students to become scientists and engineers during the space race. Russian students got higher grades, but is the country better off today?

The U.S. is not dead last, but rather just above the middle (like in Lake Wobegon, all our kids are above average).

Here are a few counterpoints:

- Americans spend the most on public education of practically any nation in the world, but get mixed results.

• A recent California study branded more than 1,000 of the state's 9,500 schools "chronic failures."

• Barring legal revisions, state officials predicted two years ago that all 6,063 public schools serving poor students will be declared in need of restructuring by 2014 when the law will require universal proficiency in math and reading.

What the hell are they supposed to do, shut down 6,000 schools?

California is not alone in facing a real dilemma. In Florida, 441 schools could be candidates for closing. In Baltimore alone, 49 schools have five years of substandard performance.

During the Bush administration's closing years, a federal survey found that 87 percent of the persistently failing schools avoided wholesale changes in staff or leadership.

What?

And Arne Duncan, Obama's education secretary, said in congressional testimony that "No Child Left Behind is broken and we need to fix it now. This law has created a thousand ways for schools to fail and very few ways to help them succeed. We should get out of the business of labeling schools as failures and create a new law that is fair and flexible, and focused on the schools and students most at risk."

The 2014 deadline for math and reading proficiency hangs in the balance. Duncan told Congress 82 percent of the schools in the country were failing the No Child Left Behind test.

Against even a dismal record, 82 percent failing is a Chicken Little "sky-is-falling" statistic.

We don't need to be so hyperbolic. The United States ranks seventeenth in the developed world in the proportion of kids graduating high school: over one-third of our kids who enter ninth grade do not graduate high school.

There are many who whistle through the graveyard on China and India. But in 2008, the United States had 1.3 million college graduates. India that same year had 3.1 million and China 3.3 million. India's budget for higher education for 2010-2015 is nine times higher than the prior five years.

As an aside, 100 percent of those three million Indian college graduates speak English.

But in 2010, a record 127,000 Chinese students (nearly 20 percent of all international students) attended college in the United States. We have our unique appeal and marquee value.

Two decades ago America had the highest proportion (compared to all other countries in the world) of its population with a high school diploma, and also with a college degree. Today we rank ninth and seventh respectively.

(Higher education provides its own set of challenges, particularly as the public universities realize that government support in some states is declining rapidly. But this chapter focuses more intently on issues with K-12.) Last year, out of 34 countries, the U.S. ranked fourteenth in reading, seventeenth in science, and twenty-fifth in math.

Make no mistake: education is a part of our national security and we are slipping.

Perhaps that explains why the federal response is to assert ever more control, when a balanced response is in order.

What in the world can a Radical Centrist do?

First you must avoid "you can't fixers," the do-nothings who say—*"You can't fix education 'til you . . ."*

—Fix poverty

—Fix the unions

—Educate parents

—Reform city hall

—Compensate teachers more highly

—Increase teacher productivity

—Implement technology

—Change curricula

—Get the federal government to back off

—End gang violence

—Improve the meals

—Upgrade the facilities

—Hire and train better teachers

—Fix the achievement gap (between rich and poor)

—Introduce vouchers

—Create charter school alternatives

—Improve security

—Increase spending

—Make schools smaller

—Close failing schools

—Hold educators accountable

—Create annual testing standards

—Recruit youthful, talented new teachers

—Lengthen the school day and the school year

OUR BASIC PROBLEM IS THAT we lurch between the silver-bullet solutions and the silver blame as if this were a battle between angels and demons. Remember the Radical Centrist promise to work to find partial and/or incremental solutions to our problems. We have to pick our spots.

The current two-party paradigm—Throw money at it vs. Starve it of funds—has failed. The answer is to *prioritize and commence,* not vice versa.

Schools are buildings with futures inside—good ones and some especially bad ones.

Troubled schools are complex ecosystems. Tinkering with them using the latest cure du jour will fail just as certainly as fixating on the villain of the day will cause you to miss the target.

Ten years ago our problem was blamed on unmotivated students and teenage pregnancy. Answer: practice birth control from the neck up.

Progress was made but the solution was incomplete.

Next, blame fell on the community and the parents. As they said in *West Side Story*, "I'm depraved on account of I'm deprived." The blamers lamented, "Parents simply don't care," or "Single-parent households can't cope," or

"'There are no male role models," or "The community itself is poisoned and no earnest student could hope to escape."

To compensate for dismal parental involvement, and sometimes to prevent it, for decades public schools behaved like closed, self-sufficient systems. But everywhere, parent-school relationships have been reframed. KIPP Academy, a charter school in the Bronx I know well, requires a partnership where parents actually sign a "contract" pledging to work with the school to improve their child's outcome.

Systemic involvement of parents is a national trend. Very exciting parent engagement activities are being embraced, specifically with English language learners (ELLs). These include parent outreach, support groups, and a superb "Natural Leader" program in which parents are encouraged to work with each other in a community setting.

Children are born learning. Tests show kids under three years old process 700 brain synapses a second. With that kind of processing power, early child development becomes a dividing line with greater impact than, "Why can't Johnnie read?"

We have to get serious about helping the poorest kids from birth to age five. With bad nutrition, no books, and no language training, these youngsters are set up to fail. We must start educating our children years before they enter school. Giving parents access to learning tools can make a difference. They are our first line.

Reforming from Below

THE PROBLEMS ARE DAUNTING. BY age three, children of working-class families have heard 30 million more words than kids from poor families. A report by the Packard and MacArthur Foundations found that by the time he or she has completed kindergarten, the average middle-class child had been read to one-on-one for between 1,000 and 1,700 hours. The average child in a low-income family has been exposed to only 25 hours of one-on-one reading.

Most school systems are too overwhelmed to reach beyond their walls to capture the up-and-coming preschoolers. Government, parents, and charities will have to create the edu-care system necessary to help these youngsters—particularly those from the poorest families among us.

Bluntly, setting up quality early child centers with edu-care is expensive, but worth it. I taught at Head Start and observed that preschoolers are absolute sponges for learning, when you can get them to sit still, and even at high velocity they absorb a great deal.

Any total economic analysis leads to the same conclusion: many of the very best after-school and charter programs come too late. Catching these youngsters as preschoolers meaningfully improves the odds that their crucial first years in school will be productive.

Again, some progress has been made, but it is incomplete.

Next on the chopping block in the blame game came teachers—the unkindest cut of all. It must be their fault.

On this matter it is time to set the record straight. Class, pay attention, please!

We are blessed with just under four million teachers in the nation's public school system. I have had the honor to meet a great many teachers and they can be subject to a few generalizations. The vast vast majority are among the most dedicated, caring professionals on the planet. They are tasked with teaching our "darlings" in what can sometimes be a thankless mission.

Most carry themselves with a dignity and professionalism that are the envy of any vocation. In the day-to-day grind of meeting the challenge of educating this country's youth they are the front line and they execute their mission admirably. And with 3.8 million in their army, we cannot win this battle without them. Study after study reveals that nothing makes more of a difference than having an outstanding teacher leading the class. Quality teachers are the key ingredient—and we should do everything we can to find, keep, and train the excellent ones—because they are the solution.

As in any field, there are good, better, best—and there is also a small minority, out of the millions, who lack commitment and command of the subject matter or the requisite patience and skill to cope with what is often a pretty entitled bunch of youngsters. But to use that small group as a center-piece for education reform is a fool's approach. And for that group, technology, accountability, and standards can be the great levelers.

There is no way we can succeed without the engagement of millions of super-dedicated and talented teachers. Having a process to weed out those who don't measure up is a tactical matter that must simply be done. But because this straightforward task has become so difficult, it distracts from the strategic need we have for the engagement of so many extraordinary professionals.

The very best leaders in education reform—Joel Klein, David Levin of KIPP, Michelle Rhee, Geoff Canada of Harlem Children's Zone, Wendy Kopp of Teach for America, David Saltzman of Robin Hood, and Melinda Gates of the Bill and Melinda Gates Foundation—have their own individual twists on how to solve the problems facing education today.

But every single one of them, as well as the major funders like Bill Gates, Warren Buffett, and Eli Broad, starts with the premise that our teacher workforce is strong and improving.

I was weaned on the philosophy of Mark Hopkins and the log. Hopkins, a Devonian-age president of Williams College, believed that great colleges required just one thing—a large, long log with an extraordinary teacher seated on one end and an exceptional student seated on the other. We all know that to be true, just like we know one other thing.

Measuring effective teachers is a great way to create a lot more logs.

The Gates Foundation has partnered with Scholastic in opening the closed classroom door with a couple of breakthrough studies. Surveying 40,000 teachers, they learned that educators believe in peer observation so long as it is fair, accurate, and transparent. In another 10,000-teacher survey, educators were uncomfortable with student feedback alone. However, student data on teachers has high predictive value.

In a broader context, teachers would welcome student reviews as a part of a multiple measure system of peers, principals, and students.

The Gates Foundation videotaped 3,000 teachers to help improve their classroom management. Every one of these tens of thousands of interactions was voluntary. Contrary to popular report, teachers are open to accountability systems. Some confirmed they vastly prefer it to principals who play favorites, and to seniority-only based advancement.

I know that bonus payment for performance works in the corporate sphere, but I'm less sure about academia. It's hard to count kids' success like so many rivets.

But recognition is always a reasonable motivator—and we need more ways to recognize excellence in the classroom.

All these approaches trump a freaky reliance upon endless standardized exams in which teachers are incentivized to teach the test rather than teaching critical thinking.

Teachers surveyed felt strongly that overreliance on a single measurement—test scores—was undesirable, even counterproductive. That is today's lesson for No Child Left Behind.

Here's another: Dozens of cheating scandals have erupted. According to the *Atlanta Journal-Constitution,* at least 178 teachers and principals in Atlanta schools were accused of cheating to raise student scores on high-stakes state curriculum tests.

Administrators and teachers are buckling to pressure—and opportunity. Some states award bonuses for high performance, others pink slips for poor showings. More than 200 teachers were fired in Washington, D.C., under an evaluation system known as IMPACT.

Even the vaunted lifetime protection of tenure has come under attack. But in a fair system good teachers have nothing to worry about.

Teachers deserve accolades, but it is hard to be complimentary when scrutinizing the administrative bureaucracy and unions governing and creating their work rules.

Please respect teachers enough not to lump them cavalierly with their union representation. Most teachers I know spend their day fully engaged in doing their very best for their students. Teachers may approve contracts, but deals are negotiated hand to hand between unions and the government entities responsible for the teachers in question.

There are more people who work for the Board of Education in New

York City than live in my birth city of Albany, the capital of the Empire State. This crowd can crush a good idea into powder with a skill one simply has to admire.

The New York City contract dictating how teachers behave runs hundreds of pages—a triumph of micromanagement and micro regulation. It creates an incentive structure tied principally to seniority, tenure, and protection of its membership to the detriment of the students, their parents, and any sensible ability to be flexible, nimble, or embrace change in an ever-changing city like New York.

Don't let anybody tell you otherwise. The massive document makes dismissing a teacher who is obstructionist, ineffective, or even morally out of bounds a virtual impossibility. Of the 55,000 tenured faculty in New York City, fewer than half a dozen are dismissed in any year.

The most prominent example was the recently shuttered rubber rooms—havens for teachers under investigation and performance and behavior review. Public outcry was so sensational against the $35 million-a-year program that it was dismantled in April 2010. Offending teachers were reassigned to non-classroom work while they await disciplinary hearings. Many will enjoy full pay and never reenter a classroom.

A huge step forward was taken when, after decades of impotence, the mayor was finally given control to hire and fire principals and to take steps to reward and punish performance in the schools, a seemingly obvious power no modern mayor before Bloomberg enjoyed.

The administration of the school system, the neighborhood oversight, the parental involvement all came to a bubbling head over the expansion of charter schools in New York City.

As an early funder of KIPP, Achievement First, Promise Academy, and many others, the organization where I have toiled for two decades called Robin Hood has helped turn New York into the Silicon Valley of charter schools. We also fought to expand the statewide cap on the number of schools from 50—a paltry number considering New York City public schools alone educate 1.1 million kids in 1300 schools, some of which were built as far back as during the Spanish-American War.

A superb organization called Inner City Scholarship Fund brings at-risk youth into the proven excellent education of the city's parochial school system run by the Catholic Church. The Church and the fund have formed an extraordinary partnership.

In New York City, I have witnessed the development of one of our nations most advanced and sophisticated education safety nets. But it still doesn't catch near enough children.

With Joel Klein, and his successor, Deputy Mayor Dennis Walcott, Mike Bloomberg has helped increase graduation rates in the city 20 percent, improved testing scores, and launched 100 charter schools.

The famous cover of *The New Yorker* magazine depicts a Manhattanite's view of the world, with the West Side highway abutting California and China just a shade further away. If Galileo were from Brooklyn we know where the center of the universe would have been.

But all across our country, exciting and bold initiatives are taking route. I mentioned Natural Leaders, a Washington State grassroots initiative which is bringing parents, particularly ELL parents, into the community of the school.

Tom Cousins, an Atlanta real estate big, has transformed the derelict East Lake community into a Purpose Built Community, hiring former mayor Shirley Franklin as CEO. Cousins, along with billionaires Warren Buffett and Julian Robertson, is expanding the model to other cities. Ed Mauro took a toxic site adjoining Providence, Rhode Island's poorest neighborhoods and built Buttonhole, a nine-hole golf course so close that poor kids can walk to it.

At local schools, few kids were signing up for the mentoring programs offered, but the line of boys and girls who wanted to play golf like Tiger stretched all the way to the first tee. Watching 60-year-olds in plaid Sansabelt slacks play a round with eleven-year-olds with their caps on sideways makes Mauro smile.

Local initiatives must bubble up from the nonprofit sector in conjunction with community school authorities. Americans understand the safety net that charity provides. With school-based initiatives, such philanthropic work must be done in partnership with the school authorities. And philanthropists must be directed to the most troubled neighborhoods, not the most promising.

It's easier said than done. Over a decade ago I arranged a dinner with Rudy Crew, the freshly minted New York City Schools Chancellor, with a group of some of the town's wealthiest patrons. We had a single agenda that night. To ask Crew what he needed. In working with his staff, I told him I thought there were tens of millions of potential donations in the room.

When asked what he needed, Crew responded with a laundry list of items like desks and chairs and blackboards.

Sometimes it's hard for administrators to be imaginative.

The situation is endlessly complex and lacks simple solutions. Taking a national perspective offers fresh color on unions. Plenty of states with weak or nonexistent unions cluster in the bottom of the rankings. So for all their recalcitrance in major cities, unions are far from the sole hurdle to clear.

Nationwide, charter schools aren't always the superior solutions publicized in the documentaries *Waiting for Superman* and *The Lottery*!

Charter performance breaks down like this, depending on which study you choose: A small percentage get astonishing results. Another group, between 17 and 25 percent, do better than public schools. Roughly half are about the same as publics; and the balance (about a third) are worse, some much worse.

A government-run monopoly is no better than a corporate one. Competition plays a role in driving improvement in every field of human endeavor, schooling children included. Researchers have for decades extolled the virtues of choice and competition. Here is the dilemma: middle-class communities have numerous choices, but most poor kids don't.

True, states like Iowa and Minnesota offer choice by allowing parents to enroll their kids in a public school they prefer. But in most major cities, if you are poor you go to your neighborhood school or not at all. That's why there is such resistance to shutting a school even if its performance and graduation rates are abysmal.

Magnet schools and special talent schools offer some alternatives but far too few.

"Public alternatives" like charters or vouchers involve a trade-off. Money leaves the neighborhood public school and flows with each student into a charter or a vouchered alternative.

If the performance of both improves then the trade-off is worth it.

Which *is* exactly the point—pitting charter schools against public schools is no longer a useful debate. I have worked with charters, getting amazing outcomes. Harlem Success Academy has one of the finest performance records of any school in our state. Isn't the point to then siphon success from the charter and to infuse it into traditional public schools?

Capacity-constrained charters are only too happy to partner with public schools.

Houston's Lee High School has been troubled for years. City Superintendent Terry Grier said, "We can't sit idly by and let parents think that only quality charter schools can educate poor kids well. . . . Why not try and replicate . . . ?"

KIPP and Lee have found common ground and the charter is pouring its lessons into the public school.

There is a big trade-off, too, in local versus national involvement.

One of the toughest things about nationwide reform is knowing which numbers to trust and what curriculum to support. Forty-two states have agreed to a set of basic standards in English and Math. Armed with unifying standards, we will be able for the first time to track regional performance.

We can examine differences: how, despite similar demographics, Texas outperforms California though spending a bit less per student; how poor African Americans in New York out-test those from numerous cities across the country.

Until now all we could do was speculate.

Tip O'Neill's admonition on localism cautions me away from too much central control. Some Republicans have called for shuttering the federal Department of Education. Don't even think about it—fix it, reform it, and focus it on building new technologies for the classroom.

What is needed is a balance of the national debate with local execution. The national view helps maintain a level playing field and create broad-based initiatives such as pushing technology and standards.

Nowhere is the tug-of-war less likely to result in one side winning than in education. Plates will have to be broken, bold initiatives will have to be implemented rather than incremental ones. Baby steps that please everyone will not work—transformational action is the only solution to the intransigence of school system inertia. Compromise won't always give us solutions. Too much entrenchment and protective instinct keeps the children from getting what they deserve. Incrementalism sounds great but is a recipe for mediocre outcomes. In education reform we need more revolution than evolution—because bureaucracy has permanently stunted our growth.

Stalling to protect a status quo is unacceptable.

Blast-Off

Two areas where we can't wait are technology and science.

Serious advances have transformed back-office and data management. Despite strides in administration of school activities, adoption of classroom technology has been painfully slow. It took a generation for computers to move from data processing rooms to executive desks. Here's the seminal difference: the technology wasn't ready and executives weren't literate. Today's youth is weaned on technology. Even uninitiated youngsters are socially conditioned (and pressured) to gain digital literacy. Kids are dying to try.

Teachers, start your engines.

Consensus is emerging. Hybrid programs which combine a teacher in front leading the lesson, followed by customized sessions online where students iterate at their own speed, are gaining traction.

Rocket Ship of San Jose, California, runs some outstanding hybrid technology schools. They combine traditional classroom instruction with individualized "Learning Labs." These labs are discreet areas where students work on educational, game-like computers, advancing at their own pace.

Their San Jose students perform at the level of nearby affluent Palo Alto, though most qualify for the free or reduced lunch plans.

Florida Virtual School's motto says it all: "any time, any place, any path, any pace." They, School of One, Michigan Virtual, and numerous others are pushing the boundaries of online learning.

Idaho Digital Learning Academy is another academic innovator. A state-sponsored, accredited online school, IDLA partners with Idaho public schools to offer online choices, particularly to schools and districts which cannot implement the technology on their own. IDLA enables understaffed rural and inner-city schools to offer upper-level Algebra 2.

We face real challenges in Math and Science. Every eighth grader in China takes one of Physics, Biology, or Chemistry. In America, only 18 percent of high schoolers take these hard science courses.

The STEM Education Coalition (Science, Technology, Engineering, and Math) pushes programs at the Department of Education but what it needs is the combining of a national initiative with local entrepreneurs. We need to leverage the good teachers into more classrooms and to create a world-class science curriculum. Software and teaching modules can't economically be done in small lots for every state and jurisdiction; and measurement against a mean is impossible without some basic nationwide standards.

No matter what central involvement, STEM depends on local innovators to bridge the gap. It's a question of balance.

THE BOTTOM MILLION

BEYOND STEM, PEOPLE WRESTLE WITH the dilemma that we aren't getting better despite obvious progress. The anchor is the bottom million.

Today we have about 49 million children in K-12 in the United States— just below four million students per grade.

Our future as a nation will be driven as much by the bottom million in each grade as it will by the top. The bottom million carries the greatest likelihood of dropouts, teen pregnancy, arrests, and incarceration. The bottom million are the most likely to be abused and to commit crimes, and the most likely to end up on public assistance.

We seem too willing to let the bottom million slip away as acceptable losses.

That's a bad return on our human capital. It costs a lot more to incarcerate than to educate, and not just in human terms. The cost to incarcerate someone at Rikers Island in New York is approaching $80,000 a year, fully loaded. Even in Manhattan, you could live at a semi-decent hotel for less.

Can we save an annuity of pain for generations by investing today in that bottom million? It is Econ 101, but still we turn our backs.

I must admit to feeling morose at times. There is no endeavor in my life where I have seen such elation at our failures and less joy in our successes.

But whenever demoralization hits, I recall the cab driver who pulled over to the side of the street when he heard me speaking on my cell phone about charter schools. With tears in his eyes he showed me pictures of his son, a KIPP star student. The school took him from a sullen, disaffected youth and turned him into a committed A student with college on his mind. The boy would be the first in his family to attend college, and his proud papa had high hopes.

The driver refused my fare money, until I insisted. He left me with the words: "God bless you, mister, you saved my boy."

That's all the encouragement I will ever need.

EDUCATION: TWENTY BELOW

THERE ARE STILL MILES TO go before we sleep. The path has hardly been straight and narrow. It has been an unceasing grind every inch of the way. But by any objective measure there is progress. There's no single silver bullet, but what might be the 20 steps to making your city or town a more effective educator of its young people?

1. Celebrate teachers. You cannot make change without them. Reward the good ones, and search for leaders.

2. Increase teacher productivity. But balance it against class sizes that are simply too big to succeed.

3. Make teachers accountable. The good ones love this, just with fair measures.

4. Create choice. Vouchers, charter schools etc. The competition has many positive consequences and few negative ones.

5. Bring the best teachers to the neediest schools. Many won't like it, but pay them to help underachievers.

6. Train and develop outstanding principals. Good leaders can fix bad schools. I have seen it happen time and again.

7. Get funding for extra help for students and for the faculty who serve that role.

8. Extend the school day and the school year. Offer tutoring at night. Too bad but this is what it takes.

9. Develop challenging courses for at-risk youth. Most often, they quit because they are bored and can't see the point.

10. Relentlessly test and measure outcomes. Again, it is just what it takes.

11. Employ technology, allow innovation, and give more than lip service to new ideas.

12. Close failing schools. But open a window whenever you shut a door.

13. Create smaller schools and build centers of excellence.

14. Co-locate charter and traditional public schools.

15. Bring parents into the equation by having them co-commit to excellence and attendance, watching that the student keeps up with studies.

16. Create central authority in the mayor's office. (And the chancellor's, if that is the construct.)

17. Police ways in which administration is clogging the ability of teachers to be their most effective in class.

18. Reconsider tenure and develop incentive compensation.

19. Make great teachers the centerpiece regardless of tenure.

20. Hire great new recruits from TFA and other groups. Encourage mentoring programs.

And always force the parties to be honest about misaligned objectives like paying the same salaries for scarce Math and Science teachers as for Physical Education teachers, or refusing to fire the few incompetent teachers. These misalignments are the keys to failure and every school system in the nation has a bad case of them.

This is not an exhaustive list for schools, but if these 20 are under control, your community is on its way in education.

But how about for incarceration?

Since New York considers 16-year-olds adults in the criminal justice system, prisoners outgrow their shoes while locked up. It's here with growing adolescents that the education and incarceration systems overlap. Painful realities dwell in prison. At New York's Rikers Island Juvenile facilities, blacks and Hispanics comprise 95 percent of the students in jail.

Minority overrepresentation translates to the biggest single problem facing prison youth today—appalling recidivism. For youth in Rikers Island they measure recidivism in days—because inside of 200 days, a significant proportion comes back, and then back, and then back again.

Almost 90 percent of New York City's incarcerated youth are rearrested before their twenty-eighth birthdays.

Did you know that there are thousands of adolescents who attend school on Rikers Island every year? At Rikers, average reading proficiency is at 5th grade for 16 to 21-year-olds. Many are illiterate.

Public School 616 of the Bronx at the New York City Correctional Institution on Rikers Island opened in 1959. Over 12,000 New York City students a year go to school behind bars. It is hard to fathom the system— the city runs 53 sites on Rikers Island and the state over 100. Most have their own unique curriculum, and detainees are switched frequently from one to another. It's a shape-shifting, tangled mess that juvenile justice reform is trying to unravel.

Island Academy was closed June 2010. The staff was let go. A new, more coordinated school program has been established with new staff. But when one visits the classrooms, school is the last thing on these kids' minds. First, it is aptly called "stir." Imagine trying to teach or to study if no one knows if the student is staying for four days or three years. The average stay in a single school there is 28 days.

Second, it is prison. Fights and watching your back trump minding your studies.

Finally, there isn't enough focus on what you do next. Reentry to society should be a focus from day one of incarceration rather than a slapdash dismissal at the end of your sentence. Increasingly, the focus is on transitions, but on this measure, we are pathetic.

For decades I have had the honor of participating in funding and evaluating Friends of Island Academy. Juveniles who go through their program experience recidivism of only ten percent.

Friends is not a cheap program, but reduction from 90 to ten percent recidivism is an economy that anyone can appreciate.

There is a teapot boiling here. The prison population in our nation is growing 13 times faster than the population at large. In 2010, over $68 billion was spent on corrections—up 300 percent from 1986.

The Bureau of Justice says half of the prisoners released this year will be back in about 1,000 days.

The program isn't working for anybody, including you. We should be looking for reasons to keep people out of jail rather than in. And when someone is in jail, we should actually try to rehabilitate them. That's not "soft on crime," that's common sense and good government.

Incarceration: Twenty Without Parole

HERE ARE 20 IDEAS FOR prison reform:

1. Abandon all "three strikes" laws. They violate the core principal of looking for ways to keep people out of jail, rather than reasons to keep them in.

2. Reconsider the wisdom of incarceration for technical parole violations.

3. Implement a Friends of Island-style training program when prisoners are first jailed—particularly first-time offenders.

4. Reconsider life sentences for nonviolent felons.

5. Create statewide sentencing policies and track how judges sentence.

6. Build a bigger system of good behavior time credits.

7. Evaluate whether juveniles should be eligible for prison or a community-based solution instead, with prison as a last resort.

8. End life sentences for juveniles.

9. Move drug court cases to community corrections facilities.

10. Move nonviolent felons to local jails. Reserve expensive prison beds for dangerous criminals and move low-risk offenders to cheaper community supervision.

11. Evaluate using prison inmates as producers of manufactured goods, perhaps having sentences reduced by output or educational attainment.

12. Consider steady work as a form of rehabilitation.

13. Train them while inside. Recognize you cannot hermetically seal society from prisons—13.5 million people spend time in prison over the course of a year and 95 percent of them eventually return to society.

14. Teach the economics of reform. Rehabilitation funding has stalled while our prison population has doubled since 1990.

15. Provide decent health services to prisoners. Medical care is generally awful in prison. Remember, 1.5 million prisoners are released each year—many carrying life-threatening and contagious diseases.

16. Create accountability for prison officials. Statistics on violence in prisons are so low as to be laughable. Learn the truth.

17. Reevaluate capital punishment burden of proof due to wrongful verdicts.

18. Make better distinctions between mental illness and addiction in sentencing.

19. Drug sentencing at the state level is out of hand—some states have to open their cells due to overcrowding.

20. Implement new tough parole standards for the 1,000,000 felons who will be paroled this year. Recognize that parole without rehabilitation equals recidivism.

Just as the teapot whistles, we find ourselves in a moment of harmonic convergence where right and left, fiscal conservatives and bleeding heart liberals, get-tough-on-crimers and prison reformers, all have a reason to cry *"Help!"*

From every corner comes an admission that our policy on mass incarceration has failed to deliver a drop-in crime rate, and it is costing us more than we can afford. These 20 recommendations may not be your 20. But even a get-tough state like Texas has moved vigorously into community systems rather than hard time. They have even slowed their rate of facilities expansion for the first time in years. We can be tough on crime without mass incarceration. We can protect our youth from the poisoning legacy that comes from multiple incarcerations. We can fix the system or the system will fix us.

You are the warden, you have the key.

___Challenge Nine___
Dread on Arrival: Homeland Insecurity

T HEY ARE BEAUTIFUL AND UGLY *in the same moment.*

The Tumacacori Highlands rise in rough, craggy canyons from low-lying desert grasslands to a mile-high elevation at a peak so remote it has no name.

These southern Arizona mountains host an incredible array of wild creatures, many of which cannot be found anywhere else in the United States. Jaguars, gray hawks, and mountain lions dot the impassable landscape. Species from well below the border line, birds like elegant trogons and five-striped sparrows, and reptiles like the Mexican vine snake, stretch to meet their northern limits in the Tumacacori. It's a daunting mural, an outlaw's frontier, but along the many summits, atop peaks of pinion pine and juniper, spreads a glorious horizon that embraces the Baboquivaris, the Sieritta Mountains, and the vast expanse of northern Mexico.

It's a gorgeous, forbidding landscape that holds many secrets.

Some call it the Devil's Highway.

The Santa Cruz River Valley has coped with cultural overlap for twelve thousand years. The valley is homeland to the Tohono O'odham, the desert people—a forgotten North American aborigine. The O'odham traversed the foothills to make mescal, collect wild foods, and every so often to seek refuge from their enemies in the steep canyons.

For generations, the forested uplands were Apache domain. From their high perch they raided with impunity across the northern Mexican border. For all its natural splendor, the Sonoran frontier bears the marks of betrayal, bloodshed, and death everywhere man has touched it.

In the late 1790s an uneasy armistice was signed with the U.S. Army, and the Apache were moved to so-called peace camps. For four decades a measure of calm embraced the Sonoran frontier. But when food supplies dwindled and the rations in the peace camps grew scarce, Apache raids resumed. Southern Arizona farmers, scratching out their living under a blazing sun, were obvious targets.

In 1872, General Otis Howard negotiated a peace with a charismatic Chiricahua Apache chief known in history by a single name, Cochise. Fierce and intelligent, Cochise ruled the Chiricahua Apache with an iron fist, unique even among the tribes of the Southwest.

During Cochise's lifetime the treaty and the word of the U.S. Army held firmly in place. However, two years after the great chief died, gold and silver were discovered on the reservation.

President Grant voided the treaty. The Chiricahua Apaches were banished to Florida and Oklahoma far, far from their ancestral mountain home.

Imagine the wide spectrum of terrain and ecosystems. On the Chihuahuan Desert, a broad, flat plain flanked on many sides by long, low-lying mountains, floor temperatures routinely exceed 120 degrees.

Up in the hills the landscape is hardscrabble and, ignoring the breathtaking views, is described as "spare in its charms."

It's always been the kind of place you go when you don't want to be found.

In January and February, cold and damp extremes in the mountains surprise outsiders who happen to trudge through. Mountain winds assault the wanderers with malefic intent.

The Tumacacori and the Sonoran Desert between Yuma in the west and Nogales in the east form the Devil's Highway. No one enters this path to paradise ignorant of the dangers—the mythology is simply too strong.

History is remembered best when it isn't written down.

Through this ancient highway pass migrants in search of something worth the risk of their crossing: a better life. Many will die for it. Growing numbers of illegal immigrant deaths in the summer of 2010 caused the area medical examiner's office to use refrigerated trucks to house the bodies. Even the most indifferent local and national authorities were bound to take notice.

Something profound is happening on those desert plains and in those inaccessible canyons. There is more than the unrelenting heat to blame.

Ten years ago, about three migrants per hundred thousand were dying. Now almost 20 times that amount expire while making the crossing. Immigrant crossing deaths at the U.S.-Mexico border peaked at just fewer than 500 in 2005. Exact numbers are obviously very difficult to ascertain because the Mexican border runs for 1,951 miles.

The numbers have begun to climb again. One Border Patrol Commissioner calls the summer "the season of death." Eighty percent of migrant deaths at the border occur between May and August. After economic ills seemed to slow the pace of entry for a year or two, the porous border, called "La Linea," has seen a rebound.

The call goes out: "10-7."

That's the Border Patrol designation of a dead migrant.

It's also the call for a broken-down automobile. There is no distinction, but there is a difference.

There is increasing political correctness about identifying individuals as "undocumented" versus "illegal." Because we are speaking of families and children who are typically in desperate straits, such labels are a distinction with an important difference. These people are willfully breaking the law. This is certainly not a conscription army. But everyone who has dealt with desperation in their lives knows that feeding the family has always trumped criminality, at least since the days of Victor Hugo.

Even as they exasperate us, we should treat these refugees with respect. Most of us could never imagine their experience.

I am reminded of a philosopher's query: What must they have suffered to be so beautiful?

The desperation that drives hundreds of thousands of migrants through treacherous terrain, often as the final phase in an already dangerous journey, means that something primal, something basic, something fierce, is propelling them forward.

It is survival.

What has happened to cause the changes in the death rates of migrants since a dozen years ago?

It appears the collision course was set when the Clinton administration militarized the borders in California and Texas. The solution to the immigrant issue was more troops, more border patrol, and more fences.

In essence, our immigration policy was a line-in-the-sand defense. And every toe-scratched furrow in the dirt brings unintended consequences.

Clinton wasn't crazy. Good fences good neighbors make. But when a border policy involves fencing but does not address the root causes and the incentives behind migration, bad things happen.

Inhospitable terrain was expected to do its part. But Mother Nature has a funny way of breaking what does not bend. Doris Meissner, the former commissioner of the INS, explained, "We did believe geography would be an ally."

We have created a gauntlet. The urban entries in San Diego and El Paso have been hermetically sealed by fences, technology, and agents. Forbidding Sonoran flatlands aren't a deterrent because the basic cost/benefit for a migrant hasn't changed.

Migrants still come—only now they cross at one of the most inhospitable places on earth.

Janet Napolitano aptly described it: "You show me a 50-foot fence and I'll show you a 51-foot ladder. That's the way the border works."

Every time we added another ten miles of wall we were driving someone farther around the wall into remote areas.

Today, migrants face a Hobson's choice: to bake on the dust-dry floor of the desert where the ground temperature reaches 120 degrees, or to freeze on the cold rocks of the Baboquivari Mountains.

Every migrant knows the risks. Every migrant knows the costs.

COYOTE CAPITALISM

HOW DOES THEIR TRAVEL TRANSPIRE? It is almost impossible to cross the border successfully today without a coyote or *pollero* (facilitator who guides a migrant's progress).

At its most basic level it involves a trip from the border, crossing a river and a barbed-wire fence, followed by a two- or three-day walk up to 50 miles through the desert wilderness. Most migrants start off with less than two gallons of water carried in plastic jugs weighing over fifteen pounds.

There is never enough water for the trip.

Sometimes a car or a truck plays a role. Sometimes it's a straight shot up Route 19 from Nogales. But whenever an easy path gets created, a checkpoint or an obstacle magically appears.

Nine migrants died when a driver of a Chevy Suburban, in which 21 Mexicans were stacked like cordwood, ran off the road in an attempt to avoid a checkpoint 30 miles north of Yuma. Another story involved a panel truck in which the air conditioning failed. Packed into the oven of a holding bin, migrants took turns breathing through a hole in the side of the truck. When they could stand it no longer they stuffed a white kerchief out the hole and waved it as best they could.

By the time a police officer pulled the vehicle over more than a dozen passengers, including a ten-year-old boy, had baked to death.

In one famous story, a couple of coyotes left a large group of migrants in the hills, saying it was just two or three miles to a major road when in fact, it was closer to 50. Fourteen of the group died an agonizing death attempting the trip.

For so many, the Mexican border represents only the last stage of a longer journey: migrants from Central and South America steal through the southern Mexican borders of Guatemala and Belize, always heading north.

The privations through Mexico are no less daunting. There are highwaymen and marauders who prey on the migrants and their families.

There are reports of rape trees. Ever seen one? Women are gang-raped by their guides according to reports from the Minuteman Project, the anti-illegal immigration organization. The victims' panties are hung in a tree to demonstrate their captors' total control.

There are purportedly many of these trees dotting the border landscapes, every one a monument to depravity.

Immigrant highways through the low mountains will startle you. Striking upward on a sandy pitch, a two-foot well-worn path indicates their road less traveled. But once you clear the lip, the sight of litter, trash bags, cast-off clothing, backpacks, shoes, and food will astonish you. It can run 200 yards in all directions. These are the bequests of life on the run: the scattered remnants, the air pungent with desperation.

Coyotes who organize these odysseys collect a few thousand dollars per person smuggled. It's a piecework cash business with no money-back guarantee.

Any business historian can tell you, a steady and desperate clientele attracts one thing: Expertise. Once a ragtag business of many sole practitioners, coyote capitalism has become a billion-dollar business. It's a long way from Butterfield and Robinson, but coyotes have gone corporate.

And when failures occur there is no bureau of complaint.

Coyotes are the same kind of capitalists on the rim you find smuggling drugs or antique artifacts. Just as drug lords saw ways to optimize their operations, so, too, did the smugglers of souls.

In Iowa in 2002, the remains of eleven migrants were found sealed in a grain hopper railcar. The Mexicans and Hondurans had literally cooked to death in the train. Later, families learned that the scheduled reopening of the car's rooftop door, planned for the train's first Texas stop, never occurred. Families feared retribution, so they never complained. Coyotes know where your wife and children live back home.

As they said in *For Whom the Bell Tolls*, "I don't provoke. . . ."

There are, it appears, good coyotes, but there are far more bad ones. Whatever their customer satisfaction rating, coyotes are cash-up-front operators in hot demand, particularly as the ugly band of 16-foot steel courses across the landscape like a Christo installation.

Because being smuggled through the services of a coyote is both a purchased and "voluntary" act, migrants are treated differently than sex slaves or other victims. Human trafficking is a crime against the individual. If you are sold into slavery or prostitution, you are a victim.

Coyote smuggling is a crime against the state.

If you are smuggled across the border because you are starving, because wage rates of $6 per day or less in Central and South America pale in comparison to the $6 per hour opportunities that await, because your family is hungry, because there is a beacon to the north, you are a criminal and can expect to be treated as such.

That is a distinction with a very big difference.

Getting caught and returned home is the downside of apprehension in all but a handful of municipalities. A few actually lock up migrants, but on a large scale such cottage solutions will not work. There are too many crossing the border to lock them all up. Border Patrol has created the equivalent of "catch and release" fishing. For hundreds of thousands attempting to cross, the hardship and risk are still a working calculus against the potential gain. So the death toll mounts.

At the current rate, in spite of increased Border Patrol, Blackhawk helicopters, and even unmanned predator drones, 2011 will hold a record for migrant deaths along the Mexican border.

An average of 500,000 migrants attempts to enter the United States every year. Some years more, some a little less, but the trend is a constant.

What is being done to help these people? Public service advertisements warn of dangers but do little to dissuade migrants. These ads are dutifully run. Target audience segmentation is changing because so many (80 percent) are under the age of 40. Increasing numbers are under 18, giving new meaning to the term "unaccompanied minor."

Migrant aid stations have been erected, though there are too many miles to cover. In Arizona, twenty Border Patrol rescue beacons have been placed in remote areas that immigrants can activate if they need help. Border Patrol rescued over 1,300 migrants last year, but sometimes help arrived too late.

No amount of responsiveness can overcome the unrelenting summer heat in the desert. Every day a few more hopes are dashed. Every day there are apprehensions and returns. One Border Patrol officer claims to have picked the same person up three times and returned him to Mexico. He has not shown up a fourth time. Has he made it, expired, or given up?

My bet is on either of the first two outcomes, and not the last.

Forget compassion for a moment, though even the most jaded Arizonians I have spoken to have sympathy in their souls. Why aren't the fences working?

There is a short answer and a longer one.

The short answer is that putting up fences is not an immigration policy and throughout history it has never really worked.

The longer answer starts with the same sentence as the short one. Anyone who ignores history misses the essential fact that immigration is a cycle and many of the fears and arguments are identical each time. Sadly, the same wrong choices are repeated.

When deploring the present, remember the past.

I have had people say to me about dying migrants, "Why don't they understand?"

So let's take a few pointers by panning back the lens of history.

Exodus

IT STARTS WITH TWO INCONTESTABLE facts we must remember. First, humans are a migratory species—always have been. And second, migration always follows trade. Always.

Boosting enforcement quickly hits diminishing returns against these immutable forces.

Take the Philippines for example. The country exports over a million and a half of its people every year. They have a culture of migration, and they are the number-three provider of immigrant talent to the United States.

Cynics say they grow people like a cash crop, nurtured, fed, and shipped to the United States and elsewhere so that funds can be sent home. Nearly

$30 billion a year is sent home by U.S. immigrant workers to their families around the world. And that is just what is recorded.

The vast majority of the immigrants from the Philippines do not suffer the tortures of a coyote-led crossing, but their burdens are still quite taxing. Nevertheless, having a source of funds in the U.S. or Europe is an economic lifeline to these families in the Philippines, so migration is a certainty.

The wage differential is a matter of survival for the folks back home.

We tend to think of immigration as a uniquely American phenomenon, but international human supply chains have sprung up, linking migrants to the demand for their work. Migration-dependent industries are the same across the globe. Farms, hospitals, restaurants, hotels, construction, and labor-intensive manufacturing are industries attracting migrant labor, no matter where the work opportunity is based.

By passing workers around, business has come to rely on human mobility. Corporations encourage the fluid motion, some of which is distinctly seasonal.

Farming in particular has come to depend on this form of "just in time" inventory. And construction trades have found that their labor travels with global liquidity too.

It was migrant workers who built much of Dubai's new skyline and there is an increasing number of migrants leaving Africa for Europe. In fact, there are countries in Europe paying people to keep them from migrating. There is a pipeline from Senegal to Europe that the Europeans are keen to manage. In the Middle East there are payments to Palestinians and others to prevent repatriations.

Countries have decided to try economics as a way to keep people from exercising the unstoppable human imperative to find opportunity.

Sometimes euros work better than fences, but neither works without a more global understanding of the problem and a broader gauged solution. So before we can recommend Radically Centrist solutions, we need to understand a few more of the facts.

How many undocumented Americans are there, and where do they come here from? There are many reports that show the number at 8 to 12 million. Obviously this is a guesstimate, but my instinct is that the number is low. Independent researchers ranging from Bear Stearns (R.I.P.) to U.S. Border Patrol point to numbers that could be a lot higher—up to 20 million. Some hyperbolically inclined state senators from Arizona have concluded that the number is 23 million.

The best we are going to have is a range. But even at the low end, immigrants have what physicists call critical mass.

The Department of Homeland Security claimed that the undocumented population was 10.8 million in January 2010, down from 11.8 million in 2007.

Such a precipitous drop raises more questions than it answers. Are we apprehending more undocumented immigrants? I've seen no such claim. The largest drop was among the Chinese and the smallest among the Mexicans.

There are many who may have returned home, but the most rational answer is tied to the most rational behavior: fewer workers are chasing fewer jobs. The eternal verity of "migration following trade" is certainly a piece of the answer.

When survival is your motivation, you act rationally. Spending thousands and risking everything to get a non-salary at a non-job is irrational. But it's also temporary. Beware the chest thumpers who claim our impenetrable protective shield is the explanation. Because when the economy returns, so will migration. Guaranteed.

According to the American Community Survey of the Census Bureau, there were about 38.5 million foreign-born Americans in 2009. The figures were 9.6 million and 4.7 percent in 1970. The rate of increase was rapid, but flattened in 2000.

In 2009, over half of the immigrants (53.1 percent) came from Latin America; 28 percent from Asia. A third came from Mexico, which was by far the largest sender, followed by China, the Philippines, then India.

Our nation has seen two great waves of immigration. They are worth comparing.

The first, from 1860 to 1920, when nearly 15 percent of the country was foreign born, came in a period of rapid industrialization. The largest immigrant group at the turn of the century was the Germans, who made up less than 15 percent of the foreign-born population. In 1910, Great Britain, Ireland, and Italy were the biggest senders of immigrants to our shores. English speakers made up the majority of the new arrivals.

Mines, mills, and factories were large employers of these immigrants.

Today's wave, reflecting the deindustrialization of our economy, provides some stark contrasts. To begin with, most new arrivals speak Spanish. And Mexico is by far the biggest provider in our history. Unlike the first wave, characterized by plant openings and new manufacturing job creation, the deindustrialization wave is characterized by plant closings and outsourcing.

In the first wave, factories brought workers to the point of production. Today, entire industries relocate. We have created a global division of labor. The trend began with New England textile jobs relocating to the south, at the end of the first wave of immigration.

In manufacturing terms, we have created a global race to the bottom.

Governments of the world compete to offer businesses lower taxes, lower wages, looser regulations, cheaper goods, and myriad other elements of a business-friendly environment. As Brazilian leaders once said, "Brazil has a lot of pollution to export."

As manufacturing jobs fled offshore, they were replaced across the country with low-wage service jobs at big-box retailers and fast-food restaurants.

In the first wave the flow of immigrants to America came to an abrupt halt because of World War I and the anti-immigration legislation that followed. Immigration did not resume for almost 45 years, until 1965, when an unheralded part of LBJ's Civil Rights Act terminated previous definitions of who could immigrate to America. For those concerned about assimilation of the latest wave, no such respite is on the horizon.

Between waves, on at least two occasions, we as a nation "imported" workers from Mexico and Latin America, only to decide later that they were less necessary than we thought, and to send them back.

This model of citizenship and worker return-to-sender provides a stencil for exportionists today. But their plan won't work. As any student of critical mass will tell them, we are way past the point of "send 'em home" today.

As a nation we have come a long way from the Ellis Island model of entry. We have become a porous membrane. Solutions will not be simple.

Any thoughtful analysis and recommendations on immigration must come face to face with Mexico. We have by any calculation between 5 million and 12 million illegal immigrants from Mexico and Latin America. You just can't arrest, detain, and send home a population the size of New York City, particularly if they keep coming back.

So in spite of all the debate, we actually know a few things with high certainty. We know where the undocumented are coming from, and given the changing face of our low-end jobs, we know what they are doing here. And judging by the $12 billion in remittances back to Mexico every year, we know why they are here.

I think we know why the numbers have slowed a bit and we know why more and more migrants are dying.

We further understand that most of the migration from Mexico is coming through that hostile, beautiful spillway in Southern Arizona. It should come as no surprise to any American that Arizona took action.

Blaming Arizona is wasted energy. As a nation we let them live with the problem and our gift back was worse than inaction. Our gift was an ill-conceived, poorly executed, ringed fence strategy that left Arizona holding the bag.

This leaves Radical Centrists with one more basic question, particularly because both poles are so tied up in their knickers they cannot produce a prudent course: What can be done?

Let's start with what cannot be done.

Mass deportation is idiotic and logistically impossible. There is even one congressman calling for the deportation of the undocumenteds' American-born babies—an interesting interpretation of the 14th Amendment, which says any child born in the U.S. is a citizen. But who needs the Bill of Rights once your lawn has been mowed?

That legislative genius parallels the Parent Trap concept that recommends deporting the parents but allows those born in the U.S., and therefore "legal," to remain—another "cost-effective" solution that would orphan hundreds of thousands—to be cared for by whom?

We also can't hermetically seal our border, even though we know most of the problem of crossing in comes from just 2,000 miles shared with Mexico. We can be more vigilant, and more humane. But the net result will not be a massive drop in crossings.

We need to recognize that throughout our history immigration has always been controversial. It's always the same three uglies: they take our jobs, they bring crime, and they won't assimilate.

Benjamin Franklin was reportedly so upset at the Germanic immigration to young Pennsylvania that he exclaimed, "We will need interpreters in the Pennsylvania Legislature so that one half will be able to understand what the other half is saying."

We recycle but we never resolve.

"THEY WILL TAKE OUR JOBS"

RADICAL CENTRISTS WOULD DO WELL to remember a simple business truth: the number of jobs in the economy is not finite but rather highly elastic.

When the economy is expanding, jobs multiply. It takes time, but jobs come with expansion. Obama is learning that job creation lags behind a turnaround but it always comes, even when outsourcing exports your jobs to another country. New jobs are created to fill what has been exported.

The Pew Hispanic Foundation has done studies that indicated that there is no consistent pattern showing that native workers either suffered or benefited from migration.

One California congressman has it all figured out. Eight million illegal immigrants working in the U.S., 15 million unemployed American citizens and legal immigrants—we could cut the number of unemployed in half if we just booted out the illegal workers. "The numbers are simple," this congressman claims.

Let's get leaders who lead with their brains.

The Migration Policy Institute finds that illegal immigrants often create the jobs they work in. They buy things and they make the economy bigger, in turn increasing the demand for labor.

The Director of the Center for Trade Policy Studies at the Cato Institute agrees. The addition of low-skilled immigrant workers expands the size of the overall economy, creating higher wage openings—because migrants spend, build, and create, even at the most menial tasks. Some undocumented who work with fake socials make payroll tax payments for benefits they will never claim. The result is higher financial reward and relatively more opportunities for those Americans who have finished high school.

Even the Economic Policy Institute, a liberal Think Tank with big labor backing, agrees that immigrant labor has a small but positive impact on the wages of native-born workers.

Cato's study went on to say that legalizing low-skilled immigrant workers would add $180 billion to U.S. GDP over a ten-year period.

Radical Centrists must keep their heads screwed on about migrant workers when the world around them cannot see straight. Illegal and legal migrants do many jobs that Americans do not wish to pursue. Their accent is on work. A New Policy Research study suggests 94 percent of undocumented workers have jobs or are seeking work versus 83 percent for all Americans.

Wage gains are trickier to explain, but are no less real. Clearly immigrants are willing to do unskilled jobs at wages below what most Americans find desirable, but study after study has shown that skilled and moderately skilled workers enjoy wage increases as immigrants assume low-skilled jobs. Migrant fruit pickers work cheaper and make fruit more affordable, expanding sales and adding moderate- to higher-skilled jobs to meet increasing demand.

Economists call this labor "price elasticity." They would.

I call it the reality of our own race to the bottom. We are outsourcing our most menial tasks locally to a willing group of immigrants. It is high time we decriminalized babysitting, gardening, and fruit picking and focused on the problem.

Legalizing unskilled workers by providing a path to citizenship, or creating a guest worker system, will ultimately create more skilled jobs and boost GDP. Wages will rise at moderate-skilled jobs and if Americans are displaced, then we owe them the training necessary to move forward into higher-skilled activity.

By the way, any sudden removal of undocumented workers en masse would have a huge impact. One study claims that a shortage of over 2.5 million workers would occur. Industries and consumers accustomed to cheaper labor and therefore cheaper prices would face staggering increases in costs. Do you want to pay $12 for a pint of blueberries?

Every American would pay more for goods and services. That's some economic solution. To be honest, I do not believe wholesale firing of undocumented workers is feasible even if it were desirable. Like the California congressman's "simple" math, it doesn't add up.

"IMMIGRANTS BRING CRIME"

ANOTHER AGE-OLD CHESTNUT. HISPANIC AND Asian street gangs provide exactly the currency that is bound to kidnap reason.

Let's examine reality and ignore the hyperbole.

Arizona Governor Jan Brewer signed her state's landmark bill cracking down on illegal immigration. She listed crime as her biggest reason.

Her signature, she said, aimed to solve a "crisis (of) border-related violence and crime due to illegal immigration."

If she'd gone to the one Arizona city that confronts Mexico most directly (Nogales, where the border separates the town into American and Mexican components), she'd have discovered the connection she identified simply does not exist.

In 2000, Nogales experienced 23 rapes, robberies, and murders. In

2009, after ten years of population growth, mostly through illegal immigration, there were 19 such crimes. Aggravated assaults dropped by one-third. There have been no murders for more than two years.

So much for the immigration-created crime wave.

Bill O'Reilly, probably the smartest of the opinionators, famously entertained Geraldo Rivera, who probably thinks he is the smartest and who may be right. These titans battled over a drunk-driving death caused by a driver who was both intoxicated and undocumented.

The claim was that a wave of drunk-driving migrants threatened the American way of life. Sadly, the drunk driving record of naturalized Americans is far worse than that of unnaturalized Americans.

Geraldo may not have persuaded O'Reilly, but he certainly persuaded me. And he should be turning your thinking as well.

There have been numerous studies, which confound the rhetoric, but the immigrant with the knife is such a potent image that politicians cling to it like a teddy. Voters need wisdom to see through the perfidy.

That's precisely why we need a Radical Center. Because we are being fed a diet of falsehoods served from the same menu that politicians cooked up in the 1880s.

THESE NON-FACTS ARE VERY, very old non-news. But no one ever accused politicians of being creative. If stoking immigration fears terrorizes the little old ladies, a scared voter is a good voter.

Tim Wadsworth, a University of Colorado sociology professor, has done groundbreaking studies. His research on crime and immigration debunks the notion that more immigration necessarily equals more crime.

Remember, with immigration nothing is ever uncomplicated. There are always balancing facts to the contrary. That's why centrists need the poise to come up with solutions and the pols are either too forbidding or too accommodating, or just plain too pissed off to think things through.

Immigration is the ultimate question of balance.

Let's face it, every illegal immigrant has broken the law, but the important thing to measure is what happens with violent crime after immigrants have landed.

Wadsworth worked only with statistics from the 1990s, a decade for which the numbers are complete. He found that cities that attracted more immigrants (like L.A., San Francisco, San Diego) experienced falls in homicide and robbery. And causality was suggested between the two trends. The same cities that saw the most foreign immigration in that decade were also the leaders in the next ten years, and in most of them, violent crime continued its downtrend.

Wadsworth didn't stop with big cities. He looked at 459 communities with populations of at least 50,000. He said distinguishing the effects of legal and illegal immigration is difficult, as the last two U.S. Census reports did not track those numbers.

He noted that immigrant citizens and non-citizens often congregate in the same areas for reasons of culture and language. He tracked robberies and homicides because they are harder to hide than other crimes.

Rather than causing crime waves, Wadsworth says, the numbers suggest that "immigration may be partially responsible for the decrease in violent crime." His statistical analysis shows that growth in the new immigrant population led, on average among the 459 cities, to a 9.3 percent decline in the murder rate and a 22.2 percent decline in robberies.

But the immigrant story is always more complex.

There are violent immigrants, and the rise of ethnic street gangs portends danger for communities, which do nothing to address that threat.

In 2010, illegal immigrants made up 7 percent of Arizona's population but were close to 15 percent of its prison population. They represent 14 percent of those held on manslaughter and 24 percent of those held on drug charges.

So despite a decrease in the overall crime rate, a disproportionate number of illegal immigrants are incarcerated for serious crimes.

There are many reasons, including immigrant recidivism. But the fact is poor immigrants have a much higher likelihood for incarceration.

What is the takeaway? There is scant evidence that major migrant influxes mean leaps in crime. But to balance that reality, there are many serious felons among the ranks of the immigrant population, and they are increasingly getting caught.

The overarching truth is that there is no clear link between increased immigration and increased crime.

"They will never assimilate"

Alexander Hamilton generally had it in 1802: "The safety of a republic depends essentially on the energy of a common national sentiment; on a uniformity of principles and habits; on the exemption of the citizens from foreign bias and prejudice; and on that love of country which will almost invariably be found to be closely connected with birth, education, and family."

Today there is good news and bad news; after all, the subject is immigration. In an oft-cited study by the Manhattan Institute for Policy Research, a libertarian Think Tank, the findings are that immigrants are adopting American mores just as quickly as they did in 1990, despite a doubling in their numbers.

Still, the study found the gap these new immigrants need to close is wider than in earlier generations in terms of their English-speaking ability and earning power. Worse, the largest immigrant population, Mexicans, has been the slowest to assimilate.

Bilingual coexistence is a characteristic of this wave. We are going to have to work hard to keep English the language of choice among the latest immigrants. But, if we have a huge underground populace, hidden in plain sight, what is their inducement to assimilate?

Here's the rub: we are focusing our energies in the wrong place. How much of the discourse has been directed to keeping low-skilled, undocumented migrants out of our country rather than something more strategic?

Is the problem that 500,000 illegals steal across our borders? Is the problem the crime and the wage pressure they create?

BECOMING CHINA'S BITCH • 373

What's missing when our broader immigration policy forces Mexicans and other Latinos into some vast underground workforce where the penalties to corporations are minor and rarely enforced?

By doing nothing for decades in Washington during the largest immigration wave in our history, we have forced Arizona and other states to craft laws to address their piece of the puzzle.

Without reading the law (the Support Our Law Enforcement and Safe Neighborhoods Act, or Arizona SB 1070)—which I have—we have decided it is a "Your papers please" throwback to a bad Sydney Greenstreet movie.

The law has a simple requirement. If a police officer, during a detention to investigate another offense, develops a reasonable suspicion that the subject is undocumented, then the officer must take specific steps to verify or dispel that reasonable suspicion.

The law says, in at least four places, that a law enforcement officer "may not consider race, color, or national origin" in making the stops. The officer must first make a "lawful stop, detention, or arrest . . . in the enforcement of any other law or ordinance of a county, city or this state."

The wording is so clear and specific: the stop must be for an offense other than immigration, it must not be subject to a scrutiny of racial profiling, and the requirements for documentation and the penalties are exactly parallel with federal statute.

After all of the hue and cry, Arizona's SB 1070 will finally be understood and it will be upheld as constitutional.

But there are clearly flaws. I have spent enough time working with police, including as a small-town police reporter. Cops have to manage adjacencies, and interpret and enforce the law as they see fit.

Put bluntly, they will never read SB 1070. They will pursue the enforcement with intent, and putting five entries in the body of the bill that say "no racial profiling" is a lawyer's guarantee of intent.

It will have little to do with what actually happens on the street. Cops enforce laws with their own verve. In the real world of immigration, the measurement of intent should also be done at street level and not just in thoughtful treatises in the *National Review*.

The Arizona law is meant to be a bridge to a solution, but we all know it is a pier.

I recall one time, fishing as a boy with my father's surf-casting rod. It was more than twice my size and the plug on the end was the size of a small football. Swirling the rod with all my might in a clumsy and agonizing arc, I managed to project the plug far out into the crashing waves. As fortune smiled on me, a massive bluefish, no doubt startled by my awkward cast, bounded across the foamy waters and bit hungrily, gut hooked and solid on the plug. After a shoulder-screaming agony of grinding on the reel, I managed to drag this monstrous fish to shore. The behemoth thrashed in the shallows and snapped its sharp teeth every time I attempted to pull the plug free.

In the fading daylight, we struck an odd tableau: a terrified and angry fish lurching in the sand around the feet of an equally terrified boy.

At that moment it struck me: What was I going to do with that fish now that I had caught him? I had no tools to cut the line or retrieve the plug. We were frozen in a stalemate of pain and there was no way out.

At last, a fisherman down the beach took pity on the fish and, with an artful thud, dispatched him. He showed no such enmity for me and lectured me sternly on thinking things through so as not to torture these magnificent fish.

The lesson stuck.

And raises a question.

What happens when they catch an undocumented worker? What will they do?

There is no doubt that a vigilant constabulary will catch as many un-documented workers as he or she chooses. Then what? Deport them? That catch-and-release concept is endlessly flawed and frightfully expensive. How about fines and imprisonment? The judicial and legal costs would be staggering and we already have the highest imprisonment rate of any coun-try in the world.

This law is not a solution—but is a dare to the feds. The best legal minds will conclude that dealing with immigration is a federal responsibility. And the debate will languish there for a long time.

There will also be numerous lookalike statutes in other states, like Alabama, but in the end they will be woefully insufficient.

The nation needs a broad response and, like it or not, we are forced by the law of critical mass to consider a single-word solution: Amnesty.

Even labor has figured this out.

Richard Trumka, President of the AFL-CIO told the City Club of Cleveland in 2010, "The truth is that in a dynamic global economy in the twenty-first century, we simply cannot afford to have millions of hard-working people without legal protections, without meaningful access to higher education, shut off from the high wage, high productivity economy. It's just too costly to waste all that talent and strength and drive."

Big corporations are also behind immigration reform, including the U.S. Chamber of Commerce, the fast-food industry, and big agriculture.

THE WAY AHEAD

WHAT MUST A RADICAL CENTRIST DO?

First, convince everyone to take a major tranquilizer. Immigration has been an explosive topic since we were colonies and the whole world is grappling with it. Dispel the notion that this is a U.S. problem.

A study in southern Europe conducted by sociologist Kitty Calavita reported that 60 percent of respondents in Spain believe immigrants were causing an increase in the crime rate. A similar study found that 57 percent of Italians believe that immigration lowers safety and quality of life.

Today's intense feelings towards Mexican immigrants are echoes of what the Irish faced in the nineteenth century. The Chinese were not permitted to naturalize at all until 1943, and then limited to no more than 100 Chinese per year. Chinese literally were entering the U.S. posing as Mexicans. The 100-per-year cap was not lifted until 1965.

Japanese were divided into those born here and those born there. The latter could not expect to naturalize.

Granted we are dealing with increasingly large numbers today, but the past does haunt us on matters of immigration.

So what should we do?

After taking our pill, second, we must focus on the debate. We cannot solve every problem but let's focus on the easier ones:

- Empower the INS to clear all naturalization backlogs.
- Arrest and deport illegal immigrants who are violent criminals and felons.
- Review the entire procedure for handing out H1 B visas and L1 visas. Some studies suggest 40 percent of H1 B visas are allowed to lapse and the folks stay here. In many cases they are working at great jobs.
- Recognize that 24 percent of the businesses started in our nation are started by immigrants.
- We need an international solution with Mexico and without a specific plan we will never solve our immigration problem.
- There is a World Health Organization, and a World Trade Organization, why not a World Immigration Organization?
- We will need a broad immigration plan that has as a centerpiece a process to help illegals become fully integrated citizens. Full registration, full taxpayer, and full participant. We need to test a guest worker visa plan. We need to beef up our enforcement. But we simply do not have the horse power.
- If we allow amnesty, the floodgates may open, so it must be paired with stricter enforcement and penalties.
- We need to prepare for the eventuality that the states will be forced to take matters into their own hands and that the federal government will keep dragging its feet. These states will keep pushing and forcing a showdown. The current administration has lost the ability to set a dialogue. So to appear activist they keep building fences . . . of all kinds.
- And yes, we will need to control our borders more effectively.
- Let's admit that migration follows trade and tax and fine corporations

who employ illegal workers. Failing to address companies' involvement in driving illegal workers to our shores guarantees a failed strategy of controlling migration.

• Consider giving outstanding college graduates in engineering, math, and science an instant green card. Dispatching these students to their home countries is like tossing away a prize you just finished assembling.

Too much energy is devoted away from the real problem. Illegal immigration could be stopped in major ways with two steps: stronger borders, and corporate penalties and sanctions with teeth. This is where Centrists must be courageous.

Repel borders alone is not the solution. Control borders, weed out violent criminals, and provide a path toward assimilation and citizenship—that's closer to a solution. Admit what we can control and bring it inside our embrace.

In times of economic duress the people need to be reassured and led. Telling them, as our leadership has, that immigrants are taking our jobs, raping our women, and refusing to read English is not the role for the Radical Centrist.

Let's pump up our GDP by legalizing illegal jobs, and by bringing in numbers that we need to make our engine hum.

More than anything else, Radical Centrists must diffuse the madness of crowds. Left to their own devices and misled by their leaders, the American people might be persuaded to do broad-brush nonsensical things to protect their homeland. Immigration is more than an economic issue; it is about who we are as a nation. We are a nation of immigrants that has become hard-hearted and unenlightened when whipped into an anti-migrant frenzy.

We need to use our brains to manage a global flow that we ourselves have encouraged. We have developed a lust for cheaper goods and services. Yet we have developed a mindset of protectivism which is inconsistent with our consumption patterns.

Worst, we have jobs we want done, and we won't do them. It's not a matter of protecting our borders; it's a matter of understanding what disease we have contracted—

And that is a case of homeland insecurity.

CHALLENGE TEN
Crude Awakening: A True Energy Policy

A DOT DEAD CENTER IN *Oklahoma's unassigned lands marks a town of a thousand souls who eked out a living in the 1930s and 40s sharecropping cotton and raising chickens.*

Lexington was a whiskey town until early 1900s statewide prohibition put a cork in the business. That left families dry and dusty with "mom and dad bending low, both of them pickin' on a double row." So said Merle Haggard.

In 1948, one of those families welcomed their thirteenth child, Harold, to their single-bedroom house without plumbing or fresh whitewash. He was enterprising, and by sixteen, determined that a fuel depot in nearby Enid held more promise than cotton farming. Two years later the boy cosigned a loan on a Ford service truck.

It was the simplest start imaginable.

Harold drilled mud and hauled water to oil rigs that were sprouting in the area.

Standing on a precipice just out of town, twenty-six oil rigs ringed his line of sight. He knew the oil business had entered his soul. Trouble was he had absolutely no geological training. But he was an incessant questioner and a canny observer.

In nearby Alfalfa County, Harold encountered derelict wells drilled decades before, but consumed by a fire. It was 1971 and the $90,000 he bet drilling the wells was far more than all he had in the world. Poring over maps and charts on his kitchen table, he trusted his growing wildcatter's instinct. It *was his first completely make-or-break decision, but it would not be his last. All three wells were producers. He was on his way.*

The oil patch is filled with characters writ in the daguerreotype of the Old West—

Waco Thomas, who buried his Cadillacs on his ranch; Boone Pickens, the raider buccaneer who has given over half a billion of his winnings to charity; Hugh Liedtke, who partnered with George H. W. Bush to drill 127 wells in the west Texas sagebrush without a single dry hole, and who later sued Texaco only to have them settle for $3 billion; and Oscar Wyatt, a Beaumont, Texas–born crop duster who learned every aspect of the oil business building Coastal States except that having partners like Saddam Hussein can get you indicted and incarcerated when you swap oil for food through the United Nations.

Harold Hamm was different. Within three years, he had thirteen rigs running all across Oklahoma. He was a millionaire by his early twenties. But he was troubled. "I needed to learn about what I was doing," he said, "so in 1975 I went to University to study geology. So I did it all backwards. I made my fortune, then I went to college."

―――――――――

IN PERSON THE SOLIDLY CONSTRUCTED Hamm comes across as folksy and earnest. He may lack a swashbuckler's color but he is a passionate and dedicated oil finder like few in our lifetime.

Harold went on to be the richest American no one has ever heard of— in fact no single American personally owns more oil and gas assets. His 73 percent ownership of Continental Resources nets him *at least* 190 million barrels of oil and natural gas equivalents, though some say the true number is quite a bit higher.

Hamm's mother lode is the controversial seven-million-acre find on the plains of western Dakota and eastern Montana known as the Bakken Formation. And if you have never heard of it, you will. Because according to a revised report by the Energy Information Administration, the Bakken is estimated to contain over 500 billion barrels of oil. If even 10 percent of it is recoverable—which is highly debatable—at $100 a barrel that sums to almost $5 trillion of value.

And who has the largest lease holding exceeding 800,000 acres? Harold Hamm and Continental Resources.

As Harold describes it, "Bakken breaks the long-standing paradigm that we could not find new fields of oil in the USA."

But nothing about the Bakken is straightforward, not the least of which is the obtaining of oil from it.

The process requires drilling very expensive wells, between $6 million and $10 million apiece. New techniques involving lateral drilling two miles down and as many as 30 stages of "fracks" (rock fracturing technology) mean the cost to lift this sweet crude is a not-so-sweet $60 a barrel. The asset Hamm describes as "fragile" was unrecoverable when discovered in 1953 because technology to do so at reasonable cost didn't exist.

As of February 2011 the vaunted Bakken was yielding less than a half a million barrels—a long way from its hoped-for peak.

Hamm says the Bakken Formation gets the U.S. "back in the game" for fossil fuel production.

While thousands join the shale rush to the basin in Williston, North Dakota, Harold Hamm keeps surveying the ridge line.

PEAK OIL

INEBRIATE OF OIL AM I, *a debauchee of crude.* Our entire society is drunk on oil—an out-and-out dependency. If you want to see a conflagration that makes the fall of 2008 look like a waltz, continue to pursue our head-in-the-Mideast-sand mentality.

Global warming and melting icecaps grab headlines, but oil is a bad drunk.

There is a theory to comprehend called Peak Oil. It refers not to a peak price—2009's $147 a barrel will be visited again and left in the dust. It points instead to peak production—we're running globally at around 85 million barrels per day right now.

The issue ain't running out of oil. There is still oil in them thar hills. The issue is the level of production, which may well have peaked globally in 2005.

Major fields of the world have indeed passed their peak production, as Matthew Simmons so artfully details in *Twilight in the Desert*. Even if you disbelieve him, we must still reassess our energy strategy. Peakists predict that demand will push against limits of supply and economic conflagration will follow. Hamm thinks his field is the antidote.

Whoever is right, the only strategy that doesn't work is staying the current course.

Our nation's oil watchdog is an operation of the Department of Energy—the Energy Institute Administration (EIA). In 2004 they forecasted Saudi oil field 2020 production at 18 million barrels a day, more than double their current rate. EIA subsequently reduced these estimates because Saudi Arabia cannot continuously produce 18 million barrels a day.

Their well hasn't run dry, nor is it the Maxwell House moment ("good to the last drop"). But we must be vigilant for the moment when Saudi Arabia can no longer increase its output. Because at that moment Saudi Arabia will cease to be oil's Ben Bernanke keeping OPEC members in line.

We are stuck in a bad luck algorithm which looks like this: world oil demand is growing at three percent a year (much faster in China and India) and production is shrinking at least two percent a year. When those two emerging economies really start to kick in (and they already have—China last year became the number-two oil user behind the U.S.), disruptions will occur.

Guaranteed.

Right now, 5 billion of the world's 6.5 billion people don't need modern energy. But that is changing. And the problem won't be running out—it will be not having it when you want it; or paying too much for it; or having to fight for it; or getting outbid and outfoxed by someone who needs it more than you do.

DEPENDENCE AND ENERGY SECURITY

SO AS WE DEBATE THE shrinking shelf and whether gas guzzlers caused the melt, we are missing a key problem. We are totally dependent on oil and we have no morning-after pill.

In his State of the Union address in January 1974, President Nixon promised: "At the end of this decade, in 1980, the United States will not be dependent on any other country for the energy we need." At the time we got just over a third of our oil from foreign sources.

Every single president since Nixon has promised to reduce dependence on foreign oil. By the second year of Obama's presidency that dependence had doubled since 1974 to nearly two-thirds.

Reports by the Department of Energy announced a downward slide to 50 percent by 2010, citing energy efficiency, higher fuel economy in autos, and the crushing effects of financial malaise on oil usage. All we need to do is tank our economy to reduce our trips to fill the tank.

By any measure, we are still besotted. In 2010, Americans consumed nearly 20 million barrels a day, about 10 million of which were imported. In one of the great wealth transfers of our age, we are spending over a billion dollars a day on imported oil rather than spending it here.

And ten of those countries on the payroll are currently on the State Department's travel warning list: Algeria, Chad, Colombia, the Congo, Iraq, Mauritania, Nigeria, Pakistan, Saudi Arabia, and Syria. What would our relationship with each of these countries be if they didn't sell us their black gold?

We also do a land office business with Venezuela, whose contempt for America is poorly camouflaged.

We don't buy from Iran but we are a price taker because oil is a world commodity. So whether we buy from them or not, our demand benefits Iran and other producing nations who wish us harm.

Similarly, no one on earth escapes the hazards of a planet overheated by combusting fossil fuels. Global warming doesn't check your zip code.

It is not simply that the United States burns 10,000 gallons of oil every second. There is a river of oil running through every element of our lives. And we have a blind faith that whenever we pull up to the pump that river will flow right into our tank, and beyond.

The next time you sit down to eat, remember the average distance your food traveled to get in your mouth is 1500 miles. Some studies say that ten calories of energy are spent for every calorie of food we eat.

Virtually every item in our homes, from the computers to the clothing to the furniture, has a significant energy subsidy baked right in. Imagine the transportation costs for starters. Then consider the oil costs of making metal—a pound of aluminum has 20 times the energy cost of a pound of iron.

Consider the oil in the chair in which you are sitting: the costs to fell trees, to transport lumber, to run a milling operation, to run the sanders and the saws, to make the petrochemicals to stain, to transport the raw materials, to heat the factory, to run the line where the chair is manufactured, to assemble the chair, to store it, pack it, and ship it to your local store, to bring it to your home. Most, if not all, powered by oil.

Your free Google searches may not be so costless. The search engine behemoth continuously draws enough electricity to power the homes of a city like Milwaukee or Kansas City. That's like powering 200,000 homes every minute of every day. And if using search engines prevents you from starting your car's engine, that's a green gain.

But the price of a gallon of gas is the least of our worries.

An oil subsidy is buried in every one of our alternative energy solutions. Biofuel eats energy as the crops are grown; the metals and plastics costs in windmills, solar panels, and nuclear power plants are significant.

What fossil fuels were likely burned to provide power for you to charge your electric car? It's not your carbon footprint—it's your carbon trail.

Today nearly one in ten American jobs ties to the oil industry. And beyond simple tax breaks, the industry is subsidized in extraordinary ways.

Richard Nixon, who presided over our first energy shock in 1973, lamented, "The price of energy does not include all of the social costs of producing it."

That's probably why we use so much.

How many hidden subsidies do oil importers enjoy? Forget the tax breaks for a moment. The obvious obscures the more important. In recent years Chevron has received half of its imports from the same ten countries on the State Department's watch list; for Exxon Mobil the percentage is about 43 percent.

How much of our defense budget is targeted at keeping sea-lanes open and protecting our access to foreign-source oil? And what proportion of our State Department and diplomatic budget is targeted at enabling our addiction?

Take our largest oil trading partner, Saudi Arabia, for example. Just how secure are they?

About half of Saudi capacity comes from one oil field, Ghawar, that nation's holiest of holies, a site that has produced about 60 billion barrels of oil so far. Two-thirds of Saudi oil goes through one huge processing plant and two terminals, one of which was a target of a foiled terrorist attack in 2002. Can you imagine?

About half of the 88 million barrels a day produced worldwide moves in tankers on fixed maritime routes. The most important choke point in all of oil-dom is the Strait of Hormuz between Oman and Iran. About 17 million barrels a day, or over a third of all seaborne oil, passes through the narrow zone—the width of the shipping lane is two miles, and the Strait is as narrow as 20 miles.

In late April 2010, Iranian Revolutionary Guards conducted three days of "Great Prophet V" exercises in the Persian Gulf. In apparent rehearsal, hundreds of fast boats called swarming boats darted in the Straits of Hormuz. Swarming exercises had been used just months before to harass U.S. Navy ships.

Just how secure is our oil?

Another choke point: Among the poorest, least stable Middle East countries, Yemen commands one side of the 20-mile wide Mandab Strait, through which all Indian Ocean shipping travels to reach the Suez Canal. Yemen also neighbors the Saudi oil fields. Al-Qaeda attacked the USS

Cole during a routine fuel stop in Yemen's port of Aden on October 12, 2000.

The deposing of Yemen's Ali Abdullah Saleh, another Middle East frenemy of the United States, means more stress for the House of Saud, and for the House of Obama.

And the ongoing costs of the Iraqi conflict are in part (some say mostly) accountable to the need for energy security. We are exposed to energy interruption at a thousand places around the globe. We are subject to the whims of a loosely coupled cartel. We face volatile countries and more volatile prices. Worst of all, it is impossible to assign a true cost to our oil.

Oil companies aren't taxed for the costs of security provided by military and diplomatic missions, nor is there a real environmental depletion levy. Every American bears these burdens. We pick up that tab. But no CPA is going to fix the energy challenge.

When an oil man draws himself to full height (plus 2-inch boot heels) and gushes like a fresh well about self-reliance and making it on their own, contain your enthusiasm. Mr. Oil Bidness had a bit of help from you.

At every step there are tax benefits and subsidies aimed at helping to lift oil. By assuring a steady flow of oil to our shores, the government protects the local provider from losing share to other energy technologies. And most of the oil bigs are huge importers.

—Which is to say the true oil market has been distorted by government for so long that we cannot openly consider alternatives—otherwise known as oil blindness.

Radical Centrists, must we depend on foreign oil? It is hard to imagine a scenario with zero dependence on imports. But we must meaningfully reduce that dependence, and limit our exposure to oil security threats.

Step back from parochial arguments and you have a dependence problem requiring 20 years to solve. Lacking a brave energy policy, we will make tiny incremental steps which alleviate the latest ache and pain but do not settle broader issues.

We need a bold multi-decade strategy which uses our domestic resources and shrewd technology development on oil, gas, and alternatives with thoughtful foreign energy policy to wean ourselves from growing dependence on foreign oil. Recent studies predict our need for imported oil will grow to 70 percent by 2025.

Every one of those studies misses the point.

A battle is brewing. And the brew is Texas tea and Chinese green tea too.

GROWING DEMAND

WE ARE THE HEAVIEST USER, but are far from the only addict. Soon our glib need for 25 percent of the world's oil will face a stark truth. Other people want our oil, and they are willing to do things and say things and promise things that we aren't willing to do to get their hands on it.

Two megatrends affect the demography of energy. By 2050 there will be nearly 10 billion people on the planet. More important, the number of people intensely reliant on energy will explode from a billion and a half to nearly four billion.

How can we continue to import nearly two-thirds of our daily requirements with surges in new demand like that? And it's not just us; today, China's oil dependence is 30 percent, and its officials predict the country will soon be closer to Japan's greater-than 50 percent reliance on foreign oil.

As the world's workshop, China has developed a staggering thirst for oil. Once the largest exporter in East Asia, China has surged to be the number-two importer of oil. It passed the United States as Saudi Arabia's biggest oil trading partner in 2010.

China's demand for petroleum was over eight million barrels a day in 2010, projected to grow to 14 million by 2030. By then as much as 70 percent of its oil might have to be imported.

Look at China's astonishing growth in car consumption alone. In the three years leading up to 2010, China's car market tripled to over 40 million vehicles. While we licked our wounds from market meltdowns, they overtook the U.S. market in auto sales by more than a million units in 2009.

China's thirty (count them) automakers had production capacity for 13.5 million autos by the end of 2009. Expansion plans will more than double domestic car output by 2015. Why are local political operators still being aggressive about giving preferential tax deals and real estate proposals to attract auto manufacturing?

In ten years, the Chinese expect to add 150 million new cars on their roads—that's more cars than we have on American roads today.

India is smaller but still highly relevant. In 2010, India consumed about three million barrels a day, about 60 percent of which was imported. India's industrial and automotive expansion should consume seven million barrels a day in a decade. As much as 85 percent may be imported.

Brazil is a huge market for major auto players. According to HIS Global Insight, Brazil will pass Germany as number-four auto market.

Emerging tigers are not simply car stories. The industrial surge exhausts their power and electricity resources.

That's why old coal will be king for another generation.

State-run Coal India, the world's biggest coal producer, is in deal mode, shopping for coal assets especially in the United States. While China has one of the world's largest coal reserves, its import rates are growing too. China alone accounted for 48 percent of the global market volume of coal in 2010.

Despite a G-20 Summit in Seoul calling for a gradual phaseout of coal-fired power plants, China and India have little intention of curbing their coal appetites. Coal supplies 80 percent of China's power needs. And even with improved rail and technology, there is so much growth forecast that Chinese authorities see no diminishment in coal's proportional usage for at least ten more years.

Worldwide coal demand should expand by 55 percent by 2035. That's bad news for environmentalists, especially since the countries of OECD (Organization for Economic Cooperation and Development), including China and India, account for 95 percent of the increase.

No matter what we do, coal pollution will cloud their skies for years to come.

SUPPLY STORM

PEAKISTS SEE A CRISIS LOOMING—an oil shortage tempest that disrupts markets and economies. But unlike most supply storms, this one has three edges.

First, staggering increases in demand create an aching need to purchase and produce more oil. Typical economic price elasticity doesn't explain behavior.

Nations must fuel their armies, their industries, and their people like a body needs blood. Some will do almost anything to ensure supply. Societal costs like pollution, war, price volatility, or doing deals with the devil are trivialities against an overarching need.

The second side hits producers who must replace oil supply they have extracted, if only to sustain their reserves—the oil treadmill syndrome. For the U.S. this means moving beyond conventional oil reserves to the harder-to-lift variety. For big producing nations like Saudi Arabia it means using "secondary recovery" to help lift oil in mature fields.

Beyond pumping stimulants into reservoirs to improve their geological vigor, a huge amount of new oil must be discovered to replace declining production.

The third edge is stealthy. Not all supply is created equal. Increases in foreign production don't entirely solve the problem because more oil is staying home. Top oil producers are finding they must hold back more oil for their own needs. Global net exports will drop for stagnating producers. For net importers like America, China, and India, this means having to find replacement oil even as global production rises. Peakist, environmentalist, or capitalist pig—no matter what your label, a storm is coming.

Radical Centrists must devise sensible energy policy amidst these three countervailing forces: demand that says "I gotta have it"; producer nations running in place to avoid eclipse; and home market supply holdback from world availability.

So let's examine the first rule of supply: Who has what?

World total proven oil reserves have expanded by nearly a third over 20 years to 1.33 trillion barrels according to BP league tables. (Proven reserves are considered reasonably certain and can be economically lifted from known reservoirs with existing techniques operating conditions.)

Proven reserves are but one lens to view the world of energy. Most folks never bother to use another, but they should and we will. Remember, Hamm is on the ridge line.

Saudi Arabia has about 20 percent of the world's conventional resources. Venezuela comes next. Iraq surged to number two with a 25-percent increase announced in late 2010 (to increase their OPEC output quota). Iran comes next with about 10 percent, followed by Kuwait and UAE.

The Middle East claims to have about 60 percent of the proven reserves in the world, though the U.S. Geological Survey shows a meaningfully lower 54 percent. Again, through a conventional lens.

The reigning kings of natural gas proven reserves are Russia, Iran, and Qatar, which combined hold nearly 3.5 quadrillion cubic feet, representing 53 percent of the world total. I am not sure what a quadrillion is, but these three have most of it—if they could only tap it all . . .

So who is producing oil? Two of the biggest three may surprise you.

Russia was the number-one producer in 2010 at ten million barrels per day. Saudi Arabia was at eight million and the United States followed at about six to eight million. After that come Iran, China, Mexico, and Canada.

The U.S. and China share the distinction of being the only net importers among the top 20 world producers.

Talk about a couple of hearty appetites.

PEEK INTO OIL'S FUTURE

JUST HOW FAR WILL COUNTRIES go to assure their supply of oil? Like any addict, we open every drawer and check every pocket in our closet. Addicts try everything.

They make unusual friends.

Oil defines China's foreign policy. Chinese ties with the military junta in Myanmar (once Burma) and significant involvement with the genocidal regime in Sudan signal their politics of necessity. The Chinese are building roads and pipelines in Kazakhstan and launching communications satellites for Venezuela with a singular aim.

The U.S. has its own strange bedfellow in Venezuela's Hugo Chavez, who calls President Bush the devil while selling us two-thirds of his country's oil exports. Chavez threatened: ". . . we will not send a drop of oil to the United States, even if we have to eat rocks." He has ample supply in his head.

The Foreign Corrupt Practices Act prevents Americans from dealing with Iran and the Sudan. So China is more than willing to extract Sudan's oil.

Addicts confront old nemeses.

Chinese President Hu Jintao opened a pipeline in 2009 that did two things at once: it linked Turkmenistan to China's Xinjiang region via Kazakhstan and Uzbekistan, and it provoked Russian interests in the region.

The United States has its own provocative pipeline: the Keystone XL, a 2000-mile, $7 billion pipe which will bring tar sand oil from Alberta to the Gulf of Mexico. Tar sand oil is dirtier than light sweet crude and environmentalists are in an uproar. Addicts never stop looking for oil, and finding it.

Conventional oil is being discovered, but most is found buried underneath deep waters or suspended in droplets and pockets in oil sands and shale. Conventional U.S. oil reserves grew by 11 percent in 2010 according to Ernst & Young. Natural gas reserves grew faster at 12 percent.

Searching for oil is perpetual motion.

Exxon Mobil's 700-billion barrel Gulf oil and gas find is just 250 miles southwest of New Orleans.

Petroleo Brasileiro SA, Brazil's state oil company, believes its Tupi field increases the nation's reserves by eight billion barrels—as much as 60 percent, which could turn the largest Latin American country into a major net exporter.

The Mexican company PEMEX drilled its deepest ocean well ever, discovering a field of potentially 500 billion cubic feet. For an important U.S.

supplier who may have overproduced its oil assets, that's an encouraging discovery.

Addicts use high prices to find proven reserves that are a good deal harder to prove.

Higher prices fuel expansion—through discovery, acquisition, and better recovery. They support technologies needed to lift shale oil—fracturing, horizontal drilling, drilling more than two miles down. But they don't reassure peakists and they fill environmentalists with dread.

Don't expect oil corporations with billions invested in oil reserves to have any incentive but to drill, baby, drill.

Their solution is *importing* less oil, not using less oil.

And where oil sees only solutions, environmentalists see only problems.

Take Canadian oil sands (coal oil), extracted by truck to concoct dark crude. Alberta's sands deposits may have more oil than the Saudi's beloved Ghawar field.

But coal oil is slower to extract and environmentally dirtier than pumping liquid oil.

However, if you use another lens than convention, it can tip the balance of power.

Hamm's estimation is that the Bakken could potentially contain recoverable reserves of 24 billion barrels of oil and equivalents, a number far larger than the U.S. Geological Survey has indicated. If Hamm is correct, then this single formation would double the total of U.S. proven reserves.

If he could only lift it all . . .

Environmentalists revile oil shale recovery in *Gasland*; Josh Fox's documentary perpetuates the belief and concern that hydraulic fracturing (fracking) used to extract gas from Appalachia's Marcellus Shale poisons the water supply and the air. The "shale industry" calls Fox's documentary misguided.

In energy's greatest gift to *New York Post* headline writers, "fracking" has become a very hot topic.

Fracking pumps water, sand, and additives at extremely high pressure miles below the surface to expand cracks in shale releasing gas. Developed by Halliburton, fracking operates below the water table, defenders argue, making water pollution impossible.

Despite years of successful operation, fracking fluid is nasty soup and using millions of gallons of river water poses disposal and pollution risks. As many as six hundred chemicals are used in the process. Recovered or "produced" water is stored in open pits and reused or disposed of while some of the chemicals evaporate into the air. The waste water is an obvious threat to the aquifer.

As many as 90 percent of all natural gas wells have already been fracked, according to the EIA. And nearly half of our natural gas is going to come from fracked wells in 20 years.

Perhaps fracking shouldn't be exempted from the Safe Drinking Water Act. And perhaps groundwater disposal should be a target for environmental review. But we face a simple dilemma. If we want our own fossil fuels, then we will surely have to frack ourselves.

Or build ourselves a very long pipe.

Beyond discovery, recovery rates must improve. Right now we extract only 20 percent of the available tar from oil sands.

Secondary recovery extends the life of diminishing fields. People think of oil fields like a shook-up can of Coke that spurts into the sky when a pin pricks the underground reservoir. Wells gush. Oil propelled by gasses and inertia plumes into the sky. Like all of us, fields have a life cycle and particularly when past their peak, need an elixir like water, steam, or gas to spur the oil on.

But reservoirs are temperamental and can be ruined if improperly managed.

Finally, addicts push every legal or natural boundary to find black gold: the Arctic (10-20 percent of conventional world reserves), federal park lands, offshore prohibited drill zones, and bigger finds in Alaska—all have eluded Big Oil's reach.

The BP spill in the Gulf and other oil disasters fuel environmentalist passions to stop the spread of "drill, baby, drill." But the requests keep coming.

PEAK AT ALTERNATIVES

THIS IRONIC TUG OF WAR is in stalemate. On one side, global warming, and on the other, oil crisis Cassandras: one says ice caps are melting; the other that Peak Oil and a supply crisis looms.

Some solutions serve both sides, most annoy everybody.

Here is the Radical Centrist Truth. Neither side can win absolutely. We cannot let go of the fossil fuel trapeze bar and float in midair, waiting for the alternative bar to swoop us to safety. We need a comprehensive plan to transition over many decades from our dependence on a diminishing asset to dependence on renewable resources.

It will require bold collaboration of business, government, and the American people. And our energy policy cannot end at the water's edge. Too many competing nations are delighted to import pollution and dependence on the fossil fuel.

We cannot achieve this maneuver with endless incremental steps everyone agrees on. Shifting from 160 years of oil means big risks and massive collaboration.

Revolution is needed. It cannot come solely from a handful of Bunker Hill zealots. It will cost trillions, but the payoff will in the long run be worth it—but not in the short run. Expect huge mistakes—the exodus is too massive.

Where will the auto industry find the $100 billion–plus necessary to convert our 140 million autos to renewable source vehicles? How will we orchestrate utilities away from a super-reliance on coal to produce cleaner power? How will consumers pay for the change to alternatives?

And most important, how will we achieve the energy independence so we are no longer prostrate to volatile pricing and uncontrollable energy suppliers whose chief allegiance is to the highest bidder?

Drill-baby-drill is not our only alternative. But with so much oil inertia, expect it. Do not look to Big Oil to desubsidize itself or to replace its hard-won billions in assets with alternative solutions. Oil companies fix problems with new oil. Only the government balance sheet is sizeable enough to instigate alternatives. Instigate, not perpetuate.

Attention, free spirits from the school of laissez faire—there is no free market in oil. Its costs are distorted because community goods like clean air, water, and global protection come essentially free to producers. These benefits tower over such multibillion-dollar trifles as domestic manufacturing deductions, and deduction of taxes (and some royalties) to foreign governments.

Oil is subsidized because we need it so desperately. What organization has the gumption and the size to cross-subsidize a business that threatens the oil behemoths? Only the federal government has the strength and the staying power to begin alternative solutions.

Price will be the long-term deliverer of alternatives, but shuttering the Department of Energy shuts the lights out on our options.

Without them there is no alternative.

THE THREE UGLIES

EVERY ALTERNATIVE SOLUTION MEANS DANCING with the Three Uglies:

Pay Ourselves vs. Pay OPEC
Find our own or buy more from them.

Cheap Gas vs. Paying for Climate
Dirty oil, cheap coal, shale vs. protecting ozone with renewables.

Cost of Displacing Oil vs. Cost of Buying It
Premium cost alternatives vs. getting more oil any way we can.

In facing the three uglies you cannot expect oil companies to transform into energy companies overnight. They have too much vested in finding and producing oil and gas.

Getting oil companies and citizens to bend to a different reality will take extraordinary leadership, big ideas, and a few dry holes.

T. Boone Pickens has just such a wildcat notion.

Today, 20 percent of our electricity comes from natural gas. Replacing methane with wind power frees up natural gas for automotive use, meaning we can break petroleum's grip on transportation.

This is a classic Texas two-step: replace fossil resources with wind and replace "international petroleum" with domestic natural gas.

It is bold as hell and worth exploring, despite protestations about wind. If wind doesn't blow your skirts up, then use nuclear power. The bold notion is to replace imported oil's grip on our transportation.

Why don't we use more methane?

Supply and utilization are both low for the same reason—it is a gas.

Transporting it scares people. But America possesses huge gas reserves and we are expert in catalyst chemistry which gets methane to liquid at scale.

Ironically, the world's worst emitter—China—has methane on the brain. China's 200-plus methanol plants have expected 2011-12 capacity of 6 to 12 billion gallons, versus 2009 global capacity of 15 billion gallons.

Clean coal is another bold concept but it appears beyond our grasp.

You've seen the industry's $20 million ad campaign selling the virtues of "clean coal," also known as Carbon Capture and Sequestration (CCS). Trouble is, CCS is so difficult and expensive to produce that not a single carbon-fired power plant in the world has been able to bring clean coal to scale.

Even the Bush administration lost patience with FutureGen, a $1.4 billion Illinois project to build the first near-zero emissions coal power plant. After FutureGen ran out of steam, China broke ground on Green Gen, their entry in the clean coal race.

Here is the truth: we are linked to coal for a long time unless we embrace our inner Francophile. France derives 75 percent of its electric power from nuclear energy. No nation exports more electricity.

Why has France been so successful? The answer is an old chestnut— "No gas, no oil, no coal, no choice." Nuclear is the price of energy independence, and the French paid it.

The UN's International Atomic Energy Agency says, despite shaken confidence, global use of nuclear power will continue to grow significantly around the world.

Has America entered a nuclear winter? Not exactly. America is the world's largest producer of nuclear power—more than 30 percent of worldwide nuclear generation of electricity.

Thirty proposed reactors across the USA were stalled by Japan's Fukushima crisis, but they were already flagging. Post-Three Mile Island, dozens of permitted reactors were canceled, without a single new construction coming on line since 1979. Twenty percent of our power comes from 104 nuclear plants built between 20 and 43 years ago. Between four and six new reactors may come on line by 2020, depending . . .

Nuclear is frozen by the pocketbook as much the heart.

A reasonably sized nuclear plant costs $6 to $10 billion, says EIA. Only five of three thousand U.S. electric utilities exceed $20 billion in market value. President Obama's proposal to boost the Department of Energy's nuclear loan programs from $18 to $50 billion has been overwhelmed by Japan's tragedy and budget constraints.

Capital requirements have driven consolidation—the 12 largest players own 54 percent of nuclear capacity.

Despite tighter regulations, nuclear power is chugging along. Indian Point nuclear facility provides 25 percent of New York City's and Westchester's power. Nearby Connecticut joins a list of states that get *most* of their power from nuclear plants. Carolina P & L's merger with Florida Progress means that nuclear provides 35 percent of the Carolinas' and Florida's electricity.

Is our nuclear renaissance stuck in neutral?

Bill Gates and a host of other entrepreneurs are betting the economics of small may drive future nuclear needs. Gates' TerraPower runs 10' by 13' reactors using slow-burn depleted uranium. NuScale is designing mini reactors one-tenth the size of current reactors.

Mini reactors can't compete with coal power plants. Their target is providing carbon-free emissions when governments tax or limit climate warming utilities.

America is kidding itself with nuclear power. It's the worst of all possible worlds—full utilization of 30- to 40-year-old plants without fresh assets. When trouble happens we will wonder how we could have been so dim.

We would rather let 104 plants age ungracefully than build fresh solutions. Sooner or later, old plants fade or have incidents, and plan B is more coal and natural gas—or worse.

Renewables face another uphill grind, but they are energy annuities which replenish and don't require exploration: wind, solar, and bio-mass-energy crops.

Wind today is the fastest growing energy technology, but it is full of hot air. Rarely blowing at what the average wind-speed maps say, it is inconsistent and unpredictable at the regional level.

Large-scale wind farms can't produce constant electricity so backup capacity is required. Utility executives are weaned on reliability—99 percent–plus availability. Load swings are accommodated by switching on additional generators at a moment's notice.

Wind blows in gusts, fanning big debates as to whether it exacerbates utility load swings. And there is concern about the amount of territory required to safely run a wind farm. The United States contains about 2.26 billion acres, not counting coastal waters. That should suffice. And of course concern for birds abounds, though Audubon says otherwise.

With the right placement wind can economically generate electricity with minimal pollutants so long as government support also blows in the right direction. Many of the ideal placement locations are in rural areas requiring miles of transmission lines to deliver power, with attendant distance transfer losses.

On a macro basis, wind is forecastable, rarely dropping across the whole country at the same moment. A coming challenge, as wind evolves beyond providing less than one percent of electrical power, is battery storage at large wind farms. Unlike residential installations, these battery systems will be enormous and costly, requiring government-size intervention and assistance.

Residential users' bugaboo is wind blockage from adjoining buildings or trees, which renders windmills uneconomical.

And windmills wear out. Each turbine requires thousands of parts. Tower sections, nacelles, and blades are large, and expensive to ship.

But study after study says there is ample breeze—some call the Southwest the "Saudi Arabia of wind." But we need extraordinary will to manage the transition.

Massive wind bets are being made. The Atlantic Wind Connection, a 350-mile backbone transmission project, will carry power from offshore wind developers. Sponsored by Google, Good Energies, and Marubeni, AWC will carry a first phase price tag of about $1.3 billion.

Wind will be a critical piece of our alternative energy mosaic, developing at its own pace. But it is not the overarching solution. It will need to find its place with solar, bio fuels, nuclear, and other ways we devise to escape our fossil fuel dependence.

Solar power includes sophisticated use of passive solar building designs; photovoltaic cells and concentrating systems which focus sunlight with mirrors. Solar is stuck at under one percent of power generation because its underlying economics are at least twice as high as fossil fuel. And paybacks even with dramatic rebates can stretch out over ten years.

Some utilities offer customers net metering credits when power excesses are generated.

No matter.

Solar fails cost comparison because daylight is fleeting, whereas fossils burn round the clock. Spread over more hours, fossil capacity always wins.

ICARUS

THE NUMBERS WE'RE BANDYING AROUND are eye-popping: billions of this; trillions of that; quadrillions of the other. Radical Centrists recognize that when the stakes are this size, government has to play a role beyond protecting our oil supply with the U.S. military.

In 2010 the Department of Energy was one of the world's largest financial backers of renewable energy, funding $30 billion of loans and guarantees.

The DOE supported one of the largest solar plants in the world, being constructed in the Mojave, with a $1.3 billion guarantee. The Ivanpah concentrating solar plant (CST) has contracts with Pacific Gas and Electric and Southern California Edison. Built by Bechtel on Bureau of Land Management property, investors behind it include Google and BrightSource.

DOE guaranteed a similar amount to fund the Caithness Shepherd's Flat Wind Farm in Oregon, the largest renewable energy project of its kind in the world.

Also in California, the Blythe CST plant secured a $2 billion loan guarantee in response to that state's commitment to get one-third of its power from renewable energy by 2020. Bets like these will kick-start the shift.

But whenever such massive bets are made, losses occur. And for its now-legendary shortcomings, Solyndra the fallible was only about one percent of the DOE portfolio. You can't be glib about flushing half a billion dollars down the proverbial black hole. But we have to be realistic about the number of dry holes we are likely to drill trying to replace our fossil fuel addiction.

Tip to government: don't pick one technology and give it unique incentives. Your role is to level the playing field so that emerging technologies get a running start. Let the market pick winners. That's what happened to ethanol—it screamed on incentives. Let's see how it fares on its own.

Incentives alone often lead to bad technology.

There has to be a reason for choosing a technology other than manufacturing cost advantages, because those can evaporate overnight. Just like your money.

Only one path exists to sustain interest in alternatives. We can loan to our heart's content. We can wink, underwrite, tariff protect, grant rebates and every type of incentive to lower costs.

Those get the ball rolling short term but they always fizzle.

Price always wins long term. Unless your price is better for a decade at least, you will not attract consumer interest or private investment.

We can't incentivize our way to major adoption of alternatives. These substitutes for oil, gas, and coal must be cheaper. Renewables can't be price competitive long term without a carbon tax or cap 'n' trade system now—in one word, subsidies.

That's how markets work—always. I don't make the rules.

If it's not cheaper or more efficient, consumers won't buy . . . especially with automobiles.

The first commercial electric cars were a fleet of New York City taxis in 1897, followed by London cabs months later. Production peaked in 1912 when gasoline automakers commercialized electric starters and new roads out of town called for longer distances. Electric cars slumbered as a mainstream product despite GM and others building prototypes in the '60s and '70s.

Toyota's 1992 "Earth Charter" pledged reduced emissions. In '93, the Clinton administration created the Partnership New Generation Vehicles (PNGV) with American makers, to create an 80 MPG vehicle. Three prototypes resulted from the billion-dollar investment.

Excluded, Toyota increased its targets. Prius launched in '97 and sold 18,000 cars. Audi and Honda followed with the Avant and Insight in the following two years. From Toyota and Honda's perspective, the race was on.

But the U.S. stalled at the gate.

Fast-forward to today, and the Obama administration wants one million electric cars on the American roads by 2014.

Popular Mechanics reported six-month 2011 sales of Chevy Volt (MSRP $40,280) and Nissan Leaf (MSRP $35,000-37,000) were 3,071 and 3,894 respectively. Despite $2500 to $7500 tax credits for hybrids and electrics, demand is spotty. The *New York Times* reported that in 2010 Costco shuttered 90 charging stations due to lack of use.

Unbending, the government launched in 2009 a $2.4 billion Transportation Electrification Initiative. *Wired* Magazine reports at least $100 million will go to expanding our 1300 public charging stations to over 22,000 by 2014.

Surveys by Deloitte and others show consumers here and in Europe share similar requirements: less than two hours to charge, 300-plus mile range, and of course reasonable price.

Deloitte predicts electric cars will be under five percent of the 2020 market while Nissan sees over ten percent. About 1.75 million hybrids were on U.S. roads by 2010 according to Green Energy-Efficient-Homes.com, giving hybrids one percent penetration. Sales have slowed from 45,000 per month in 2008, to below 25,000 a month since.

A Prius is relatively expensive—$23,500 starting price for your 50 MPG. And it's not just a price issue—a blogger sniped "I drive a gas burner. You drive a coal burner."

The Rocky Mountain Institute and others espouse additional ways to cut emissions, like ultralight and superlight cars.

But in the end, much of the battle will come down to batteries.

Japan dominated the lithium-ion battery market until 1998 when the Chinese government turned its attention on the powerful lightweight devices. China was determined to power our cell phones and laptops.

Naturally, they wanted to dominate electric vehicles too. EVs depend upon a quality "pack"—an intricate connection of batteries to run the car. Nothing is more temperamental and price determining in EV design.

Chinese subsidies worth millions were directed to companies like Tianjin Lishen Battery so it could supply Apple, Samsung, and Motorola. In 2008 China granted nearly $3 million for the company to develop electric cars. Coda, an American electric car company aimed at mainstream buyers, signed a global joint venture with Lishen Power Battery of Tianjin and together they developed the pack and the cell for transportation and utility applications.

As of December 2010, China had 52 rechargeable battery makers according to Fourin, a Japanese research house, and 94 pure electric vehicles had been approved for production, 80 percent using lithium-ion batteries. Warren Buffet invested $232 million in the Chinese company BYD to develop its own lithium-ion battery.

Will lithium-ion be the lasting battery technology? Some say lithium-air and nano batteries are the Holy Grail.

It feels like the industry is just getting warmed up.

Imagine the opportunity to replace America's 140 million autos with emission-free technology. Whoever breaks the cost code will seize one of the greatest replacement market opportunities in history.

We're Not Kicking the Habit.

And our addiction is challenging us right now.

Alternative energy will play a major role and it has just one reality: Public investment is essential to kick-start a revolution. There are only two players on the field. One is the U.S. government, the other is the combined might of the oil giants with tens of billions invested in the ground. They are not about to undermine their own business.

Government must combine a comprehensive strategy with private sector incentives to partner in massive bets on alternatives. (They can take public-private initiatives in health-care breakthroughs as a model.) Together they must offer pricing that can change consumer sentiment.

We have tilted the playing field in the direction of foreign oil. Unless that changes, alternative energy will be peripheral power in every sense of the word.

We need to modernize our transmission and distribution infrastructure to accommodate alternatives. Can you spell investment incentives?

And despite the breakup of the congressional love affair with ethanol, we need an expansion of our biofuel facilities infrastructure.

The maligned "Corn Con" that directed four out of every ten ears into ethanol production has been a magnet for controversy. But check the results. Ethanol exploded from 1.6 billion gallons in 2000 to 13.3 billion gallons in 2010.

Combined with a tariff on foreign ethanol, cheap ethanol imports stalled at the border. But then we exported ethanol because its subsidized cost was lower than gasoline.

Let's get this straight: We exported a gasoline alternative when the subsidy was designed to create a cheaper alternative to foreign oil?

That's why we need a *comprehensive* plan.

There is no revolution without government lighting the fuse. Only the government's balance sheet can possibly handle these massive development expenditures, despite the many demands we Americans place on it. In the end, these things are only affordable if they become our national priorities. Again, there are times it would be nice to have a planned economy like you-know-whose.

The federal government is trying, give them that. It is we who are duping them. And, to be balanced, Uncle Sam is doing a better job than he gets credit for.

That said, the din around the $535 million Solyndra deal highlights some things that *are* wrong with the government program. We picked an untested technology, we structured the loan to incent building a new factory when the company was losing money on every item sold, we misjudged competitor pricing, and we structured a government-takes-all-in-bankruptcy deal, which scared investors away. Okay, lessons learned.

But losing a half a billion is almost irrelevant in the context of how much money it will cost to make this change. We obviously don't want to screw up repeatedly, but in a trillion-dollar global sweepstakes for energy, such losses are inevitable.

In short, we love our planet, but we just aren't in the mood to pay extra for it. We need our Uncle's help but some think any government support is anticompetitive. That's just wrongheaded. Oil thrives on parental support. We will need to create pricing schemes where alternatives are cheaper, or Americans will not purchase. The solution cannot lie only with the market. But in the end the market will persevere. If you are looking for Adam Smith's invisible hand . . . it is either around our throat or theirs.

CODA:

Where Do We Go From Here?

T ODAY, WE ARE IN SHORT supply of uniters.

No longer do our eyes cast naturally to the corners of the room. Jefferson, Washington, and Adams all had passion for social fairness, even as they allowed slavery to prosper. So, imperfect or not, they stretched for solutions. We have always held to the truth of equal status that the Founding Fathers aspired to, but occasionally it takes us some time.

This is one of those occasions when we need to stretch.

Now, as then, the toughest part of political leadership is knowing when to stand firm on a principle and when to compromise.

The framers instinctively understood that about our nation.

Common sense in the center teaches us this delicate balance. It also teaches us to acknowledge when change is needed, especially when it is difficult.

Any rational review of our history will reveal that important and lasting change begins with civil disobedience. But we have put up blinders against change, even when it is desperately needed. We have lost our peripheral vision. Gone are leaders who embrace change as it happens.

Pundits have scared us to the poles, where we sit, frozen. Our reaction is to be reductionist and dismissive. It is safer to be aligned, and more comforting to be assured that we are right. On-air palliative cures have hijacked our discomfort. We have been robbed of our skill at uniting.

We must become the change we seek.

Imagine the courage of Ben Franklin as he sat locked in the cavernous

Independence Hall, hashing through the harrowing debates of the Constitutional Convention. In his eighties by then, the gentle sage had returned to his Philadelphia for steamy and overheated July meetings. Debate raged between the most and least populated states about how best to govern the nation: by a body representing the proportion of population, or a body equally representing each state.

Equilibrium seemed impossible. Powerful argument and irrefutable logic sat on both sides. Without concession, the founders could reach no agreement.

And no agreement meant no constitution.

And yet there would be one. Franklin dared to stretch, proposing a bicameral body with one part representing proportional population and another reflecting the equal value that each individual state brought to the equation.

And thus, the eventual: A constitution for a new nation.

Franklin's persuasive compromise became the birth of Congress, a cornerstone of the Republic.

Examples of leadership by stretching abound in our history. We stretched to end slavery; we stretched in the Depression; and we stretched in World War II. Yet stretching for civil, religious, and human rights has become a lost art. And for a country with an unconditional love of freedom, we have become a paradox, because today, for more Americans than ever before, the promise of liberty is unfulfilled.

Ask any foreigner what the essence of America is and they will tell you it is our unfettered ability to dream the big dreams. And then make them happen.

We excel at both parts.

Those sweaty days at the Constitutional Convention were moments when dreamers forged the foundation of our nation. They were the ultimate eventualists. They dared the big dreams, but they also shaped and compromised so that we might all share the dream together. That eventualism was built by stretching personal philosophies to fit across the widest set of tent poles.

Let's not shrink the tent now.

What I have found in thousands of conversations on this very topic is this:

Deep down, Americans have not entirely left home. We've never strayed far from our national adolescence.

Henry Adams wrote his expansive nine-volume history of the United States and covered only 17 years. He postulated that by 1817 (the end of the Madison presidency), America was a settled country in terms of its national temperament. At an extremely young age, the American character was already determined.

With that stirring conclusion he ended his history there.

This temperament is a complex one. It's seemingly simple, but is able to exist with contradictions, ambiguities, and imperfections better than the temperament of any nation in the history of man.

Together we possess a uniquely American ability. The singular genius of the United States is that it is able to create out of chaos and multiplicity an order that allows for collegial leadership. Empires throughout time have created order with varying degrees of success, but none has really ever equaled the United States in creating a leadership that is mutually respectful.

Most never cared enough to try.

This American genius, set by the time of our country's adolescence, is the very key to winning the twenty-first-century prosperity that we all seek. This endowment lies deep like a seed in every one of us, fourth-generation Americans and newcomers alike.

We will make a better nation, truer to itself and its principles, if we stretch from the poles and meet in the center. Leadership is not the braying and dogmatic repetition of strongly held positions in the face of opposing strongly held positions.

World leadership involves making complicated choices between conflicting values, often of equal merit, and selecting laws and policies, here and abroad, that consider ambiguities. It will require that Americans acknowledge shifts in worldwide power that have altered our long-held and coveted status.

408 ♦ PETER D. KIERNAN

We are *a* superpower, not *the* superpower, and we must admit that.

Machiavelli archly advised his Prince, "It is better to be feared in the world than loved."

By that standard the United States is doing well—very well—but is fear the most effective way to counteract a terrorist threat? Can we evaluate our actions in Iraq, Afghanistan, and elsewhere with an honest assessment of whether we are advancing or hurting our cause without being disloyal to our outstanding men and women in uniform?

The uniters I seek may not be folk heroes. They may not enjoy the same adulation and scorn from their admirers and detractors in turn. But one thing is certain: a radical return to the center will make America a great democracy once again.

That's precisely where you and I come in.

You probably found both something to love and something to despise about this book. For anyone who agreed with all of it, well, thanks, Mom.

For the rest of you, particularly if you're most comfortable in one ideology or another, I ask you to reframe your relationship with your party. No ideology ever really solved a problem without a tip of its hat to pragmatism.

It's time to doff yours in the gallant hope that we can chart a reasonable course together. Our enemies have never been more vexing or more powerful. They choose feint and dodge rather than frontal assault. And our richest competitors also count some of the world's poorest as their countrymen.

We fight adversaries out of uniform, against soldiers of indeterminate rank. And the pure power of largeness, in both body count and resources, threatens our ability to rule and advocate in the manner of our prior 230 years.

I ask you to find your inner American voice and pay less attention to the external one you use every day. Feel the way you felt when you pledged allegiance as a grade schooler. Try taking an extreme view with that voice, and you will choke on the words.

In *Saving Private Ryan,* perhaps the most realistic war movie ever made, the amiable and doomed captain, played by Tom Hanks, pulls Private Ryan close at the end and demands of him that he "Earn this!"

As Americans, be worth it. Have the fortitude to demand more of your leaders and of yourselves. Can you defy the harsh forces on the right and left? Even in the thorniest of stalemates common sense can lead to brilliant solutions if you just think about it long enough.

The impossible chasms can always be crossed so long as a few people make the first push.

All good things start with an independent initiative. Always.

Practice this personal patriotism. Brave men and women who spend themselves defending our freedom are not the only patriots. Become one of them. Make sacrifices; give a little. Virtually every signer of the Declaration of Independence died penniless and ruined by virtue of his patriotism.

For us, the consequences are less dire, but the need for individual patriotism has never been greater. Spend yourself in this noble cause.

Our history exalts in the parable of an isolated voice, unheard at first by the throngs, ignored by powers and principalities, that lingers like a solitary musical note suspended in air—constant, unbending, hovering above the din.

Time after time an ear turns, and another, and another, each joining the harmony until the whole of the nation, some grudging, some with brio, all take up the melody.

United, this is the American chorus.

INDEX